Folkloristics

An Introduction

FOLKLORISTICS
AN INTRODUCTION

Robert A. Georges and Michael Owen Jones

INDIANA University Press

Bloomington & Indianapolis

Cover illustration: Adapted from Smithsonian Institution, photo no. 69039; biblical quilt by Harriet Powers.

This book is a publication of

Indiana University Press
601 North Morton Street
Bloomington, IN 47404-3797 USA

http://iupress.indiana.edu

Telephone orders 800-842-6796
Fax orders 812-855-7931
Orders by e-mail iuporder@indiana.edu

TM

Manufactured in the United States of America

Library of Congress Cataloging-in-Publication Data

Georges, Robert A.
    Folkloristics : an introduction / by Robert A. Georges and Michael Owen Jones.
      p. cm.
    Includes bibliographical references and index.
    ISBN 0-253-32934-5 (cl : alk. paper). — ISBN 0-253-20994-3 (pa : alk. paper)
    1. Folklore—Methodology. 2. Folklore—Philosophy. I. Jones, Michael Owen. II. Title.
GR40.G46   1995
398'.01—dc20   95-14400

5 6 7 8 07 06

Contents

Acknowledgments

For permission to quote from the following selections under copyright, grateful acknowledgment is made to the following publishers, authors, agents, and trustees of authors' estates:

ROGER D. ABRAHAMS, "The Language of Festivals: Celebrating the Economy." Reprinted from *Celebration: Studies in Festivity and Ritual*, Victor Turner, ed. (Washington, D.C.: Smithsonian Institution Press), pp. 174–177, by permission of the publisher. Copyright 1982.

ROGER D. ABRAHAMS, "Playing the Dozens." Reproduced by permission of the American Folklore Society from *Journal of American Folklore* 75:297, July–September 1962. Not for further reproduction.

MARK AZADOVSKII, *A Siberian Tale Teller*, trans. James R. Dow (1974). Reprinted by permission of the Center for Intercultural Studies in Folklore and Ethnomusicology, The University of Texas, Austin, Texas.

FLORENCE E. BAER, "'Give me ... your huddled masses': Anti-Vietnamese Refugee Lore and the 'Image of the Limited Good,'" *Western Folklore* 41 (1982). Reprinted by permission of the California Folklore Society.

WILLIAM R. BASCOM, "Four Functions of Folklore." Reproduced by permission of the American Folklore Society from *Journal of American Folklore* 67:266, October–December 1954. Not for further reproduction.

H. M. BELDEN, *Ballads and Songs Collected by the Missouri Folk-Lore Society*, University of Missouri Studies 15 (1960), text of "Naomi Wise." Reprinted with the permission of the University of Missouri Press.

RUTH BENEDICT, *Zuni Mythology*. Copyright © 1935 by Columbia University Press. Reprinted with the permission of the publisher.

BERTRAND HARRIS BRONSON, *The Traditional Tunes of the Child Ballads*, vol. 4, © 1972, text and musical transcription of "Our Goodman." Reprinted with the permission of Princeton University Press.

DONALD J. COSENTINO, *Defiant Maids and Stubborn Farmers: Tradition and Invention in Mende Story Performances*, © 1982. Reprinted with the permission of Cambridge University Press and the author.

FRANCIS A. DE CARO and ROSAN A. JORDAN, "The Wrong *Topi*: Personal Narratives, Ritual, and the Sun Helmet as a Symbol," *Western Folklore* 43 (1984). Reprinted by permission of the California Folklore Society.

RICHARD M. DORSON, ed., *Buying the Wind: Regional Folklore in the United States*, © 1964. Reprinted with the permission of the University of Chicago Press.

CARLOS C. DRAKE, "Jungian Psychology and Its Uses in Folklore." Reproduced by permission of the American Folklore Society from *Journal of American Folklore* 82:324, April–June 1969. Not for further reproduction.

ALAN DUNDES, "Earth-Diver: Creation of the Mythopoeic Male." Reproduced by permission of the American Anthropological Association from *American Anthropologist* 64:5, pt. 1, October 1962. Not for sale or further reproduction.

DOROTHY EGGAN, "The Personal Use of Myth in Dreams," in *Myth: A Symposium*, ed. Thomas A. Sebeok. Reproduced by permission of the American Folklore Society from the *Bibliographical & Special Series of The American Folklore Society, Volume 5, 1955*. Not for further reproduction.

R. J. EVANCHUK, "Inside, Outside, Upside-Down: The Role of Mainstream Society Participants in the Ethnic Dance Movement," *Folklore and Mythology Studies* 11–12 (1987–88). Reprinted with the permission of the UCLA Folklore Graduate Students' Association.

GARY ALAN FINE, "The Kentucky Fried Rat: Legends and Modern Society," *Journal of Folklore Research* 17 (1980). Reprinted with the permission of the *Journal of Folklore Research*.

GLADYS-MARIE FRY, "Portrait of a Black Quilter," in *Missing Pieces: Georgia Folk Art 1770–1897* (1977). Reprinted with the permission of the Georgia Council for the Arts.

KENNETH S. GOLDSTEIN, "Strategy in Counting Out: An Ethnographic Folklore Field Study," in *The Study of Games*, ed. Elliott Avedon and Brian Sutton-Smith (1971). Reprinted by permission of John Wiley & Sons, Inc.

JOSEPH P. GOODWIN, *More Man Than You'll Ever Be: Gay Folklore and Acculturation in Middle America.* Copyright © 1989 by Indiana University Press. Reprinted with the permission of the publisher.

MARIA HERRERA-SOBEK, "*Corridos* and *Canciones* of *Mica, Migra,* and *Coyotes*," in Stephen Stern and John Allan Cicala, eds., *Creative Ethnicity: Symbols and Strategies of Contemporary Ethnic Life*, © 1991. Reprinted by permission of the Utah State University Press.

DAVID HUFFORD, "Folklore and Medicine." Reprinted from Michael Owen Jones, ed., *Putting Folklore to Use*, copyright © 1994 by the University Press of Kentucky. Reprinted by permission of the publishers.

PAMELA JONES, "'There Was a Woman': *La Llorona* in Oregon," *Western Folklore* 47 (1988). Reprinted by permission of the California Folklore Society.

ROSAN A. JORDAN, "The Vaginal Serpent and Other Themes from Mexican-American Women's Lore," in *Women's Folklore, Women's Culture*, ed. Rosan Jordan and Susan Kalčik, © 1985. Reprinted with the permission of the University of Pennsylvania Press.

ADRIENNE L. KAEPPLER, "Tongan Dance: A Study in Cultural Change," *Ethnomusicology* 14 (1970). Reprinted by permission of the author and the Society for Ethnomusicology.

KENNETH L. KETNER, "A Study of the Use of Madstones in Oklahoma," *The Chronicles of Oklahoma* 46 (Winter, 1968–69). Reprinted with the permission of the Oklahoma Historical Society.

BARBARA KIRSHENBLATT-GIMBLETT, "A Parable in Context," in *Folklore: Performance and Communication*, ed. Dan Ben-Amos and Kenneth S. Goldstein, © 1975. Reprinted with the permission of Mouton de Gruyter Publishers, a division of Walter de Gruyter & Co., Publishers.

BARBARA KIRSHENBLATT-GIMBLETT, ed. *Speech Play: Research and Resources for Studying Linguistic Creativity*, © 1976. Reprinted with the permission of the University of Pennsylvania Press.

ELLI KÕNGÄS MARANDA, "Folklore and Culture Change: Lau Riddles of Modernization," in *Folklore in the Modern World*, ed. Richard M. Dorson, © 1978. Reprinted with the permission of Mouton de Gruyter Publishers, a division of Walter de Gruyter & Co., Publishers.

WOLFGANG MIEDER, "The Proverbial Three Wise Monkeys," *Midwestern Journal of Language and Folklore* 7 (1981). Reprinted with the permission of *Midwestern Folklore*.

CAROL A. MITCHELL, "The Sexual Perspective in the Appreciation and Interpretation of Jokes," *Western Folklore* 36 (1977). Reprinted by permission of the California Folklore Society.

LYNWOOD MONTELL, "Cemetery Decoration Customs in the American South," in Robert E. Walls and George H. Schoemaker, eds., *The Old Traditional Way of Life: Essays in Honor of Warren E. Roberts*, © 1989. Reprinted by permission of the Trickster Press, Indiana University Folklore Institute.

AXEL OLRIK, "Epic Laws of Folk Narrative," in Alan Dundes, ed., *The Study of Folklore*, © 1965. Reprinted by permission of Prentice-Hall, Inc., Englewood Cliffs, N.J.

MARVIN K. OPLER, "Japanese Folk Beliefs and Practices, Tule Lake, California." Reproduced by permission of the American Folklore Society from *Journal of American Folklore* 63:250, October–December 1950. Not for further reproduction.

ELLIOTT ORING, "Whalemen and Their Songs: A Study of Folklore and Culture," *New York Folklore Quarterly* 27 (1971). Reprinted with the permission of the New York Folklore Society.

HARRY OSTER, "Negro Humor: John and Old Master," *Journal of the Folklore Institute* 5 (1968). Reprinted with the permission of the *Journal of Folklore Research*.

GUY OWEN, "Using Folklore in Fiction," *North Carolina Folklore* 13 (1965): 147-155 passim. Reprinted with the permission of Mrs. Dorothy Owen.

SOLEDAD PÉREZ, "Mexican Folklore from Austin, Texas." Reprinted by permission of The Texas Folklore Society from *The Healer of Los Olmos and Other Mexican Lore*, Publications of the Texas Folklore Society 25 (1951), pp. 74 and 76.

The Fairy Tales of Charles Perrault, trans. GEOFFREY BRERETON, © 1957. Text of "Little Red Riding-Hood" reprinted with the permission of Penguin Books Ltd.

JAMES PORTER, "Jeannie Robertson's *My Son David*: A Conceptual Performance Model." Reproduced by permission of the American Folklore Society from *Journal of American Folklore* 89:351, January-March, 1976. Not for further reproduction.

CHARLES FRANCIS POTTER, the entry "Eenie, Meeny, Miney, Mo" from *Funk & Wagnalls Standard Dictionary of Folklore, Mythology, and Legend* by Maria Leach. Copyright 1949, 1950, 1972 by Harper & Row, Publishers, Inc. Reprinted by permission of Harper Collins Publishers, Inc.

PAUL RADIN, *The Trickster: A Study in American Indian Mythology*, © 1972 by Routledge and Kegan Paul. Reproduced with the permission of Routledge, Chapman & Hall Ltd.

SHARON SHERMAN'S videotape *The Chainsaw Art of Skip Armstrong* (1991). Quoted with the permission of Sharon Sherman.

C. W. SULLIVAN, III, "Johnny Says His ABCs," *Western Folklore* 46 (1987). Reprinted by permission of the California Folklore Society.

ARCHER TAYLOR, *The Shanghai Gesture*, Folklore Fellows Communications 166 (1956). Reprinted with the permission of Folklore Fellows Communications, Turku, Finland.

BARRE TOELKEN, "The 'Pretty Language' of Yellowman: Genre, Mode, and Texture in Navaho Coyote Narratives," *Genre* 2 (1969). Reprinted with the permission of *Genre*.

"We Shall Overcome" (videotape, 1988). Quoted with the permission of Resolution, Inc./California Newsreel.

EVELYN KENDRICK WELLS, *The Ballad Tree: A Study of British and American Ballads, Their Folklore, Verse, and Music* (New York: The Ronald Press, 1950). Reprinted with the permission of John R. Wells.

D. K. WILGUS AND ELEANOR R. LONG, text and musical transcription of "Arch and Garden," from *"The Blues Ballad* and the Genesis of Style in Traditional Narrative Song," in Carol L. Edwards and Kathleen E. B. Manley, Eds., *Narrative Folksong, New Directions: Essays in Appreciation of W. Edson Richmond*. © 1985. Reproduced with the permission of Kathleen E. B. Manley and Susan Szymczyk, sister of Carol L. Edwards (deceased).

WILLIAM A. WILSON, "On Being Human: The Folklore of Mormon Missionaries," 64th Faculty Honor Lecture, Utah State University, © 1981. Reprinted by permission of the Utah State University Press.

Folkloristics

An Introduction

1. Introduction: Folklore and Its Study

As we interact with each other on a daily basis, we continuously express what we know, think, believe, and feel. We do so in a variety of readily distinguishable, often symbolic ways: by singing and making music, for example, or by uttering proverbial expressions, dancing, and creating objects. Much of what we express and the ways we do so have the behaviors of our predecessors and peers as sources. We learn most of the stories we tell and the games we play not in the classroom or through print or other media, but rather informally and directly from each other. With time and repetition,

some examples of human expression become pervasive and commonplace. When they do, we conceive them to be traditions or traditional; and we can identify them individually or collectively as *folklore*.

The word *folklore* denotes expressive forms, processes, and behaviors (1) that we customarily learn, teach, and utilize or display during face-to-face interactions, and (2) that we judge to be traditional (a) because they are based on known precedents or models, and (b) because they serve as evidence of continuities and consistencies through time and space in human knowledge, thought, belief, and feeling. The discipline devoted to the identification, documentation, characterization, and analysis of traditional expressive forms, processes, and behaviors is *folkloristics* (alternatively identified as *folklore studies* or *folklife research*).[1] Those who are trained in that discipline and who pursue its objectives in their work are *folklorists*.

The Pervasiveness of Folklore

Folklore is an integral and vital part of our daily lives. In stating that our hands are "as cold as ice" or that a room is "as hot as an oven," we speak folkloricly, using familiar, widely disseminated proverbial comparisons. In order not to "tempt the Fates," many of us knock on wood when we mention our well being or ongoing successes, perpetuating a practice that has roots in ancient Greek, Druidic, and early Christian beliefs and rituals. Sneezing evokes immediate responses worldwide, including the uttering of such traditional expressions as "God bless you," "Praise to Allah," "Good

Figure 1–1: Mary Alicia Owen (1850–1935), the most famous American woman folklorist of her time, produced field-based studies of Gypsy, Native American, and African-American folklore; her research on voodoo resulted in a presentation to the International Folklore Congress in 1891, covered by the (London) Times, *and publication of* Old Rabbit the Voodoo and Other Sorcerers, *which rivaled Joel Chandler Harris's Uncle Remus books in popularity (photo by Simon J. Bronner).*

life," and "Gesundheit," each of which is an example of folklore.[2]

The pervasiveness of folklore is readily apparent on holidays. Regardless of what calendars they follow, for instance, people everywhere mark the end of one year and the beginning of another by following established customs. The new year may be ushered in by singing certain songs ("Auld Lang Syne" in Scotland and the United States) and eating particular foods (pork and blackeyed peas in the American South). Celebrants may exchange gifts or coins; shoot off guns or fireworks; jump over small outdoor fires; or insure that a healthy or wealthy person is the first to cross their thresholds. Wearing new clothing insures good luck for the upcoming year, while bad luck inevitably results if one washes clothes or removes ashes from the hearth on New Year's Day.[3]

Numerous beliefs, rituals, and customs surround important life-cycle events, such as pregnancy and childbirth. Records dating back 5,000 years indicate that certain visual tests have been employed to determine pregnancy, such as the condition of a woman's eyes or puffiness in the neck (modern medicine recognizes thyroid enlargement as a common occurrence in pregnancy). Some people practice divination rituals to foretell the sex of the unborn child, including the ancient technique of dactyliomancy—that is, suspending a ring or other object tied to a string over the pregnant woman's abdomen and noting whether it swings back and forth in pendulum fashion (usually indicating a boy is involved) or moves in a circle (for a girl).[4]

That storks bring babies is a familiar saying and belief (identified by folklorists as Motif T589.6.1[5]), associated with the worldwide notion of children coming from watery places. While pink and blue flowers, napkins, and decorations dominate at baby showers in the United States, a tradition has developed of using yellow as a nonsexist color. Many women carefully avoid breaking the ribbons on shower gift packages; to some, the number of broken ribbons indicates the number of children one will have.

Current warnings that the expectant mother should avoid viewing frightening films and violent television programs parallel notions about fearful sights and strong emotions marking or deforming the unborn child. A gravid woman should remain calm and pleasant so the baby will have a good disposition. She should also avoid eating certain foods, such as strawberries, which might mark the child.

Nurses in American hospitals report finding scissors and knives in patients' beds, the presence of which some believe magically cuts birth pangs. Instructions to untie knots, release locks, and open cupboard doors supposedly have the same effect. Many people around the world plant a "birth tree," believed to maintain a mysterious union with the child; as one thrives or suffers, so does the other. The day of a child's birth may be thought significant; for example, a baby born on New Year's will be lucky always, regardless of the particular day on which this date falls.

Literary works and mass media productions make use of folklore, thereby contributing to its pervasiveness. The title of Joyce Carol Oates's novel *Do with Me What You Will* (1973) derives from a girl's words to her father in the traditional tale identified by folklorists as Type 706, *The Maiden without Hands,*[6] a story in which the daughter encourages her father to mutilate her in order to save himself. Police officers' jokes, anecdotes, and ethnic slurs provide telling remarks about individuals' values and beliefs in Joseph Wambaugh's novels. Short stories like Flannery O'Connor's "A Good Man Is Hard to Find" and Katherine Mansfield's "Bliss" (as in "ignorance is bliss") use familiar proverbs as thematic strategies.[7]

Many of the "classics" in American literature embrace folklore. Traditional accounts of supernatural events and figures, such as "The Legend of Sleepy Hollow" (1819–20), inform Washington Irving's works. A German tale about Peter Klaus, the goatherd, inspired *Rip Van Winkle* (1819–20). John Greenleaf Whittier includes village superstitions, supernatural tales, and other lore in many of his poems, such as "Telling the Bees" (1858), a work based on the belief that bees will leave the hive if not informed of a death in the family. Herman Melville took advantage of seafarers' tales, proverbs, and superstitions in penning *Moby-Dick* (1851) and other works. Joel Chandler Harris derived the bulk of the animal tales in *Uncle Remus: His Songs and Sayings* (1880) from African Americans on Southern plantations. Beliefs, including death portents, play an important role in *The Adventures of Huckleberry Finn* (1885) by Mark Twain (Samuel Langhorne Clemens). (See Box 1–1.)

Willa Cather includes a Bohemian folk custom of a burial at the crossroads in *My Antonia* (1918). Paul Lawrence Dunbar incorporates African American dialect and folk speech in his poetry.[8] Josephina Niggli's *Mexican Village* (1945) is replete with local legends and superstitions, and laced with folksongs and proverbs. In *The Color Purple* (1982) and other novels, Alice Walker includes a conjure woman as well as other examples of African American folklore, often to define characters and illustrate relationships between them as well as to develop the plot.[9] Maxine Hong Kingston's writings, such as *Tripmaster Monkey* (1989), make use of legends, folktales, and other lore from Chinese tradition.

Folklore is often the principal means a writer uses to convey, illustrate, or reinforce a major theme in a literary work. In his novel *Bread and Wine* (1936), for instance, Italian writer Ignazio Silone reveals

BOX 1–1

Excerpt from Mark Twain, *The Adventures of Huckleberry Finn* (1885)

I set down in a chair by the window and tried to think of something cheerful, but it warn't no use. I felt so lonesome I most wished I was dead. The stars were shining, and the leaves rustled in the woods ever so mournful; and I heard an owl, away off, who-whooing about somebody that was dead, and a whippowill and a dog crying about somebody that was going to die; and the wind was trying to whisper something to me, and I couldn't make out what it was, and so it made the cold shivers run over me. Then away out in the woods I heard that kind of a sound that a ghost makes when it wants to tell about something that's on its mind and can't make itself understood, and so can't rest in its grave, and has to go about that way every night grieving. I got so downhearted and scared I did wish I had some company. Pretty soon a spider went crawling up my shoulder, and I flipped it off and it lit in the candle; and before I could budge it was all shriveled up. I didn't need anybody to tell me that that was an awful bad sign and would fetch me some bad luck. . . . I got up and turned around in my tracks three times and crossed my breast every time; and then I tied up a little lock of my hair with a thread to keep witches away. But I didn't have no confidence. You do that when you've lost a horseshoe that you've found, instead of nailing it up over the door, but I hadn't ever heard anybody say it was any way to keep off bad luck when you've killed a spider.[10]

why activist Pietro Spina (alias priest Don Paolo) is frustrated in his attempts to rally Abruzzi peasants to left-wing political causes. Silone dwells on the peasants' fear of the evil eye (see Box 1–2) and other traditional supernatural phenomena and describes the many ways the people try to protect themselves from sinister unseen forces. In doing so, Silone reveals that the principal obstacle to change in Italy's Abruzzi region is the inhabitants' collective, conservative, and fatalistic worldview.[11]

Peruvian author Mario Vargas Llosa titles one of his novels *The Storyteller* (1989), playing that role himself to tell the tale of Saúl Zuratas, commonly known as Mascarita because the right side of his face is covered by a dark birthmark. But the novel's narrator's story reveals that the East European–Peruvian Creole–Jewish-Christian Mascarita is transformed culturally as he learns the traditional tales of the indigenous Machiguengas and discovers so much about their way of life from the stories that he becomes not just a convert to the tribe but also its storyteller. Llosa acknowledges his indebtedness to "Father Joaquin Barriales, O.P., the collector and translator of many Machiguenga songs and myths that appear in my book."[13]

Authors usually draw upon recent experiences or childhood memories when relying on and incorporating folklore into their fiction. An example is Guy Owen, who authored a novel that was made into a Hollywood movie, *The Flim Flam Man*

BOX 1–2

References to the Evil Eye in Ignacio Silone's Novel *Bread and Wine* (1936)

When Magascià is taking Don Paolo to Pietrasecca, [these two characters in the novel] pass a family of poor peasants.

> "How are the crops?" Magascià asked the man on the donkey.
> "Bad, very bad," was the answer.
> "That means he'll have a good harvest," Magascià whispered in the priest's ear.
> "Then why did he say the opposite?"
> "To save himself from the evil eye, of course," said Magascià.

Despite precautions against the evil eye, . . . unexplainable happenings are believed to result from its power. Matalena attributes the 1915 earthquake to the evil eye and fears it so much that she remains buried in the ruins of her house for several days rather than permit rescuers to dig her out. She is also convinced that the bad eye caused the death of her late husband, who was run over by an automobile.

> "I started weeping and wailing and crying that it was the evil eye that had got him because he had just been coming home to live in a new house. But the clerk insisted that it wasn't the evil eye, but an accident that might have happened to anybody. But it must really have been the evil eye. Of course priests say they don't believe in the evil eye, but if they really didn't believe in it they wouldn't wear black."

In at least one instance the results of the penetrating glance are even more mystical. Donna Evangelina, a student, had this experience:

> "She went to Rome for the government party anniversary celebration, and the head of the government . . . seems to have looked at her. He was two hundred yards away! Ever since Donna Evangelina has done nothing but talk of the devastating glance that penetrated her from two hundred yards' distance. It made the poor girl pregnant."[12]

(1967), directed by Irvin Kershner and starring George C. Scott as a veteran Southern con-man. Owen has published other novels as well as short stories. In an article titled "Using Folklore in Fiction" he explains how and why he purposely utilizes folklore in his writings.[14]

> Like most Southern novelists, I grew up listening to people spinning yarns. . . . I listened to the tall tales of a ghost named Caleb, who walked the Elkton trestle at night carrying his head like a jack-o'-lantern under his arm. I listened to the yarns of the deer and coon hunters about a mythical wild cat that could never be treed, and of the old days when dark "painters" [panthers] leaped from the woods on my grandfather Burney's house and the bears walked like men into the cornfields, carrying out arms of roastenears stacked like stove wood. I grew up hearing the tall tales of moonshiners who outwitted the law. . . . And many is the tale I heard of pinhookers, those cunning speculators, and the trickery they used in gypping country folk out of their tobacco. . . . Because of my background, then, it is only natural that I should people my fictional world with moonshiners and pinhookers and country folk who outwit the law at every turn, as is the case in *The Ballad of the Flim-Flam Man.*

Owen also learned dialect and superstitions from African American sharecroppers with whom he grew up.

> I noted the graves covered with sea shells, much later learning that the shells were an ancient symbol of immortality. . . . I heard dark tales of Negroes who used "conjuring powders" or other means to cast spells or "put the bad mouth" on their enemies, and I knew an old woman who sold love potions.

One of the examples of stories that influenced Owen's writing came from an African American friend, Frank Gillings, who became known as Geechee.

> Geechee and I practically grew up together, and I learned unconsciously a great deal of Negro lore from him. . . . Of the many

stories he told me, one concerned the way he outwitted three bootleggers at Lake Waccamaw. . . . In those days the Negroes in our section celebrated the sixth of July, not the fourth, as Independence Day. . . .
> As the story goes, Geechee had given out of money before his thirst for white lightning was slaked, and when he asked for credit the moonshiners had given him short shrift. He brooded about this serious blow to his full participation in the 6th of July festivities and was bound and determined to pay back the men who had so grossly offended him.
> He set into spying on them, discovering that they had a large number of cases of illegal whiskey stacked in the bushes and carefully guarded. He hid behind a tree and the next time the men drove up in their car for a fresh supply, Geechee leaped from hiding and ran toward them shouting, "Run for your lives. The sheriff is on to you and is right behind me!" The moonshiners dived into their car and betook themselves from Lake Waccamaw, leaving my friend with a lavish amount of bottle-in-barn. According to his version, he passed out the whiskey gratis to all his friends and became the hero of the 6th of July celebration. . . .
> Now Geechee told me this and swore it was the gospel. I have my doubts about it, for he was known to stretch his blanket on occasion. Nevertheless, the story stuck with me for over twenty-five years, and it forms the basis for Chapter 7 in *The Ballad of the Flim-Flam Man.* I merely substituted my con-man hero Mordecai Jones for Geechee and Doodle Powell for the insensitive, ungenerous Negro bootleggers.

In this and other instances, Owen bases his own literary creation on folklore. "In my new novel, Curley Treadaway, the narrator of *The Ballad of the Flim-Flam Man,* is almost caught one night raiding Doodle Powell's still in Slade Swamp. To escape, he climbs the nearest tree, pretends he is 'Belzybub,' an angel of the Lord's, and successfully converts the dangerous moonshiner, and escapes without being detected. (Of course, there are numerous folk tales in which a man hides in a tree and pretends to be God.) But it does not end there," writes Owen, who explains that he elaborates events for many pages. "In other words, out of this nugget of a folk yarn I have fashioned two chapters of a comic novel—at least they are funny to me."

Dialect and folk sayings aid in establishing a sense of place in Owen's novels, he writes. "Most of the folk speech I picked up listening to my grandfather. . . . He was a gifted teller of tales in his quiet way, and his speech was peppered with dialect words." Like Mark Twain (in *Huckleberry Finn*) and many other novelists before him, Owen sprinkles his fiction with dialect and proverbial speech. "It is easy to see why such folk sayings would appeal to a writer of fiction," Owen contends. "They are concrete, vivid and, unless overused, fresh and charged with energy and surprise. Above all, they are authentic and they add color and flavor to the Southern writer's style."[15] As evidence, Owen notes that Orville Prescott, reviewing *The Ballad of the Flim-Flam Man* in the *New York Times*, wrote: "Who can resist a hero who says, 'He moved as slow as smoke off a manure pile?'"[16]

In sum, writers often base their creations on folklore as plots or incorporate folklore as structural devices. Beliefs, proverbs, narratives, and other examples of folklore may set the tone or alter a mood. Dialect and traditional sayings can convey character and a sense of place. Stories may serve as a way to communicate precepts and values.

Television shows also incorporate folklore. On the 1980s sitcom "Night Court," the defense attorney (Ellen Foley as Billy) knocks on wood for good luck. In an episode of "Evening Shade" during the 1990–91 season, Burt Reynolds as Wood tells a lawyer joke, one of many in the cycle portraying attorneys negatively. Jonathan Winters as Gunny Davis on "Davis Rules" tries to calm Randy Quaid, who frets while awaiting news of whether or not his son made the baseball team. "You know, Dwight, a watched boy never arrives," he says, changing the wording but not the meaning of the proverb "A watched pot never boils." In an episode of "Roseanne," Roseanne Barr divines the sex of her friend Crystal's baby using a ring suspended from a string. When Roseanne makes fun of Crystal for insisting on having a girl baby instead of the boy that is foretold, Roseanne's daughter says cynically, "God, Mom, get a life!" In so remarking, she employs a slang expression current at the time.

Films, too, use examples of folklore. Years ago, Walt Disney produced three animated features based on fairy tales: *Snow White and the Seven Dwarfs* (Type 709, 1937), *Cinderella* (Type 510, 1950), and *Sleeping Beauty* (Type 410, 1959). More recently the studio added *Beauty and the Beast* (Type 425C, 1991), the title song for which won an Academy Award in 1992, and *Aladdin* (Type 561, 1992), recipient of two Oscars in 1993.

Other films center on omens, witches, and evil spirits. In having a hideous, eellike creature burst forth from a man's chest, Ridley Scott's 1979 box-office hit *Alien* offers a theme that parallels oral accounts of the "Bosom Serpent" (or the frog or lizard in the stomach) which date back several centuries. The legend "Bloody Mary" (Mary Whales, Mary Worth, etc.),[17] in which someone conjures up a spirit by repeating into a mirror in a darkened room, "Mary Whales [or other name], I believe in you," is analogous to the legend and ritual in Barnard Rose's 1992 psychological chiller, *Candyman*. The central character, played by Virginia Madsen, is a Master's Degree student in Chicago completing her study of modern legends, particularly the one about a mysterious serial killer named Candyman who, one of her informants insists, is real.

National Lampoon's Vacation (1985) offers a comedic transformation of "The Runaway Grandmother." As in oral accounts, an elderly woman on vacation with her family dies (in this case it's Aunt Edna). Stranded in the middle of nowhere, the family wraps her in a tarp and ties her to the luggage rack on top of the car. Usually in oral accounts the car is stolen, the body along with it, whereas in the film the family deposits Aunt Edna on the patio at the home of her nephew (who is away), an umbrella propped in her arms to shield her from the rain.[18]

Legends in particular have been favored in mass media. In Ethan and Joel Coen's farcical film *Raising Arizona* (1987), a pair of bumbling fugitives kidnaps an infant, then accidentally loses him by leaving him atop their getaway car during an inept gas-station robbery. This resembles the "Baby on the Roof" story told by people to one another a decade before. John Sayles's 1980 horror film *Alligator* seems to be based on the alligators-in-the-sewers legend (which also appears in Thomas Pynchon's 1963 novel *V.*). (See Box 1–3.)

The most frequently collected legend in the United States, "The Vanishing Hitchhiker" (Motif E332.3.3.1.), has served as the basis for several television plots and popular songs. It usually concerns a driver who picks up a young woman walking along the road, only to discover on arriving at her destination that she has vanished. She had died several years before, but returns annually as a ghost. Dickey Lee's "Laurie," subtitled "Strange Things Happen," is one of the best-known songs based on the legend.[21]

Advertising has long included folklore. In the 1950s, a print ad for Borden milk advised, ". . . and here's how to keep healthy, wealthy and wise!" Another by the Industrial Rayon Corporation read, "Pennies saved are pennies earned . . . and panties of Spun-lo are still only about 69¢."[22] Both proverbs are associated with Benjamin Franklin, but many of these aphorisms he printed were orally communicated.[23] In the 1960s, Skippy peanut butter's commercials, print ads, and billboards urged us to "Swallow [follow] the leader." A commercial for Imperial margarine put to use the tune and part of the text of the nursery rhyme "Sing a Song of Sixpence." Procter and Gamble invoked *Cinderella* (Type 510) to promote the cleaning agent Mr. Clean:

> *One older sister:* "Cinderella, wash the floor."
> *Other older sister:* "Yeah, wash it, and then re-wax it."

BOX 1–3
Alligators in the Sewers

Full-grown alligators prowled the sewers of New York. It seems that Miami vacationers returning to New York in the winter brought back baby alligators as pets for their children. The more the alligators grew the less ideal they appeared as playmates, and their owners, too tenderhearted to skin them for their hides, flushed them down the toilet. Some survived in their new environment and confronted sewer maintenance workers, who publicly protested at this unnecessary additional hazard to their occupation.
—Richard M. Dorson[19]

*   *   *

Did he remember the baby alligators? Last year, or maybe the year before, kids all over Nueva York bought these little alligators for pets. Macy's was selling them for fifty cents; every child, it seemed, had to have one. But soon the children grew bored with them. Some set them loose in the streets, but more flushed them down the toilets. And these had grown and reproduced, had fed off rats and sewage, so that now they moved big, blind, albino, all over the sewer system. Down there, God knew how many there were. Some had turned cannibal because in their neighborhood the rats had all been eaten, or had fled in terror.
—Thomas Pynchon[20]

(Sisters leave for the ball.)
Cinderella: "Wash, wax, pfui!"
(Fairy Godmother appears.)
Fairy Godmother: "Phew, ammonia. That strips wax. But use Mr. Clean with no ammonia. Mr. Clean gets the dirt but leaves the wax shining and you get a sheen.
Cinderella: "Wow!"
Fairy Godmother: "And now off to the ball?"
Cinderella: "Ball-schmall. Tonight's my bowling league. Bye."[24]

In 1974, McDonald's touted its new "quarter pounder" in a two-page ad with two giant juicy hamburgers and the headline, "Man does not live by bread alone" (that is, the quarter pounder provides more meat for the money). Numerous transformations of this biblical proverb (Matthew 4:4) appeared during the period. For example, "Man cannot live by clothes alone," contended a print ad for a men's cologne by Pierre Cardin. "Man cannot live by blue jeans alone" read an ad by Wrangler, the maker of jeans in 37 colors and numerous styles.[25] Volkswagen relied heavily on folklore in its advertising in the early 1970s. Among other examples were its use of proverbial expressions such as "Ugly [Beauty] is only skin deep," "For people who can't stand the sight of a Volkswagen [blood]," and "It won't eat you out of house and home"; slang and traditional phrases like "We do our thing; you do yours" and "Different strokes for different folks"; and slogans of the period that had become conventional, such as "More power to the people."[26]

Advertising today continues to draw heavily upon folklore. "Man does not live by toast alone," states the headline for an ad illustrating nine different foods that can be prepared in the General Electric Ultra Oven Broiler. Proclaiming Bermuda to be a desirable getaway, the caption below a photograph of golfers on the green states: "It's not whether you win or lose, it's where you play

Figure 1–2: Print ad inspired by the folktale "Little Red Riding Hood" (by permission of Ford Parts and Service Division, Ford Motor Company).

the game," a twist on the traditional "it's how you play the game." An ad for a car stereo by Pioneer ("The Best Sound Going") is headlined: "Supertuner. Nobody can steal our thunder." A Ford/Mercury/Lincoln print ad showing a young woman driving a convertible through a dark forest with a wolf lurking behind a tree contains the headline "Little Red Rotting Hood—A tale of consumer rights, insurance companies and some very well-disguised auto parts." Below is a cautionary tale based on "Little Red Riding Hood" that begins, "Once upon a time, the differences between imitation auto replacement parts and genuine parts were obvious." In utilizing old adages, current slang, customs, nursery rhymes, and even fairy tales, advertisers assume readers' familiarity with the examples of folklore while simultaneously perpetuating them.

Authors of printed cartoons and comic strips also assume reader familiarity with folklore examples. For instance, a "Kit 'N' Carlyle" cartoon shows a kitten lapping up milk spilled from a carton on the floor. Alluding to a familiar proverb, the cat thinks to itself, "Why would anyone ever cry over spilt milk?" In a "Good News—Bad News" cartoon by Henry Martin, one man in a bar explains to another, "As I see it, Al's problem is threefold: (1) He isn't hitting on all cylinders. (2) He isn't cooking on all burners. (3) He isn't dealing from a full deck." Other cartoons make use of children's rhymes ("Rain, rain, go away, come again another day," sing the animals on Noah's ark); traditional sayings ("I get advice from every Tom, Dick and Harriet [Harry]," remarks Stanley Parker to a neighbor while his wife Harriet oversees his work); and elves, witches, and fairy tales ("Read me about Snow White and The Seven Divorces," Dennis the Menace requests of his father at bedtime).

With their multiple frames or panels, comic strips offer the chance to develop more of a storyline involving folklore. A "Cathy" strip by Cathy Guisewite illustrates this. In the first frame, the title char-

Figure 1–4: Cartoon incorporating reference to two children's games, "Simon Says" and "Mother, May I?" (the "Bizarro" cartoon by Dan Piraro is reprinted by permission of Chronicle Features, San Francisco, California).

Figure 1–3: Highway sign whose message derives from combining "Georgia, the peach state" with the slang "peachy keen" (photo by M. O. Jones).

acter (garbed in a robe and holding a telephone) thinks to herself, "Grant's phone is busy. That's an omen that I shouldn't be calling him." In the next frame Cathy thinks, "My hair is tangled. That's an omen that I shouldn't be going out with him today." Finally coifed and dressed, she thinks, "He's 3 minutes late, an omen that this whole relationship is out of sync." The final frame shows Grant inside the front door, dripping wet. "It's pouring out, Cathy," he says. "Maybe we shouldn't be going to the game today." Cathy responds: "Men are so superstitious."

Whether we live in remote areas or in urban centers, folklore pervades our lives. We all tell stories. We celebrate events, take part in rituals, and use figurative language. As children we sing jingles, participate in counting-out rhymes to determine who will be "it," tell jokes and riddles, and play

Figure 1–5: Strip cartoon using a familiar proverb (by permission of Johnny Hart and Creators Syndicate, Inc.).

games. At work we learn and use the jargon of our trade, follow custom and tradition to accomplish tasks, and tell stories about job-related experiences. At home we develop and engage in rituals such as family outings, holiday observances, or shared meals. Among friends we joke, tell stories about our common experiences, employ slang expressions or dialect terms, and offer advice in the form of beliefs or practices. If we watch television, go to the movies, or look at ads, we see and hear examples of folklore that have been removed from the interactional setting and incorporated into another context.[27]

The Varied Nature of Folklore

Because we express what we know, think, believe, and feel in wide-ranging and varied ways, those expressive forms, processes, and behaviors that are traditional and hence identifiable as folklore are also diverse. Folkloristics includes in its data base examples of myriad forms or genres, many of which have language as the principal medium of communication, such as fairy tales, ballads, myths, proverbs, and rhymes. But the nonverbal can be more dominant than the linguistic, as is the case with many games (Hopscotch, Hide-and-

Seek) and innumerable customs and rituals. Language may play no direct part at all. This is true for much music and dancing and for beliefs (unless they are verbalized) and objectmaking (unless craftspeople explain how they make what they do). Since neither the medium of expression nor genre is a defining criterion for data in their field,

---

BOX 1-4
Crime Victim Stories

One of the most popular traditions among New Yorkers is telling stories about significant events in their daily lives. The specific content of these urban tales may vary, but they often share common characteristics and themes. Many New Yorkers, for example, recount their experiences with power blackouts, transit or garbage strikes, battles at traffic court, or eccentric characters. As storytellers, they select their accounts from an extensive repertory of narratives that includes other stories, perhaps more personal or intimate. Yet, whether intimate or commonplace, many of these tales deal with some aspect of crime victimization or some feature of urban life. . . . Everyone has such stories to tell, whether about crime-victim situations, urban foul-ups, or some other, equally dramatic, aspect of city life.
—Eleanor Wachs[28]

A
ROUND TUIT

At long last we have a sufficient quantity of these so that each person may have one of his own. Guard it with your life. These TUITS have been hard to come by, especially the round ones. This is an indispensable item. It will help you become a much more efficient person. For years you have been saying, "I'll do that as soon as I get 'A Round Tuit'." Now that you have a round tuit of your very own, all those things that have been needing to be accomplished will surely get done.

*****

Figure 1–7: An example of commodification of folklore (see Fig. 1–6) in the form of a potholder advertised and sold through a mass-distributed catalogue (photo by M. O. Jones).

THIS IS AN INDISPENSABLE ITEM FOR EVERYBODY FOR YEARS, PEOPLE HAVE BEEN SAYING, "I'LL DO IT AS SOON AS I GET A ROUND TUIT"

THE ABOVE IS A ROUND TUIT. CUT IT OUT. KEEP IT HANDY, AND YOU WILL HAVE NO MORE TROUBLE GETTING ALL THOSE EXTRAS DONE. YOU FINALLY GOT A ROUND TUIT

Figure 1–6: Two examples of photocopier lore, illustrating diversity of and variation in folklore.

folklorists focus their inquiries on examples as varied as autograph album verse, visual riddles, legends, jumprope rhymes, photocopy machine lore, quiltmaking, nursery rhyme parodies, fiddle tunes, latrinalia (writing on restroom walls), and ethnic jokes.

Diversity in folklore also occurs because of *variation*. By definition, every folklore example exists in multiple *versions* or *variants* (see Box 1–5). Each version is distinctive because it is generated at a given time and under a unique set of circumstances. Differences among multiple versions of a particular folklore example range from the imperceptible to the obvious. There is usually no difference, for instance, in wording each time the proverb "A rolling stone gathers no moss" is spoken, even though there may be notable contrasts in stress and intonation or in the situations they comment on. By contrast, verbatim repetition is rare, if not impossible, in telling fairy tales such as *Cinderella* (Type 510) or *Rapunzel* (Type 310), whether the narrators and audience members are the same or different from telling to telling.

Folklore learned in one era or language and perpetuated in another time or tongue also results in variation. The English-language proverb "A bird in the hand is worth two in the bush," for example, has been documented in such historically earlier variant forms as "A birde in the hand is worth ten in the wood" (1562) and "A byrde yn hond ys better than thre yn the wode" (1530). Equivalents in other languages include "Better a sparrow in the hand than two flying" (Portuguese), "Better one bird

By its very nature, folklore is traditional and its preservation depends upon custom and memory. It is, therefore, subject to all the variations that come from the attempt to repeat exactly the customary action, or to tell or perform that which has been learned from listening to someone else. Every performance of such an act and every repetition of such a tale or song displays differences from all others. These variations may be involuntary, where the aim is an exact repetition, or they may represent a conscious attempt at creation within the framework of the tradition. Since every repetition thus displays variations, it is customary to call each example of an item of folklore a variant. If the idea of variation is not foremost in the mind of the speaker, he is more likely to use the term *version*. There is otherwise no difference in the use of these two terms.
—Stith Thompson[29]

in the pot than ten in the wood" (Swedish-Finnish), and "Better a hawk in the hand than two in flight" (Icelandic).[30]

Variety in the folkloristic data base comes about as well because the same events are reported or memorialized in more than one way, either in the same or different forms. The murder and decapitation of a pregnant young woman named Pearl Bryan near Fort Thomas, Kentucky, in January of 1896, for example, was the source and subject of six different ballads, all of which became traditional.[31] A bridge in Arta, Greece, that remained structurally unsound and uncrossable until the wife of the master craftsman was walled up alive in its foundation became and remains widely known through the characterization of the event in legend as well as ballad.[32] The sinking of the ocean liner *Titanic* in 1912, the 1963 assassination of President John F. Kennedy, and the explosion of the American space shuttle *Challenger* in 1986 became subjects of jokes as well as multiple songs and legends, all of which have endured through time and spread through space, principally by word of mouth.[33]

Finally, there is variety in the folkloristic data base because folklore gives rise to

Figure 1–8: The Bridge of Arta in Greece, which is the subject of legend and ballad (photo by R. A. Georges).

folklore. Joke cycles and parodies illustrate this process. Once they are created and become current, for instance, narratives of particular kinds (knock-knock jokes, shaggy-dog stories) proliferate, as do those about historical and fictional characters, such as legends about singer Elvis Presley, anecdotes about Mormon elder J. Golden Kimball, and jokes about the fictional Irishmen Pat and Mike and Swedes Ole and Sven. Folklore examples are also regularly parodied, and the parodies themselves frequently become folklore, as is the case, for instance, with the following nursery rhyme and the two parodies that follow it:

Mary had a little lamb,
Its fleece was white as snow;
And everywhere that Mary went
The lamb was sure to go.
It followed her to school one day,
Which was against the rule;
It made the children laugh and play
To see a lamb at school.

* * *

Mary had a little lamb,
Her father shot it dead.
Now Mary takes the lamb to school
Between two hunks of bread

* * *

Mary had a little lamb,
She also had a bear.
I've seen her lamb a dozen times,
But I've never seen her bear [bare].

Folklore is self-perpetuating too when aspects of specific traditions are incorporated into other folklore examples. A given musical score, for instance, may serve as the tune for several songs with entirely different words; and the words of a particular song may be sung to different tunes. This is the case with the hymn "Amazing Grace," which is sung to numerous tunes, including one called "New Britain," which is also integral to five other hymns commonly sung by white Primitive Baptists.[34] The same plot is often communicated through both narrating and singing, as is the case with a widely disseminated story about a musical instrument made from body parts of a murder victim that reveals the identity of the slayer.[35] Narrative sequences are frequently found in multiple folklore examples, such as those that depict a hero's accomplishment of impossible tasks (planting fields and then making the crops mature and harvesting them within a few days' time), or that portray his eventual success in rescuing a princess held by a powerful captor (a giant, a seven-headed dragon) or in some inaccessible place (atop a glass mountain). Different stories often begin and end with the same formulaic language ("Once upon a time," "And they lived happily ever after"); and distinctive songs often share the same refrains ("Hey derry, derry, down," "Fa la la diddle"). In sum, any aspect of a folklore example may serve as the basis for, or be made a part of, another one, either of the same or different kind.

How Is Folklore Documented?[36]

Since folklore is such an integral part of human existence, opportunities to observe, elicit, and document it are limitless. Children play familiar games (Tag, London Bridge) in village squares and on city streets, for example, where their behavior is subject to scrutiny by the casual observer or the interested passerby. Joketelling occurs regularly on the job and at social gatherings. Music-making, singing, and dancing frequently evolve spontaneously at family and small-group gatherings.

Greetings ("What's happening?"), slang ("blockhead," "the real McCoy"), and proverbial speech (She "holds the upper hand," I guess I just "lost my head") recur with surprising frequency during casual conversations and formal addresses. Objects characterized by conventional patterns (patch-work quilts) and identifiable decorative motifs (bent-arm crosses) are produced, exchanged, and utilized by people everywhere. Human groups ranging from hunters and farmers to students and doctors all develop special lexicons and create and perpetuate rituals, the existence of which may be known only to group members. Thus, one need not travel to exotic places, seek out some preselected segment of the human population, or wait until some special time to find folklore.

While opportunities to discern examples of folklore arise spontaneously and unexpectedly whenever and wherever human beings interact face to face, they are also often generated at predetermined times or in predesignated places. In all societies, for example, the telling of certain kinds of stories is a family or community event, the time and place for which are known or stipulated in advance. Weddings, funerals, and initiation ceremonies are always prearranged, with the kinds of activities marking these major transitional or liminal stages in life being based on well-established mod-

els. Dates and sites for such calendrical celebrations as agricultural rituals, religious ceremonies, and ethnic festivals are known in advance, as are the nature and sequence of the activities that distinguish these occasions from all others. Preplanning enables one to witness or obtain information about such scheduled events and to test hypotheses about the part folklore plays in their unfolding, enactment, and perpetuation.

Examples of folklore can also be elicited, described, and discussed through impromptu questioning or systematic interviewing. The expressive nature of folklore makes it readily distinguishable from other experiences. The ability to differentiate such modes of communicating enables all individuals to characterize or describe songs and stories they and others know, beliefs to which they and others subscribe, objects they and others make, expressions they and others use, and so forth. Therefore, an interviewer can elicit examples of, and information about, folklore from others; and such information and examples serve as data for a folklorist's inquiries.

Figure 1–9: Zora Neale Hurston (L), eliciting folklore from Rochelle French and Gabriel Brown (R) in Eatonville, Florida, in 1935 (USZ61–1777, John and Alan Lomax Collection, courtesy Prints and Photographs Division, Library of Congress).

Figure 1–10: In doing fieldwork to study folklore in its naturally occurring environment, Linda Gastañaga interviews Circle A Ranch foreman Dennis Brown during spring branding, Humboldt County, Nevada (NV–6–19754–32, photo by Carl Fleishhauer, courtesy American Folklife Center, Library of Congress).

tal note of examples of proverbial speech and of specific occasions on which they are used. Jokes, riddles, jargon terms, gestures, rhymes, and simple songs and melodies can be readily committed to memory. When later recollected, these examples of folklore can be easily characterized, either orally or in writing.

Secondly, folklorists make written records. The words a singer sings or a storyteller speaks can be represented fairly accurately in writing; and drawings or written descriptions can characterize such tangible objects as buildings or cooking utensils. Whether they are verbatim transcriptions of riddles or myths, summaries of epics or ballads, or sketches of house floorplans or body decorations, written records are more permanent than human recollections. They have served as folklorists' primary docu-

Systematic questioning and observation are techniques of fieldwork. Once referring to laborious agricultural tasks performed by hand, the word *fieldwork* has come to designate the act of inquiring into the nature of phenomena by studying them at first hand in the environments in which they naturally exist or occur.[37] Long associated with the activities of anthropologists, sociologists, and linguists, and now common in psychology, education, and oral history research, fieldwork as a data-gathering process began in earnest with those who first systematically recorded folklore during the late eighteenth and early nineteenth centuries.

Folklore can be documented in numerous ways. The oldest and most fundamental is simply remembering what one experiences. Aware that proverbial expressions may be employed during virtually any firsthand interaction, for instance, folklorists can condition themselves to make men-

Figure 1–11: W. D. Hand in the UCLA Archive of American Folk Medicine examines some of the 200,000 cards containing data from both field collections and published works (photo by Bill Bebee, courtesy UCLA Folklore and Mythology Archives).

Figure 1–12: A set of cards in the UCLA Archive of American Folk Medicine documenting treatments for warts (photo by Bill Bebee, courtesy UCLA Folklore and Mythology Archives).

est amount of scholarly attention include storytelling and stories, singing and songs, music-making and tunes, riddling and riddles, and speaking and speech forms such as proverbs. The aural aspects of all of these can be easily and accurately recorded on magnetic tape. Second, while folklorists gather their data by participating, observing, and interviewing, it is the last of these that always has been, and continues to be, the principal means of eliciting folklore and information about it. Since interviewing entails questioning and answering, and hence relies heavily on speech, tape recording is an efficient and effective way of documenting interviews. Finally, the tape recorder has proved to be the least intrusive or objectionable mechanical recording device available. For these reasons, folklorists have come to regard the tape recorder as a useful, and often essential, piece of equipment; and sound recordings have taken their place alongside written records as primary documents in folklore research.[39]

The documentation techniques the folklorist employs depend on a number of factors, including availability, appropriateness, local custom and belief, and personal preference. In addition, the choice rests on the information the folklorist seeks in order to test some hypothesis or to illustrate a particular phenomenon. An investigator interested in opening and closing formulas in fairy tales, for instance, could document these in memory, in writing, or on magnetic tape; but it might seem inappropriate as well as unnecessarily cumbersome and expensive to film multiple storytellings in order to obtain such information. On the other hand, folklorists wishing to document and analyze the nonverbal aspects of narrators' performances or listeners' responses could not capture such information on audio tape and would miss much of it while trying to take notes; therefore they would likely choose to film the event. Though some recommend that folklorists

ments since the inception of their discipline in the early nineteenth century.

Increasingly over the years, folklorists have relied on mechanical recording devices, both as substitutes for and supplements to mental and written records. Still pictures and photographic slides can record shapes, colors, and designs of such material objects as items of clothing or pieces of pottery; and they can freeze for all time a moment in a dance or a movement pattern of people at play. Motion picture and video cameras enable one to document the dynamic nature of narrator-audience interactions; the finger, hand, and body movements of musicians; and the actions and reactions of participants in rituals. Whether presented alone or in conjunction with oral or written descriptions, photographic records of folklore capture on film visual images that could otherwise only be documented by the human eye.[38]

Of all the available mechanical recording devices, the tape recorder is the one that folklorists have used most extensively and that has had the greatest impact on their work. There are several reasons why this is so. First, the expressive forms, processes, and behaviors that have received the great-

BOX 1–6
Folklore Texts

A text, in the parlance of the folklorist, represents the basic source, the pure stream, the inviolable document of oral tradition. It comes from the lips of a speaker or singer and is set down with word for word exactness by a collector, using the method of handwritten dictation or mechanical recording. What the state paper is to the historian and creative work to the library scholar, the oral traditional text is—or should be—to the student of folklore. He [or she] cannot discuss and appraise the aesthetics of oral style if the sources at his [or her] disposal mingle the spoken words of an informant with the written intrusions of an editor. Nor can he [or she] be sure that the beliefs and values revealed in folklore are accurate testimonials of a given culture if an alien hand from an outside culture has refined and "improved" the raw texts. . . .

The oral text differs in important ways from the literary text, which must always be relegated to a secondary position by the professional folklorist. A spoken narrative comes from the speaker's mouth with the freshness and spontaneity—and the garbled syntax and meanderings—of everyday talk. A written retelling is pruned and polished and often enough altered to suit the bias of the author and the expectations of the reader. . . .

Literary revisions of folklore will always concern the folklorist, both for their revelations of folk influences on the great masters and for their preservation of perishable folkstuff. Lacking field collections before the nineteenth century, the folklorist must turn to a thousand literary sources to capture and to date the traditions of yesteryear. He [or she] has recourse to Herodotus and Boccaccio and Chaucer, to medieval romances and jestbooks and saints' legends, to the Thousand and One Nights and the Ocean of Story, to popular songsters and county histories and local newspapers. But his [or her] ultimate test to determine the traditional character of a literary text must always be its approximation to a field-collected text. In the hierarchy of folk tradition, Homer ranks below Frank Alley of Jonesport, Maine; for to determine if each has retold the same hoary sailor's yarn, we hold Homer's version up to the one told by the old lobsterman . . . , as he heard it from a fellow who heard it from a fellow—and then surmise that Homer too must have tapped an oral source.

—Richard M. Dorson[40]

Figure 1–13: Videotaping breakdancing in New York City in 1981 (photo by Martha Cooper).

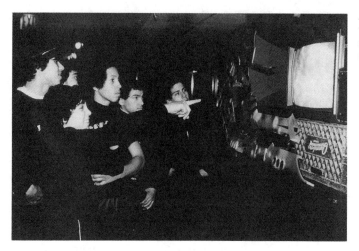

Figure 1–14: Breakdancers
watch themselves on videotape (photo by Martha
Cooper).

BOX 1–7
Making Films about Folklore

The successful documentary film can transport viewers, however briefly, to places
and events they would never see on their own. Likewise, the sheer carrying of the
camera can give the photographer an "excuse" to enter and observe places he or she
doesn't necessarily belong. However, at least with documentary films about folk
culture, the medium of film also offers a chance to support, verify, and reinforce the
indigenous subject matter of the film. Hopefully made with trust and understanding
from the subjects of the film, this kind of documentary becomes not only a collabora-
tive effort among the film makers, but also a kind of collaboration between the film
makers and the people or community represented in the film.
     —Tom Rankin[41]

Figure 1–15: Vance Ran-
dolph audiotaping "Dea-
con" Hembree's fiddling,
1941 or 1942 (photo by
Townsend Godsey, courtesy
Lyons Memorial Library,
College of the Ozarks).

Figure 1–16: Church deacon Leonard Bryan (L) and folklorist Pat Mullen read an illustrated article in the Washington Star *about Mullen's recent visit to Bryan's home to collect folklore (BR8–2–20424–16, photo by Gerald N. Johnson, courtesy American Folklife Center, Library of Congress).*

record as much information as possible from or about those who serve as their research subjects or informants, it is neither practical nor necessary for them always to utilize the most technically sophisticated devices or to make multiple kinds of records simply because the equipment or opportunity exists to do so. Inquiry is, by definition, always selective and focused.

How Are Folklorists Employed?

More than 500 colleges and universities in the United States and Canada offer folklore courses. There are 16 degree-granting programs, four of which confer the Ph.D.— the University of California, Los Angeles (UCLA), Indiana University, the University of Pennsylvania, and Memorial University in St. John's, Newfoundland. At 80 institutions undergraduates may minor or take a concentration in folklore.[42]

Those trained in folkloristics find employment in a variety of professions. Many

teach in universities and colleges, either in folklore programs or departments or in such other fields as English, history, anthropology, ethnic studies, American studies, music (or ethnomusicology), dance ethnology, and area studies programs. Public school teachers take courses or earn degrees in folklore studies to enrich their curricular offerings in language arts, social science, and history through their knowledge and increased understanding of the folklore of different groups, cultures, and eras.

Some with training in folkloristics become information and library science specialists, finding employment as archivists and librarians. Others launch careers in historical, art, and science and industry museums, where they work to preserve and display material manifestations of culture and behavior that are vital and integral to all societies. Some folklorists work in living history and open-air museums that preserve or re-create typical villages, farms, and ways of life from earlier eras.

Most of the 56 states and territories of the United States as well as many cities

Figure 1–17: Martha Warren Beckwith (1871–1959) began her career studying folk dance but extended her research to a wide range of expressive forms among Native Americans, Native Hawaiians, and Jamaican Blacks; she held the first academic chair of folklore in the United States (Vassar College, beginning in 1920), presided over the American Folklore Society in 1932–33, and published six books, a dozen monographs, and more than fifty essays and reviews (courtesy Mt. Holyoke College Library/Archives).

employ folklorists on the staffs of historical commissions, humanities committees, and arts councils. Several not-for-profit organizations have been founded by folklorists and/or employ those trained in folkloristics. The folklorists' responsibilities include identifying, documenting, and presenting folk art, ethnic foods, dancing, music-making, singing, and narrating. Often this takes the form of planning, coordinating, and scheduling festivals and exhibits. Folk arts coordinators, cultural conservationists, or folklife specialists, as they are variously called, also produce publications, radio programs, and films or videotapes about local or regional folklore and the traditions of various ethnic and occupational groups, families, and neighborhoods.

Others who study folklore work in the entertainment industry. Some are musicians, singers, and dancers or choreographers; others are technicians. A few develop, direct, or produce special programming. Some advise film studios or write scripts.

Many folklorists apply their training in service professions. Some work in public health and social welfare programs. Their knowledge of traditional beliefs and practices, coupled with their training in observ-

---

BOX 1–8
Folklore Research and Museums

What museums can offer folklife . . . is an intellectually congenial home and a forum for public education. Ideas from the world of folklife are finding expression in more and more museum-sponsored exhibitions; each passing year adds dozens of new entries to the burgeoning list of important folklife exhibits.

. . . [B]eyond the access to particular subjects, folklife [study] seems to offer museums an approach to democratizing their exhibits, research, and other activities. Where other disciplines are national or international in thrust, folklife can highlight the local and regional. Where other approaches seem a bit elite or upper-crust, folklife can be homespun and evoke life at the grassroots. Where other approaches emphasize the extraordinary, folklife can explore and celebrate the ordinary life. Folklife offers a way of seeing form and splendor in what before seemed ordinary, and its emphasis on tradition presents possibilities for reconnecting the past with the present.
 —Alan Jabbour[43]

Figure 1–18: Sister Diana Akhgar leading a social studies class on Iran (1982) dressed in a chaddor, *the outer garment of the women of Iran (196610–4–24A, photo by Susan Dwyer-Shick, courtesy American Folklife Center, Library of Congress).*

BOX 1–9
Folklorists' Use of Media

In the broadest sense of bringing information and ideas before a public, folklorists routinely publish in all the common media: speech, sound recordings, radio, television, films, videotapes, still photographs, drawings and sketches, print, exhibits of material objects, firsthand demonstration and performance. I cannot think of another discipline that claims all those media, singly or in combination.
—Judith McCulloh[44]

---

ing and interviewing, equips them to advise medical practitioners or help patients and clients. Some develop and supervise programming for the elderly, designing life-review projects with the aging, for example, in which they record, characterize, or present family, ethnic, and work traditions. Yet others with degrees in folkloristics are employed in environmental planning, assessing the potential impact of development projects on people's traditional ways of life, helping generate government policies on cultural preservation, or documenting and publicly presenting the local customs, objects, and other traditions. Some are employed in agencies involved in economic development, often through crafts assistance programs.

Others trained in folkloristics work in public relations, using their knowledge of folklore and their abilities to elicit and document traditions to better design convention activities and publicity information. Some are employed in marketing and advertising. Folklorists also serve as travel agents and tour organizers or guides, using their knowledge of local customs and regional cultures to better serve their clients. Yet other folklorists work for management consulting firms or serve as inside consultants to organizations. They document and analyze occupational traditions and traditional aspects of corporate cultures to facilitate communication, enhance working

Figure 1–19: Gladys-Marie Fry (L) holds a workshop with Alabama quilters Eloise Dickerson and Mamie McKinstry at the 1986 Cultural Conservation program, "Traditional Crafts in a Post-Industrial Age" (86–7304–120, photo by Dale Hrabak, courtesy Smithsonian Institution Center for Folklife Programs & Cultural Studies).

relations, and participate in organizational development planning.[45]

How Is Folklore Conceived and Studied?

People commonly conceive and study folklore in three ways. One way is to regard folklore as individual items that exemplify specific forms—folktale, folksong, folk speech, or folk art, for instance—and to make these "folklore genres" and examples of them the foci of study.[46] Another approach is to consider folklore study a disciplinary subfield (of literary studies, anthropology, history, linguistics, or psychology, for instance) and to study folklore as one studies other things that serve as data for that discipline.[47] A third view is that folklore is the product and possession of certain groups, making these "folk groups" and their traditions the sources and subjects of folklore study.[48]

This book differs in that it focuses on the study of folklore as a discipline, identifiable

as *folkloristics*. For there has long been a community of scholars who focus upon folklore solely or principally in their inquiries and who have created through their research, teaching, and publications a distinctive field of study. We have organized the book around the principal perspectives that have developed in and guided this discipline.

In terms of the history of folkloristics, and from the viewpoint of a professional folklorist, folklore can be conceptualized and studied in four ways: as (1) *historical artifact*, (2) *describable and transmissible entity*, (3) *culture*, and (4) *behavior*. Each of these has as its intellectual foundation a set of assumptions about the nature and province of folklore. These assumptions determine what concepts are central to a folklorist's inquiries and what questions he or she poses and attempts to answer. They also dictate what kinds of investigative and documentation techniques the folklorist uses and how she or he represents and presents folklore to others.

Each of these four ways of conceptualizing and studying folklore is treated as a

BOX 1-10
Understanding the Species

The performance of folklore—whether it provides us with delight and amusement or causes us to fear and tremble—is one of our most fundamental human activities. The study of folklore, therefore, is not just a pleasant pastime useful primarily for whiling away idle moments. Rather, it is centrally and crucially important in our attempts to understand our own behavior and that of our fellow human beings.
—William A. Wilson[49]

how questions investigators address and what they conclude relate to the perspective under discussion. At the same time, we show that the four perspectives supplement and complement one another and are all necessary for a full understanding and appreciation of folklore.

Notes

1. These are three of the terms that have been coined in English to differentiate the folklorist's field of study from the phenomena folklorists study. For information about these terms, see Bruce Jackson, "Folkloristics," *Journal of American Folklore* 98 (1985):95–101; Don Yoder, "The Folklife Studies Movement," *Pennsylvania Folklife* 13 (1963):43–56; Richard M. Dorson, "Introduction," in *Folklore and Folklife: An Introduction* (Chicago: University of Chicago Press, 1972), pp. 1–50; and Simon J. Bronner, *American Folklore Studies: An Intellectual History* (Lawrence: University Press of Kansas, 1986), pp. 13, 57, 93, 108, and 122. Throughout this book, we use the term *folkloristics* rather than proposed alternatives because to us it denotes the study of folklore as a discipline with its own assumptions, concepts, lexicon, issues, and hypotheses.

2. For videotapes that indicate the pervasiveness of folklore in people's lives, see *Harmonize: Folklore in the Lives of Five Families* (1981, Steve Zeitlin and Paul Wagner, Center for Southern Folklore, color, VHS, 21 min.), and *Everywhere You Look: Folk Art in New York's Public Spaces* (1992, Varick Chittenden, Traditional Arts in Upstate New York, color, VHS, 16 min.). For a phonograph album with narratives, music, songs, and riddles of a single family, see the Archive of Folksong's *The Hammonds Family: A Study of a West Virginia Family's Traditions*, recorded and compiled by Carl Fleisshauer and Alan Jabbour (AFS L65-L66 [1973]).

3. "New Year" in Maria Leach, ed., *Funk & Wagnalls Standard Dictionary of Folklore, Mythology, and Legend*, 2 vols. (New York: Funk & Wagnalls, 1949–50), vol. 2, pp. 790–791. For additional information on folklore related to the new year, see "New Year's Day,"

perspective in folkloristics in this book. The perspectives are presented in the order in which folklorists emphasized them in their inquiries historically. However, it is our thesis that these four perspectives are inherent in all folklorists' studies, even though one or some combination of them may receive greater attention than the others. For example, a folklorist concerned principally with the cultural nature of the Potawatomi game *"kus-a-kee"* (squaw dice) is identifying the phenomenon according to genre (game) and by type (squaw dice). Furthermore, she or he either assumes or attests to its nature as a historical artifact by noting its traditionality. Finally, her or his description of the way the game is played amounts to a characterization of how the players behave. A behaviorally oriented study of storytelling that focuses on the ways an individual narrator adapts American tall tales (genre) to different audiences reveals the persistence of the stories over time (historical artifact) and the part their telling plays in varied cultural contexts.[50]

Characterizing the perspectives is the principal objective of, and the organizing principle for, the chapters that follow. We illustrate each perspective by describing and quoting from a variety of works, noting

"Islamic New Year," and "Emancipation Day" in Hennig Cohen and Tristram Potter Coffin, eds., *The Folklore of American Holidays* (Detroit: Gale Research, 1987), pp. 1–23. For works on the use of food in celebration, see Theodore C. Humphrey and Lin C. Humphrey, eds., *"We Gather Together": Food and Festival in American Life* (Ann Arbor: UMI Research Press, 1988).

4. See *Funk & Wagnalls Standard Dictionary*, especially entries for afterbirth, birth omen, birthstone, birth tree, caul, divination, life token, and twins. Other information about pregnancy beliefs presented here is taken from the following sources: Frances Maybell Cattermole-Tally, "From the Mystery of Conception to the Miracle of Birth: An Historical Survey of Beliefs and Rituals Surrounding the Pregnant Woman in Germanic Folk Tradition, Including Modern American Folklore" (Ph.D. diss., University of California, Los Angeles, 1978); Frances Cattermole-Tally, "Folk Customs of Pregnancy and Childbirth" (unpublished paper, 1980); and Vance Randolph, *Ozark Superstitions* (New York: Columbia University Press, 1947), chapter 9, "Pregnancy and Childbirth," pp. 192–210.

5. See Stith Thompson, *Motif-Index of Folk-Literature*, rev. ed., 6 vols. (Bloomington: Indiana University Press, 1955–58). Folklorists usually use the word *motif* to refer to phenomena, behaviors, and relationships found in traditional prose and poetic narratives (e.g., epics, ballads, fairy tales, legends, myths) that stand out because they contrast in obvious ways with one's sense of what is real or normal. Thus, pregnancy presented in a narrative as resulting from sexual intercourse between a male and female would not have the status of a motif, but pregnancy resulting from a woman's having faced the west wind or having eaten a particular food would. The concept of motif is discussed in greater detail in chapter 4. See also Dan Ben-Amos, "The Concept of Motif in Folklore," in Venetia J. Newall, ed., *Folklore Studies in the Twentieth Century: Proceedings of the Centenary Conference of the Folklore Society* (Totowa, N.J.: Rowman and Littlefield, 1980), pp. 17–36.

6. See Stith Thompson, *The Types of the Folktale: A Classification and Bibliography*, 2d rev., Folklore Fellows Communications 184 (Helsinki, 1961). Folklorists use the term *tale type* to identify a group of stories configured into a set and identified in a common way because the similarities discernible in their plots are judged to be too striking and significant quantitatively or qualitatively to be attributed to chance or coincidence. To identify a story as a *version* of "Cinderella" or "Little Red Riding-Hood" or "Rapunzel," for instance, indicates that each of these stories has been documented as having been told often over time and through space. The construct of the tale type is discussed in greater detail in chapter 4.

7. Kay Stone, "Things Walt Disney Never Told Us," *Journal of American Folklore* 88 (1975):42–50, and Francis A. de Caro, "Proverbs and Originality in Modern Short Fiction," *Western Folklore* 37 (1978):30–38.

8. For specific studies of works by many of these authors, see Steven Swann Jones, *Folklore and Literature in the United States: An Annotated Bibliography of Studies of Folklore in American Literature* (New York: Garland Publishing, 1984).

9. African American artist Romare Bearden (1912–88) also depicts conjure women in his works. See, for instance, his 1964 photolithograph titled "The Conjure Woman."

10. Mark Twain, *The Adventures of Huckleberry Finn* (New York: Holt, Rinehart and Winston, 1961), pp. 3–4.

11. Robert A. Georges, "Silone's Use of Folk Beliefs," *Midwest Folklore* 12 (1962):197–203, reprinted in Kenneth and Mary Clarke, eds., *A Folklore Reader* (New York: A. S. Barnes, 1965), pp. 197–206.

12. Georges, p. 200.

13. Mario Vargas Llosa, *The Storyteller*, trans. Helen Lane (New York: Penguin Group, 1990), p. 247.

14. Guy Owen, "Using Folklore in Fiction," *North Carolina Folklore* 13 (1965):147–155. Quotes are from pp. 150, 151, 152, 153, and 154. For books and articles concerning the use of folklore in American literature, see the work by Jones cited in n. 9.

15. Owen, p. 154.

16. Guy Owen, "The Use of Folklore in Fiction," *North Carolina Folklore* 19 (1991):73–79. The quote is from p. 75.

17. Janet Langlois, "'Mary Whales, I Believe in You': Myth and Ritual Subdued," *Indiana Folklore* 11 (1978):5–33, and Bengt af Klintberg, "'Black Madam, Come Out!'" *Scandinavian Yearbook of Folklore* 44 (1988):155–167.

18. See Stone; Harold Schechter, "If This Movie Seems Familiar," *New York Times* (Oct. 5, 1990); Daniel R. Barnes, "The Bosom Serpent: A Legend in American Literature and Culture," *Journal of American Folklore* 85 (1972):111–122; Rosan Jordan de Caro, "A Note about Folklore and Literature (The Bosom Serpent Revisited)," *Journal of American Folklore* 86 (1973):62–65; Harold Schechter, *The Bosom Serpent: Folklore and Popular Art* (Iowa City: University of Iowa Press, 1988); and Linda Dégh, "The Runaway Grandmother," *Indiana Folklore* 1 (1968):68–77. See also Larry Danielson, "Folklore and Film: Some Thoughts on Baughman Z 500–599," *Western Folklore* 38 (1979):209–219.

19. *America in Legend: Folklore from the Colonial Period to the Present* (New York: Pantheon Books, 1973), pp. 291–292.

20. *V* (New York: Bantam Books, 1964), p. 33.

21. For the story "The Baby on the Roof," see Jan Harold Brunvand, *The Choking Doberman and Other "New" Urban Legends* (New York: W. W. Norton, 1984), pp. 55–57. For "Alligators in the Sewer," see Loren Coleman, "Alligators-in-the-Sewers: A Journalistic Origin," *Journal of American Folklore* 92 (1979):335–338, and Jan Harold Brunvand, *The Vanishing Hitchhiker: American Urban Legends and Their Meanings* (New York: W. W. Norton, 1981), p. 92. In regard to "The Vanishing Hitchhiker," see Jan Harold Brunvand, *The Study of American Folklore: An Introduction,* 2d ed. (New York: W. W. Norton, 1978), p. 110; Brunvand, *The Vanishing Hitchhiker,* esp. pp. 41 and 46; Richard K. Beardsely and Rosalie Hankey, "The Vanishing Hitchhiker," *California Folklore Quarterly* 1 (1942):305–335; Richard K. Beardsely and Rosalie Hankey, "A History of the Vanishing Hitchhiker," *California*

Folklore Quarterly 2 (1943):13–25; Katharine Luomala, "Disintegration and Regeneration, the Hawaiian Phantom Hitchhiker Legend," *Fabula* 13 (1972):20–59; and William A. Wilson, "The Vanishing Hitchhiker among the Mormons," *Indiana Folklore* 8 (1975):80–97.

22. Julian Mason, "Some Uses of Folklore in Advertising," *Tennessee Folklore Society Bulletin* 20 (1954):58–61.

23. Stuart A. Gallacher, "Franklin's *Way to Wealth:* A Florilegium of Proverbs and Wise Sayings," *Journal of English and Germanic Philology* 48 (1949):229–251.

24. See this and other examples in Tom Burns, "Folklore in the Mass Media: Television," *Folklore Forum* 2 (1969):90–106.

25. Barbara Mieder and Wolfgang Mieder, "Tradition and Innovation: Proverbs in Advertising," *Journal of Popular Culture* 11 (1977):308–319.

26. Alessandro Falassi and Gail Kligman, "*Folk-Wagen:* Folklore and the Volkswagen Ads," *New York Folklore* 2 (1976): 79–86.

27. For further discussion of the use of folklore in media, see Linda Dégh, *American Folklore and the Mass Media* (Bloomington: Indiana University Press, 1994).

28. *Crime-Victim Stories: New York City's Urban Folklore* (Bloomington: Indiana University Press, 1986), p. xi.

29. "Variant," in *Funk & Wagnalls Standard Dictionary,* vol. 2, pp. 1154–1155.

30. Archer Taylor, *The Proverb and An Index to the Proverb* (Hatboro, Pa.: Folklore Associates, 1962), pp. 22–24.

31. Anne B. Cohen, *Poor Pearl, Poor Girl! The Murdered-Girl Stereotype in Ballad and Newspaper,* Publications of the American Folklore Society, Memoir Series 58 (Austin: University of Texas Press, 1973).

32. John Cuthbert Lawson, *Modern Greek Folklore and Ancient Greek Religion: A Study in Survivals* (New Hyde Park, N.Y.: University Books, 1964), pp. 262–268.

33. See, for instance, F. A. de Caro and Elliott Oring, "JFK Is Alive: A Modern Legend," *Folklore Forum* 2 (1969):54–55; Elizabeth Radin Simons, "The NASA Joke Cycle: The Astronauts and the Teacher," *Western Folklore* 45 (1986):261–277; and

Willie Smyth, "Challenger Jokes and the Humor of Disaster," *Western Folklore* 45 (1986):243–260.

34. Beverly Patterson, "Amazing Grace [film review]," *Journal of American Folklore* 104 (1991):362–364.

35. The folktale is identified as Type 780, *The Singing Bone.* The ballad is most often called "The Twa Sisters" in English.

36. Much of this section was published previously as Robert A. Georges, "Folklore," in David Lance, ed., *Sound Archives: A Guide to Their Establishment and Development,* International Association of Sound Archives, Special Publication 4 (1983), pp. 134–146.

37. For a characterization of the nature of, and problems in, fieldwork see Robert A. Georges and Michael O. Jones, *People Studying People: The Human Element in Fieldwork* (Berkeley and Los Angeles: University of California Press, 1980). Among other works on folklore fieldwork and ethics are Kenneth S. Goldstein, *A Guide for Field Workers in Folklore* (Hatboro, Pa.: Folklore Associates, 1964), "Experimental Folklore: Laboratory vs. Field," in D. K. Wilgus, ed., *Folklore International: Essays in Traditional Literature, Belief, and Custom in Honor of Wayland Debs Hand* (Hatboro, Pa.: Folklore Associates, 1967), pp. 71–82, and "The Induced Natural Context: An Ethnographic Field Technique," in June Helm, ed., *Essays on the Verbal and Visual Arts* (Seattle: American Ethnological Society, distributed by the University of Washington Press, 1967), pp. 1–6; Tom Ireland, "Ethical Problems in Folklore," in Gerald Cashion, ed., *Conceptual Problems in Contemporary Folklore Study* (Bloomington, Ind.: Folklore Forum Bibliographic and Special Series, No. 12, 1974), pp. 69–74; Edward D. Ives, *The Tape-Recorded Interview: A Manual for Field Workers in Folklore and Oral History* (Knoxville: University of Tennessee Press, 1974); Bruce Jackson, *Fieldwork* (Urbana: University of Illinois Press, 1987); Susan I. Scheiberg, "A Folklorist in the Family: On the Process of Fieldwork among Intimates," *Western Folklore* 49 (1990):208–213; Guntis Smidchens and Robert E. Walls, "Ethics and the Student Fieldworker," in George H. Schoemaker, ed., *The Emergence of* *Folklore in Everyday Life: A Fieldguide and Sourcebook* (Bloomington, Ind.: Trickster Press, 1990), pp. 11–14; and Michael Ann Williams, "'Come on Inside': The Role of Gender in Folk Architecture Fieldwork," *Southern Folklore* 47 (1990):45–50.

38. On filming and videotaping, see Sharon R. Sherman, "Visions of Ourselves: Filming Folklore, Present and Future," *Western Folklore* 50 (1991):53–63. Several filmmakers have published essays about their fieldwork experiences in conjunction with their films or videotapes. Sharon R. Sherman discusses her video *Passover: A Celebration* (1983, Folklore and Ethnic Studies, University of Oregon, color, VHS, 28 min.) in "'That's How the Seder Looks': A Fieldwork Account of Videotaping Family Folklore," *Journal of Folklore Research* 23 (1986):53–70. Elaine Lawless and Elizabeth Peterson, who produced and directed *Joy Unspeakable* (1981, Audio-Visual Center, Indiana University, color, VHS, 59 min.), respond to questions raised in a review by Larry Danielson in *Western Folklore* 41 (1982):320–323; their comments are on pp. 323–326. Karen Lux, who worked with videographer Pieter Biella to produce *God's Mother Is the Morning Star* (1990, Documentary Film, color, VHS, 28 min.) writes about her experiences in "The Making of 'God's Mother Is the Morning Star': A Case Study in Videotaping an Elderly Folk Artist," *New York Folklore* 15 (1989):33–46.

39. For further discussion, see Ives's book and the videotape *An Oral Historian's Work,* with Dr. Edward Ives (1987, by David Weiss and Karen Shelden, Northeast Archives of Folklore and Oral History, University of Maine, color, VHS, 33 min.).

40. *Buying the Wind: Regional Folklore in the United States* (Chicago: University of Chicago Press, 1964), pp. 1–3.

41. "The Folklorist as Filmmaker," in Charles Camp, ed., *Time & Temperature: A Centennial Publication of the American Folklore Society* (Washington, D.C.: American Folklore Society, 1989), p. 33.

42. Ronald L. Baker, "Folklore and Folklife Studies in American and Canadian Colleges and Universities," *Journal of American Folklore* 99 (1986):50–74, and Elliott Oring, ed., *Folk Groups and Folk-*

lore Genres (Logan: Utah State University Press, 1986), p. ix.

43. "Foreword," in Patricia Hall and Charlie Seemann, eds., *Folklife and Museums: Selected Readings* (Nashville: American Association for State and Local History, 1987), pp. xiii–xiv.

44. "Writing for the World," *Journal of American Folklore* 101 (1988):293.

45. For more on folklorists' skills, knowledge, and abilities, see Richard M. Dorson, "Introduction: Concepts of Folklore and Folklife Studies," in Dorson, ed., *Folklore and Folklife: An Introduction* (Chicago: University of Chicago Press, 1972), pp. 1–50, and the essays in Michael Owen Jones, ed., *Putting Folklore to Use* (Lexington: University Press of Kentucky, 1994).

46. Form or genre is the sole or principal organizing criterion in leading introductory textbooks, including Brunvand, *The Study of American Folklore*; Dorson, *Folklore and Folklife*; and Oring.

47. See, for instance, Sandra Dolby Stahl, *Literary Folkloristics and the Personal Narrative* (Bloomington: Indiana University Press, 1989). Rosemary Lévy Zumwalt compares what she characterizes as "literary folklorists" and "anthropological folklorists" in her book *American Folklore Scholarship: A Dialogue of Dissent* (Bloomington: Indiana University Press, 1988).

48. For instance, Oring treats children and ethnic, religious, and occupational groups as folk groups; and Dorson, *Buying the Wind*, defines folk groups by locale and region and focuses on selected groups of people in Maine, Pennsylvania, the Southern mountains, Louisiana, Illinois, the Southwest, and Utah.

49. Quoted on the inside front cover of Bruce Jackson, Judith McCulloh, and Marta Weigle, eds., *Folklore and Folklife* (Washington, D.C.: American Folklore Society, 1984).

50. These examples refer to two published studies: Alan Dundes and C. Fayne Porter, "Potawatomi Squaw Dice," *Midwest Folklore* 13 (1963–1964):217–227, and Richard Bauman, "'I Go into More Detail Now, to Be Sure': Narrative Variation and the Shifting Contexts of Traditional Storytelling," in *Story, Performance, and Event: Contextual Studies of Oral Narrative* (New York: Cambridge University Press, 1986), pp. 78–111.

Folklore as Historical Artifact

2. Folkloristics as a Historical Science

A concept of folklore can be said to develop when individuals first become aware that much of what they express and most of the ways they express themselves while interacting face to face are not unique to them. The discovery that there are striking similarities in people's expressive behaviors leads one to realize that individuals learn, imitate, and perpetuate selected forms and examples of expression that are created more often by others than by themselves. With time and repetition, these can become readily familiar and widely known. When they do, they tend to be objectified and conceptualized as collective traditions that multiple individuals know and share with one another.

A concept of folklore and an interest in the expressive traditions from which the concept is derived existed long before the word *folklore* was coined. From the beginnings of recorded history, writers called attention to what they considered to be fantastic stories and exotic customs. The ancient Greeks were among the first to commit to writing oft-told tales they called *myths* and to make such narratives the subjects of discussion and debate.[1] Popular songs employing everyday speech and expressing the interests and concerns of common people make up the bulk of the *Chih Cheng*, the oldest Chinese poetry anthology, whose definitive edition dates back to Confucius' time (551–479 B.C.). In his *Germania* (A.D. 98), the Roman historian Tacitus (ca. A.D. 56-ca. 120) paints a broad word portrait of early Germanic tribes, largely by describing their traditional customs (see Box 2–1). The oldest extant Japanese texts—two commissioned histories, *Kojiki* (Records of Ancient Matters) (A.D. 712, English translation 1882) and *Nihongi* (A.D. 720, English translation 1896)—include many myths, legends, and folksongs as integral parts of their chronological narratives.

Interest in what was to become known as folklore continued after the decline of ancient civilizations, with traditional tales in particular serving as major sources and models for written works. Early chroniclers such as the Venerable Bede (673–735) and William of Malmesbury (ca. 1090–1143) incorporated popular stories about the miracles of the Virgin Mary and lives of Christian saints into their writings. Compilations of short moralistic tales or *exempla* served as source works which medieval priests told to their congregations to illustrate points in their sermons. Writers throughout Europe drew liberally as well on story collections from the Near East, such as the pre-eighth century Sanskrit fable book the *Panchatantra* and Somadeva's eleventh-century work *Kathasaritsagara* (Ocean of Story). Because of the tendency and freedom among writers of the time to copy, recopy, and edit, many of the same stories appeared in writing again and again. Such tales became even more widely known as individuals who learned them from written sources told them to live audiences in varied settings, including courts, churches, marketplaces, drinking establishments, and homes.

From the Middle Ages through the first half of the eighteenth century, folklore served principally as a source and resource for writers. Narratives by the Italian author Giovanni Boccaccio (1313–75) and the English poet Geoffrey Chaucer (1342?–1400), for instance, share plots with well-known

BOX 2–1
Tacitus on the Germans

Marriage in Germany is austere, and there is no feature in their morality that deserves higher praise. They are almost unique among barbarians in being satisfied with one wife each. The exceptions, which are exceedingly rare, are of men who receive offers of many wives because of their rank; there is no question of sexual passion. The dowry is brought by husband to wife, not by wife to husband. Parents and kinsmen attend and approve of the gifts, gifts not chosen to please a woman's whim or gaily deck a young bride, but oxen, horse with reins, shield, spear and sword. For such gifts a man gets his wife, and she in her turn brings some present of arms to her husband. In this interchange of gifts they recognize the supreme bond, the holy mysteries, the presiding deities of marriage. A woman must not imagine herself free to neglect the manly virtues or immune from the hazards of war. That is why she is reminded, in the very ceremonies which bless her marriage at its outset, that she is coming to share a man's toils and dangers, that she is to be his partner in all his sufferings and adventures, whether in peace or war. That is the meaning of the team of oxen, of the horse ready for its ride, of the gift of arms. On these terms she must live her life and bear her children. She is receiving something that she must hand over unspoilt and treasured to her children, for her son's wives to receive in their turn and pass on to the grandchildren.[2]

folktales, suggesting that these literary creations were inspired by or derived from oral storytellings.[3] (For instance, versions of Type 882, *The Wager on the Wife's Chastity*, and Type 1186, *With His Whole Heart*, appear respectively in Boccaccio's *Decameron* and in Chaucer's *Canterbury Tales*.) Jestbooks popular during the Renaissance

include numerous widely told humorous stories, such as those of fools who cut off branches of trees on which they are sitting (Type 1240, *Man Sitting on Branch of Tree Cuts It Off*), who burn down their houses to rid them of pesky rodents or insects (Type 1282, *House Burned Down to Rid It of Insects*), and who don't mend their roofs when the weather is fair and can't do so while it is raining (Type 1238, *The Roof in Good and Bad Weather*).[4]

Historical legends and classical myths served as sources and provided the subject matter for playwrights ranging from the anonymous creators of medieval mystery and miracle plays to such major Elizabethan dramatists as John Lyly (ca. 1554–1606), Christopher Marlowe (1564–93), and William Shakespeare (1564–1616).[5] Poetical miscellanies from such late sixteenth century works as Thomas Deloney's *The Garland of Good-Will* (1593) to such early eighteenth century ballad collections as the anonymous *A Collection of Old Ballads* (1723–25) drew heavily on historical and local legends and drinking and popular songs.

In all such works, an awareness of, and indebtedness to, folklore are readily apparent. But a particular kind of model of reality was required before individuals began to conceive of folklore as something deserving of documentation and study in and of itself. Since folkloristics evolved as a discipline in Europe, and since *folklore* is an English word coined by an Englishman, it is to the intellectual life of Europe—and particularly that of Great Britain—that one must turn to understand what kind of model of reality was prerequisite to the evolution of folkloristics, and when and why that model evolved.

To describe a "model of reality" is to sketch a view of the world that seems to be common to, or shared by, a sizable number of individuals. In characterizing such a model, one attempts to describe what is normative, not unanimous. No one can poll all members of a collectivity or determine all the commonalities in their individual worldviews. But one can infer from written records and (when possible) observable behaviors what similarities seem to be significant for a majority of a group and then explain what those are. Models of reality, then, are always constructed and hypothetical; but like all hypotheses, they can be presented confidently when available evidence makes proposing them defensible.

From a Mechanistic to an Organic Model

Philosophers characterize the intellectuals of seventeenth and early eighteenth century Europe as being committed to a worldview that was essentially mechanistic in nature. The central metaphor in this model is a machine. In this view, the physical universe operates as a machine does—constantly, repetitiously, and predictably, according to a set of mathematical principles and physical laws that are determinable and hence knowable and describable. The universe and everything in it came into being through an initial act of creation, and they have been operating uniformly like a machine ever since. Because assumptions about the constancy and predictability of reality predominate, time is largely irrelevant in such a view. Things presumably remain stable and unchanging after they come into being. The universe, once created, is fixed and closed.

Human beings, in this scheme of things, are separated from, and hence are detached observers of, the universe. Like the physical world, living species are assumed to have remained essentially the same since their creation. Fossil evidence suggests that some species may have become extinct (though fossils could have been put on earth by God or the Devil to test humans' faith); and new species might have come into existence (but presumably only because of hybridization). For the most part, the same generalizations about consistency and regularity were thought to apply to both the physical and the human aspects of this dualistic reality.[6]

During the latter half of the eighteenth century, European thinkers presented an alternative model of reality which gained increasing popularity, in large part as a reaction against the intellectualism and utilitarianism inherent in a mechanically oriented worldview. According to this model, nature cannot be understood solely in mathematical terms. Instead, human beings' views of reality are dependent on their conceptions of, and personal reactions to, perceived phenomena and ways they conceptualize those phenomena relative to each other and to themselves. Everything in the universe—including human beings—is what it is by virtue of its relationships to other parts of a whole. The whole, moreover, is equal to more than the sum of its parts because of the fundamental importance of the relationships as well as the components.

The central metaphor in this Western model is an organism. Like organisms, reality is evolving and ever-changing. This implies development over time, and movement through time from the simple to the increasingly complex. Progress is inevitable. The past and things associated with it become important because time is regarded as a fundamental dimension of reality, and the present is considered to be an outgrowth and further development of what preceded it chronologically.[7]

The concept of progressive development from the simple to the complex provided new motivations and suggested alternative directions for the study of humanity. It gave rise to the notion of relative rates of progress—i.e., that some things, including people, progress and change more rapidly

BOX 2-2
Comparison of Two Models

MECHANISTIC MODEL

Reality is like a machine.

Mathematical principles and physical laws are the sources and bases for human views of reality.

Constancy, repetition, and predictability are inherent in nature and fundamental to one's view of the world.

Human beings are separate from, and detached observers of, everything else in the universe.

Things have remained essentially the same since the creation of the universe, making a concept of time irrelevant to one's view of reality.

ORGANIC MODEL

Reality is like an organism.

Human beings' perceptions and conceptions are the sources and bases for their views of reality.

Development and change are inherent in nature and fundamental to one's view of the world.

Human beings are an integral part of, and related to, everything else in the universe.

Things have been ever-changing since their creation, making a concept of time integral to one's view of reality.

than others. It sparked interest in the past and in objects and behaviors that seem to have survived from bygone eras and to persist through time despite ongoing changes that make them incompatible with contemporary norms. Phenomena associated with past and passing lifestyles came to be conceptualized as artifacts. They were valued because of the insights they could potentially provide into a people's roots, heritage, and continuity.

The emerging organic model and its underlying assumptions evoked growing interest in, and provided specific justification for, the documentation and study of antiquities. Antiquarianism had a lengthy history in Europe, particularly in Great Britain. Merely uncovering and describing antiquities had long been ends in themselves. But making "collections of things which have no other merit than that of being old" was no longer appropriate, as Francis Grose (1731–91) noted in 1775. Such studies should be undertaken only if they can provide insights into human history, he insisted.[8] Others concurred. Writing two

years after Grose, for example, John Brand (1744–1806) admitted, in his *Observations on Popular Antiquities* (1777), the impossibility of ever determining the *"prime* Origin of superstitious Notions and Ceremonies of the People"* (Brand's emphasis). But Brand stressed the importance of tracing "backwards, as far as possible, the Courses of them on those Charts, that remain, of the distant Countries from whence they were first perceived to flow."[9]

Organicism and the Evolution of Folkloristics

Organicism and its underlying assumptions thus provided a justification and goal for preserving and disseminating expressive behaviors that seemed to be antiquities. The potential historical and literary value of a manuscript collection of archaic poems and songs, for instance, sufficed to motivate Bishop Thomas Percy (1729–1811) to publish the three-volume *Reliques of Ancient English Poetry* in 1765. For Sir

Walter Scott (1771–1832), making available a selection of songs sung traditionally along Scotland's boundary with England was justified because the songs and accompanying examples of popular superstitions and legendary history were significant indicators of the social and political history of that area (in *Minstrelsy of the Scottish Border, Consisting of Historical and Romantic Ballads, Collected in the Southern Counties of Scotland; with a Few of Modern Date, Founded upon Local Tradition,* 3 vols., 1802–1803).

Recognition of the potential historical importance of antiquities was coupled with an awareness that surviving remnants of the past were rapidly disappearing with the growth of urbanization, industrialization, and compulsory education. Scotsman Hugh Miller (1802–56) expressed in 1835 a widespread fear that "the stream of tradition" was "rapidly lessening" and that "oral knowledge of the past" would soon be lost.[10] Englishman William John Thoms (1803–85) pleaded for help in documenting antiquities in the August 22, 1846, issue of the periodical *The Athenaeum.* "I am not without hopes of enlisting your aid in garnering the few ears which are remaining, scattered over that field from which our forefathers might have gathered a goodly crop," he wrote. "No one who has made the manners, customs, observances, superstitions, ballads, proverbs, &c., of the olden time his study, but must have arrived at two conclusions," Thoms continued: "—the first, how much that is curious and interesting in these matters is now entirely lost—the second, how much may yet be rescued by timely exertion."[11]

For Thoms, the lack of a distinctive word was a hindrance to the task he challenged readers to undertake. He found the two terms commonly used in England—*popular antiquities* and *popular literature*—to be inappropriate, noting that "it is more a Lore than a Literature, and would be most aptly

Figure 2–1: William John Thoms who, writing in The Athenaeum *of August 22, 1846, coined the term "folk-lore" (from* The Academy, *11 November 1899).*

described by a good Saxon compound, Folk-Lore—*the Lore of the People*" (Thoms's emphasis).[12] In proposing the word *folklore,* Thoms gave a collective name to "the manners, customs, observances, superstitions, ballads, proverbs, &c., of the olden time" and provided a linguistic basis for subsequently designating a distinctive field of study (*folkloristics*) and those who make "the lore of the people" the focal point of their inquiries (*folklorists*).

By the time Thoms coined the word *folklore* in 1846, numerous individuals had already taken it upon themselves to begin to collect folklore, to preserve it in writing, and to share it with others through print. Thomas Crofton Croker (1798–1854), for instance, focused in his Irish fieldwork on beliefs and stories about fairies and other supernatural beings. He published descriptions of local scenery and dialect as well as narrative texts in his book *Fairy Legends and Traditions of the South of Ireland* (1825). In the United States, John Fanning Watson (1779–1860) included a mass of "traditionary lore" in his *Annals of Philadelphia and Pennsylvania in the Olden Time.* First published in 1830, the book saw numerous printings throughout the century. Watson, who employed the motto "To note and to observe," avidly sought remembrances from older people regarding artifacts, beliefs, legends, and sayings "of olden time." An admirer of Sir Walter Scott, Watson emulated his methods. "When a young man," Watson wrote, "Scott was wont to make frequent journeys into the country, *among strangers*, going from house to house, with his boy George,—and particularly seeking out the residences of *the old people*, with whom he delighted to enter into conversation, and exciting them to dilate upon the reminiscences of their youth" (Watson's emphasis).[13] Particularly noteworthy was the fieldwork of a Finnish physician, whose efforts resulted in the creation of a folklore-based literary epic that immediately became a source and symbol of Finnish identity, both in Finland and abroad.

While a medical student, Elias Lönnrot (1802–84) began collecting folklore in Karelia and other provinces to the east of Finland bordering on Russia, an area particularly rich in orally recited poetry. Concerned about the Swedish and Russian domination of their country, Finnish intellectuals in the late eighteenth and early nineteenth centuries turned their attention to the rural population, convinced that the "soul and special quality of the Finnish nation was hidden in the oral tradition that had been preserved by the common people."[14] Lönnrot's teacher, Reinhold von Becker, was the first to begin piecing together from different folk poems the character and story of Väinämöinen, the oldest of the Finnish deities.

Lönnrot made his first field trip in 1828. It was a four-month vacation during which he hoped to learn various dialects in Karelia and particularly to "collect products of its remarkably beautiful folklore." He met Kainulainen, a "wise man" (possessor of magical powers), healer, and hunter. From him Lönnrot recorded 49 poems, including songs about divinities of the ancient Finns.

Later employed by the government and posted to various provinces as a roving medical examiner, Lönnrot often met masters of narrative poetry and noted down a wealth of spells, epic runes, wedding songs, and customs. He also took leaves of absence from his medical post in order to collect folk poetry.

In 1834, on his fifth major field trip, Lönnrot spent a week in Uhtua, where he cared for the sick, who repaid him by singing poems. He met Arhippa Perttunen, who in two days sang for him 4,100 lines. Full and clear, these 60 songs were exceptional aesthetically.

In 1835, Lönnrot published some of this material in the two-volume *Kalevala*

Figure 2–2: In the earliest photo of Finnish folksingers, Jyrki and Ohvo Malinen from Vuonninen are seen clasping hands for support as they sing long epic poems or runes (photo by A. Berner, courtesy Finnish Literature Society).

taikka vanhoja Karjalan runoja Suomen kansan muinaisista ajoista (The Kalevala, or Old Karelian Songs from the Ancient Times of the Finnish People). This became known as the *Old Kalevala* because the author later doubled its length through his own collecting efforts and those of others he inspired, bringing out a new edition in 1849. The *New Kalevala* consists of 50 poems concerning such heroes as Väinämöinen—"the steadfast one," "the eternal sage"—who is the oldest, born of an air-maiden. Ilmarinen is a smith who forges the Sampo, a three-sided mill that produces grain, salt, and money in unlimited quantities. Lemminkäinen is the "reckless" one, the wanton lover boy. The three reside with others in the Kaleva District on a misty headland and foggy island.

The 22,795 lines of the poem tell of common activities like making beer and hollowing out a boat. They also describe marvelous occurrences and extraordinary beings such as forest deities, a demon's elk, and a fire-breathing gelding. After a cattleherd kills Lemminkäinen, his mother rakes the water to recover the cut-up pieces, which she assembles; miraculously, Lemminkäinen is resurrected. The heroes' boat becomes stuck on the back of a giant pike. Väinämöinen kills the fish, making a *kantele* (harp) of its jawbone, which only he can play and with which he enchants all creation. There are traditional charms, incantations, and magic spells as well as lyrical poems and wedding laments in Lönnrot's *Kalevala*, a work that quickly became and remains today the national epic of Finland.[15]

Perhaps the most influential early work that predated Thoms's 1846 coining of the word *folklore* was the *Kinder- und Hausmärchen* (Children's and Household Tales) by the Grimm brothers, Jakob (1785–1863) and Wilhelm (1786–1859). This anthology of traditional stories (2 vols., 1812, 1815)—some recorded by the Grimms from

---

BOX 2-3
Opening Lines of *Kalevala*

The second edition (1849) of *Kalevala*, Finland's national epic based on folk poetry collected by Elias Lönnrot, begins:

I am driven by my longing,
And my understanding urges
That I should commence my singing,
And begin my recitation.
I will sing the people's legends,
And the ballads of the nation.
To my mouth the words are flowing,
And the words are gently falling
Quickly as my tongue can shape them,
And between my teeth emerging. . . .
Let us clasp our hands together,
Let us interlock our fingers;
Let us sing a cheerful measure,
Let us use our best endeavours,
While our dear ones hearken to us,
And our loved ones are instructed,
While the young ones are standing
    round us,
Of the rising generation,
Let them learn the words of magic,
And recall our songs and legends,
Of the belt of Väinämöinen,
Of the forge of Ilmarinen,
And of Kaukomieli's sword-point,
And of Joukahainen's crossbow:
Of the utmost bounds of Pohja,
And of Kalevala's wide heathlands.[16]

---

living narrators and others selected, edited, and reprinted by them from a variety of written sources—was an instant success. It quickly won an international readership and introduced the world at large to such now-famous stories as "The Frog King" (Type 440), "Cinderella" (Type 510), "Sleeping Beauty" (Type 410), "Hansel and Gretel" (Type 327A), "Little Red Riding Hood" (Type 333), and "The Wolf and the Seven Kids" (Type 123).[17]

The Grimms characterized these stories as artifacts with long histories. They

BOX 2–4
Closing Lines of *Kalevala*

Lönnrot's national epic concludes with the immaculate conception of the virgin Marjatta. Her son is baptized and hailed as the King of Karelia. Väinämöinen (the oldest of the ancient Finnish divinities) departs in anger, vowing to return one day when needed once again "to fetch a new moon, free a new sun."

Then the aged Väinämöinen
Went upon his journey singing,
Sailing in his boat of copper,
In his vessel made of copper,
Sailed away to loftier regions,
To the land beneath the heavens.
There he rested with his vessel,
Rested weary, with his vessel,
But his kantele he left us,
Left his charming harp in Suomi
  [Finland],
For his people's lasting pleasure,
Mighty songs for Suomi's children.[18]

Figure 2–3: Portrait of Kinder- und Hausmärchen *compilers Wilhelm and Jacob Grimm (from the frontispiece to* Deutsche Wörterbuch, *vol. 1, Leipzig: S. Hirzel, 1854).*

pointed out in commentaries and notes the existence, in written documents and literature from the past, of narratives with the same or analogous plots. An earlier version of "Cinderella" (Type 510), for instance, had appeared in Giambattista Basile's *Il Pentamerone* (1634–36). Charles Perrault's 1697 *Contes de ma mère l'oye* (Stories of Mother Goose) included among its eight prose tales literary renderings of "Sleeping Beauty" (Type 410), "Little Red Riding Hood" (Type 333) (see Box 2–5), "Cinderella" (Type 510), and "Bluebeard" (Type 312). This demonstrated to the Grimms the traditionality of the stories and attested to the antiquity of the cultural base of the Germanic and other peoples among whom such narratives were known.

The Grimms also noted the importance of documenting tales as they were remembered and told by the seemingly dwindling number of people who still knew them. They emphasized as well the need to preserve the stories and to present them in print as the Grimms indicated they themselves had done—in the language and natural way the tales were told by living narrators. This was what they had done, they pointed out, with the stories of their revered informant Frau Katherina Viehmann of Niederzwehren (see Box 2–6).

Because the Grimms' work indicated that the *Märchen*telling tradition was still alive, and that such stories were known and told throughout most of Europe, many fieldworkers used the *Kinder- und Hausmärchen* as a collector's handbook. They listened for, and asked informants if they were familiar with, stories with plots like those of the tales in the Grimm collection.

BOX 2-5

Charles Perrault's "Little Red Riding-Hood"
(1697)

Once upon a time there was a little girl, the prettiest you could hope to see. Her mother doted on her and her grandmother was even more fond of her. The kind old woman had a little red hood made for her, which suited her so well that everyone called her Little Red Riding-Hood.

One day her mother baked some cakes and said to her:

"Go and see how your grandmother is, for I hear that she is ill. Take her a cake and this little pot of butter."

Little Red Riding-Hood set off at once to see her grandmother, who lived in another village. As she was going through a wood she met Master Wolf, who had a great mind to eat her but did not dare to because of some woodcutters who were working near by. He asked her where she was going. The poor child, who did not know that it was dangerous to stop and talk to a wolf, said:

"I am going to see my grandmother and am taking her a cake and a little pot of butter from my mother."

"Does she live far from here?" asked the wolf.

"Oh yes," said Little Red Riding-Hood, "it's beyond that mill which you see over there, in the first house in the village."

"Well," said the wolf, "I am going to see her, too. I will go this way and you go that way, and we will see who gets there first."

The wolf ran off at full speed along the shortest path, while the little girl took the longest one, dawdling on the way to gather nuts, chase butterflies and pick little bunches of wild flowers.

The wolf soon reached the grandmother's house. He knocked: *rat-a-tat*.

"Who's there?"

"It's your granddaughter, Little Red Riding-Hood," said the wolf, imitating her voice. "I've brought you a cake and a little pot of butter from my mother."

The grandmother, who was in bed because she was feeling rather poorly, called out:

"Pull the catch and you'll loose the latch."

The wolf pulled the catch and the door opened. He sprang on the old lady and devoured her in a twinkling, for he had had nothing to eat for over three days. Then he shut the door and got into the grandmother's bed to wait for Little Red Riding-Hood.

Presently she arrived and knocked at the door: *rat-a-tat*.

"Who's there?"

At first Little Red Riding-Hood was afraid when she heard the gruff voice of the wolf, but then she thought that her grandmother must have a cold, so she answered:

"It's your granddaughter, Little Red Riding-Hood. I've brought you a cake and a little pot of butter from my mother."

Making his voice a little less gruff, the wolf called out:

"Pull the catch and you'll loose the latch."

Little Red Riding-Hood pulled the catch and the door opened.

When the wolf saw her coming in, he hid himself under the bedclothes, and said:

"Put the cake and the little pot of butter on the bread-bin and get into bed with me."

Little Red Riding-Hood undressed and got into bed, but she was very surprised to see how her grandmother looked in her nightclothes. She said to her:

"What big arms you have, grandmother!"

"The better to hug you with, my dear!"

"What big legs you have, grandmother!"

"The better to run with, my child!"

"What big ears you have, grandmother!"

"The better to hear with, my child!"

"What big eyes you have, grandmother!"

"The better to see with, my child!"

"What big teeth you have, grandmother!"

"They're to eat you with!"

So saying, that wicked wolf sprang on Little Red Riding-Hood and ate her up.

MORAL

This story teaches that the very young,
And little girls more surely than the rest,
—sweet, dainty things, clothed in their
    Sunday best—
should never trust a stranger's artful tongue.
    Small wonder if these guileless young
      beginners
    Provide the wolf with some of his best
      dinners.
I say the wolf, for every wolf that roams
Is not the same.
Some, in appearance tame,
Gentle, well-mannered, affable and gay,
Trotting beside them in the friendliest way,
Follow young ladies right into their homes.
    Alas, how many to their cost do find
    These plausible wolves are the most
      dangerous kind.[19]

BOX 2-6
The Grimms' Description of Frau Viehmann

She has a firm and pleasant face, a bright and keen look in her eyes, and was probably beautiful when she was young. She preserves these old tales firmly in her memory, a gift, as she says, which is not given to everyone, for many people can retain nothing. She narrates thoughtfully, confidently, very lively and with special pleasure in doing so, at first quite fluently, and then, if one wants, repeats slowly, so that one can copy down what she says. . . . Whoever believes in the easy falsification of tradition, carelessness in retention, and therefore in the impossibility of long-term memory, should hear how precisely she sticks to the same narration and is zealous about its correctness. She never changes anything when repeating and corrects any mistake, as soon as she notices it, right in the middle of her speech. Attachment to tradition is stronger among people who continue without any change in the same form of life than among us who tend to change can understand.[20]

Figure 2–4: Frau Viehmann, the Grimms' house-keeper and source of many of the folktales appearing in the Grimms' collection of children's and household stories (from the first volume of the second edition of Kinder- und Hausmärchen, *1819).*

Furthermore, the names the Grimms gave to previously untitled or variably identified tales ("Snow White," "Hansel and Gretel," and "Rumpelstiltskin," for example) became widely known, translated, and used. The stories in the *Kinder- und Hausmärchen* served as exemplars of orally told tales and as the foundations for a rapidly growing folk narrative data base. Thus, the fairy tale became the principal kind of story upon which folklorists focused, and it remained so from the early nineteenth until the middle of the twentieth century.

By conceptualizing and characterizing folklore as historical artifact, pioneering fieldworkers such as the Grimms, Croker, Watson, and Lönnrot assumed and implied not only that folklore was a survival from the past, but also that it was transmitted through time intergenerationally and primarily through an oral tradition. This suggested that the ongoing existence of folklore constituted conclusive evidence of continuity in culture through time, and that examples of folklore could provide insights into the national character and cultural heritage of peoples.

Nationalism and Comparativism

As stated earlier, the Grimms demonstrated through their commentaries and comparative notes that the *Märchen* they documented and presented were nationally significant because parallels and analogues to these stories existed in early records of Germanic peoples. At the same time, the Grimms' notes and comments also revealed that many of the *Märchen* were not unique to the Germans, but that they were a part of the heritage of other European peoples as well. From the inception of its systematic collection and study, then, folklore was viewed in a dual way. On the one hand, it was seen as something that embodies the ethos of peoples and that provides evidence of their continuity and national distinctiveness. On the other hand, folklore reveals that different peoples have much in common with each other culturally and that the similarities are often too numerous or striking to be attributed solely to chance or coincidence.

An alternative hypothesis was necessary to account for significant cross-cultural similarities. The one advanced had evolved and was adopted from nineteenth-century European scholars' studies of language. It posited that many of the similarities discernible in the folklore being recorded in different places—like the striking similarities uncovered through the comparative study of different languages—must be indicative of, and attributable to, the fact that different peoples can share a common ancestry.[21]

Folklorists' adoption and application of this *Indo-European hypothesis*, as students of language came to call it, provided a means of avoiding a potential conflict between a monocultural and multicultural approach to folklore study. Folklore found in only one society could be conceived as artifacts that were unique to the people in question. Folklore found in multiple societies could be viewed as artifacts that had their origins in the ancestral society of peoples who were related historically by virtue of their descendancy from a single cultural base. Furthermore, folklore found in multiple, historically related societies could still be regarded as being distinctive to particular peoples. For folklores, like languages, that were rooted in a common cultural base had necessarily evolved and changed in different ways for the different groups that were created when the single

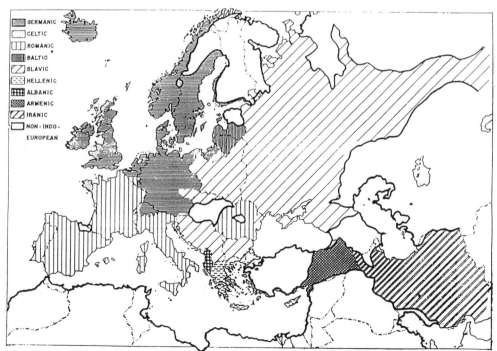

Figure 2–5: Indo-European languages in modern Europe (from Cassidy/Robertson, Development of Modern English *© 1954, by permission of Prentice-Hall, Inc., Englewood Cliffs, N. J.).*

ancestral culture evolved into multiple so-cieties. Each societal offshoot had retained and perpetuated a common set of ancestral traditions. However, all had transformed and perpetuated shared ancestral folklore in somewhat different ways; all had also created new and distinctive folklores as they had developed historically.

As folkloristics evolved in Europe during the nineteenth century, the two ways that folklore was viewed—as a nationally unique, and as an ancestrally and culturally shared, artifact—served as both the conceptual foundations and the subjects of debate for the developing discipline. Nationalistic pride, competitiveness, and self-conscious-ness motivated individuals in countries throughout Europe to collect their peoples' folklores and to demonstrate through folk-lore the antiquity and the cultural richness and distinctiveness of their heritage. The influence of the organic model of reality and its emphases on the time dimension, development from the simple to the in-creasingly complex, and relatedness of phe-nomena inspired researchers to study folk-lore comparatively in order to gain insights into the prehistory and nature of the hypo-thetical Indo-European society from which peoples who were speakers of the major languages of Europe and Western Asia had evolved.

Throughout the first three-quarters of the nineteenth century, then, folkloristics was Eurocentric and Indo-European fo-cused. Fieldworkers collected folklore in their European homelands, for the most part, and, to a lesser extent, in other coun-tries (mostly in Europe) to which they traveled or in which they lived or worked. For example, Svend Grundtvig (1824–83) amassed and published impressive collec-tions of ballads and folktales from singers and storytellers in his Danish homeland;[22] and Austrian consul Johann Georg von Hahn made the first field collection of fairy tales in Albania and Greece (published as

Griechische und Albanische Märchen, 1864). By the last quarter of the century, folklore documentation and study had be-gun or were well underway on every conti-nent. But it was in Europe that folkloristics evolved as a field of study. It was European and Indo-European-derived folklore that was the foundation of the discipline's data base. And it was the study of folklore col-lected in Europe that provided the models and inspiration for the development of folkloristics both subsequently and in other places around the globe.

Evolutionism and Its Effects on Folkloristics

European and Indo-European-derived folklore remained the focus of folkloristics during the closing quarter of the nineteenth and well into the twentieth century. But the folklore data base and the assumptions upon which its study was built were af-fected significantly by the ongoing evolu-tion of the organic model of reality in which folkloristics had its intellectual roots. The concepts of development, progress, and change—basic to an organically oriented worldview—logically and perhaps inevita-bly evolved eventually into a concept of evolution itself. Emergent in the work and pronouncements of such individuals as French naturalist Jean-Baptiste de Monet de Lamarck (1744–1829), geologist Sir Charles Lyell (1797–1875), and philosopher Herbert Spencer (1820–1903), the principles of evolutionism were first articulated con-sciously and systematically in 1859 in *Ori-gin of Species* by Charles Darwin (1809–82).

As philosopher Harry Girvetz notes,

> The main tenet of the evolutionary prin-ciple as it applies to biology is that species have a common origin and are thereby chang-ing and related. The immutability of species is denied and so, too, is the idea that they were separately created. Over vast stretches

of time complex organisms have derived from simpler organisms and ultimately from the simplest microscopic organisms. Thus species change in form: new species come into being; existing species become extinct. This is the minimal claim.[23]

Darwin makes only one statement in *Origin of Species* about the possible implications of evolutionism for human beings: "Much light will be thrown on the origin of man and his history."[24] In his 1871 book *Descent of Man*, however, Darwin asserts that humans are descended from simpler organisms and are products of natural selection. He comments on the implications of this conclusion:

> The main conclusion arrived at in this work, namely that man is descended from some lowly organized form, will, I regret to think, be highly distasteful to many. But there can hardly be a doubt that we are descended from barbarians. The astonishment which I felt on first seeing a party of Fuegians on a wild and broken shore will never be forgotten by me, for the reflection at once rushed into my mind—such were our ancestors. Those men were absolutely naked and bedaubed with paint, their long hair was tangled, their mouths frothed with excitement, and their expression was wild, startled, and distrustful. They possessed hardly any arts and like wild animals lived on what they could catch; they had no government and were merciless to everyone not of their own small tribe. He who has seen a savage in his native land will not feel much shame, if forced to acknowledge that the blood of some more humble creature flows in his veins. For my own part I would as soon be descended from that heroic little monkey, who braved his dreaded enemy in order to save the life of his keeper, or from that old baboon, who descending from the mountains, carried away in triumph his young comrade from a crowd of astonished dogs—as from a savage who delights to torture his enemies, offers up bloody sacrifices, practices infanticide without remorse, treats his wives like slaves, knows no decency, and is haunted by the grossest superstitions.[25]

Darwin's pronouncements implied that much more than biological development was involved in human evolution. Not only had the human species developed physically from simpler and hence lower life forms. There was also an ongoing evolution intellectually and culturally within the species itself, as attested by the existence and behavior of "barbarians" or "savages" such as the Fuegians. The analogy that Darwin implied and others made explicit between biology and culture and between biology and intellect led to the development of a concept of *unilineal cultural evolution*— that culture evolves like biological species do, from the simple to the increasingly complex, with the cultures of all peoples passing through the same developmental stages in their evolution, though at differing rates. Furthermore, peoples whose cultures were judged to be at early or primitive stages of cultural evolution were also conceived to be at low evolutionary stages intellectually, with their thinking being conceived and characterized as prelogical and associative rather than logical and analytical.

These notions provided the motivation and justification for documenting and studying the behaviors of "primitive peoples" systematically. By knowing and understanding the culture and intellect of such peoples, one could presumably gain insights into the origins and early development of human thought and culture and determine what had survived and what had been changed and lost as humans ascended the evolutionary ladder.

The Primitiveness of Folklore

Sir Edward Burnett Tylor (1832–1917) applied evolutionism to human history in *The Origins of Culture*, the first book in his two-volume *Primitive Culture: Researches into the Development of Mythology, Phi-*

losophy, Religion, Language, Art, and Custom (London: John Murray, 1871). With sections on culture, survivals and revivals, magic and occult arts, animism, mythology, and similar topics, Tylor's work had an immediate and significant impact on folkloristics. Many were quick to accept his view of history and emulate his methods.

Tylor assumed that humankind had evolved through three stages: savagery, barbarism, and civilization. The educated world of Europe and America of his day served as the standard of the highest stage of civilization, while the "savage tribes" of his time most closely approximated the earliest, primitive condition.[26]

Tylor considered folklore forms such as myths, riddles, and proverbs to be products of a mythologic stage of thought. Particular examples survived among the "modern rude tribes" and "even higher and later grades of civilization," including European peasants, as survivals or relics of a "savage condition prevalent in remote ages among the whole human race." The original "sense-riddles" ("such as the typical enigma of the Sphinx"), as opposed to modern-day verbal conundrums, have ceased to be created, writes Tylor. But "many ancient specimens have lasted on in the modern nursery and by the cottage fireside," surviving largely "in remnants for children's play." By the Middle Ages in Europe, proverbs, too, were "mostly heirlooms," the "remnants of an earlier condition of society."[27]

According to Tylor, "the stream of civilization winds and turns upon itself, and what seems the bright onward current of one age may in the next spin round in a whirling eddy, or spread into a dull and pestilential swamp." These eddies and swamps are "survivals."

Survivals are ways of thinking and doing things perpetuated "by force of habit" from their original creation into current culture. They change in the process, lose utility, and

BOX 2-7
Proverbs from the Mythologic Stage of Thought

At the level of European culture in the middle ages, they [proverbs] have indeed a vast importance in popular education, but their period of actual growth seems already at an end. Cervantes raised the proverb-monger's craft to a pitch it never surpassed; but it must not be forgotten that the incomparable Sancho's wares were mostly heirlooms; for proverbs were even then sinking to remnants of an earlier condition of society. As such, they survive among ourselves, who go on using much the same relics of ancestral wisdom as came out of the squire's inexhaustible budget, old saws not to be lightly altered or made anew in our changed modern times. We can collect and use the old proverbs, but making new ones has become a feeble, spiritless imitation, like our attempts to invent new myths or new nursery rhymes.
—Edward Burnett Tylor[28]

cease to have a reason for being. Making little sense in terms of modern society, they appear "irrational." Tylor cites the example of an elderly Somersetshire woman whose handloom dates from before the introduction of the flying shuttle, a newfangled appliance she refused to learn to use. He writes: "This old woman is not a century behind her times, but she is a case of survival. Such examples often lead us back to the habits of hundreds and even thousands of years ago."

There are also "revivals" in culture of ideas and practices that should have faded from the scene, but suddenly burst "forth again with a vigour often as marvellous as it is unhealthy," writes Tylor. He gives as an example spiritualism in his own day, with its mediums and seances, its communicating with the spirit-world by rapping and

BOX 2–8

The Riddle of the Sphinx (Also Called the Oedipus Riddle)

The old Oedipus riddle was part of another riddle contest—between Oedipus and the Sphinx. The fabled lion-bird woman, sent from Ethiopia by Hera to Thebes to punish that city for the crimes of Laius, took her stance on a rock overlooking the city, and threw to death from the rock every passer-by who could not answer her riddle: "What walks on four legs in the morning, on two at noon, and on three in the evening?" When Oedipus gave the correct answer "Man, who creeps in infancy on all fours, walks erect on his two legs in the prime of life, and hobbles with a cane for a third leg when an old man," the Sphinx threw herself to death from the rock; Oedipus thus saved Thebes, and was given the queen, Jocasta, as a reward. She proved to be his own mother. . . . The suicide of disappointed riddlers, even in a fable, seems to us rather drastic, but the ancients took their riddles very seriously.
    —Charles Frances Potter[29]

* * *

English-Language Examples of the Sphinx Riddle

What is that in the morning upon foure legges doth goe, / and about noone it standeth fast upon two and no moe. / In the evening againe it hath no lesser than three in store. / Which tell me, Ser, art thou not he, whom I doe take thee for?—It's a man; for when he is a childe, then doth hee creep upon hands and feet; but when he is a man, then he standeth straight upon two leggs; but when he is old and decrepit, besides his legs then he useth a staffe to support his body (1631).

* * *

Four feet it has in the morning,
Yet fast movement is a-lacking.
With two about mid-day
He can manage much better.
Though he gets at nightfall three,
He moves but soft and slow (1938).

* * *

What kind of animal is that that stands on four legs in the morning, two in the day, and three in the evening?—Child creeping (two legs and two hands), man with two feet, and old woman with a stick (1943).[30]

BOX 2–9

Survivals in Culture

These are processes, customs, opinions, and so forth, which have been carried on by force of habit into a new state of society different from that in which they had their original home, and they thus remain as proofs and examples of an older condition of culture out of which a newer has been evolved. . . . The serious business of ancient society may be seen to sink into the sport of later generations, and its serious belief to linger on in nursery folk-lore.
    —Edward Burnett Tylor[31]

BOX 2-10
Cultural Revivals

Sometimes old thoughts and practices will burst out afresh, to the amazement of a world that thought them long since dead or dying; here survival passes into revival, as has lately happened in so remarkable a way in the history of modern spiritualism.

—Edward Burnett Tylor[32]

writing, and the feat of a table or other object rising in the air.

Survivals continue in culture "in the very teeth of common sense," writes Tylor; but once they had a rationale. How does one ascertain their earlier meanings? As an illustration of his methods, Tylor analyzes three traditions in modern society whose rationale had eluded others, of which "one is ridiculous, the others are atrocious, and all are senseless." The first of these "is the practice of salutation on sneezing, the second the rite of laying the foundations of a building on a human victim, the third the prejudice against saving a drowning man."

To interpret customs connected with sneezing, Tylor turns to data about "the less cultured races," beginning with the Zulus among whom sneezing is a sign that a sick person will be restored to health. After sneezing, ill persons return thanks to the ancestral spirit (Itongo) which had caused them to sneeze to let them know the Itongo is with them. If a sick person doesn't sneeze, others express grave concern. "So, then, it is said, sneezing among black men gives a man strength to remember that Itongo has entered into him and abides with him," writes Tylor.

Tylor also examines early accounts of traditions among peoples in Guinea, New Zealand, Samoa, North America (Indians), and Eastern Asia (Hindus). He considers beliefs and practices among European peasants in earlier centuries and the classic ages of Greece and Rome. He notes that Jews employ the formula "Tobim chayim!" that is, "Good life!" and Moslems say, "Praise to Allah!" after sneezing. He mentions a twelfth-century example from England of saying, "waes hael!" ("may you be well!"—"wassail!"), used to avert being taken ill after a sneeze. He also refers to "God bless you!" in English, "Got hilf!" in German, and "Felicità!" in Italian.

Back to the Zulus, Tylor notes that "repeated yawning and sneezing are classed together as signs of approaching spiritual possession." Hindus, Persians, Jews, and others ascribe yawning and sneezing to demoniacal possession or the invitation of such. "In comparing the modern Kafir ideas with those of other districts of the world, we find a distinct notion of a sneeze being due to a spiritual presence," writes Tylor. "This, which seems indeed the key to the whole matter, has been well brought into view" by stories in Celtic folklore "turning on the superstition that any one who sneezes is liable to be carried off by the fairies, unless their power be counteracted by an invocation, as 'God bless you!'"

In conclusion, "it was not originally an arbitrary and meaningless custom, but the working out of a principle," writes Tylor. "The plain statement by the modern Zulus fits with the hints to be gained from the superstition and folk-lore of other races, to connect the notions and practices as to sneezing with the ancient and savage doctrine of pervading and invading spirits, considered as good or evil, and treated accordingly." Thus, "The lingering survivals of the quaint old formulas in modern Europe seem an unconscious record of the time when the explanation of sneezing had not yet been given over to physiology."

Having explained a "ridiculous" custom, Tylor then takes up an "atrocious" one, that of sacrificing human victims when building foundations. As before, he cast about in collections of folklore from earlier eras and among contemporary peasants and tribal peoples. For example, he cites a current belief in Scotland that Picts of antiquity had bathed foundation stones with human blood, and rumors in Germany in 1843 that a child was sought to be built into the foundation of a new bridge. He notes European legends from the fifteenth century to the present. For instance, "Thuringian legend declares that to make the castle of Liebenstein fast and impregnable, a child was bought for hard money of its mother and walled in." According to the story, the child was eating a cake while the masons worked. The child cried out, "Mother, I see thee still." Later, it cried out, "Mother, I see thee a little still." Finally, as the masons put in the last stone, "Mother, now I see thee no more."

Tylor also cites Slavonic, German, Danish, Greek, and other legends. From all this evidence, he writes, it appears that tradition preserves "the memory of a bloodthirsty barbaric rite, which not only really existed in ancient times, but lingered long in European history." Turning "to less cultured countries" (in Africa and Asia), "we shall find the rite carried on in our own day with a distinctly religious purpose, either to propitiate the earth-spirits with a victim, or to convert the soul of the victim himself into a protecting demon."

Finally, Tylor takes up the most "senseless" of the three practices, that of not saving a drowning person. Once again he cites examples from European peasantry and tribal societies. Finding much evidence of spiritualistic belief, he concludes, "From this point of view it is obvious that to save a sinking man is to snatch a victim from the very clutches of the water-spirit, a rash defiance of deity which would hardly pass unavenged."

To summarize, Tylor made cross-cultural comparisons using accounts by explorers, travelers, local clerics, missionaries, administrators, physicians—anyone who had documented peoples' traditions for whatever reason. He sought both examples and explanations of the practices whose original meaning he attempted to reconstruct. The purpose for studying survivals, states Tylor, is that they constitute evidence "aiding us to trace the course which the civilization of the world has actually followed." He had wanted to call them superstition, meaning "residium," but "the term superstition now implies a reproach." Therefore, "it is desirable to introduce such a term as 'survival,' simply to denote the historical fact which the word 'superstition' is now spoiled for expressing" (see Box 2–11).

Committed to rationalism and believing it to be an index of progress, Tylor assumed the stance of a social reformer, tolerating irrational concepts only as historical documents. In terms of a reformer's science, the purpose of ethnography is "to expose the remains of crude old culture which have passed into harmful superstition, and to mark these out for destruction," which was the objective of many who succeeded him.

Sir James George Frazer (1854–1941) took E. B. Tylor's cultural evolutionism to an extreme. He assumed all peoples go through the same stages of cultural development, postulating the evolution of cultural thought from magic, through religion, to science. Frazer's best known work is *The Golden Bough: A Study in Magic and Religion* (1890), reissued in 12 volumes between 1911 and 1915 (a one-volume abridgement appeared in 1922). In the second edition (1900), he subdivides *sympathetic magic* into *homeopathic* and *contagious magic*. These categories appear in subsequent discussions of magic and superstition, indicating their general acceptance among scholars.

According to Frazer, magic is based on two principles of thought. One is that like

BOX 2-11
Fear of the Gods

There seems always to have been a body of thought inherited from an earlier time, a residual element, a *superstes*, or a *superstites*. This residuum often carried the connotation of a suspect or rejected element. The exact etymology of "superstition" has never been agreed upon, but the Germanic equivalents would seem to support the notion of a faith or a false faith that has either lived on or has grown up outside the bounds of an accepted faith or belief. The German *Aberglaube*, the Dutch *overgeloof*, and the Danish *overtro* are terms that bear out both aspects. . . .

Still another facet is seen in the closest Greek equivalent to superstition, namely, *deisidaimonia*, "fear of the gods." More clearly than any other definition, this Greek word expresses man's concern for the imponderable forces that lie behind the visible universe, awakening in him not only feelings of awe, but those of fear as well.

While it is commonly supposed that these old beliefs and superstitious practices are the legacy of people still in a primitive or benighted state, on the one hand, or that, on the other, these quaint and erroneous ideas are kept alive in the civilized community only by the unlettered folk, experience has taught otherwise. Superstition exists in all strata of society and is encountered among people of all degrees of formal education.
—Wayland D. Hand[33]

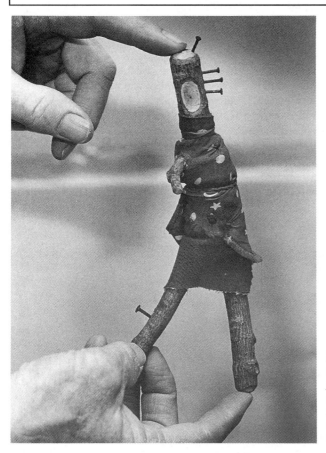

Figure 2–6: "Voodoo doll" into which nails have been driven to produce pain in a victim by means of the principle of homeopathic magic (photo by Bill Bebee, courtesy UCLA Folklore and Mythology Archives).

produces like. As an example of imitative or homeopathic magic involving the "Law of Similarity," Frazer refers to "North American Indians" who, "we are told, believe that by drawing the figure of a person in sand . . . and then pricking it with a sharp stick . . . , they inflict a corresponding injury on the person represented."[34]

The imitative principle, scholars since Frazer's time have also noted, is found in much folk medicine as *similia similibus curanter*, "like cures like." For instance, "a leaf shaped like a kidney, or a liver, or an ovary, or what not is supposed to designate a remedy for disorders of the organ which it resembles," reports Vance Randolph in *Ozark Superstitions* (New York: Columbia University Press, 1947).[35] "A strong tea of red-clover blossoms is highly regarded in some quarters as a blood purifier and general tonic," he writes. "The shell of a black walnut is supposed to represent the human skull, and the meat is said to resemble the brain; therefore people who show signs of mental aberration are encouraged to eat walnuts."

The second principle of thought underlying many magical beliefs and practices,

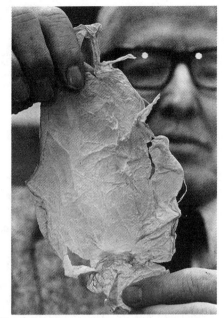

Figure 2–7: The caul or "veil," a fetal membrane sometimes covering the head or face of a newly born child, has been used as a talisman to protect against drowning; a person born with a caul is said to be gifted with healing and to possess second sight (clairvoyance, precognition), the capacity to see remote or future objects or events (photo by Bill Bebee, courtesy UCLA Folklore and Mythology Archives).

BOX 2–12
Sympathetic Magic

If we analyse the principles of thought on which magic is based, they will probably be found to resolve themselves into two: first, that like produces like, or that an effect resembles its cause; and, second, that things which have once been in contact with each other continue to act on each other at a distance after the physical contact has been severed. The former principle may be called the Law of Similarity, the latter the Law of Contact or Contagion. . . . Charms based on the Law of Similarity may be called Homoeopathic or Imitative Magic. Charms based on the Law of Contact or Contagion may be called Contagious Magic. . . .

If my analysis of the magician's logic is correct, its two great principles turn out to be merely two different misapplications of the association of ideas. Homoeopathic magic is founded on the association of ideas by similarity: contagious magic is founded on the association of ideas by contiguity. Homoeopathic magic commits the mistake of assuming that things which resemble each other are the same: contagious magic commits the mistake of assuming that things which have once been in contact with each other are always in contact.
          —Sir James George Frazer[36]

Figure 2–8: Smöjning, or passing through a tree, in Uppland, Sweden (1918), in order to transfer the disease from the child to the tree (courtesy Nordiska Museet).

contends Frazer, is that things which have once been in contact with each other continue to act on one another at a distance after being physically separated. (This idea is also known as *pars pro toto,* "the part for the whole.") He cites as an example of contagious magic involving the "Law of Contact or Contagion" the worldwide belief that magical sympathy exists between a person and any severed portion of his or her body, such as hair or nails, as well as blood, saliva, or mucous. Whoever gains possession of these parts may, at a distance, affect

the person. For example, burning an individual's hair or cutting the nail parings into smaller pieces can injure or perhaps even kill the person from whom they were obtained.

One may also affect another individual by allowing discarded parts of oneself to touch him or her, a notion for which Frazer's followers have also found evidence. For instance, in his article "The Magical Transference of Disease" (1980), Wayland D. Hand cites many examples of contagious magic to get rid of illnesses by transferring

---

BOX 2–13
Superstitious Los Angeles

In "Superstitious L.A." in the *Los Angeles Times Magazine*, April 17, 1988, Paul Ciotti notes some current superstitions.

It's bad luck to:
Look back when getting on an airplane.
Count the cars in a funeral cortege.
Let your wife pack your parachute.
Say to an undertaker, "I'll be seeing you."
Wash your husband's coffee cup until he comes home again at night.

It's good luck to:
Hang baby shoes from your rear-view mirror.
"Die" on screen at the start of your movie career.
Buy your lottery tickets from a hunchback.

Ciotti quotes former UCLA basketball coach John Wooden, who used to pick up hairpins on his daily five-mile walk around the track and stick them in the wood of a tree for good luck: "It was an old baseball superstition—'find a hairpin, stick it in the nearest wood and get a base hit.'"

He also cites a Century City stockbroker who bases his decisions on how well or how hideously a colleague dresses. "If he's dressed badly, I buy, and if he's looking good, I sell. In the two months I've been charting him, I've been 100% right. I'm not kidding. I turned one $140,000 account into $240,000" by making trading decisions on this basis.

Other beliefs include "Sitting too close to the TV makes your eyes change color. If you curse your computer, it will trash your files. Photocopying with the cover up gives you cancer. . . . When caught in a traffic jam, the lane you end up in will always be the slowest." Finally, a screenwriter who dropped a page from his screenplay immediately retyped it lest the sale of his story be jinxed.

---

them to others, such as a belief recorded in Kansas that a wart should be pricked, "and the blood collected in brown paper which is thrown into the road without looking where it falls, . . . destined to pass to the person finding the bundle."[37]

According to Frazer, both the law of similarity and the law of contact or contagion fall under the rubric "sympathetic magic." This is because "both assume that things act on each other at a distance through a secret sympathy." Imitative or homeopathic magic is based on the association of ideas by similarity, and contagious magic is founded on the association of ideas by contiguity. Both are mistaken, he con-

tends. Hence, "magic is a spurious system of natural law as well as a fallacious guide of conduct; it is a false science as well as an abortive art."[38]

For his categories of magic, Frazer seems to have been influenced by Tylor. In the second of two chapters on "Survival in Culture" in his book *Primitive Culture*, Tylor examines magic, which he considered to belong "to the lowest known stages of civilization." The "lower races, who have not partaken largely of the education of the world, still maintain it in vigour."[39] The key to understanding "Occult Science," writes Tylor, is that it is based on "the Association of Ideas." Thus, "Man, as yet in a low intellectual condition, having come to associate in thought those things which he found by experience to be connected in fact, proceeded erroneously to invert this action, and to conclude that association in thought must involve similar connexion in reality."

An example of the "magic arts" resulting from "mistaking an ideal for a real connexion" is that of "practices whereby a distant person is to be affected by acting on something closely associated with him—his property, clothes he has worn, and above all cuttings of his hair and nails." This is what Frazer came to call "contagious magic." Tylor also gives numerous examples of "magical arts in which the connexion is that of mere analogy or symbolism," such as the Cornishman who, on cutting himself, "will rub the knife with fat, and as it dries, the wound will heal; this is a lingering survival from days when recipes for sympathetic ointment were to be found in the Pharmacopoeia." Frazer labeled such practices and beliefs "homeopathic magic," and he subsumed contagious and imitative magic under the general term "sympathetic magic."

Scholars' continuing use of terms developed by researchers such as Tylor and Frazer within a survivalistic framework attests to their ongoing meaningfulness.[40] The notion of survivals itself in Tylor's and Frazer's sense also remains relevant in today's world, according to Wayland D. Hand. He writes that while many superstitions "are now barely believed, or only half believed, they somehow linger on as heirlooms of the hoary past, finding harbor with succeeding generations of people in all walks of life." Hand attributes this to several factors, including idle curiosity, important symbols and associations, and the creative imagination of human beings in devising new beliefs and practices modeled on the old. Moreover, "the uncertainties and hazards of life, and the myriad unexplored and un-

explained facts that man constantly faces, will always serve to inspire approaches and modes of thought that inevitably lead to the speculations and irrationalities that underlie superstition."[41]

Conclusion

By characterizing cultural and intellectual development in evolutionary terms and demonstrating that folklore can be found not only in Europe and Indo-European-derived societies, but also among non-Western and even "primitive" peoples, researchers such as Tylor in the late nineteenth and Frazer in the early twentieth century established the fact that folklore is universal. The data base for folkloristics, their work indicated, cannot be limited to examples of folklore recorded and reported only in certain parts of the world, such as Europe. Instead, it must include data from all cultures and from people of all kinds.

Incorporating examples of folklore from around the globe into the folkloristic data base made Western researchers aware of previously unknown and unacknowledged similarities among human beings. Certain forms of expression—such as riddles, proverbs, rituals, games, and myths—were soon found to be pervasive, and perhaps even universal. Furthermore, the folklores of peoples everywhere, it soon became apparent, are pervaded by recurrent preoccupations and themes, such as animal-human liaisons; magical acts, objects, and transformations; interactions between deities and humans; and intercourse between natural and supernatural beings and realms.

Scholars hypothesized that similarities discernible cross-culturally in examples of folklore could be explained in one of two ways. When different peoples with similar folklore examples (e.g., specific stories, games, songs) were known or assumed to

Figure 2–9: Drawing by a reporter who covered the American Folklore Society meeting in Baltimore, December 28–29, 1897, published in the Baltimore American, *29 December 1897; scholarly papers included H. C. Bolton's "Relics of Astrology," C. C. Bombaugh's "Bibliography of Folklore," W. W. Newell's "Opportunities for Collecting Folklore in America," and A. S. Chessin's "Russian Folklore" (photo by Simon J. Bronner).*

have had a common ancestry (as speakers of Indo-European-derived languages presumably do) or to have interacted with each other historically (as have speakers of Indo-European and non-Indo-European languages, for example), then the existence of the similarities in folklores was attributed either to a shared cultural heritage or to intersocietal borrowing. The folklore examples in question were conceived to be artifacts from past historical eras. Each was hypothesized to have had a single origin (*monogenesis*) and to have become traditional from having been transmitted over time, either intergenerationally within, or interactionally between, societies.

When neither common ancestry nor historical contact was documentable or seemed possible, then similarities in the folklore examples of different peoples were explained in developmental terms. Similar beliefs, customs, and stories were conceived to be artifacts of the primitive cultural and prelogical intellectual stages through which all peoples presumably pass in the natural course of the evolution that occurs within the human species. Thus, similar folklore examples found among peoples not related through cultural ancestry or historically shared experiences were hypothesized to have originated independently, and hence to have had multiple origins (*polygenesis*). Moreover, such folklore examples were judged to be traditional not only for the peoples among whom they are found, but also for the human species as a whole.

These hypotheses were subjects of considerable discussion and debate during the closing decades of the nineteenth and the early part of the twentieth century. The view that folklore is universal was quickly accepted. It was convincingly supported by the rapidly growing number of folklore examples from non-Western societies that fieldworkers were recording from living informants and that library researchers were uncovering in older written works authored, for the most part, by European travelers, missionaries, and government officials residing or working abroad. But scholars differed about what the universality of folklore implied. Some individuals, such as the English researchers Andrew Lang (1844–1912) and Edwin Sidney Hartland (1848–1927), inferred from this discovery that all folklore must have had primitive origins. They regarded all forms and examples of folklore as manifestations and artifacts of prelogical thinking and primitive stages of cultural evolution.[42] Other investigators, such as Joseph Jacobs (1854–1916) and Moses Gaster (1856–1934), argued that there are formal and qualitative differences among folklores and that one cannot treat all forms and examples of folklore indiscriminately or compare them arbitrarily or unsystematically.[43] They criticized those who cited the superficial similarities they found among selected stories, customs, and beliefs to support the view that *all* folklore examples must necessarily be survivals from primitive stages in cultural and intellectual evolution. The fact that folklore examples often have seemingly primitive concepts and ideas in them, they contended, did not necessarily mean that the examples themselves had survived from primitive times. Furthermore, different examples of folklore often have very different histories, they insisted, and must therefore be treated individually rather than collectively.

Scholars eventually compromised, conceding that it is defensible to hypothesize polygenesis for many beliefs and customs, for simple stories (such as humorous anecdotes and animal tales), and for basic games (e.g., those involving tagging and hiding), regardless of the ancestry or history of peoples among whom they are found. For lengthy or complexly structured folklore forms and examples such as *Märchen* and ballads, however, monogenesis is the only

BOX 2-14
On the Primitiveness of All Fairy Tales

With regard . . . to the *Origin* of the peculiar and irrational features of myth and *märchen* we believe them to be derived and inherited from the savage state of man, from the savage conditions of life, and the savage way of regarding the world. . . . The essence both of *märchen* and myths is a number of impossible and very peculiar incidents. These incidents are due to the natural qualities of the savage imagination. Again, the incidents are combined into various romantic arrangements, each of these arrangements being a *märchen*. The *märchen* were originally told, among untutored peoples, about anonymous heroes,—a boy, a girl, a lion, a bear,—such were the leading characters of the earliest tales. As tribes became settled, these old stories were localised, the adventures (originally anonymous) were attributed to real or imaginary named persons or gods, and were finally adorned by the fancy of poets like the early singers of Greece. Thus, while a savage race has its *märchen* (in which the characters are usually beasts or anonymous persons), the civilised race (or the race in a state of higher barbarism) has the same tale, developed and elaborated into a localised myth, with heroes rejoicing in such noble names as Perseus, Odysseus, Jason, Leminkainen, or Maui.
  —Andrew Lang[44]

BOX 2-15
On the Nonprimitiveness of European Fairy Tales

The rigid Anthropological School of folktale research [i.e., evolutionists such as Andrew Lang and Edwin Sidney Hartland] have had the merit of drawing our attention to savage custom, as explaining the unnatural incidents of folktales. Mr. Farrer went somewhat farther, and drew attention to savage fairy tales themselves. Since his time several sets of savage tales have been published. . . . Those who have read these tales will agree with me, I think, that they are formless and void, and bear the same relation to good European fairy tales as the invertebrata do to the vertebrate kingdom in the animal world. Judging by them, at any rate, we should not be disposed to think that the majority of European folktales have descended unchanged from the time when the European world was savage. Yet when Europeans were savages they probably told fairy tales, and these were probably as amorphous as the fairytales of Samoa or the Torres Straits.
  —Joseph Jacobs[45]

tenable hypothesis. From the late nineteenth century to the present, this commonsensical compromise has enabled researchers to conduct their inquiries in terms of either a universal or a culturally delimited data base and to pose and attempt to answer questions that are historical or panhuman in their concerns, implications, and applications.

But folklorists choosing either of these sets of options conceptualize folklore first and foremost as artifact—from early stages in human evolution, from earlier periods in the histories of particular peoples, or both.

Notes

1. Our earliest information about Greek mythology is found in the epic poems the *Iliad* and the *Odyssey*, attributed to Homer and hypothesized to have been written in the ninth or eighth century B.C., and *The Theogony* of Hesiod (fl. ca. 800 B.C.). There are numerous characterizations and retellings of

the Greek myths. Among the most popular and widely read are Edith Hamilton, *Mythology* (New York: New American Library, 1940); Robert Graves, *The Greek Myths*, 2 vols. (Baltimore: Penguin Books, 1955); H. J. Rose, *Gods and Heroes of the Greeks: An Introduction to Greek Mythology* (New York: Meridian Books, 1958); and *New Larousse Encyclopedia of Mythology*, new edition (New York: Hamlyn, 1968), pp. 85–198.

2. From *Germania* (A.D. 98), in *Tacitus on Britain and Germany*, trans. H. Mattingly, Penguin Books Edition (Baltimore: Penguin Books, 1948), pp. 115–116.

3. For a discussion of Chaucer's indebtedness to storytelling and possible relationships between traditional narratives and the stories he has his Canterbury pilgrims tell, see Carl Lindahl, *Earnest Games: Folkloric Patterns in the Canterbury Tales* (Bloomington: Indiana University Press, 1987).

4. Jestbook titles are telling of their contents, as the following reveal: *A C. Mery Tales* (1525); *Merry Tales, Witty Questions, & Quick Answers* (1567); and *Tarleton's Jests* (1609).

5. See, for example, Lyly's *Endimion* (1586–87) and *Midas* (1589); Marlowe's *The Tragicall History of Dr. Faustus* (1604); and Shakespeare's *The Taming of the Shrew* (1594–95) and *King Lear* (1606–1607).

6. This characterization of the mechanistic model is derived, for the most part, from Harry Girvetz, George Geiger, Harold Hantz, and Bertram Morris, *Science, Folklore, and Philosophy* (New York: Harper & Row, 1966); see especially pp. 227–230 and 291–306. The model is characterized similarly in Bertrand Russell, *A History of Western Philosophy* (New York: Simon and Schuster, 1945), pp. 561–563.

7. This characterization of the organic model is derived, for the most part, from Girvetz et al., pp. 294–306.

8. Francis Grose, *The Antiquary Repertory*, vol. 1 (London, 1775); reprinted in Richard M. Dorson, ed., *Peasant Customs and Savage Myths: Selections from the British Folklorists*, vol. 1 (Chicago: University of Chicago Press, 1968), p. 5.

9. Reprinted in Dorson, vol. 1, pp. 7–8.

10. Hugh Miller, *Scenes and Legends of the North of Scotland* (Edinburgh: Adam and Charles Black, 1835), p. 3.

11. Reprinted in Dorson, vol. 1, pp. 52–54.

12. Reprinted in Dorson, vol. 1, p. 52.

13. Simon J. Bronner, *American Folklore Studies: An Intellectual History* (Lawrence: University Press of Kansas, 1986), p. 6.

14. Lauri Honko, "The Kalevala Process," in *Kalevala 1835–1985: The National Epic of Finland* (Helsinki: Helsinki University Library, 1985), p. 17.

15. Michael Owen Jones, "Folk Poetry, Finnish Identity, and Lönnrot's *Kalevala*," in *The World of the Kalevala: Essays in Celebration of the 150 Jubilee of the Publication of the Finnish National Epic* (Los Angeles: UCLA Folklore and Mythology Publications, 1987), pp. 1–25; Michael Branch, "Kalevala: From Myth to Symbol," in *Kalevala 1835–1985*, pp. 1–11; and William A. Wilson, *Folklore and Nationalism in Modern Finland* (Bloomington: Indiana University Press, 1976), pp. 35–42.

16. Poem 1, lines 1–10, 21–36, in *Kalevala: The Land of the Heroes*, trans. W. F. Kirby (London: J. M. Dent and Sons, 1907).

17. The popularity of the *Kinder- und Hausmärchen* is indicated by the fact that seven editions of the book were published during the Grimms' lifetimes (1812 and 1815, first edition; 1819, second edition; 1837, third edition; 1840, fourth edition; 1843, fifth edition; 1850, sixth edition; and 1857, seventh edition). The work was also widely translated—into French in 1830, for example, and into English in 1884 (with earlier partial English translations). The French translation was the basis for the Russian one and the 1884 English edition for a partial Japanese translation (1887). Writes Murray B. Peppard, "The Grimms were fortunate in being translated early and well. . . . English has been one of the important mediums for carrying the tales to the corners of the earth" (*Paths through the Forest: A Biography of the Brothers Grimm*, New York: Holt, Rinehart and Winston, 1971, p. 72).

18. Poem 50, lines 501–512, in Kirby.

19. From *The Fairy Tales of Charles Perrault* (1697), trans. Geoffrey Brereton (Baltimore: Penguin Books, 1957), pp. 21–25.

20. Cited in Peppard, pp. 61–62.

21. For further discussion of this point, see Stith Thompson, *The Folktale* (New York: Dryden Press, 1946), pp. 370–380.

22. Grundtvig's principal works are his col-

lections of folksongs, *Danmarks gamle Folkeviser*, 7 volumes (1853–1912); sagas, *Danske Sagn* (1854–61); and folktales, *Danske Folkeæventyr, efter utrykte Kilder* (1876, 1878, and 1884).

23. Girvetz et al., p. 309.

24. Quoted in Girvetz et al., p. 313.

25. Charles Darwin, *Descent of Man*, 2d ed. (London: A. L. Burt, 1874), p. 707.

26. For further information about Tylor's views on culture and stages of development, see his *Primitive Culture*, vol. 1, pp. 1–25; E. B. Tylor, *Anthropology*, 2 vols. (London: Thinker's Library, 1930, originally published 1880), vol. 1, pp. 18–19; and David Bidney, *Theoretical Anthropology* (New York: Columbia University Press, 1953), p. 191. References to *Primitive Culture* throughout the text are to the 7th ed., 2 vols. in 1 (New York: Brentano's Publishers, 1924). Quotes are from pp. 16, 71–72, 89–90, 93, 97–110, 134, and 136–137.

27. For further discussion of Tylor's influence on folkloristics, see Ellen J. Stekert, "Tylor's Theory of Survivals and National Romanticism: Their Influence on Early American Folksong Collectors," *Southern Folklore Quarterly* 32 (1968):209–236.

28. *Primitive Culture*, pp. 89–90.

29. "Riddles," in Maria Leach, ed., *Funk & Wagnalls Standard Dictionary of Folklore, Mythology and Legend*, vol. 2 (New York: Funk & Wagnalls, 1950), p. 942.

30. From Archer Taylor, *English Riddles from Oral Tradition* (Berkeley and Los Angeles: University of California Press, 1951), pp. 23–24.

31. *Primitive Culture*, p. 16.

32. *Primitive Culture*, pp. 16–17.

33. "'The Fear of the Gods': Superstition and Popular Belief," in Tristram Potter Coffin, ed., *Our Living Traditions: An Introduction to American Folklore* (New York: Basic Books, 1968), pp. 216 and 217.

34. Sir James George Frazer, *The Golden Bough: A Study in Magic and Religion*, 12 vols., 3d ed., 10th reprinting (New York: St. Martin's Press, 1955), p. 55.

35. The quotes are from pp. 105, 106, and 114.

36. Frazer, pp. 52–54.

37. Wayland D. Hand, "The Magical Transference of Disease," in *Magical Medicine: The Folkloric Component of Medicine in the Folk Belief, Custom, and Ritual of the Peoples of Europe and America* (Berkeley and Los Angeles: University of California Press, 1980), pp. 17–42. The quote is from p. 20.

38. Frazer, p. 53.

39. The quotes are from Tylor, *Primitive Culture*, pp. 112, 116, and 119.

40. Some works that illustrate this point are Jan Harold Brunvand, *The Study of American Folklore: An Introduction*, 3d ed. (New York: W. W. Norton, 1986), pp. 317–318; Don Yoder, "Folk Medicine," in Richard M. Dorson, ed., *Folklore and Folklife: An Introduction* (Chicago: University of Chicago Press, 1972), pp. 191–215; Wayland D. Hand, *Popular Beliefs and Superstitions from North Carolina*, The Frank C. Brown Collection of North Carolina Folklore, vol. 6 (Durham, N.C.: Duke University Press, 1961), pp. xix–xlvii passim; entry on magic in Leach, vol. 2, pp. 660–661; and Kenneth W. Clarke and Mary W. Clarke, *Introducing Folklore* (New York: Holt, Rinehart and Winston, 1963), pp. 83–84.

41. Hand, "'The Fear of the Gods,'" p. 226.

42. Among Lang's best-known works are a collection of essays published as *Custom and Myth* (London: Longmans, Green, 1884) and his introduction (vol. 1, pp. xi–lxx) to Margaret Hunt's English translation of the Grimms' *Kinder- und Hausmärchen*, titled *Grimm's Household Tales*, 2 vols. (London: George Bell and Sons, 1884). Hartland's works include *The Science of Fairy Tales: An Enquiry into the Fairy Mythology* (London: Walter Scott, 1891), and *The Legend of Perseus: A Study of Tradition in Story, Custom, and Belief*, 3 vols. (London: D. Nutt, 1894–96).

43. Jacobs is best known as an editor of fairy tale collections, including *English Fairy Tales* (London, 1890), *Celtic Fairy Tales* (London, 1892), and *Indian Fairy Tales* (London, 1892). Gaster devoted most of his career to a study of Jewish folklore and authored, among other works, *The Exempla of the Rabbis* (London and Leipzig: Asia Publishing Co., 1924) and *Ma'aseh Book: Book of Jewish Tales and Legends* (Philadelphia, 1934).

44. "Introduction," in Hunt, vol. 1, pp. xli–xlii.

45. "The Problem of Diffusion: Rejoinders," *Folk-Lore* 5 (1894):136–137.

3. Survival, Continuity, Revival, and Historical Source

The phenomena that folklorists focus upon can be viewed as artifacts because they have histories. At some point in time, particular human beings create ordered ways of expressing themselves. These expressive forms and certain examples of them come to be regarded as traditional—and hence become identifiable as folklore—when, over time, others repeat or imitate what particular individuals were the first to say or do. Viewing folklore as artifact thus acknowledges its historicity and attests to its durability and utility for human beings.

From the inception of their discipline in the early nineteenth century to the present, researchers have recognized and discussed the artifactual nature of folklore. They have hypothesized that some forms, examples, and aspects of folklore must hearken back to early stages in the development of the human species, while others must have been created during earlier eras in the histories of particular peoples. Folklorists have studied diverse kinds of phenomena from this perspective—including ballads, stories, children's games and rhymes, art and crafts, and festivals. They have concluded that folklore viewed as artifact may be conceptualized as *survival, continuity, revival,* or *historical source.*[1]

Survival

Francis B. Gummere observes in a 1907 book on the ballad that "curious old ideas prevail" in English and Scottish narrative songs, and "minor superstitions abound which are derived from a lapsed mythology and a superseded habit of dealing with the other world."[2] Louise Pound writes in her 1921 work on the same phenomenon that "ballads preserve many archaic literary traits along with the emotions and culture of a vanished age,"[3] an opinion shared by her student Lowry Charles Wimberly and expressed in a book he published seven years later.[4] Evelyn Kendrick Wells states and amplifies these notions in her 1950 work *The Ballad Tree.*[5]

In her discussion of the supernatural in these traditional narrative songs, Wells assumes that ballads are survivals from the past which have suffered alterations through time. She focuses on ballad content, discussing examples of "ancient attitudes and beliefs" and "evidences of primitive thought and custom which have been swept into the stream of tradition." These ideas and practices, she writes, have been "preserved in the ballads in a fragmentary, or vestigial, or only faintly reminiscent state." Thus, folklore is a survival, and there are survivals in folklore.

Animals can speak in ballads, notes Wells, a "vestige of" totemistic belief in a kinship between them and human beings. Spirits dwell in blood, light, and personal possessions; when his name is uttered, a man dies. Here is evidence of animism, the notion of the presence of souls or spirits in various parts of the body, in objects, and even in one's name. People are transformed into animals, and vice versa. Mortals disappear into the otherworld. Fairies appear at the slightest provocation, steal children, and cast spells. There are omens and portents.

Of the three dozen ballads that Wells

cites, few "carry forward so much ancient folklore as 'Tam Lin,'" writes Albert B. Friedman.[6] Robert Burns collected this song and contributed it to James Johnson's *Scots Musical Museum* (1792). Later Francis James Child included it as ballad number 39, variant A, in his ten-part compilation *The English and Scottish Popular Ballads*, published in five volumes between 1882 and 1898, on which Wells draws heavily for her examples.[7]

The setting of "Tam Lin" (see Box 3–1) is Carterhaugh, off limits to young women (verses 1–2). Janet, whose father gave her ownership of this plain, defies the taboo. While visiting the grounds she plucks a rose, a flower protected by elves and fairies. Her action provokes Tam Lin to appear (verses 5–7). An amorous encounter apparently ensues. Desiring a father for the child she carries, Janet spurns the landlords and "earthly knights" in her father's hall in favor of her "elfin" love (verses 12–16). Back at Carterhaugh, she summons Tam Lin by plucking another rose (verses 19–20). She learns that fairies had stolen him as a child (verses 22–23), and that he is anxious to return to the human world. Every seventh year the fairies must pay a tithe to hell. They usually pass off an abducted mortal in order to save one of their own. Tam Lin, being "so fair and full of flesh," fears he is the next victim (verse 24).

To disenchant her lover, Janet must pull him from his horse while he rides in the fairy troop on Halloween at midnight (verses 25–26), holding him fast as he passes through a series of repulsive or dangerous shapes (verses 31–33). A bath in well water, his nakedness then covered with Janet's cloak, will complete Tam Lin's transformation from elf back to human being (verses 34–35). Janet follows instructions, redeeming him (verses 36–39). However, Tam Lin now knows the secrets of the fairy world, to the chagrin of the queen of fairies, who regrets not having torn out his "two grey

eyes" and replaced them with wooden ones as a security precaution (verses 40–42).

"This fine ballad stands by itself, and is not, as might have been expected, found in possession of any people but the Scottish," writes Francis James Child, who presumed a national origin for "Tam Lin." "Yet it has connections, through the . . . retransformation of Tam Lin, with Greek popular tradition older than Homer."[8] Child describes a fairy tale from Crete containing a similar theme of shape-shifting and transformation, told about 1820 or 1830 by a peasant who had heard it from his grandfather and similar to one recorded 2,000 years earlier in Greece. In suggesting that elements in the ballad might have originated in historically related societies, Child echoes Sir Walter Scott, who devotes a 40-page introduction to "Tam Lin" in his *Minstrelsy of the Scottish Border*, focusing on "fairies of popular superstition." Scott attributes the English "elf" to the *berg-elfen* of the Scandinavians and the word *fairy*, or *faerie*, to *fae*, "derived from the Persic through the medium of the Arabic." He then examines modifications to these concepts over time in Indo-European tradition, before considering current survivals.[9]

Similarly, as she develops her discussion of folklore in "Tam Lin" and other ballads, Wells scans "survivals in primitive thought around us," thus interpreting modern examples of folklore as survivals. For example, "An everyday phrase may hark back to some hinterland of thought; a flippant 'My stars!' may be descended from the ritual of swearing by the sun, the stars, the moon, turning oneself about thrice and repeating runes [mysterious ancient rhymes]," she writes. "Animal superstitions abound," such as beliefs that "rats leave a sinking ship, and dogs howl at the approach of death. Cats, crows, black dogs, white horses, as every child knows, are the bringers of good and bad luck." Further, "'I have a hunch' is said . . . to have evolved

BOX 3–1
"Tam Lin"

1 O I forbid you maidens a' [all],
   That wear gowd [gold] on your hair,
   To come or gae [go] by Carterhaugh,
   For young Tam Lin is there.

2 There's nane [none] that gaes [goes] by
      Carterhaugh
   But they leave him a wad [forfeit],
   Either their rings, or green mantles,
   Or else their maidenhead.

3 Janet has kilted [tucked up] her green
      kirtle [petticoat]
   A little aboon [above] her knee,
   And she has broded [braided] her yellow
      hair
   A little aboon her bree [brow],
   And she's awa [away] to Carterhaugh,
   As fast as she can hie [go quickly].

4 When she came to Carterhaugh
   Tam Lin was at the well,
   And there she fand [found] his steed
      standing,
   But away was himsel.

5 She had na pu'd [pulled] a double rose,
   A rose but only twa [two],
   Till up then started young Tam Lin,
   Says, "Lady, thou's pu [will pull] nae
      mae [no more].

6 "Why pu's thou [do you pull] the rose,
      Janet,
   And why breaks thou the wand [twig]?
   Or why comes thou to Carterhaugh
   Withoutten my command?"

7 "Carterhaugh, it is my ain [own],
   My daddie gave it me;
   I'll come and gang [go] by Carterhaugh,
   And ask nae [no] leave at thee."

            *   *   *

8 Janet has kilted [tucked up] her green
      kirtle [petticoat]
   A little aboon [above] her knee,
   And she has snooded [tied with a rib-
      bon] her yellow hair
   A little aboon [above] her bree [brow],
   And she is to her father's ha [hall],
   As fast as she can hie [go].

9 Four and twenty ladies fair
   Were playing at the ba [ball],
   And out then cam [came] the fair Janet,
   Ance [once] the flower amang them a'
      [all].

10 Four and twenty laides fair
   Were playing at the chess,
   And out then cam the fair Janet,
   As green as onie [any] glass.

11 Out then spak [spoke] an auld [old] grey
      knight,
   Lay oer the castle wa [wall],
   And says, "Alas, fair Janet, for thee
   But we'll be blamed a' [all]."

12 "Haud [hold] your tongue, ye auld fac'd
      [old-faced] knight,
   Some ill death may ye die!
   Father my bairn [child] on whom I will,
   I'll father nane [none] on thee."

13 Out then spak [spoke] her father dear,
   And he spak meek and mild;
   "And ever alas, sweet Janet," he says,
   "I think thou gaes wi [are with] child."

14 "If that I gae wi [am with] child, father,
   Mysel [myself] maun [must] bear the
      blam [blame];
   There's neer a laird [not a lord] about
      you ha [hall]
   Shall get the bairn's [child's] name.

15 "If my love were an earthly knight,
   As he's an elfin grey,
   I wad na gie [would not give] my ain
      [own] true-love
   For nae [any] lord that ye hae [have].

16 "The steed that my true-love rides on
   Is lighter than the wind;
   Wi siller [silver] he is shod before,
   Wi burning gowd [gold] behind."

17 Janet has kilted her green kirtle
   A little aboon her knee,
   And she has snooded her yellow hair
   A little aboon her bree,
   And she's awa [away] to Carterhaugh,
   As fast as she can hie.

18 When she cam to Carterhaugh,
   Tam Lin was at the well,
   And there she fand his steed standing,
   But away was himsel.

19 She had na pu'd a double rose,
   A rose but only twa,
   Till up then started young Tam Lin,
   Says, "Lady, thou pu's nae mae.

20 "Why pu's thou the rose, Janet,
   Amang the groves sae green,
   And a' to kill the bonnie babe
   That we gat [begot] us between?"

21 "O tell me, tell me, Tam Lin," she says,
   "For's sake that died on tree,

If eer ye was in holy chapel,
Or christendom did see?"

22 "Roxbrugh he was my grandfather,
Took me with him to bide [dwell],
And ance [once] it fell upon a day
That wae [wo] did me betide.

23 "And ance it fell upon a day,
A cauld [cold] day and a snell [frosty],
When we were frae [from] the hunting
    come,
That frae my horse I fell;
The Queen o Fairies she caught me,
In yon green hill to dwell.

24 "And pleasant is the fair land,
But, an eerie tale to tell,
Ay at the end of seven years
We pay a tiend [tithe] to hell;
I am sae [so] fair and fu of flesh,
I'm feard it be mysel.

25 "But the night is Halloween, lady,
The morn is Hallowday;
Then win me, win me, an ye will,
For weel I wat ye may.

26 "Just at the mirk [dark] and midnight
    hour
The fairy folk will ride,
And they that wad [would] their true-
    love win,
At Miles Cross they maun bide [must
    wait]."

27 "But how shall I thee ken [know], Tam
    Lin,
Or how my true-love know,
Amang [among] sae mony unco [so many
    strange] knights
The like I never saw?"

28 "O first let pass the black, lady,
And syne [then] let pass the brown,
But quickly run to the milk-white steed,
Pu [pull] ye his rider down.

29 "For I'll ride on the milk-white steed,
And ay [always] nearest the town;
Because I was an earthly knight
They gie me that renown.

30 "My right hand will be glovd, lady,
My left hand will be bare,
Cockt up shall my bonnet be,
And kaimd [combed] down shall my
    hair,
And thae's [these] the takens [tokens] I
    gie [give] thee,
Nae [no] doubt I will be there.

31 "They'll turn me in your arms, lady,
Into an esk [newt] and adder;

But behold me fast, and fear me not,
I am your bairn's [child's] father.

32 "They'll turn me to a bear sae [so] grim,
And then a lion bold;
But hold me fast, and fear me not,
As ye shall love your child.

33 "Again they'll turn me in your arms
To a red hot gaud of airn [iron bar];
But hold me fast, and fear me not,
I'll do you nae [no] harm.

34 "And last they'll turn me in your arms
Into the burning gleed [ember];
Then throw me into well water,
O throw me in wi speed.

35 "And then I'll be your ain [own] true-
    love,
I'll turn a naked knight;
Then cover me wi your green mantle,
And cover me out of sight."

36 Gloomy, gloomy was the night,
And eerie was the way,
As fair Jenny in her green mantle
To Miles Cross she did gae [go].

37 About the middle o the night
She heard the bridles ring;
This lady was as glad at that
As any earthly thing.

38 First she let the black pass by,
And syne [then] she let the brown;
But quickly she ran to the milk-white
    steed,
And pu'd the rider down.

39 Sae weel she minded what he did say,
And young Tam Lin did win;
Syne coverd him wi' her green mantle,
As blythe's a bird in spring.

40 Out then spak the Queen of Fairies,
Out of a bush o broom:
"Them that has gotten young Tam Lin
Has gotten a stately groom."

41 Out then spak the Queen o Fairies,
And an angry woman was she:
"Shame betide her ill-far'd face,
And an ill death may she die,
For she's taen awa the boniest knight
In a' my companie.

42 "But had I kend [known], Tam Lin," she
    says,
"What now this night I see,
I wad hae taen [would have taken] out
    thy twa grey een [two grey eyes],
And put in twa een o tree [two eyes of
    wood]."[10]

from the belief that good luck followed from touching a hunchback."

Carrying a rabbit's foot for good luck, contends Wells, is " a vestige of totemism, the early belief that man's descent from animals gave him a kinship with them and involved their worship," sacrifice, and use in divination (reading the entrails) and adornment (wearing a bit of its fur or skin to gain special powers). "Children today show us something of a primitive reasoning in attributing to animals powers similar to their own," writes Wells. "They still live in a world where any bird or dog or horse may speak to them, and the presence of speaking animals in fairy tales finds them completely and uncritically receptive." Furthermore, "The child who looks out the window chanting, 'Rain, rain, go away,' or who pettishly kicks the chair he has stumbled against, is animating the rain or the wood, as did his pagan ancestor."

Wells also refers to spirits, which "might dwell in something intangible, like light . . . Today we have a relic of it in the emanation from a ghost, or more crudely, the light in the Hallowe'en jack-lantern." She discusses witchcraft, too, including the magical transformation of human beings into animals, "a primitive belief, not yet outgrown." Much of witchcraft "consisted of mimetic or imitative magic, the dramatic representation of a desired occurrence." For instance, the Eskimo play a game of "cat's cradle" with thread strung between their fingers to ensnare "the rays of the sun and store them against winter's darkness. . . . We tear up a letter that has hurt us, in an unconscious wish to hurt the sender."

Like Wells, other folklorists have dwelt on concepts and customs in the modern world as relics, inferring, for instance, that some children's games and songs—such as "London Bridge"—contain reference to ancient rites. Lady Alice Bertha Gomme, for example, puzzled over this song's stanzas (which emphasize the difficulty of building

Figure 3–1: A harvest figure with jack-o-lantern head in the New Jersey Pine Barrens, 1984 (PFP–216651–2–35, photo by Sue Samuelson, courtesy American Folklife Center, Library of Congress).

a bridge) and also over why a prisoner had to be taken (when the children sing "London Bridge is falling down, My fair lady!" and the keepers of the bridge lower their arms around one child who is thereby captured).[11] Influenced by cultural evolutionism, Gomme concludes that the game is a survival among modern children of an ancient foundation sacrifice demanding human victims to make bridges and buildings steadfast.[12]

Charles Francis Potter also opts for a survivalistic interpretation of children's lore. He differs in seeking "word fossils" rather than evidence of ancient beliefs and rites per se, especially in counting-out

---

BOX 3–2
"Word Fossils" in Children's Counting-out Rhymes

> Eena, meena, mona, mite
> Basca, lora, hora, bite,
> Hugga, bucca, bau;
> Eggs, butter, cheese, bread,
> Stick, stock, stone dead—O-U-T!

Here is one of the oldest known rimbles . . . betraying its age by the word-fossils so thickly sprinkled through it. Mixed with the English words are Latin, Cornish, and Cymric (Old Welsh). We are back in Druid times, about the first century B.C., when we chant some of these words. It was in 61 B.C., so Tacitus tells us, that the Roman conqueror Suetonius commanded the holy Druid groves of the sacred isle of *Mona* (now Anglesea) cut down to end the bloody rites of Druidism. To get to that island . . . you must cross the *Menai* Strait. *Hora* and *lora* are Latin for hour and binding-straps, and *bucca* was Cornish for hobgoblin or evil spirit.

Of course, we have only etymological evidence coupled with historical coincidence . . . , but it is certainly possible that our common eeny, meeny, miny, mo is a descendant of an ancient magic rime-charm used in Druid times to choose the human victims to be ferried across the Menai Strait to the isle of Mona to meet a horrible fate under the Golden Bough of the sacred mistletoe amid the holy oaks.

Since one known method of Druid sacrifice was to burn victims alive in wicker cages, perhaps the words . . . reflect the scene when the man chosen by this sacred lot of the magic rime was told his *hora* had come and was bound by the *lora* inside the *stick* and *stock* wicker cage or huge *basca* (basket) and burned until he was *stone dead*. We still have the *eggs, butter, cheese,* and *bread* to account for. . . . [T]hese four have been deemed powerful magic foods. Significantly enough, they are still employed in incantations in rural midsummer festivals still celebrated in former Druid regions. . . .

The remaining word eeny is probably also from the same land and period, for it occurs in the very ancient Anglo-Cymric 'shepherd's score' by which West of England shepherds count their sheep and Cornish fishermen their mackerel, even to this day, again illustrating the persistence of oral tradition.

—Charles Francis Potter[13]

---

rhymes. Basically, he makes two points regarding what these survivals in children's rhymes reveal. One is "the propensity of children to weave into their play-rimes references to much-discussed current events" and experiences or words which they do not fully understand (such as Latin terms in the Mass).[14] Potter's other point is that "in folklore as everywhere else, ontogeny recapitulates phylogeny," that is, the development of an individual repeats the evolution of the tribe or race. Thus, "the children's game-rimes reproduce the thought-forms, dance patterns, and even the language of our primitive forebears."[15]

Several implications of folklore as survivals need to be mentioned. Conceived of as relics from an earlier age and no longer functional or feasible in society, survivals must inevitably die out (see Box 3–3). And indeed, the numbers of people among whom certain folklore forms or examples are known may diminish, for various reasons. To explain the very existence of survivals, however, researchers have hypothesized factors corresponding to the view

BOX 3-3
Vanishing Material Folk Culture

Material folk culture is not yet a thing of the past alone—there are informants by the thousands, artifacts by the millions waiting to be studied—but there is little place for material folk culture in our world. It cannot last. Many material traditions were developed as solutions to practical problems which no longer exist, and modern technologies provide easier solutions than folk ones do for the problems that remain. The material traditions for which a modern need can be found are few. Some material traditions are carried on despite practical reasons for their discontinuance because they remain satisfying to their practitioners. A tourist market has been found to replace a portion of the withering market for folk crafts. Many ethnic groups have selected some annual customs and associated traditional foods as safe things to which they can cling in order to preserve some group identity. But daily, there are fewer who can provide the fieldworker with detailed information about their material folk culture. When all the active bearers of material traditions are dead, the objects they have left behind will continue to be instructive and a century from now fieldworkers will be bringing in fresh data. But daily, there is less to study and the answers become more difficult to obtain.

—Henry Glassie[16]

that these customs and ideas are out of place and time; thus, explanations tend to emphasize the negative. For example, the "tradition bearers" are said to perpetuate certain forms and examples because they are isolated from the mainstream geographically or culturally (by language, religion, or values). They lack education, being unlettered or untutored. Or they are irrational, uncritical, unreflective, or unusually conservative.

Some folklore examples *can be* considered "survivals" in the sense that they are known or thought to have been more common during the past, and they seem more compatible with former than with present norms. But folklore examples identifiable as "survivals" are not merely vestiges carried on out of habit, through ignorance, or because of uncritical acceptance. Rather, they are phenomena that have purposes and meanings for the human beings among whom they are found, even though the origins of these phenomena may be obscure and their initial purposes and meanings

may be unknown or may have been different (see Box 3-4).

In his discussion of tongue twisters Charles Francis Potter provides evidence that folklore has purposes and meanings for people.[17] Called "cramp words" in some Southern states, tongue twisters consist of a word, stanza, or whole poem. The name comes from the fact that the word or phrase is difficult to repeat aloud several times because of the initial consonants or the sequence of slightly varied consonantal combinations. When Potter "innocently asked the readers of a short piece [in a national magazine] listing a dozen tongue twisters" to send him some—apparently assuming tongue twisters to be survivals on the wane—he "received more than 13,000 of them from country crossroads and great cities alike." He hit this "rich jackpot of American oral tradition and folklore" not only because people had communicated them to one another intergenerationally through time, but also because they were meaningful and useful.

BOX 3-4
Survivals and Continuities in American
Festivals

[Americans'] notions of festival and increase emanate from observances still carried out at those points in the agricultural year in which the work of the season has been translated, by tradition, into the work of the gods and maintained in the notion of *holiday*. . . . With us, *custom* and *tradition* are translated into a sentimental backward look, which we call, ambivalently, *old-fashioned* ways. Almost by sentiment alone, certain practices and values are maintained long after the particulars of the agricultural economy have lost their hold on us. In fact, at the center of this sentiment is a simplified version of farming; no longer is work involved, but only the fairs, games, festivals, and of course, the holiday dinners and picnics that remain to remind us how to live by the seasons. . . . Many of our most powerful holiday symbols continue to speak in terms of the processes of life, of death and rebirth, of maturing, reaping, and lying fallow.

. . . [T]hough we do cling to many kinds of clean, old-fashioned observances, we also have innumerable ways of celebrating that face forward and emphasize the new. In fact, our holidays have two sides to them: the old practices that are commonly carried out in the home or some homelike place, and the emergent, the glittering new, which is, as often as not, a street affair. . . .

Parades have easily become advertisements for business, much as they did on the frontier, where they were hastily organized to show off the new goods that had just hit town. The pageant, then, becomes a symbolization of the forward march of commerce and industry. Festive intensification in such cases is rendered gigantically, with the immense floats, the amplified size and sounds of the marching band, and the skyscraping balloon representations of animals and comic characters. . . . Moreover, we sneak all kinds of other festive occasions onto our calendars by making such a to-do about birthdays and anniversaries.

—Roger D. Abrahams[18]

As a child in the 1890s in Massachusetts, Potter himself recited tongue twisters as part of winter evening games. "They were permitted and even encouraged by our elders because they were supposed to train us to speak more distinctly." One of his correspondents, a Rhode Island woman, wrote him that her dentist father required patients with new plates to practice reciting a tongue twister. A California Jesuit priest said he learned the following poem half a century earlier from an old Shakespearean actor who taught elocution in a private academy in San Francisco:

Amidst the mists and frosts the coldest,
With wrists the barest and heart the boldest,
He stuck his fists into posts the oldest,

And still insisted there were ghosts on Sixth Street.

Others wrote to Potter informing him that as sorority members in girls' schools they used tongue twisters to tease candidates being initiated; that as pathologists they employed them to test for speech disorders; and that as judges or police officers they required suspected inebriates to try to pronounce them (for example, "Sister Susie sat in the soup").

A New Yorker informed Potter that frequently those who are given auditions for the stage must repeat:

Three gray geese in the green grass grazing:
Gray were the geese and green was the grazing.

Radio announcers also reported having been required to recite difficult tongue twisters as tests. A Detroit woman claimed she was cured of teenage stammering by rapidly repeating, "The sun shines on shop signs." An Ohio woman wrote that when a little girl she was told she could make her mouth smaller if she pursed her lips (as if whistling) and said repeatedly: "Fanny Finch fried five floundering fish for Francis Fowler's father."

Often tongue twisters are recited for purposes of entertainment, an important use. A favorite from the South and West, reports Potter, is easy to say the first time, but almost impossible three times quickly: "Black bug's blood." Many correspondents attributed their cure of hiccuping to saying certain tongue twisters. Potter cites a seventeenth-century work on English grammar that presents ten tongue twisters to cure the hiccup, among which is the famous

> Peter Piper picked a peck of pickled peppers;
> Did Peter Piper pick a peck of pickled peppers?
> If Peter Piper picked a peck of pickled peppers,
> Where's the peck of pickled peppers Peter Piper picked?

Potter also lists "older short twisters," including

> Gigwhip.
> Truly rural.
> Troy boat.
> Peggy Babcock.
> A cryptic cricket critic.
> Shave a cedar shingle thin.
> Pure food for four poor mules.

"Yet new ones keep appearing," writes Potter, such as

> Preshrunk shirts.
> Tillie's twin sweater set.
> Six twin-screw cruisers.
> Old oily Ollie oils old oily autos.
> Platinum, aluminum and lightly linoleum.

In other words, not only does this folklore form survive, but new examples are created and perpetuated as word play or for various practical applications.

Continuity

Whether or not they are judged to be survivals, all examples of folklore provide evidence of continuity in human behavior through time. Behaviors sometimes continue because there are no known alternatives or because known alternatives are rejected. Wayland D. Hand presents numerous examples, recorded in Western Europe and the United States from the nineteenth to the mid-twentieth centuries, of "ridding a person of a disease by transferring the malady to another person, to animals, plants, and to various kinds of objects," based on sympathetic magic.[19]

Many of Hand's examples involve chills (fever), a stye in the eye, boils, and warts. Techniques of transfer include recommendations to touch or rub the afflicted area, or collect drops of blood, using paper or cloth which is tied into a parcel and left for someone to pick up. According to Hand, "clear reference is made to the new victim, e.g., 'the one who finds it will take your wart'; 'if anyone picks up the paper, your wart will pass to him'; 'whoever picks up your blood will take your wart,' etc., etc." Or one is instructed to count beans, peas, or kernels of corn to equal the number of warts, then package them and leave the parcel for a passerby. Or one is told to wish the malady onto someone else, perhaps using a verbal formula such as "the command of the stye to leave and go to . . . 'the next one that passes by.'"

Another case in point is the dreaded illness of the late twentieth century, AIDS, or Acquired Immuno-Deficiency Syndrome (breakdown of the immune system), a condition identified in 1981. Mystery surrounds where and when the deadly virus first emerged. Reliable information on cause and treatment is lacking, which causes anxiety and confusion. The only certainty is that AIDS is infectious, progressive, and irreversible. As is the case with other illnesses in the past, some blame it on a subgroup in society which they fear, distrust, or dislike—hence, the attribution of the disease as divine retribution or well-deserved punishment for allegedly sinful or perverse behavior (e.g., drug use, homosexuality, prostitution), or rumors of a political conspiracy against certain segments of society, biochemical warfare perpetrated by a foreign government, genetic experiments run amok, lab mutations, and so on.

Stories and beliefs about the ways of getting AIDS express fear of contact with other people through shaking hands, holding hands, or kissing; being near a person who coughs, sneezes, or spits; and even brushing up against a sweaty person, breathing the same air as others, or being in the same room or elevator or on a public bus. Some fear contagion from hot tubs and swimming pools, and hypothesize a possible infection of clothing in public laundromats. Others recommend avoiding contact with money, telephones, doorknobs and handrails, hotel beds, and public toilet seats and water fountains. Some are wary of food and its preparation in cafeterias, open salad bars, and restaurants owned by homosexuals. Many fear needles piercing the skin (e.g., tattooing, ear piercing, needle injection, hair electrolysis, acupuncture). Some wonder about the possible danger posed by insects that feed on human blood, like mosquitoes, bedbugs, fleas, and flies. Lacking a cure, those who have AIDS use a range of self-treatments to strengthen the immune system, such as acupuncture, herbal concoctions, diets, vitamin supplements, and special foods.[20]

In addition to behaviors continuing because alternatives are unknown or unac-

Figure 3–2: Silver votive offerings and discarded crutches, Shrine of Saint Michael Taxiarchis, Tarpon Springs, Florida, 1962 (photo by R. A. Georges).

ceptable, they may also persist along with newly developed or recently adopted alternatives. Cemetery decoration customs in the American South, discussed by Lynwood Montell, serve to illustrate this.[21] For example, "The older custom of erecting nondescript fieldstones or shale is still practiced in some areas of the South by less affluent members of society such as tenants and sharecroppers," contends Montell. Most markers contain pictorial representations and epitaphs (word messages) expressing both the individuality of the deceased and conventional sentiments, such as the following popular rhyme:

Remember friend as you pass by,
As you are now so once was I;
As I am now so ye shall be,
Prepare in death to follow me.

A common custom, originating about 1890, was to mount a photograph of the deceased on the face of the gravestone, thereby filling "the human need for visible, tangible reminders of those who had died. Although it is not utilized as frequently as it once was, the custom . . . is still practiced." Few people now build gravehouses (gravesheds, graveshelters, spirit houses), but examples of "rapidly vanishing structures" may still be seen. "Most of these tiny houses are of wood, but brick, brick and wood, and metal examples have also been observed," writes Montell. "Gravehouses may have served early people's presumed needs to control the spirit of the deceased." Presently, however, they keep "pigs, dogs,

Figure 3–3: Discarded crutches and thanskgiving plaques expressing gratitude for miraculous healing and answers to prayers, St. Joseph's Oratory, Montreal, Canada, 1994 (photo by Mary R. Georges).

and other scavenging animals away from the corpse" and shelter "the grave from rain."

Montell describes annual social customs in cemeteries. "Decoration Day, as it is known and practiced today, began in the South, a fact that helps to explain its continued popularity there." Because older community cemeteries have no business manager or endowments, they must be cared for on a volunteer basis. "For this reason many of the rural people of the South still come together on a community basis once or twice each year to clean and decorate the cemetery, and to share in fellowship around the graves of their deceased family members and friends." The "cleanings serve not only as a means of preserving and maintaining the physical appearance of the cemetery, but also as a social gathering for the area or as a family reunion, drawing relatives together again."

Decorations typically consist of floral arrangements. The art of making flowers by hand out of construction paper dipped in wax "declined rapidly with the introduction of plastic flowers following World War II, and is now virtually nonexistent." Items having personal meaning to the deceased adorn the graves, such as toys, dolls, images of animals, light bulbs, vacuum tubes from radio and television sets, and telephone line insulators. Stones, broken dishes and crockery, lamps, clocks, and shells also decorate graves in both Euro-American and African American cemeteries. "The custom has been practiced since early times by blacks on the Sea Islands and in the historic Cotton Belt, where it appears to be a continuation of an African custom," writes Montell. "Southern whites likely borrowed the custom from black neighbors, but the possibility of an inheritance from Scotland exists."

"Certain of the older, one-time-only folk practices, such as the choice of gravemarker forms and types, erecting tiny houses, house-like forms, or other perma-

Figure 3–4: Gravehouses, Powersburg, Wayne County, Kentucky, 1993 (photo by Lynwood Montell).

nent covers over graves, placing photographs of the deceased on the gravestones, and building fences and walls around entire cemeteries and/or individual graves, are radically on the decrease and their complete demise will likely occur with the passing from the cultural landscape of the extant examples," Montell contends. By contrast, "social gatherings and other ongoing activities . . . represent tenacious folk customs and indicate a continuing cohesiveness and sense of identity with a particular hallowed spot by the persons involved in these social activities. Even these 'never-say-die' customs are subject to change, however, as modern funeral technology makes deeper and deeper inroads into regional folkways." He concludes: "We must bear in mind, however, that customs and traditions seldom die out altogether, and that evolving human activities are understood only as we understand societal change and the factors that attend upon change."

Behaviors that continue may be in evidence only privately. Sometimes they remain unshared because they are judged to be no longer relevant or appropriate, or not compatible, with the times, the place, or

Figure 3–5: Shell-covered grave in Mount Pleasant, South Carolina, 1976 (photo by John Michael Vlach).

others' expectations. With changing circumstances these behaviors become manifest, only to diminish once again. Marvin K. Opler's study of folk beliefs and practices among Japanese-Americans interned at

Tule Lake, California, during World War II suggests aspects of this complex process.[22]

In the role of community analyst from 1943 to 1946, Opler noted behaviors among the 19,000 internees that had been documented historically in rural Japan but rarely appeared among immigrants (Issei) or their American-born children (Nisei) in California until the internment experience. A subsequent rechecking of data from 1946 to 1949 "outside Center confines with original informants and former research staff . . . revealed that the folkloristic beliefs and practices had again largely vanished . . .

once the American scene was substituted for the Center." Among the examples of folklore that intensified during internment were citings of *hinotoma* (a ball of fire, taken to mean a ghost presaging death), stories about bewitchment and shape-shifting, omens, pregnancy and infancy beliefs, and folk medical practices by traditional specialists. "Folklore which had been remembered by a handful of Issei, and perpetuated by a small circle, was seized upon by Issei and Nisei alike in a broadening sphere," writes Opler.

For instance, beliefs documented his-

Figure 3–6: In Akita Prefecture in Japan, rice straw effigies called Kashima-sama *are constructed to guard a village from evil influences (FP 86–269, photo by Kozo Yamaji, courtesy Smithsonian Institution Center for Folklife Programs & Cultural Studies).*

torically among Japanese peasants concerned a ball of fire, *hidama,* and a fluorescent-like light representing the human soul, *hitodama.* If a person should treat rice with disrespect, as in careless burning, then it may become a fireball that whirls out of the house and thereafter is a bad omen. As difficulties at the Relocation Center increased, according to Opler, "the Nisei came to regard the crematory ('graveyard') area as especially dangerous, and around the time of citizenship renunciation—a most tempestuous period in the Center— we noted all people, old and young, for the first time in camp history, making a wide arc around these buildings," suggesting they had recalled and communicated these bad luck omens to one another. One internee said:

> There are ghosts seen over there, *hinotama.* Greenish lights, they say, bigger than a fist. Last winter, I heard only one story of light coming out of the camp smoke above the field on a foggy morning, but now all sorts of stories are going around. We wouldn't go near too early in the morning or at night around that barrack. It's the worst place.

Another told Opler about a young girl who was walking to her apartment in Block 32

> when something prompted her to look over her shoulder. She glanced up and was chilled by a strange glow hovering over the latrine roof. She shivered violently and hurried home to tell her mother, fully expecting her not to believe it. But her mother looked worried, opens the door, looks out, but says nothing. The girl insisted on knowing what it was and her mother told her she must have seen *hinotama.* A few days later an elderly bedridden block resident died.

Historically some Japanese had postulated complex notions about Fox, a transformer who could bewitch the unwary, and Inari, a ricefield and fertility god of popular Shinto. At Tule Lake, rumors circulated of Fox as well as Dog and Badger entering humans in spirit form. A woman outspoken in dealings with Block residents, who was married to a part-Caucasian, after late 1944 was said to be possessed with the spirit of the Fox, changing form with it, talking in a strange language, and harming people when the beast's spirit invested her. In 1945, an attractive divorcee whose son was famous in his Block for intending not to renounce citizenship also was charged with Fox possession (*kitsune-tsuki*); and her daughter was called "immoral, like her mother" for no apparent reason.

No one reported actually seeing a fox in the compound, but a badger was captured in Block 36 in February 1945. Rumor had it that, like Fox, it could bewitch people. One person said, "After the Badger in Ward III, my grandmother told this one," a story of personal experience in Japan involving a supernatural light that appeared to guide her through the darkness from a shrine to her home. Remarked another individual, a Nisei, "I had never heard much of Fox, Badger or Cat until this camp. Back in Gilroy [California], where I was born, I had heard it only once and forgot it until here." He then told about a newcomer who, the old people had discovered, kept several foxes on his farm. "They talked about it until it became a choice story among the young that he could set these foxes to bewitch anyone he didn't like. It started when he threatened an old-time resident, but it's not like that here where everyone knows such stories now." Opler notes that after 1946, outside the Tule Lake camp, accounts of transformation and bewitchment were not told. He quotes one man who said, "Oh, those fox and badger stories back at the Center; well, people used to believe a lot of things in that Center they never believed before and haven't believed since!"

Similarly, in the camp many people referred to omens of death, such as "If you point at a funeral line, you are next to die";

"If three persons are photoed together, the middle one is first to die"; and "If you feel sorry for a sick animal, you will become ill; if, then it dies, you will die." Pregnant women were urged to eat *kobu* (kelp, seaweed) to give the baby thick hair; admonished not to quarrel so the child would be amiable; refrain from staring at fires, which would cause the infant to have blotchy skin; avoid frightening experiences on pain of making the baby nervous; and avoid eating sour foods lest the child's bones be soft. According to Opler, "the claim was made increasingly that more girls are born in wartime and this, over time, presages the coming of peace. While peace was remote in 1944, the story went the rounds that more girls were being produced at the Center hospital and peace was certainly near." The number of traditional healing specialists had jumped phenomenally by 1945, with "no less than 75 thriving Chiryoists as against less than a dozen [American] doctors." This was due, contends Opler, to "the strain on hospital facilities and the growth of interest in things specifically Japanese."

After the Center's dissolution, writes Opler, "every belief and practice here recorded" was checked "with original informants. While the 'ball of fire' legend was recast into . . . scientific sounding rationalizations . . . , even the girl in Block 32 could not recall seeing it." He continues: "The Nisei . . . all scoffed at the accounts and showed little interest in the ideas. Life crisis beliefs and bad omens, when checked with the same persons, found little support, except here and there the notions of determining the male foetus [i.e., omens and signs, such as 'the mother's eyes become fiercer and sharper,' 'the foetus is active,' and 'the mother eats coarse foods'], the custom of *miso shiru* for infant girls [feeding them soybean soup to aid blood circulation], and one or two of the food beliefs. *Chiryo* practitioners, outside camp surroundings, were in a variety of other callings and in thirty-odd cases checked found not the slightest call for their talents. And so it went. Conditions of life had changed and with them culturally rooted beliefs."

In other words, current circumstances in combination with a climate of anxiety and fear among people who were densely concentrated and segregated from the rest of the population had triggered recall and then discussion of, and narrating about, beliefs, practices, and stories learned earlier. After tensions faded and residents of the internment camp dispersed, these topics were no longer a frequent matter of conversation and speculation. Indeed, their earlier manifestation was even denied by some, explained away, or dismissed as unimportant because they were considered no longer relevant or appropriate.

Other behaviors may continue precisely because of their ongoing appropriateness. This is apparent in the case of behaviors related to tensions caused by social stresses based on differentiation or stratification. "Inevitably, the experiences of slavery and the social marginalization that arose in the plantation world came to be recorded in the stories blacks told about the interactions between themselves and whites," writes Roger D. Abrahams.[23] These stories provide insights "regarding the black response to exclusion and exploitation. . . . Humorous and often subversive, these stories commonly report an especially brazen or subtle act in the face of Old Master's authority, or they record the ways in which dispossessed and often hungry people reacted to the presence of food around them."

Velma McCloud, in *Laughter in Chains* (New York: Lenox Press, 1901), provides an example called "Grandpa Roasts a Pig." She writes, "My father, in his boyhood, heard this tale many times from his grandfather, a slave on the Hammond plantation in Georgia." According to the story, the grandfather had become expert in stealing and cooking pigs for himself and other slaves because his master, Planter Hammond, would give them no meat. Suspecting the grandfather, and wanting to catch him in the act, Hammond visited unexpectedly at the very moment he was preparing pork stew. Great-Grandpa tried to keep him outside; failing that, he told Hammond that the aromatic smell from the stove came from "possum stew." Hammond demanded a taste. Thinking quickly, Great-Grandpa said it was done to a turn. "Must be all dat good spittin' we done," he muttered under his breath. "The *what!*" said Hammond. "Spittin'," said Great-Grandpa, who explained that the blacks "allus spits in possum gravy. Makes de meat mo' tenduh. Aunt Janie done spit in it; Uncle Amos done spit in it; de chilluns done spit in it; an' I spit in it myse'f fo' er five times." Then he picked up some meat on a fork. "You wants a nice big piece, Massa?" Appalled, Hammond exclaimed, "That's the most disgusting habit I ever heard of. . . . You're a pack of damned savages."

Abrahams notes that the story centers on a "capping conversation," that is, a perfect comeback in a contest of wits. It also contains ironic implications: "the master who does not hesitate to wander into his slave's quarters to taste the food there . . . , the technique the great-grandfather uses of 'loud talking' (that is, seeming to mutter, but in loud enough tones that he is sure to be overheard), the seeming acceptance of the white stereotype of blacks as dirty in their personal habits. All these stories repeat traditional means of getting around Old Master," writes Abrahams.

Other stories make use of black stereotypes of whites, such as the idea that blacks had that whites would bet on anything; in this case, the black character in the tale manages to outwit, manipulate, or exploit the whites. Yet others concern contests of strength or wit between blacks and whites. Some stories revolve around the white ste-

reotype of blacks as stupid or lazy, but often in tales this trait is only feigned by a clever black. "The contemporary folklore of Afro-Americans continues to reflect social tensions of this sort, and to record equally ingenious black responses to indignity and inequality," writes Abrahams.

Why do many tellers and listeners find humor in some of these accounts? Harry Oster writes that they appeal to "the ordinary person's need to deaden the pangs of a sense of inferiority. . . . Moreover, where the protagonist is physically puny or poverty-stricken, the narrator and his audience enjoy identifying with the little man who either through luck or through shrewd trickery defeats frighteningly powerful opponents."[24] In regard to "Two at the Gate" (see Box 3–5), Eddie "Son" House, the narrator, "found the story amusing and memorable as a result of the comic reversal of roles: the ignorant chicken thieves outwit the educated and supposedly wise master. But whatever slave first told this story (adapting a central motif from English tradition), he was engaging in double-edged satire, poking fun at the gullibility of both master and slave. The original teller and those who repeated the story relished the discomfiture of the Olympian Old Marster, but the sophisticated narrator and the amused listeners also relished their sense of superiority to those above them in power and those below them in intelligence."[25]

This story and its variants have a long history. Identified as combining Type 1791, *The Sexton Carries the Parson,* and Motif X424, "The devil in the cemetery," the anecdote has been claimed to be "as old as the *Thousand and One Nights,* and appears in nearly every medieval and Renaissance tale collection. But it is widely told by oral story-tellers all over Europe and, for some reason, is about the best known of all anecdotes in America."[26]

A tradition no longer popular may be revitalized accidentally and perpetuated

BOX 3-5
"Two at the Gate"

"One I can remember my father used to tell me about it a lotta time[s] when I was quite young. . . . An' so he'd sit down an' tell me what his father used to tell him an' his father told him. So the old story kep' a-goin'.

"An' so he told me this one about one of the slaves, how he tricked his—in a way— tricked his master into somethin' that he wasn't expectin'.

"So his master couldn't walk so he had this guy, his slave, to roll him aroun' in a wheelchair. An' so that night he let him off. An' so this guy, this colored guy, he goes to see his girl friend that night. . . .

"An' at the same time it was two more Negroes went out stealin' one night, stealin' chickens. An' so they had these gunny sacks with them to put the chickens in after they steal 'em. They steal the chickens, they would tie thei' legs together so in case-a one would get a-loose he couldn't get very far. They could ketch him easy. So, anyway they stole the chickens an' they put 'em in the sacks. An' so in walkin' along goin' back home, one says to the other, says, 'Say, listen, we got to divide these chickens. . . .' Says, 'We don't wanta sit alongside the road to do it. Somebody may come along an' see us with the chickens. Say, wonder where could we go?'

"So the other guy says, 'I tell you a good place we won't be bothered with nobody. Nobody passin' or nothin'. They sho' ain't comin' there. . . .' He says, 'Let's stop in the cemetery. Say, nobody visits there, not at night, especially. . . .'

"So they stopped at the cemetery. An' goin' in at the gate two of the old hens got out the bag an' the other . . . [man] stopped to try an' get'm. He says, 'No, that's all right. Let's hurry on in here an' we can get these two when we be comin' out.' Say, 'They can't get nowhere, thei' legs tied. . . .'

"So they went up there in the cemetery. An' either one of them didn't have any kind o' education or nothin'. They didn't know how to count good. So . . . [one] says, 'I'll tell you how we'll do it. . . . [A]s I get one chicken out I'll say, "That one yours," an' I get the next one, I'll say, "This one mine." We can divide 'm like that. . . .'

"So they was doin' that. An' this guy was comin' back from his girl friend's. It was gettin' kinda late an' the road went right by the cemetery. So he got along there an' he heard 'em countin'. One said, 'This one mine, that one yours.' Well, he knowed that was the cemetery. 'Oh my God!' he said, 'Must be Judgment Day! God an' the Devil dividin' souls!'

"So he took out an' run home. He got home, poundin' on the door, 'Wake up Old Marster, wake up, wake up!'

"He said, 'What's the matter with you?'

"Say, 'Wake up, it's Judgment Day!'

"He says, 'You crazy?'

"Says, 'No, I'm not crazy. God an' the Devil is down there in the cemetery dividin' souls, right now. If you don't believe it, get up an' get in your chair, an' I'll roll you down there an' let you hear 'em yourself.'

"He says, 'All right, I'm goin', an' I'm gonna take my shotgun with me. An' if you fool me down there, an' they ain't that, I'm gonna shoot ya.'

"He says, 'Well, okay, you welcome, Old Boss, you welcome. Get in your chair.'

"So . . . [he] rolled him on down there an' rolled him up to the gate, near the gate. An' he say, 'Now you listen.' An' they was near about through countin', 'This one mine, that one yours.'

"Say, 'You hear'm don't ya?' Old Boss then he commenced to get interested in it too. He believed it too hisself then.

"An' so way after a while they got the last chickens in. An' the other one remembered, says, 'Wait a minute. . . . [Y]ou remember we got two at the gate.'

"An' Old Marster thought he was talkin' about him an' the guy he had . . . wheelin' him. He says, 'It's two at the gate.'

"Then the Negro said, 'Yeah, say, Old Boss, two at the gate, talkin' about us!'

"An' Old Marster jumped out the wheel chair—he hadn't walked in years, jumped out the wheel chair. He say, 'You can bring the chair on with you.'

"That's the first time he's walked in years. He thought it was Judgment Day too. He fooled him."[27]

because of positive reinforcement and, in the case of handmade objects, owing to financial benefits. The invention of the Storyteller figurine by Pueblo artist Helen Cordero illustrates this. According to Barbara A. Babcock,[28] evidence exists of a long and continuous tradition among Pueblo peoples of making human and animal figures out of clay (dating from perhaps as early as between 300 B.C. and 100 A.D.). The tradition of clay figure making seems to have been difficult to sustain, however, once contact between Pueblo peoples and "outsiders" took place. Spanish clergy of the sixteenth and seventeenth centuries found "muchos idolos" throughout the Rio Grande Pueblos which they zealously destroyed and prohibited from being made. From the sixteenth until the late nineteenth century, clay figure making was limited mainly to the creation of effigy vessels and small unfired animals.

By 1880, however, Cochiti potters had begun producing figures in Anglo garb. Rather than being primitive idols or eccentric "grotesques," they were a caricature and mockery of whites. The Indians increasingly became subjected to curious Anglo tourists; the railroad also brought the carnival, circus, and vaudeville. In addition, Cochiti men were taken to Washington, D. C., and to New York, where they were introduced to opera. "Their mimings of countless versions of the whiteman in stereotypical operatic poses were re-presented in clay, as were the two-headed, no-legged freaks and dancing bears of the carnival and circus," writes Babcock.

At the end of the nineteenth century, figurines were seen as a debasement of Pueblo art. Well into the 1960s, dealers and collectors called them *mono* (monkey, silly fool, mimic, mere doll). The most popular figure at Cochiti between 1920 and 1960 was the Singing Mother or Madonna. Only a few women made them. By the mid–1980s, however, more than 175 potters throughout the New Mexico Pueblos made Storytellers and related figures, thanks to a chance event and a quickly developing market worldwide. "When Helen Cordero shaped the first Storyteller doll in 1964, she made one of the oldest forms of Native American self-portraiture her own, reinvented a longstanding but moribund Cochiti tradition of figurative pottery, and engendered a revolution in Pueblo ceramics," writes Babcock.

Helen Cordero was 45 years old in the late 1950s when she began making clay figures. She had been doing beadwork and leatherwork with her husband's cousin, Juanita Arquero. One day her husband's aunt remarked that instead they should make pottery, because the materials are cheap; "Mother Earth gives it all to you." Juanita, who had learned to make pottery as a child, began again, assisted for six months by Helen Cordero, who wanted to learn the craft. Because Helen produced such misshapen bowls and jars, Juanita suggested she try figures instead. It "was like a flower blooming," with small animals and, eventually, "little people" coming to life.

At a show of her work, folk art collector Alexander Girard bought all her "little people" (standing male and female figures eight to nine inches high). He asked her to make more and larger figures, eventually commissioning a 250-piece Nativity set. Then he requested a larger seated figure with children, perhaps thinking of the Singing Mothers made by a few other women. Helen pondered his request. "I kept seeing my grandfather [Santiago Quintana]. That one, he was a really good storyteller and there were always lots of us grandchildrens around him." He had wanted his traditions preserved and maintained, and went to great lengths to assure that anthropologists got it right. "When Helen remembered her grandfather's voice and shaped that first image of him telling stories to five grandchildren in 1964," writes Babcock, "she

Figure 3–7: Pueblo potter Helen Cordero of Cochiti, New Mexico, making a Storyteller figure, 1979 (4–79082–9A, photo by Dudley Smith; all rights reserved, Photo Archives, Denver Museum of Natural History).

These rewards and recognition had several consequences. "In Helen's own work, it resulted in both technical refinements and the invention of new forms." She developed an increasingly finer finish to the figures by increased sanding and applications of white slip before painting. Also she began making children separately, rather than pulling them out of the primary piece of clay, enabling her to increase the number of children and vary their placements and postures around the Storyteller. "By the early 1970s her Storytellers not only had more children and finer painted garb, but the main figure itself had become taller, thinner, and better proportioned. . . . By

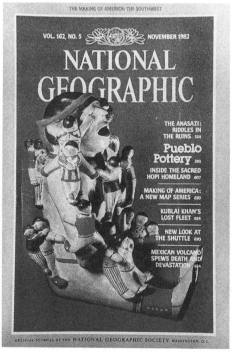

Figure 3–8: Storyteller figure by Helen Cordero which appeared in a 1975 book, a 1977 issue of a journal of American Indian art, and on the 1982 cover of National Geographic (by permission of National Geographic Society).

made two significant modifications in the Singing Mother tradition: (1) she made the primary figure male, rather than female, and (2) she placed more than a realistic number of children on him." The first Storyteller had five children; subsequent ones have up to 30.

The Storyteller brought Helen Cordero almost immediate fame and success. In 1964, her figures won first, second, and third prizes at the New Mexico State Fair, and other awards subsequently. She has been honored with two museum exhibits of her work. *Sunset Magazine* (April 1972) featured her Storyteller on its cover and in an article; one of her Storytellers appeared on the cover of *National Geographic* (November 1982). Demand for her work rose.

Figure 3–9: Storyteller figures by other potters inspired by Helen Cordero's success (photo by M. O. Jones, from the collection of R. A. Georges).

1970, she had also developed the distinctive face which has become her trademark," writes Babcock, who quotes Helen Cordero: "his eyes are closed because he's thinking; his mouth is open because he's singing." In addition, Helen had begun signing her pieces. Success led her to produce other images from her experience, including Nativities, Singing Mothers, Drummer, Pueblo Father, Nightcrier, Water Carrier, Hopi Maiden, Owl, Turtle, and so on. The Storyteller, however, remained her favorite and the most requested.

Helen Cordero's success prompted as many as 175 other potters in recent years to produce figures, including Storytellers. A tradition, once looked down upon and engaged in by few, was reinvigorated because of an offhand remark to work with clay, which costs nothing, and a serendipitous experiment with molding figures. Interest by others facilitated perpetuation because of the positive reinforcement through public acclaim and financial rewards. This in turn led to experimentation and transformation, as well as imitation and perpetuation.

Revival

Unless individuals communicate the folklore they know, others are unaware of it and are unable to learn it; and while that folklore persists in memory, it does so only as long as those who can recollect it remain alive. Because *people* are the creators and perpetuators of folklore, it is they who are the determiners of its history. Tales and songs, for instance, become *folk*tales and *folk*songs because individuals find them meaningful, relevant, or appealing enough to want to tell and sing them over and over again. But tales and songs, like such material objects as clothing, go in and out of fashion; and when people judge a once-oft-told story or frequently sung song to have little or no meaning, relevance, or appeal, then they are not motivated to perpetuate it by sharing it with, or teaching it to, others.

Metaphorically and by analogy with living things, folklore is often characterized as something that is "born, lives, and dies." But sometimes when it seems destined to "die out," individuals come to conceive it to be meaningful, relevant, or appealing once again; and they communicate and share it anew, occasionally only once, but often on multiple occasions and through time. Folklore on the verge of "dying out" is thus "revived," in metaphorical terms; and its traditionality may be reestablished if people again come to communicate it with notable frequency as they interact over time. As Raymond Firth writes about oral narratives, if "traditional tales no longer describe the kind of society which is generally desired by the people, and the continuity itself either has ceased to have meaning or is actively opposed . . . the reaction of a people is to let the traditional tales go altogether, not bothering to impart them or to listen to them any more."[29] However, Firth adds, a people "may come to find in time that they want these tales again . . . as a validating resource for their own general continued existence as a society." They may then revive the stories in order to "maintain their social identity in a wider social universe." Firth continues: "The tales can be maintained as true, they can be held to have a symbolic character, with their true meaning ascertainable only to those who are patient to inquire and sympathetic to the interpretation, or they can be regarded as simple recreation." Alternatively, states Firth, the tales "can be maintained as overtly or symbolically true by the community concerned, and issued to the world outside as recreational or aesthetic products. In any case," he concludes, "as a property that is indubitably belonging to the group concerned, the traditions can serve as an identity badge, and as a social rallying point."

Such was the case during the early twentieth century with English folk dancing, in which a diminishing number of rural villagers participated. Cecil Sharp (1859–1924) witnessed a group of ten men doing the Morris Dance in Headington on Boxing Day in 1899.[30] Spellbound, Sharp queried the dancers, asking particularly about the music one of them played on a concertina. The next day, 27-year-old musician William Kimber played five tunes that Sharp wrote down. This experience made Sharp realize that "the normal musical education, based on German music, did not supply all that was needed for young people." It motivated him to search for more tunes like that played during the Morris dancing—"good, strong, simple melodies which were essentially English in character."

In 1905, Sharp introduced William Kimber, the musician for the first group of Morris dancers he had encountered six years earlier, to a woman named Mary Neal. Neal was secretary to the Esperance Working Girls' Club, a group made up mostly of London area seamstresses who got together regularly to sing, dance, and act. Mary Neal had contacted Cecil Sharp initially about sources for English folksong and folk music, which the club members wanted to learn and perform. So enthusiastic were they with what Sharp told and taught them that they soon wanted to add English folk dancing to their repertoire as well. Sharp brought Neal and William Kimber together; and Kimber taught the women enough in two evenings to enable them to perform Morris Dances at a Christmas party.

A repeat performance was held the following April (1906), preceded by a lecture

Figure 3–10: William Kimber, Headington Morris dancer.

study of English folk dances. Between 1907 and 1913, he published *The Morris Book* in five parts, assisted by Herbert C. Mac-Ilwaine on parts 1 through 4 and George Butterworth on part 5. The 11 dances described in the first edition of part 1 include eight from Headington, where Sharp had first seen Morris dancing. Subsequent parts include dances he documented in such other English counties as Oxfordshire, Gloucestershire, Warwickshire, and Northamptonshire. The 83 Morris Dances Sharp published (about half the number he documented) were from 14 distinguishable traditions; and 59 of the dances he characterized in print (with descriptions, notations, and music) were reconstructed from information and demonstrations provided by elderly individuals, with most of whom Sharp actually danced in order to learn.

Sharp broadened his folk dance collecting, focusing not only on Morris Dances, but on sword, processional, and country dances as well.[31] In 1911, he cofounded The English Folk Dance Society, "with the object of preserving and promoting the practice of English folk-dances in their true traditional form" (see Box 3–6). Sharp "knew that the dances, though for the most part lying dormant, were not moribund." So "he threw all his energies and talents into reviving the tradition" in order "that it might take its rightful place" in English "national culture." Vacation Schools were set up to train teachers, and classes were held both in London and other parts of England. The students "came from all walks of life with a good sprinkling of professional people including musicians and university dons." Most of those who participated felt "the urge to pass on their experiences to others."

Sharp made personal presentations to supplement actual dance instruction in the Vacation Schools and classes. He also "lectured on song and dance (with illustrations) in nearly every boys' private school in En-

on English folk dancing by Cecil Sharp. "This aroused great interest and Miss Neal was besieged with inquiries as to how the songs and dances could be learned." Club members began to instruct others, and "performances continued to be given in London and also in the provinces." While not officially connected with the club, Sharp "cooperated with it whenever opportunity offered and often lectured at its performances."

Public response to these efforts motivated Sharp to pursue more actively his who were invited to give a matinee performance at London's famous Savoy Theater on December 2, 1912.

Traditional dancing, which had all but "died out" in England by the end of the nineteenth century, thus underwent a revival, thanks largely to the efforts of one person. Because of Sharp's work, English folk dances—together with folksongs and folk music—enjoyed a renaissance, not only in the villages in which they had once been regularly performed, but also in towns and cities throughout England and abroad. The dances that Sharp was the first to document and describe in print are regularly performed in England today; and they have, as Sharp had hoped, indeed come to be regarded as a fundamental part of England's national culture.

The United States, too, witnessed a "revival" of sorts earlier in the twentieth century, this one of folksinging during the 1930s and 1940s. Woody Guthrie, Aunt Molly Jackson, Jim Garland and, later, Pete Seeger sang songs from oral tradition or composed their own in a "folk" style, performing at labor union meetings and urban "hoots."[33] In the late 1950s and early 1960s, "folksongs" entered the mainstream of popular entertainment with the Kingston Trio's hit "Tom Dooley" (1958–59) and Joan

gland," but he "made no serious endeavour to get the dances generally taught in the public schools, knowing that the curriculum would not allow of it." He trained and taught a team of demonstration dancers, who performed Morris and other traditional English dances regularly on weekends and

Figure 3–11: The Kennet Morris Men of Reading performing at the Centenary Conference of the (English) Folklore Society, Royal Holloway College, 1978 (photo by M. O. Jones).

Baez's appearance on the cover of *Time* magazine (November 23, 1962).

Four groups of "folksingers" or "singers of folksongs" held sway, according to Ellen J. Stekert.[34] Those who learned their songs and style from oral tradition as they grew up included the likes of white Southern mountain singers Almeda Riddle and Sarah Ogan Gunning and African American blues performers Reverend Gary Davis and Son House. They appeared at festivals and on college campuses. Imitators learned the skills of those they admired, dedicating themselves to becoming part of that style and culture, such as bluegrass and old timey music (e.g., John Cohen and the New Lost City Ramblers) or Negro blues. Utilizers included urban pop performers like the Kingston Trio, Bob Dylan, Harry Belafonte, and others who altered traditional tunes, texts, and/or style of presentation to conform to an existing mass media aesthetic, as well as urban art performers such as Alfred Deller and Richard Dyer-Bennet, who incorporated traditional songs into their classical music repertoires. A fourth group (e.g., Joan Baez, Judy Collins, Peggy Seeger, and the trio Peter, Paul, and Mary) merged vocal and instrumental folk, classical, jazz, and pop styles to create a new aesthetic.

This revival appealed largely to individuals who celebrated others' traditions rather than their own. Writes Bruce Jackson: "[Negro] Blues were popular in the folksong revival, but the audiences were mostly whites; rural songs and performers were popular, but the audiences were mostly urban; labor songs were popular, but the audiences were mostly middle-class students." He contends that "the revival can be fairly characterized as romantic, naive, nostalgic and idealistic; it was also, in small part, venal, opportunistic, and colonialistic."[35] Nevertheless, the revival made many people aware for the first time of the existence of traditional songs and

tunes; provided those among whom the songs and tunes were traditional with a new sense of the nature and value of an integral part of their cultural heritage; and attracted individuals to the academic study of folklore.[36]

Revivals in local communities and among native populations differ from the American folksong and folk dance revivals of the 1960s in that usually individuals consciously perpetuate their own traditions rather than those of other people. *Preserving a Way of Life: People of the Klamath, Part II*, a 28-minute video produced by James Culp (New Day Films, 1989), illustrates this. The film depicts efforts by several members of the Karuk tribe in Northern California to revitalize the language and such traditions as games and dances and chipping arrowheads, making drums and baskets, preparing acorn soup, and using nets and traps to fish for salmon. In the nineteenth century, whites forced the Karuk off their lands in order to mine and log the area. (*Karuk* means "the upriver people," that is, those living above the Klamath.) They killed many Indians. Whites also forced the children to learn English and shun native ways. Eventually many whites and Karuk married, so few full-blooded Indians remain. "When I was young, it was all around me. The Indians and their ways was all here," said Lew Wilder (age 67 at the time of filming, but now deceased). "I could visit an old Indian while he was settin' making buckskin mocassins and an old lady doing something, making baskets—that was just *common*," he continued. "I waited years and years before I took any interest in it. Then I realized that somebody had to learn something about it. But it was rather late. . . . I learned from different old timers, but they didn't last very long. I could have learned from an awful lot more." He added: "I seen it all done, yeah. But the fine points, they missed me. I didn't realize it. I always could go to an old timer and get what I wanted to know. And first thing I know, *I* was the old timer."

Leaf Hillman, in his 20s, became Lew Wilder's protegé. In the film we see him watching Wilder chip stone points and learning how to make drums and soapstone pipes. From others Hillman reconstructed the Karuk language, which he now teaches to the youth. As Hillman remarks in the film, "There's no way that we can carry on our traditions unless the young people learn. If the young people just learn what these old people have to say, and take it down. Everyone has an important part in it. If we all do our part we can save it," he contends. "Like my personal feeling is, if I *don't* do it, then who is going to do it? Who is? And that's the way we should all feel about it."

Toward the end of the film we see Hillman with his wife and their infant. Hillman says, "I think I'm doing my part. And I'm trying to pass it on. I want to learn it so I *can* pass it on to my kids. If it's not passed on, it'll just be dead. It'll be dead." Lew Wilder remarks, "By keeping these old things a-going—like the dances and the original outfits they used—why, they'll know what their ancestors had, you know. This way they can see, and *feel*, what their ancestors had." Preston Arrow-Weed (one of the film's narrators) concludes, "By keeping the old ways alive, our elders give us the gift of the future."

Revivals of folklore may be large scale and long term, such as the English folk dance and the American folksong revivals described above; or they may be limited in scale and small group in their orientation, as is the case with the selective cultural revival among the Karuk. But revivals may also be short term, sometimes occurring during only a single interpersonal encounter. This often happens in the kinds of interviews that folklorists regularly conduct. In their attempts to elicit and docu-

ment folklore examples, fieldworkers frequently discover that they stimulate informants to recollect long-forgotten or rarely thought about traditional sayings, games, tales, songs, etc., and motivate interviewees to communicate or share them with the researcher. Such an incident occurred in September 1959, when Elli Kaija Köngäs was interviewing 69-year-old Mrs. Fannie Jurva in St. Albans, Vermont.[37]

Köngäs, a native of Finland, was interested in documenting Finnish folklore found in the United States. Shortly after meeting, she and Mrs. Jurva discovered that both were from the same province, Northern Ostrobothnia. Having recently done folklore fieldwork in that area, Köngäs asked Mrs. Jurva if she knew any *vainolaistarinat*, historical-supernatural legends that recount exploits of guerrillas in two wars that had occurred between Finland and neighboring countries in the early eighteenth and early nineteenth centuries. "Fannie Jurva was well acquainted with the Enemy Cycle," as this group of tales was called, writes Köngäs, having learned her stories from her grandmother, who was born in Finland in the 1840s. Mrs. Jurva told Köngäs stories she had learned from her grandmother about Laurukainen, "'the blond boy' (*valkeapää poika*)" and hero of the cycle, "who plays many tricks on the Russians"; tales of *Musta-Nykyri*, a local hero; and other narratives including Finnish treasure tales and one "humorous belief tale." The latter, untitled (like most narratives told during firsthand interactions), concerns the devil dividing souls (translated by Köngäs):

> They thought it was the devil that carried the souls around there in the graveyard. Two boys had, at one time, stolen apples from somewhere close to the graveyard. Then they went there by the cemetery fence to divide the apples. Then someone was walking there in the cemetery. He heard how the boys were saying:

"One for you
and one for me,"

and as the man thought that the devil was dividing the souls there, he went away, because he thought that the reckoning had come.

The boy said that one was missing, and it was said:

"One is missing, said the devil as he divided souls,"

or

"One is missing, said the devil as he counted souls."

"She obviously enjoyed her story-telling," writes Köngäs about Mrs. Jurva, who was "deeply moved by the fact that there was someone to listen to her and even write down her stories." Mrs. Jurva, moreover, "was surprised . . . that she still remembered her variants [of the traditional tales she told] and that someone was interested in them." She had immigrated to the United States 43 years earlier, and had had little contact with other Finns from her own district. "I asked very few and very general questions, such as 'Did they tell about any treasures in Muhos?'" writes Köngäs. "This was quite enough to carry her away to the midst of treasure tradition for quite a while." Many of Mrs. Jurva's stories fared as well as or better than variants one could collect in Muhos contemporaneously. She told them "in a good and very pure Ostrobothnian dialect," not English.

To Köngäs, the experience provided clear-cut evidence that "folklore indeed can . . . be a survival" in an individual's memory. For "there was nobody to listen to it, there was nobody to understand it, not to speak of appreciation. The local legends which faithfully referred to villages, houses, and persons in Muhos could not interest even a Finnish listener in the U.S. if he were not familiar with the localities and persons." Obviously, folklore can not only survive in memory, but it also can be revived, if only momentarily, when that person interacts with someone else who has the requisite background, knowledge, and interest to make him or her an appropriate, appreciative, and understanding audience.

Historical Source

In addition to being historical phenomena themselves—whether conceptualized as survivals, continuities, or revivals—examples of folklore also frequently serve as *sources* of historical information. Epic poems and songs, for instance, often have noteworthy wars as their sources and subject matter, as *The Iliad* of Homer illustrates; and many ballads detail military encounters (e.g., "The *Constitution* and the *Guerrière*," about an 1812 naval battle off the coast of Nova Scotia); violent crimes (for instance, "Pearl Bryan," recounting the 1896 murder of an unmarried pregnant woman in a Kentucky field); and historical personages and events (for example, "The Death of Queen Jane," detailing the 1537 passing away, twelve days after giving birth to Prince Edward, of Jane Seymour, the third queen of Henry VIII). When used as historical sources, folklore examples enable researchers to reconstruct past events and to supplement, corroborate, and challenge or correct existing historical records and interpretations.

William Lynwood Montell relied almost exclusively on tape recordings he made of orally told tales he elicited from former residents and neighbors to reconstruct the history of a community in Cumberland County, Kentucky.[38] Founded by a family of ex-slaves after emancipation (in 1866), the "tiny Negro colony" of Coe Ridge was significant locally and historically because of its African American citizenry and the ways events which occurred there affected community members and area Caucasians as the two groups interacted.

Before Montell undertook his investigation, the existence and history of Coe Ridge were known only locally and principally through oral tradition. The town never had its own newspaper; no letters, diaries, or manuscripts survive; and most official public records were destroyed in a 1933 county courthouse fire. Brief passing references are made to Coe Ridge in two books focusing on local history; in occasional stories in newspapers from nearby communities; and in a privately published book of childhood recollections by a former community resident (Samuel Coe, *The Chronicles of the Coe Colony*, 1930). But these few printed sources, Montell discovered, are highly selective and often biased. To obtain the information needed to reconstruct the 90-year history of Coe Ridge, Montell relied on his skills as a folklore fieldworker and analyst.

Thirty-eight people served as informants for Montell (16 African Americans, 22 Caucasians) during the four years he conducted his field research (1961–65). Individually and collectively, they provided the data needed for him to describe the beginnings of Coe Ridge and to trace its development and transformations from its founding until its demise in the late 1950s. Originally a farming community, its citizens turned to lumbering when demand made it profitable, and to moonshining as natural resources became increasingly scarce. The stories Montell recorded reveal that throughout its history, Coe Ridge was a site for both confrontation and cooperation between blacks and whites and that the fate of its citizenry was closely bound up with its geographical location, politics, economics, and evolving race relations.

In demonstrating "the usefulness of oral tradition" in reconstructing local history"—the "central purpose" of his investigation—Montell states that he "was able to set down in print an account that could never be written by most historians who are accustomed to doing research solely in libraries and archives." This "folk history,"

he states, "articulate[s] the feelings of a group toward the events and persons described." Acknowledging that not all "oral traditions are historical truths," Montell also asserts that "personal recollections *are* history, however, from the viewpoint of the folk who perpetuate them." By documenting multiple individuals' accounts of the same event and collating them, Montell contends, one "is able to determine precisely what happened." People don't "consciously falsify information when discussing a historical event," he discovered; and while "oral tradition frequently confuses places and details," it "seldom varies concerning the actual event and chief actors." Moreover, Montell determined from his data analysis that variation in firsthand oral accounts of local historical events usually provides complementary, not incompatible, information. "In the absence of written records," concludes Montell, "the historian should gather and analyze historical traditions of the local people." Otherwise, the histories of "numberless folk groups like those of Coe Ridge . . . will remain unwritten."

That folklore can and should be examined along with available written documents by those attempting to reconstruct history is a view expressed repeatedly and perhaps most emphatically by Richard M. Dorson.[39] Convinced that a consideration of folklore is essential for comprehensive, balanced accounts of the past, Dorson enumerates ways that insights gained from scrutinizing folklore can supplement those obtained by perusing printed sources. Folklore is an important "source for popular attitudes, prejudices, [and] stereotypes," notes Dorson, as well as for information about "national myths," images, and symbols. Folklore can also be used in historical studies "to illustrate the veracity of tradition" and to "enable the historian—especially the local historian—to separate fiction from fact." Dorson writes, "Oral traditions offer the chief available records for the beliefs and concerns and memories of large groups of obscured Americans." He concludes, "The historian can find history alive in the field as well as entombed in the library."

One historian who concurs with the view that students of history should be familiar with folklore as well as with conventional written documents and official records is Lawrence W. Levine.[40] He acknowledges the importance of folklore specifically in historical studies of African Americans. Levine notes that familiarity with African American folklore has "allowed recent scholars to move beyond assumptions which for too long structured historical understanding of black life and culture in slavery." Among these are the assumptions that "African culture disappeared almost completely in the English colonies"; that "slaves were left no choice but to meekly copy white culture"; that "the vast gulf between African and European culture made it impossible for a blend of the two cultures to take place"; and that "black slaves and their descendants had little sense of group cohesion, pride, or history and had no sources of power or authority independent of the whites."

Levine gives examples of folklore that challenge each of these assumptions. He notes, for instance, that African American cosmology, humor, song style, and performance behavior have closer affinities with African than with European analogues. By contrast, he states that insofar as religion, folk beliefs, folk medicine, and music are concerned, "it is clear that the African and West European systems, long assumed to be totally different, had enough in common to facilitate interchanges between whites and blacks." Writes Levine, "The historical use of folklore helps us to gain some sense of a people's angle of vision, to better understand the inner dynamics of a group and the attitudes of its members, and to comprehend their sense of worth."

Levine demonstrates not only how folklore study can supplement information found in conventional historical source documents or challenge interpretations, but also how it can challenge long-standing assumptions. Montell, however, found that the stories which individuals told him in the early 1960s about events in Coe Ridge "closely parallel" those included in Samuel Coe's 1930 book *The Chronicles of the Coe Colony*, a work "none of the informants had read." In this case, then, the folklore Montell documented and the "most important [published] work dealing with Coe Ridge" agree, and hence confirm each other. Thus, as noted above, folklore can be used as a source on the basis of which individuals can reconstruct past events and supplement, corroborate, and challenge or correct existing historical records.

Conclusion

The forms and examples of folklore dealt with in this chapter provide evidence of continuities in human behavior through time. Sometimes viewed as survivals from, or as sources of or for information about, earlier stages of intellectual or cultural development or from earlier historical periods, these forms and examples of folklore are not merely vestiges perpetuated habitually or uncritically. They have purposes and meanings for people, even though their origins may be obscure and their initial purposes may have differed or even be unknown today. These forms and examples are artifacts in that (1) they have a history, having been generated in the past and continued in the present, and (2) they have been isolated from the continuum of human experience and identified categorically as stories, beliefs, ballads, or art, and specifically as "Two at the Gate," *hinotoma,* "Tam Lin," and Storyteller. Having originated (or been modeled after phenomena originating) in another time and place, they may also be regarded as describable and transmissible entities, which is the subject of the next section; and they also may be viewed as aspects of culture and behavior, two perspectives in folkloristics discussed in later chapters.

Notes

1. For filmic examples of survival and continuity, see *The Meaders Family: North Carolina Potters* (1980, Robert Glatzer, Ralph Rinzler, and Robert Sayers, Audio Visual Services, Pennsylvania State University, University Park, color, VHS, 31 min.); *Tradition Bearers* (1983, Michael Loukinen, Northern Michigan University, color, 16mm. and VHS, 47 min.); and *Traditions in Clay: C. J. and Cleater Meaders* (1993, Bob Wheeler, Bob Wheeler Film/Tape, Cartersville, Georgia, color, VHS, 10 min.). *The High Lonesome Sound* (1963, John Cohen, Joel Agee, and Patricia Jaffe, Audio Brandon Films, black and white, 16mm., 30 min.) emphasizes continuity of folksongs in Southeastern Kentucky and the popularity of new music as well, while *Sam Li'a: The Legacy of a Hawaiian Man* (1989, Myrna and Eddie Kamae, Asian-Pacific Foundation of Hawaii, color, 16mm. and VHS, 60 min.) concerns continuity and revival of folk music. *The Screen Painters of Baltimore* (1988, Elaine Eff, Direct Cinema Limited, color, VHS, 28 min.) focuses on a form of painting that began in East Baltimore in 1913, flourished during the 1930s and 1940s, and then fell into abeyance until revived in recent years, partly through the folklorist's efforts. An example of folklore (quilts) used as historical source is *Hearts and Hands* (1987, Pat Ferrero, Ferrero Films, San Francisco, color, VHS, 63 min.); see also the companion publication *Hearts and Hands: The Influence of Women and Quilts on American Society* by Pat Ferrero, Elaine Hedges, and Julie Silber (San Francisco: Quilt Digest Press, 1987). An example of how a community has developed folklore about an historical event and then used this to promote tourism is *Norma Jean: A Shocking Story* (1987, John H. Behnke, Aurora Boralis Films, color, 16mm. and VHS, 15 min.). Regarding the search for surviving accounts about an historical figure, see *Blood Memory: The Legend of Beanie Short, An Oral History of a Civil War Raider* (1992, Robby Henson with W. Lynwood Montell, color, VHS, 56 min.), which could be supplemented with the article by D. K. Wilgus and Lynwood Montell called "Beanie Short: A Civil War Chronicle in Legend and Song," in Wayland D. Hand, ed., *American Folk Legend: A Symposium* (Berkeley and Los Angeles: University of California Press, 1971), pp. 133–156. *A Singing Stream: A Black Family Chronicle* (1987, Tom Davenport, Daniel Paterson, and Allen Tullos, Davenport Films, color, 16mm. and VHS, 57 min.) traces twentieth-century African American history through the musical and cultural traditions of one Southern family who used music to promote family loyalty and purposefulness as members dispersed to jobs in the North. Finally, for a film about oral accounts as a basis for reconstructing the history of an occupational group, see *Miles of Smiles, Years of Struggle: The Untold Story of the Black Pullman Porter* (1982, Jack Santino and Paul Wagner, Benchmark Films, color, 16mm. and VHS, 59 min.) in conjuction with Jack Santino, *Miles of Smiles, Years of Struggle: Stories of Black Pullman Porters* (Urbana: University of Illinois Press, 1989).

2. Francis B. Gummere, *The Popular Ballad* (Boston: Houghton Mifflin, 1907). Quotes are from p. 298.

3. Louise Pound, *Poetic Origins and the Ballad* (New York: Macmillan, 1921). The quote is from p. 109.

4. Lowry Charles Wimberly, *Folklore in the English and Scottish Ballads* (Chicago: University of Chicago Press, 1928).

5. Evelyn Kendrick Wells, *The Ballad Tree: A Study of British and American Ballads, Their Folklore, Verse, and Music* (New York: Ronald Press, 1950). Quotes are from pp. 124, 125, 127, 128, 130, 134, and 136.

6. Albert B. Friedman, ed., *The Viking Book of Folk Ballads of the English-Speaking World* (New York: Viking Press, 1956, paperback reprint, 1963). The quote is from p. 41.

7. For examples of "Tam Lin" on phonograph albums, see Peggy Seeger and Ewan MacColl, *Cold Snap: Traditional and Contemporary Songs and Ballads* (Folkways FW 8765, 1978); *Scottish Tradition 5: The Muckle Sangs—Classic Scots Ballads* (Tangent Records TNGM 199/3, 1975); and *Folk Ballads from Donegal and Derry*, collected and edited by Hugh Shields (Leader Records LEA 4055).

8. Child, vol. 1, p. 336.

9. Walter Scott, "Introduction to the Tale of Tamlane: On the Fairies of Popular Superstition," *Minstrelsy of the Scottish Border*, ed. Thomas Henderson (London: George G. Harrap, 1936), pp. 288–327.

10. From Francis James Child, *The English and Scottish Popular Ballads*, 10 vols. in 5 pts. (Boston: Houghton Mifflin, 1882–1898), pt. I, pp. 340–343.

11. Alice Bertha Gomme, *The Traditional Games of England, Scotland, and Ireland*, 2 vols. (London: Folk-Lore Society, 1894, 1898, reprint ed., New York: Dover Publications, 1964). "London Bridge" is discussed on pp. 332–350 in the Dover reprint edition.

12. See also William Wells Newell, *Games and Songs of American Children* (New York: Dover, 1963, reprint of second [1903] edition of the work originally published in 1883), pp. 204–211, 253–254; and Mary and Herbert Knapp, *One Potato, Two Potato . . . The Secret Education of American Children* (New York: W. W. Norton, 1976), pp. 4–5 and 15.

13. "Eeny, Meeny, Miny, Mo," in Maria Leach, ed., *Funk & Wagnalls Standard Dictionary of Folklore, Mythology, and Legend*, vol. 1 (New York: Funk & Wagnalls, 1949), p. 340.

14. Potter, "Eeny, Meeny, Miney, Mo," in *Funk & Wagnalls Standard Dictionary*, vol. 1, p. 340; see also Potter's entry "Counting-Out Rimes," vol. 1, pp. 254–255.

15. Potter, "Shepherd's Score," in *Funk & Wagnalls Standard Dictionary*, vol. 2, pp. 1006–1007. The quote is from p. 1007.

16. *Pattern in the Material Culture of the Eastern United States* (Philadelphia: University of Pennsylvania Press, 1968), pp. 237–238.

17. Charles Francis Potter, "Tongue Twisters," in *Funk & Wagnalls Standard Dictionary*, vol. 2, pp. 1117–1119.

18. "The Language of Festivals: Celebrating the Economy," in Victor Turner, ed., *Celebration: Studies in Festivity and Ritual* (Washington, D.C.: Smithsonian Institution Press, 1982), pp. 174–177.

19. Wayland D. Hand, "The Magical Transference of Disease," in *Magical Medicine: The Folkloric Component of Medicine in the Folk Belief, Custom, and Ritual of the Peoples of Europe and America* (Berkeley and Los Angeles: University of California Press, 1980), pp. 17–42. Quotes are from pp. 21 and 24.

20. Betty Blair, "AIDS," in the forthcoming *Encyclopedia of American Popular Beliefs and Superstitions*, edited by Donald J. Ward.

21. Lynwood Montell, "Cemetery Decoration Customs in the American South," in Robert E. Walls and George H. Schoemaker, eds., *The Old Traditional Way of Life: Essays in Honor of Warren E. Roberts* (Bloomington: Trickster Press, Indiana University Folklore Institute, 1989), pp. 111–129. Quotes are from pp. 111, 113, 114, 117, 118, 119, 121, 122, and 123.

22. Marvin K. Opler, "Japanese Folk Beliefs and Practices, Tule Lake, California," *Journal of American Folklore* 63 (1950):385–397. Quotes are from pp. 385, 386, 387, 388, 389, 390, 391, 394, 395, and 397.

23. Roger D. Abrahams, "Getting around Old Master (Most of the Time)," in *Afro-American Folktales: Stories from Black Traditions in the New World* (New York: Pantheon Books, 1985), pp. 265–295. Quotes are from pp. 265, 266, and 267.

24. Harry Oster, "Negro Humor: John and Old Marster," *Journal of the Folklore Institute* 5 (1968):42–57.

25. Oster, pp. 48–49.

26. Stith Thompson, *The Folktale* (New York: Dryden Press, 1946), p. 214.

27. From Oster: told by Eddie "Son" House, originally a native of Mississippi, and recorded in Iowa City, Iowa, April 24, 1965.

28. Barbara A. Babcock, "The Figurative Tradition" and "The Invention of the Storyteller," in Barbara A. Babcock and Guy and Doris Monthan, *The Pueblo Storyteller: Development of a Figurative Ceramic Tradition* (Tucson: University of Arizona Press, 1986), pp. 3–20 and 21–27. Quotes are from pp. 3, 11, 15, 21, 22, 23, and 24. For research on the impact of women's creation and sale of storyteller dolls on the men's political and economic domains, see Barbara A. Babcock, "'At Home, No Womens Are Storytellers': Potter-

ies, Stories, and Politics in Cochiti Pueblo," in Joan Newlon Radner, ed., *Feminist Messages: Coding in Women's Folk Culture* (Urbana: University of Illinois Press, 1993), pp. 221–248.

29. Raymond Firth, chapter 10, "Oral Tradition in Relation to Social Status," in *History and Traditions of Tikopia*, Memoir 33, The Polynesian Society (Wellington, New Zealand, 1961), pp. 170–171.

30. Maud Karpeles, *Cecil Sharp: His Life and Work* (Chicago: University of Chicago Press, 1967). Quotes are from pp. 25, 26, 69, 70, 86, 109, 110, 111, 118, and 127.

31. Sharp's publications on these dances include *The Country Dance Book*, 6 parts (parts 3 and 4 with George Butterworth, part 5 with Maud Karpeles, London: Novello, 1909–24); and *The Sword Dances of Northern England*, 3 parts (London: Novello, 1911–13).

32. Reprinted in Karpeles, p. 86.

33. For the origins of "hootenanny," see Peter Tamony, "'Hootenanny': The Word, Its Content and Continuum," *Western Folklore* 22 (1963):165–170.

34. Ellen Stekert, "Cents and Nonsense in the Urban Folksong Movement: 1930–1966," in Bruce Jackson, ed., *Folklore and Society: Essays in Honor of Benj. A. Botkin* (Hatboro, Pa.: Folklore Associates, 1966) pp. 153–168. See also B. A. Botkin, "The Folksong Revival: Cult or Culture?" in David A. DeTurk and A. Poulin, Jr., eds., *The American Folk Scene: Dimensions of the Folksong Revival* (New York: Dell, 1967), pp. 95–100.

35. Bruce Jackson, "The Folksong Revival," *New York Folklore* 11 (1985):195–203. Quotes are from p. 195.

36. To name a few (with their present institutional affiliations): Ellen Stekert (University of Minnesota), Bruce Jackson (State University of New York, Buffalo), Lydia Fish (State University College of New York, Buffalo), Roger D. Abrahams (University of Pennsylvania), Edward D. Ives (University of Maine), Roger Welsch (University of Nebraska), Richard Bauman (Indiana University), Neil V. Rosenberg (Memorial University of Newfoundland), Ralph Rinzler (Smithsonian Institution), and Joseph Hickerson (American Folklife Center, Library of Congress). Most of these individuals not only performed in coffeehouses or on college campuses but also appeared on phonograph records. Kenneth S. Goldstein (now at the University of Pennsylvania) produced folk music albums. University of California professors Bertrand Bronson, Charles Seeger, and D. K. Wilgus played an active role in the 1958 Berkeley Folk Festival, and Wilgus subsequently directed four folk festivals at UCLA. For more information, see Jackson, "The Folksong Revival," and Richard A. Reuss and Jens Lund, eds., *Roads into Folklore: Festschrift in Honor of Richard M. Dorson*, Folklore Forum Bibliographic and Special Series 14 (Bloomington: Indiana University Folklore Institute, 1975).

37. Elli Kaija Köngäs, "Immigrant Folklore: Survival or Living Tradition?" *Midwest Folklore* 10 (1960):117–123. Quotes are from pp. 118, 119, 120, 121, 122, and 123.

38. William Lynwood Montell, *The Saga of Coe Ridge: A Study in Oral History* (Knoxville: University of Tennessee Press, 1970). Quotes are from pp. vii, xxi, 7, 192, 193, 194, 196, and 197.

39. See the set of reprinted essays in Richard M. Dorson, *American Folklore and the Historian* (Chicago: University of Chicago Press, 1971). Quotes are from the essay "Oral Tradition and Written History: The Case for the United States" in that volume, pp. 132, 134, 138, 140, and 144.

40. Lawrence W. Levine, "How to Interpret American Folklore Historically," in Richard M. Dorson, ed., *Handbook of American Folklore* (Bloomington: Indiana University Press, 1983), pp. 338–344. Quotes are from pp. 340, 341, 342, and 343. In his book *Black Culture and Black Consciousness: Afro-American Folk Thought from Slavery to Freedom* (New York: Oxford University Press, 1977), Levine demonstrates in detail the ways that information obtained from an analysis of folklore supplements that derived from the examination of conventional historical source documents. See also works by Charles Joyner, such as "Reconsidering a Relationship: Folklore and History," *Kentucky Folklore Record* 32 (1986): 17–33, and *Down By the Riverside: A South Carolina Slave Community* (Urbana: University of Illinois, 1984). On the difference between written history and orally communicated history, see Barbara Allen, "The Personal Point of View in Orally Communicated History," *Western Folklore* 38 (1979):110–116.

Folklore as Describable
and Transmissible Entity

4. Folklore as Genre and Type

The second of the four perspectives to be discussed in this work views *folklore as describable and transmissible entity.* It establishes folklore's categorical variety by focusing on the expressive forms of which the data for folkloristics are most often examples (e.g., fairy tales, ballads, proverbs, riddles, jokes, legends). In addition, it orders the folkloristic data base by (1) grouping together similar folklore examples (multiple versions of a tale, song, tune, etc.); (2) labeling them in common ways (for instance, the story "The Dragon Slayer," the ballad "Lord Randall," the game "Simon Says"); and (3) describing and systematizing the resulting sets. Finally, it acknowledges the fact that folklore is transmissible through space as well as time, and it addresses questions about the nature and consequences of transmission. To view folklore as describable and transmissible entity, then, is to configure folklore examples into sets, to define those sets, and to chart their distribution in space. In the remainder of this chapter, we discuss the concept of folklore as a describable entity.[1] Folklore as a transmissible entity is the subject of chapter 5.

The Concept of Form/Genre

The fundamental tasks in folkloristics, as in other disciplines, are to identify and order the phenomena that are the subject of inquiry. From the inception of their field to the present, the data that folklorists have collected have been examples of expressive forms that are readily identifiable by well-established and commonly used names. Words such as *myth, legend, proverb,*

riddle, and *ballad,* for example, all had lengthy histories of use in English long before folkloristics evolved in the early nineteenth century. This was the case in other languages as well. It is not surprising, therefore, that pioneering folklorists labeled their data in familiar ways, employing everyday words whose meaningfulness was taken for granted.[2] Often these words were used by themselves (e.g., *joke, game, tongue twister, ritual*). Sometimes they were prefixed with *folk* (or its equivalent in other languages) to indicate the traditionality of the phenomena they modified (for instance, *folktales, folksongs, folk beliefs, folk customs*).[3] Furthermore, the categories these words designate became—and remain—the bases for conceptualizing, identifying, and classifying folklore by *form* or *genre.* Following the practice of most folklorists, we regard the words *form* and *genre* as synonyms and use them interchangeably throughout this work.

The very act of labeling a folklore example as a *tale, song, belief, game, fence, barn,* etc., categorizes it. Therefore, all folklore examples identified in a common way—as *myths, superstitions, houses,* for instance—presumably belong to the same *generic set* because they share some characteristic(s). Determining the distinctiveness of a form, then, entails discerning what the members of a generic set have in common.

Material objects that are traditional and that thus constitute data for folkloristics (barns, baskets, pots, fences, for instance) have physical characteristics that can be observed and examined directly and at first hand. However, a wide range and variety of folklore examples are not material objects (e.g., stories, songs, beliefs, customs). Since they cannot be weighed, measured, or physically handled, their nature and characteristics must be hypothesized. Folklore examples that are material objects are thus identifiable generically on the basis of observable physical properties, while the generic identity of those that are intangible must be determined by intuition, inference, or analogy.

Because of their large number and variety, the generic sets of which folklore data are examples are definable on the basis of diverse and often quite different criteria. Individuals' conceptualizations of given forms understandably vary, depending on (1) what folklore examples they conceive to be members of particular generic sets, (2) what similarities they discern among those set members, and (3) which of the discerned similarities they judge to be important. Hence, although folklorists share a scholarly lexicon and a basic set of concepts, there are differences as well as similarities—both through time and at any given point in time—in their individual conceptions and explanations of what generic designators such as *myth*, *legend*, and *ritual* mean.

Many material objects made traditionally, and therefore frequently documented and studied by folklorists, are identified categorically as examples of *pottery*. Objects are so designated because they are made of clay and because their makers shape the objects and subsequently fire or heat them, transforming the plastic substance of which they consist into a material that is hard, brittle, and durable. All examples of pottery, then, have two different things in common: the material of which, and the processes by which, they are created.

Examples of pottery can be grouped into numerous kinds of subsets on the basis of differing criteria. Charles G. Zug III describes some of the options.[4] Zug notes, for example, that one way the people he studied classify their pottery indicates the intended purpose or use of the objects, a criterion that also influences the specific form in which they are made. Included in this purpose-oriented subset are such objects as sugar jars, cream pitchers, butter jars, molasses jugs, milk crocks, preserve jars, medicine jars, butter tubs, beanpots, coffeepots, candle sticks, spittoons, birdhouses, rabbit feeders, grave markers, and

Figure 4–1: Burlong Craig with a harvest of wares, Catawba County, North Carolina, 1978 (photo by Charles Zug).

flowerpots. *Puzzle jugs* can also be included in the purpose-oriented subset, for a puzzle jug is a vessel whose purpose is to trick people. It has "a perforated neck, hollow handle and rim, and assorted mouthpieces, all designed to embarrass anyone attempting to drink its contents."[5]

Materials other than clay used in creating pottery can also serve as criteria to define and distinguish subsets. One example Zug provides is pottery pieces that are ordered into a subset on the basis of the nature of their glazes, with the materials used to create the glazes—salt, lead, and alkaline, for instance—serving as part of name given to individual set members.

Another way that folklorists define forms is to focus on the fundamental components and relationships that members of a given generic set share. Such definitions are based principally on analyses of *structure* and have as their objective to discover and describe what the "building blocks" of sets are and how these basic components interrelate. For folklore examples that are material objects, it is primarily their structure that determines what generic sets those examples belong to and what the labels given to those sets mean. To illustrate the primacy of structural analysis in defining generic sets whose members are material objects, let us consider fences.

Fence, like *myth* and *superstition*, is a word with a long history and a meaning that seems obvious because we are familiar with and frequently use it. It denotes an object created to mark boundaries, to confine phenomena (usually animals or human beings) to a predetermined space, and/or to serve as a barrier. Fences are configurable into subsets that are definable on the basis of the materials of which they are constructed. *Wood fences* constitute such a subset, one to which many folklore data can be assigned because many examples of wood fences are traditional.

Wood fences themselves are divisible into subsets principally on the basis of the nature of their component parts and the ways those parts are interrelated to create a fence. Two of the subsets to which folklore examples are most often assigned are identifiable as the *snake* and *jack*.[6]

The snake fence (also known as *worm*, *Virginia*, and *zigzag*) consists of eight-to-ten-foot split rails that are interlocked, supported by crossed poles, and arranged angled at about 60 degrees in zigzag fashion. The overall height is four to five feet, with the fence taking up from six to eight feet of ground space width because of the angled pattern in which it is built.

The jack fence (also called *jack pole* and *jack and pole*) "consists of two wooden posts with butts resting on the ground from three to five feet apart and joined at or near their apex." A horizontal timber lies "in the crotch formed by the extended upper ends of the members forming the jack." The number of horizontal poles varies from one to six; they can be attached to the x-crossed posts with wire, spikes, or nails.[7]

Because material objects can be observed and examined directly and at first hand, components and relationships can be readily perceived, thus making structure the principal basis for classifying such objects and defining sets and subsets into which they fall. As noted earlier, however, folklore data are often examples of generic sets consisting of phenomena that are not material objects. Although they can only be hypothesized, the structures of these phenomena, too, often serve as either the principal means or one way of defining the forms those set members exemplify. One such nonmaterial form that can be defined structurally is *superstition*, as Alan Dundes demonstrates.[8]

In terms of their structure, superstitions can be said to be "*traditional expressions of one or more conditions and one or more results with some of the conditions signs and others causes*" (emphasis in the origi-

Figure 4–2: Snake or zigzag split rail fence, Cooperstown, New York, 1994 (photo by Mary R. Georges).

Figure 4–3: Four-pole jack fence with mortise and tenon joints, Lima, Montana, 1948 (from Austin E. Fife, Exploring Western Americana, *UMI Research Press, 1988, p. 162, by permission of Alta Fife).*

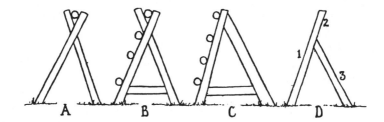

Figure 10.   Construction of Different Types of Jack Fences

Figure 4–4: Construction of different types of jack fences (from Austin E. Fife, Exploring Western Americana, *UMI Research Press, 1988, p. 160, by permission of Alta Fife).*

nal). Some superstitions involve single conditions and single results. This is the case with "If a dog howls, it's a sign of death"; "If it rains on the wedding day, the groom will die first"; "If you step on a crack, you'll break your mother's back"; and "If you sing before breakfast, you'll cry before supper." Multiple conditions may also occur, as with "If you steal a dishcloth, rub it over a wart, and hide it under a rock, the wart will go away," and "In the spring the first mourning dove you hear cooing, take off one of your stockings or socks, turn it wrongside out and in the heel will be a hair, the color of the hair of the person you're going to marry." There may be multiple results, too, as in "In dog days [i.e., the hot, sultry summer days between early July and early September], dogs are liable to go mad and snakes are blind."[9]

Superstitions can be configured into subsets on the basis of the nature of the relationship that exists between condition and result. Sometimes the relationship is temporal and noncausal. Examples include "When there's a ring around the moon, it's going to rain"; "If your hand itches, you're going to receive some money"; "If a black cat crosses your path, you'll have bad luck"; and "Someone in your family will die if you see a falling star." The condition mentioned in each of these is one over which human beings have no control and which they regard and interpret as an omen. Moreover, no causality is intended or implied in these *sign superstitions*. The ring around the moon is not said or believed to actually *cause* subsequent rain, nor is someone supposed to die *because* a star falls. The signs merely portend what will come to pass; they are conditions from which results follow in time, but not because of a cause-and-effect relationship.

The relationship between condition and result in another subset of superstitions *is* causal, however. These superstitions sometimes prescribe practices that human beings may carry out to bring about a particular effect or result. Thus, one may "Put an ax under the bed to cut the pain in two during childbirth"; "Take three swallows of strong coffee to cure hiccoughs"; "Put the right stocking and shoe on first, and all will go right through the day"; and "Use a new pen when taking a test to avoid making mistakes." These *magic superstitions*, as this subset can be called, may also prescribe actions to be avoided because carrying them out will lead to negative consequences. Since it is unlucky to "sit on a table," "bid a person goodbye twice," "tell a dream before breakfast," or "count the cars in a funeral procession," one should not do these things (condition) in order to avoid negative consequences and maintain the status quo (result). Moreover, one may change things for the better by behaving in ways that bring good luck, such as hanging a horseshoe over the front door, walking around a chair when playing cards, carrying a rabbit's foot, and wearing a dime in one's shoe or stocking.

In addition to sign and magic superstitions, structural analysis reveals a third subset, *conversion superstitions*. These sometimes stipulate actions that one can take to avoid negative results that follow from the appearance or accidental creation of signs. For instance, seeing a priest the first thing in the morning is bad luck. But one can avert the bad luck by going back home and starting out again, or by tying a knot in a handkerchief. Spilling salt brings bad luck, too, unless one throws some of the spilled salt over one's left shoulder, in which case the bad luck can be averted. Two people who let an object such as a tree come between them while they are walking along together will quarrel, unless they say, "Bread and butter," an action that enables them to avoid a spat.

Sometimes actions prescribed not only enable one to avoid a negative consequence of signs or actions, but even make it possible for one to create a positive result instead. If you drop a comb, for instance, you will be disappointed. But if you step on the comb, you'll avoid disappointment. Furthermore, if you also turn around three times and make a wish when you step on the comb, then your wish will come true, thus turning a potentially negative result into a positive one.

A structural analysis, then, reveals that superstitions can be organized into three subsets. The nature of the relationship between condition and result (temporal for sign superstitions and causal for magic superstitions) is the criterion for identifying and differentiating these two subsets structurally. The act of creating an alternative, positive result by behaving in a prescribed way defines and distinguishes the third subset (conversion superstitions).[10] Some alternative definitions of superstition are presented in Box 4–1.

Other generic sets exhibit greater structural complexity and variety than superstitions. This is the case with *riddles*, as

demonstrated by Robert A. Georges and Alan Dundes.[14] The basic structural component of riddles is a *descriptive element*, which consists of a *topic* and a *comment*. In every riddle there is at least one object or item that is allegedly described (topic) and about which an assertion is made (comment). In the riddle "Twenty-four horses set upon a bridge" (answer: teeth in your gums), the topic is "twenty-four horses" and the comment is "set upon a bridge." The riddle "A crowd of little men [topic] livin' in a flat-top house [comment]" (answer: matches in a box) similarly has a single descriptive element.

When riddles have two or more descriptive elements, they may either be compatible or conflict. In "A lady in a boat / With a yellow petticoat" (answer: egg), for instance, there are two descriptive elements: a lady in a boat and the lady wears a yellow petticoat. The two are compatible, for the second merely adds another detail to the description presented in the first. However, in the riddle "What has eyes, but can't see?"

BOX 4–1
Some Alternative Generic Definitions of Superstition

A superstition . . . is a mode of fear based on some irrational or mythological belief and usually involves some taboo in practice.
—David Bidney[11]

    *   *   *

There is no objective means of distinguishing "superstitions" from other types of belief and action. In order to escape from this impasse it will be necessary to fall back on a convenient device used by lawyers, namely the notion of the "reasonable man." . . . [H]ereafter the word "superstition" will be used in the sense of the kind of belief and action a reasonable man in present-day Western society would regard as being "superstitions."
—Gustav Jahoda[12]

    *   *   *

"Superstitions". . . include divinations, spells, cures, charms, signs and omens, rituals and taboos. . . . [M]ost superstitions can be seen to be based on unauthorized or out-moded religion.
—Iona Opie and Moira Tatem[13]

(answer: potato), the two descriptive elements are in opposition, since the second (it can't see) seems to deny a function (seeing) of a part (eyes) that is stipulated in the first of the two descriptive elements (it has eyes). Structurally, then, a riddle can be defined as a *"verbal expression which contains one or more descriptive elements, a pair of which may be in opposition; the referent of the elements [the riddle answer] is to be guessed"* (emphasis in the original).

The optionality of oppositions makes the riddle generic set divisible into two subsets: *nonoppositional and oppositional.* Furthermore, each of these can in turn be subdivided when the content of riddles is more closely focused upon in the analysis. As riddle content clearly reveals, nonoppositional riddles may be either *literal or metaphorical.* In posing the riddle "My fader had a tree, it bear fruit, outside brown and inside white," a riddler presents a literal description of a coconut; and coconut is the answer to the riddle he or she poses. Literal descriptions of the riddle answer are also illustrated by "It dips in and out" (answer: paddle) and "Where they appear it is white" (answer: water lilies). By contrast, the riddle "Two brothers side by side all day and at night they go to rest" provides a metaphorical description of its referent, for the answer is a pair of boots. Metaphor is also fundamental to the riddles "A house on a single pole" (answer: mushroom) and "A little steel trap that keeps snapping closed" (answer: eyelashes).[15] Thus, nonoppositional riddles can be further subdivided into two subsets, with the literal/metaphorical dichotomy being the basis for the division.

Oppositional riddles are also divisible into subsets because the nature of the oppositions in them can create three different kinds of contradictions. The riddle "What goes to the branch [stream] and drinks and don't drink?" (answer: cow with a bell around its neck) consists of three descriptive elements: it goes to the branch [stream], it drinks, and it doesn't drink. Of the three, the second and third are in opposition, since they contradict each other. Furthermore, the contradiction is antithetical, since the "it" that is the topic of all three descriptive elements cannot both drink and not drink at the same time. Hence, this riddle is an example of a subset of oppositional riddles that can be called *antithetical contradictive* since the opposition created by the contradiction it drinks/ it doesn't drink is an antithesis.

Oppositional riddles may also describe phenomena in ways which deny that an object has an attribute, function, or part that is either fundamental to it or that is usually associated with it. "What has legs / but cannot walk?" (answer: chair) consists of two descriptive elements: something has legs, and "the something" can't walk. The descriptive elements are in opposition because the second assertion ("but [it] cannot walk") denies to the object being described a function (the ability to walk) that is usually associated with legs, which the first descriptive element indicates the unnamed object has. Denial of an associated part is the basis for the contradiction in "What has hands / and no fingers?" (answer: clock), for hands and fingers usually go together, and both therefore are expected to be present when one is said to exist. "Something has fingers but no toes" (answer: glove) similarly denies the existence of an expected other object since fingers and toes are usually both parts of the same thing—a body. All three of these examples belong to a subset of oppositional riddles that can be identified as *privational contradictive* since the contradictions that create the oppositions in all three are deprivations.

A third subset of oppositional riddles consists of those in which a natural or expected consequence of an action specified in the first descriptive element is denied, or the consequence that is described is not the natural or expected one. In the riddle "What eats and eats and never gets full?" (answer: a sausage grinder), for instance, the expected effect of repeated or continuous eating is that the eater will eventually be full; but that consequence is explicitly denied. Similarly, one expects something that goes in and out of water to get wet; but that is stated not to be the case in the riddle "What jumps into the water and out again and don't get wet?" (answer: an egg in a duck's belly). An unexpected effect occurs in the riddle "What grows larger the more you contract it?" (answer: debt), since one meaning of the verb *contract* is obviously to make or become smaller, not the opposite. This is also the case with "My father make a door an' it was too short; he cut it and it became longer" (answer: grave), since the image evoked by the words *cut it* is that an object will be smaller, not larger, after that action is taken. In all of these riddles, the descriptive elements in opposition are *causally contradictive* because logical or anticipated effects do not follow in time from described actions that usually cause them to come about.

As this description reveals, members of a generic set are sometimes divisible into multiple subsets—seven in the case of riddles. Moreover, the kinds of characteristics common to members of subsets can vary considerably. As the identifying labels

indicate, members of the nonoppositional subset of riddles share a lack of opposition in their descriptive elements, while members of the oppositional subset have in common a stated or implied opposition. The nature of the relationship between the structural components (topic and comment) of a descriptive element or between two or more descriptive elements is thus the basis for identifying and differentiating these two subsets.

Both of these subsets of riddles, in turn, are also divisible into subsets, each on a different basis. The two subsets of non-oppositional riddles—literal and metaphorical—are defined and distinguished by the nature of the description each provides of the phenomenon that is the riddle referent (and hence its answer). By contrast, the three subsets of oppositional riddles—antithetical contradictive, privational contradictive, and causal contradictive—are identified and differentiated on the basis of the nature of the contradictions that create the oppositions in each. The number, variety, and hierarchical ordering of these subsets are represented diagrammatically in Box 4–2. For comparison, alternative definitions of the riddle distinguishing the genre on the basis of criteria other than structure are presented in Box 4–3.

Folklorists are necessarily aware of and must consider structure when attempting to describe the expressive forms of which

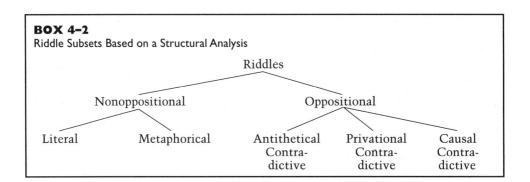

BOX 4–2
Riddle Subsets Based on a Structural Analysis

BOX 4–3
Some Alternative Generic Definitions of the Riddle

The true riddle or the riddle in the strict sense compares an object to another entirely different object. Its essence consists in the surprise that the solution occasions: the hearer perceives that he has entirely misunderstood what has been said to him. . . . The true riddle may also contain an introductory and a concluding element. Both of these are ordinarily conventional, and either one or both may be lacking.
  —Archer Taylor[16]

  *   *   *

Riddles are questions that are framed with the purpose of confusing or testing the wits of those who do not know the answer.
  —Roger D. Abrahams and Alan Dundes[17]

  *   *   *

The riddle is a puzzling question with an answer that seems arbitrary because the hearer receives meaning B in the riddle answer while expecting to react to meaning A in the riddle question; but the riddle question and answer are compatible because meanings A and B share some semantic relationship."
  —Brian Sutton-Smith[18]

their data are examples. But they do not always focus solely or mainly on structure. Frequently, members of the generic sets to which folklore examples are assigned share multiple kinds of characteristics, making it difficult and sometimes impossible for folklorists to determine or agree about which kind or combination of similarities is most important for defining a set. When this occurs, forms are understandably conceptualized and characterized in alternative ways.

As noted in earlier chapters, folklorists configure into a single generic set tales such as *Cinderella* (Type 510), *Snow White* (Type 709), *Bluebeard* (Type 312), and *Hansel and Gretel* (Type 327A). Because these are the kind of stories the Grimms highlighted in their groundbreaking and influential collection *Kinder- und Hausmärchen* (discussed in chapter 2), folklorists throughout the world often follow precedent and call such tales *Märchen*. Alternative designators include the French *conte populaire*, the Norwegian *eventyr*, the Swedish *saga*, the

Russian *skázka*, and the English *fairy tale* and *folktale*. In this work, we follow the widespread practice in the United States and use *Märchen* and *fairy tale* interchangeably to identify such stories.

With the Grimms' work as both model and fieldwork guide, collectors throughout the world have elicited and documented myriad *Märchen*. The result is that such stories have always constituted a sizable portion of the folkloristic data base. Furthermore, recording examples of fairy tales from living narrators remains a primary goal and often even a preoccupation of many folklorists. Yet while documenting *Märchen* has been relatively easy and quite successful, determining and describing what characteristics such stories have in common have been much more difficult tasks.

In part, the difficulty is attributable to the fact that the word *Märchen* simply meant "story" in German at the time the Grimms decided to make it a part of the title of the work for which they became and remain famous. Contrary to what is often assumed, the Grimms did not set out to provide a sampling of a specific narrative genre in the initial edition and volumes of their *Kinder- und Hausmärchen* (1812, 1815). Instead, they were motivated to present a set of traditional stories for an adult audience that could also be read to, and provide instruction for, children.[19] As the Grimms revised the *Kinder- und Hausmärchen* and prepared subsequent editions, and as others began to elicit and document analogous stories, the word *Märchen* came increasingly to be used in a technical sense to denote tales of a particular kind—those like "Cinderella," "Snow White," and "Rapunzel." Neither the Grimms nor any other pioneering folklorists provided an explicit definition for this set of tales, however; and folklore examples were identified as *Märchen* and assigned to that generic set by intuition and analogy.

Scholarly attempts to characterize the fairy tale generically were rare during the nineteenth, and have been sporadic throughout the twentieth, century. What the results reveal is that defining *Märchen* is a difficult task because the stories that are grouped into that generic set do not share only one common element, but rather exhibit a number and variety of similarities.

Russian folklorist Vladimir Propp (1895–1970) postulated in his 1928 book *Morfológija skázki* (Morphology of the Folktale) that "fairy tales possess a quite particular structure which is immediately felt and which determines their category, even though we may not be aware of it."[20] Propp selected for his structural analysis a set of 100 Russian *Märchen* recorded by A. N. Afanás'ev and published in *Naródnye rússkie skázki* (Russian Folktales) between 1855 and 1864. Propp's perusal of these narrative texts revealed the recurrence in fairy tales of a maximum number of 31 functions, with *function* being conceived

as a structural component that is "*an act of a character, defined from the point of view of its significance for the course of the action*" (emphasis in the original). (A listing and brief characterization of Propp's functions are provided in Box 4–4.[21])

BOX 4–4

The Structure of Fairy Tales According to Vladimir Propp's Analysis of Their 31 Functions

Initial Situation

The members of a family are enumerated, or the future hero is identified by name and/or status (e.g., Ivan, a soldier, a poor farmer).

Preparatory Section

1. *Absentation:* One of the members of a family is absent from home.
2. *Interdiction:* An interdiction is addressed to the hero/heroine (e.g., don't look in a particular place, don't venture away from a specified site, take a stipulated person or object along when going to a designated destination).
3. *Violation:* The interdiction is violated (i.e., someone disobeys what has been commanded).
4. *Reconnaissance:* The villain makes an attempt at reconnaissance (e.g., tries to obtain information about the nature or whereabouts of the victim or a particular being or object).
5. *Delivery:* The villain receives the information, succeeding in the attempted reconnaissance.
6. *Trickery:* The villain attempts (by magic, disguise) to deceive the victim in order to take possession of him/her or of his/her belongings.
7. *Complicity:* The victim submits to deception and thereby unwittingly helps the enemy.

Inauguration of the Plot

8. *Villainy:* The villain causes harm or injury to a member of a family (e.g.,

through abduction, plundering, theft, physical violence, enticement, expulsion, casting of a spell, seizure of a magical agent).

8a. *Lack:* One member of a family either lacks something or desires to have something (e.g., a bride, a magical object, money or material possessions).

9. *Mediation:* Misfortune or lack is made known; the hero/heroine is approached with a request or command; he/she is allowed to go or is dispatched (e.g., responds to a call for help or an announcement of misfortune and departs from home).

10. *Beginning counteraction:* The seeker agrees to or decides upon counteraction.

11. *Departure:* The hero/heroine leaves home.

＊   ＊   ＊

12. *The first function of the donor:* The hero/heroine is tested, interrogated, attacked, etc., which prepares the way for receiving either a magical agent or helper (e.g., the hero/heroine must accomplish difficult or impossible tasks, free a captive, resolve a property dispute, win a fight or battle).

13. *The hero's/heroine's reaction:* The hero/heroine reacts to the actions of the future donor.

14. *Provision or receipt of a magical agent:* The hero/heroine acquires the use of a magical agent (e.g., by chance, transference, or offer of help in time of need).

15. *Spatial transference between two kingdoms, guidance:* The hero/heroine is transferred, delivered, or led to the whereabouts of an object of search (e.g., flies through the air on a magical steed or bird, travels across earth/water on a person's/animal's back).

Struggle with Villain and Villainy

16. *Struggle:* The hero/heroine and the villain join in direct combat (e.g., in a physical fight or battle, in a contest of strength or wits, in a game).

17. *Branding, marking:* The hero/heroine is branded (in the form of a wound or other perceptible sign or by being given an object to be used subsequently for recognition).

18. *Victory:* The villain is defeated (e.g., beaten in a fight or battle, defeated in a contest or game, banished, killed).

19. (no designator) The initial misfortune or lack is liquidated (e.g., the object of search is found or seized, a spell on a person is broken, a slain person is resuscitated, a captive is freed).

20. *Return:* The hero/heroine returns (to the place from which he/she commenced the journey or search).

21. *Pursuit, chase:* The hero/heroine is pursued (e.g., by an ogre, demon, threatening being or animal, enchantress, potential assassin).

22. *Rescue:* Rescue of the hero/heroine from pursuit (e.g., by helpful animals or natural elements, by hiding or being hidden, by magical transformation or aid, by creating obstacles that impede the progress of a pursuer).

23. *Unrecognized arrival:* The hero/heroine, unrecognized, arrives home or in another country.

24. *Unfounded claims:* False hero/heroine presents unfounded claims.

Task and Solution

25. *Difficult Task:* A difficult task is proposed to the hero/heroine (e.g., to endure an ordeal by fire, to answer a riddle, to hide undetected, to accomplish a specified test).

26. *Solution:* The task is resolved.

27. *Recognition:* The hero/heroine is recognized (e.g., by the brand made or the token given earlier).

28. *Exposure:* The false hero/heroine or villain is exposed.

29. *Transfiguration:* The hero/heroine is given a new appearance (e.g., becomes handsome/beautiful, puts on new garments).

30. *Punishment:* The villain is punished (e.g., banished, tortured, killed).

31. *Wedding:* The hero/heroine is married and ascends the throne.

According to Propp, all fairy tales must have a villainy (function 8) or a lack (function 8a); and the villain must be defeated (function 18) or the lack liquidated (function 19), making at least one of these pairs of functions obligatory in every *Märchen*. All other functions are optional, in the sense that no particular ones *must* be present, although some of them always are. Since most of the remaining functions are also either paired or ordered into longer sets, however, the occurrence of the first member of an optional pair or group of functions makes the other pair or set member(s) obligatory. For example, when an interdiction occurs in a *Märchen* (e.g., don't go into a particular room of a castle, take your brother with you when you go into the woods), it is invariably violated, making function 3 (violation) obligatory when function 2 (interdiction) occurs. Similarly, when a test is proposed to a protagonist to determine his or her worthiness of receiving a magical object or helper (function 12), the protagonist responds to the test (function 13) and receives the magical object or helper (function 14). Thus, the presence of optional function 12 (the first function of the donor) makes functions 13 (the hero's reaction) and 14 (provision or receipt of a magical agent) obligatory.

Regardless of their number, the functions that are present in *Märchen* always occur in the same sequence, Propp asserts, unless the plots of the stories have been subject to a process of transformation. Furthermore, Propp notes, it is the stability of structure that accounts for the *Märchen*'s "striking uniformity" and "repetition," while it is content and style that are variable and responsible for the fairy tale's "amazing multiformity, picturesqueness, and color."

Other researchers allude to the structural sameness of fairy tales by noting their length, plot complexities, and multiepisodic nature. Stith Thompson, for example, begins his definition with a somewhat general comment about structure when he writes, "A *Märchen* is a tale of some length involving a succession of motifs or episodes." As he continues, however, Thompson shifts his focus to content, commenting in some detail (though still somewhat generally) on the kinds of actors and settings that such stories have in common. "It moves in an unreal world without definite locality or definite characters and is filled with the marvelous," states Thompson. "In this never-never land," he continues, "humble heroes kill adversaries, succeed to kingdoms, and marry princesses."[22]

Implicit in Thompson's definition are a number of characteristics besides structure that are frequently cited by other folklorists as well. The emphasis on the "never-neverland" settings suggests that fairy tales are fictional in nature, a criterion commonly cited to distinguish them from such other traditional narrative forms as legends and myths. Mention of the "marvelous" implies the imaginative and even magical, further reinforcing a view that *Märchen* are fictional and not factual stories, and hence tales that are told principally to entertain. That fairy tales are usually populated by general character types and set in indefinite locales adds further to the view that structure alone does not suffice to describe this generic set, since the nature of what is depicted (content) and the way it is portrayed (style) are essential qualities of *Märchen*. Definitions quoted in Box 4–5 provide additional evidence of the multiple and differing kinds of characteristics that researchers conceive to be common to members of the fairy tale generic set.

The ballad, another expressive form of which innumerable folklore data are examples, also cannot be defined generically on the basis of a single criterion. The assertion most commonly made about ballads is that they are songs which tell stories. This statement acknowledges that ballad is a

BOX 4–5
Some Generic Definitions of the *Märchen* (Fairy Tale)

By *fairy tale* we mean a continued narrative generally of a certain length, practically always in prose, serious on the whole, though humour is by no means excluded, centering in one hero or heroine, usually poor and destitute at the start, who, after a series of adventures in which the supernatural element plays a conspicuous part, attains his goal and lives happy ever after.
—Alexander Haggerty Krappe[23]

*   *   *

[*Märchen*] are prose narratives which are regarded as fiction. They are not considered as dogma or history, they may or may not have happened, and they are not to be taken seriously. Nevertheless, although it is often said that they are told only for amusement, they have other important functions. . . . [*Märchen*] may be set in any time and any place, and in this sense they are almost timeless and placeless. They have been called "nursery tales" but in many societies they are not restricted to children. They have also been known as "fairy tales" but this is inappropriate both because narratives about fairies are usually regarded as true, and because fairies do not appear in most [*Märchen*]. Fairies, ogres, and even deities may appear, but [*Märchen*] usually recount the adventures of animal or human characters.
—William Bascom[24]

*   *   *

The . . . category . . . of . . . *Märchen* includes those narratives which are told primarily for entertainment—though they may well reflect themes also expressed in myths and legends and thus serve to reinforce the didactic functions served by the latter, especially as far as children are concerned—and are indeed open to rational interpretation. Their factual content, however, may be as minimal as that of the most fabulous of myths. It is this sort of "popular tales and traditions" that William Thoms sought to distinguish when he coined the term "folk-lore" in 1846. Examples here are legion in any tradition, in large measure, it would seem, because the relatively secular character of such narratives permits a range of variation and adaptation far wider than that generally present among myths and, to a lesser extent, legends.
—C. Scott Littleton[25]

subset of a broad, varied genre (song) and that it is a means of ordering, characterizing, and communicating information about a noteworthy or memorable event (telling a story by singing). Two different criteria are implied by this assertion: *what a ballad singer's objective is* (to tell a story) and *how she or he accomplishes that objective* (by singing). But there are some notable differences in how ballad singers reach their common goal, resulting in the configuring of ballads into subsets that are also definable on the basis of differing and multiple criteria.

Sometimes ballad singers tell their stories by focusing on selected details of an event while ignoring others or giving them short shrift. Often referred to as *leaping and lingering*, this narrating technique is reportorial and objective, for the singer selectively characterizes aspects of the event and withholds personal response and judgment. This can be illustrated by innumerable examples, including the ballad "Babylon."

In "Babylon" (also known as "The Bonnie Banks o Virgie O"), a stranger (called variously such things as a robber or a banished or wicked man) confronts three maidens (sometimes identified as sisters).[26] He takes the girls by the hand one at a time and asks each if she prefers to become his wife or to die. The first two refuse to marry the man, and he does indeed stab and kill each of them. The third maid says she will neither wed him nor be his victim. In some versions of the song, this woman turns the tables and kills the man; in other versions she warns him that her brother, who is nearby, will come to her rescue and kill the stranger. When he asks and is told the girl's brother's name—Babylon—the man stabs himself, for *he* is Babylon; and he realizes that he has unknowingly killed two of his sisters. The focus in the song is on the confrontations and murders.

The listener (or reader of a text of a singer's words) is not told initially (if ever) who the man in the ballad "Babylon" is. There is no information given about where he comes from, why he wants to marry, or why he threatens the three young women and kills two of them. No judgments are made or morals pronounced in available texts, thus illustrating the detached and objective way singers present the story. Furthermore, the tale is told principally through dialogue between the man and the young women. The words they speak differ only slightly during each of the three confrontations, a plot development technique known as *incremental repetition*. (See Box 4–6 for a text of "Babylon.")

Ballads exhibiting these characteristics are usually identified as a distinctive subset and identified in one of two ways. They are sometimes called *Child ballads* because they are the kind of song that the American ballad scholar Francis James Child (1826–96) focused upon in his comprehensive and widely known and used published collection *The English and Scottish Popular Ballads* (5 volumes in 10 parts, Boston: Houghton Mifflin, 1882–98). Such songs are also often called *traditional ballads*, since

Figure 4–5: Francis James Child, compiler of The English and Scottish Popular Ballads, *5 vols., 1882–1898 (frontispiece, vol. I).*

scholars hypothesize that the principal way of learning and perpetuating them historically has been by oral tradition, and hence when people interact at first hand, or face to face.[27] Calling such ballads by these alternative labels introduces other distinguishing criteria for the subset. *Child ballad* makes source or model a shared characteristic of the members of the subset, while *traditional ballad* stresses the ways the songs are learned and perpetuated. No one of these criteria defines the subset by itself; rather, it is a combination of quite different kinds of criteria that give the subset its distinctiveness.

Another ballad subset consists of songs whose singers tell their stories in great detail rather than by leaping and lingering. These songs also present evaluative comments about how the players in the drama

BOX 4–6

A Version of the Ballad "Babylon" (Here Called "The Bonny Banks of Virgie O") (Child Ballad No. 14)

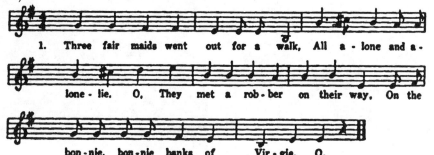

1. Three fair maids went out for a walk, All a-lone and a-lone-lie. O, They met a rob-ber on their way, On the bon-nie, bon-nie banks of Vir-gie, O.

1   Three fair maids went out for a
       walk,
     All alone and a-lonelie, O,
     They met a robber on their way,
     On the bonnie, bonnie banks of
       Virgie, O.
2   He took the first one by the hand,
     And he whipped her around and he
       made her stand.
3   "O will you be a robber's wife?
     Or will you die by my pen-knife?"
4   "I will not be a robber's wife;
     I would rather die by your pen-
       knife."
5   Oh, he took out his little pen-knife,
     And it's then he took her own sweet
       life.
6   He took the second one by the hand,
     And he whipped her around and he
       made her stand.
7   "Oh, will you be a robber's wife?
     Or will you die by my pen-knife?"
8   "I will not be a robber's wife,
     I would rather die by your pen-
       knife."

9   Oh, he took out his little pen-knife,
     And it's then he took her own sweet
       life.
10 He took the third one by the hand,
     And he whipped her around and he
       made her stand.
11 "Oh, will you be a robber's wife,
     Or will you die by my pen-knife?"
12 "I will not be a robber's wife.
     Nor will I die by your pen-knife.
13 "Oh, if I had my brothers here,
     You would not have killed my sis-
       ters dear."
14 "Oh, where are your brothers, pray
       now tell?"
     "Oh, one of them is a minister."
15 "And where is the other, pray now
       tell?"
     "He's out a-robbing like yourself."
16 "The Lord have mercy on my soul,
     For I have killed my sisters dear."
17 Then he took out his little pen-
       knife,
     And it's then he took his own sweet
       life.[28]

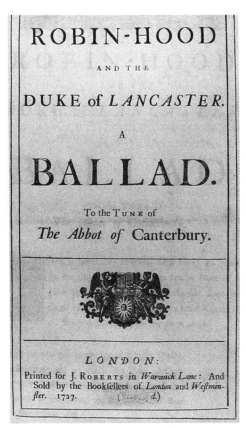

Figure 4–6: Broadside ballad, London, 1727 (photo by Diane Dugaw; courtesy UCLA Folklore and Mythology Archives).

Figure 4–7: Broadside ballad (photo by Diane Dugaw; courtesy UCLA Folklore and Mythology Archives).

behave, and they moralize about the consequences of characters' actions. Because they include judgments and points of view as well as detailed descriptions of events, such songs are often sentimental and explicitly didactic. Many of them were printed on, made popular by, and learned from inexpensive broad sheets that were peddled on city streets in Europe and America from the mid-seventeenth into the nineteenth century.[29] Principal characteristics shared by members of this *vulgar ballad* subset, then, are the ways the singer tells the story and assesses the event that the tale depicts. A text of the vulgar ballad "Naomi (Omie) Wise" is presented in Box 4–7.[30]

A third subset of ballads is identifiable as the *blues ballad*, described in detail by D. K. Wilgus and Eleanor R. Long.[31] Unlike their traditional and vulgar counterparts, blues ballads do not tell their stories directly and chronologically. Instead, they mention and comment on selected aspects of an event without recounting it fully or providing much detail. Implicit in the performance of such songs is the assumption that singer and audience members already know the story, since understanding what

---

BOX 4–7
"Naomi (Omie) Wise": A Vulgar Ballad Version of an 1808 North Carolina Murder

Come all you young people, I pray you
    draw near,
A sorrowful ditty you quickly shall hear.
The truth I will tell you about Omie
    Wise,
How Omie was deceived by Lewis's lies.

Come all ye pretty maids take warning
    from me,
. . . .
Let this be a warning to all who pass by
That you be not deceived by Lewis's lie.

He promised to wed her at Adam's
    springs,
Some money he'd give her and other fine
    things.
Neither of them he gave her but
    flattered the case,
Saying, "We will be married; will be no
    disgrace."

He said he'd go with her right straight to
    the town,
There they would be married, in union
    be bound.
He took her on behind him and away
    they did go
Till they came to the banks where the
    river did flow.

"Now, Omie, poor Omie, I'll tell you my
    mind;
I intend for to drown you and leave you
    behind."
"Have mercy, have mercy!" poor Omie
    did cry,

Saying, "I'm a poor rebel and not fit to
    die."

"No mercy I'll have," this hero did cry,
"In the bottom of the river your body
    shall lie."
"Have mercy, have mercy, and spare me
    my life!
Let me go rejected and not be your
    wife."

This hero did choke her, as we under-
    stand,
And threw her in the river below the
    mill dam.
Some count this high treason; but oh!
    what a crime
To murder poor Omie and leave her be-
    hind.

Now Omie is missing, as we all do
    know,
And down to the river a-hunting they
    go.
They found her a-floating on the water
    so deep,
Which caused many people to sigh and
    to weep.

The people they gathered to behold a
    great sight.
They left her on the shores all the dark
    stormy night.
The next day a-following the inquest
    was held.
No doubt but the jury their minds they
    could tell.[32]

---

these songs are really about requires the listener to supply the missing specifics. Those who can't are likely to be perplexed, as the illustrated blues ballad text illustrates.[33]

Inferable from the text are only a few specifics: that "Louieville" was the site of the event being referred to; that someone named Gordon shot someone named Arch in the right arm; that Arch apologized to Gordon for some unspecified reason; and that Arch is the only son of the "Guvnor," who is told not to cry, since Arch "has to die" because of what living "a sporting life" has done to him.

To understand and appreciate the song,

one must be able to supply the missing details by knowing the whole tale beforehand. The story, in this case, is that of an actual event that occurred on April 30, 1895. A man named Fulton Gordon discovered Archibald Dixon Brown, the only son of Kentucky Governor John Young Brown, in a Louisville bawdy house. Archibald was there with Gordon's wife, who was also Archibald's paramour. Gordon surprised the couple; and when he found them together, he shot them both.

How a ballad tells the story it communicates, then, is one criterion that defines and differentiates the traditional, vulgar, and blues subsets of ballads. The "how" includes the nature and number of story details presented through the song and the presence or absence of viewpoint, judgment, or assessment. But some scholars regard these as only minimal criteria, citing additional characteristics that members of given ballad subsets have in common. Wilgus and Long, writing about the traditional ballad, for instance, state, "Its formal structure is the couplet or quatrain, rhyming *aa, abcb,* or *aabb* with or without refrain (melody frequently playing a major role in this respect)." They also assert that the meter of traditional ballads—at least those in English—is "based upon a pattern of stressed syllables (4–3–4–3) and relatively indifferent to the number of unaccented syllables between." Vulgar ballads, they note, also employ the quatrain as the stanzaic pattern; "[b]ut its rhyme scheme is more likely to be in couplet form and/or to incorporate internal rhyme, and its meter is markedly regular, with stereotypical relationships between stressed and unstressed syllables (e.g., iambic, anapestic)." There is nothing unique stanzaically or metrically about the blues ballad, Wilgus and Long contend, since it shares features with both other ballad subsets.

That ballads can be readily configured

and reconfigured into varied subsets is exemplified by other "linguistic labels" that researchers use to identify them. American folklorists often single out ballads that are known or hypothesized to have been created in North America and call them *native American ballads,* making place of origin the principal criterion for creating a specific subset. A *religious ballad* subset recognized by some scholars obviously has the nature of the characters or subject matter of the stories that the songs tell as the distinguishing criterion. Those ballads that are groupable into a subset because they have the potential to make listeners/readers laugh are sometimes called *humorous ballads.* Some other designators for ballad subsets include *cowboy, Robin Hood, historical, Negro, outlaw, tragic, romantic,* and *supernatural* ballads, with the elements common to members of those subsets being obvious from the everyday language used to designate them.[34]

The fact that individual folklore examples such as ballads may be configured into multiple and often quite different subsets might seem, to some, to be indicative of a lack of intellectual rigor in ordering the phenomena that constitute the data base for folkloristics. Yet what the multiplicity and variety of sets and subsets reveal is that folklore not only takes many forms, but that it is also multifaceted, with purpose, use, structure, content, style, and function all being relevant and important. Any one or combination of these multiple and varied aspects of a folklore example might emerge as dominant in a specific situation or for a particular inquiry, for all folklore examples can be found in multiple and varied contexts, and all are conceptualized and characterized in multiple and varied ways by all human beings, including scholars. It is for this reason that a particular story, for example, may be identifiable in one situational context as a fairy tale, in another as a legend, and in yet another as a myth, as the eminent folktale scholar Stith Thompson notes repeatedly in his publications.[35] It is also the reason why, as Wilgus and Long point out, certain versions of a song (such as "Young Beichan") can be identified as traditional ballads on the basis of one criterion (e.g., because of the song's inclusion as ballad number 53 in Child's collection) and also as vulgar ballads on the basis of another criterion (e.g., because of the way they tell the story they communicate).[36]

The processes of ordering phenomena into sets and subsets are essential for classifying data. Yet all classification schemes, like the sets and subsets that are their foundations, are hypothetical and hence tentative and potentially temporary. As inquiry evolves, the folkloristic data base, like data bases in all fields, inevitably grows. As new data come under scrutiny, classification schemes and the sets and subsets that undergird them are continuously scrutinized and assessed. Some sets and subsets in folkloristics, as in other fields, endure over time; others become irrelevant or indefensible, for the continuous and ongoing processes of defining and classifying phenomena involve selection and evaluation as well as accommodation. Furthermore, new "unions" can result, as has been the case in folkloristics with the recognition of hybrid sets such as the *mythological legend* ("legends [that] have grown up around such Biblical stories as the Garden of Eden and the Flood"[37]) and the *riddle joke* (also known as the *joking riddle*)—e.g., "How does an elephant hide in the jungle?" ("It wears green sneakers"); "Why did the Moron cut a hole in the rug?" ("To see the floor show"); "How many poets does it take to change a light bulb?" ("Three—one to curse the darkness, one to light a candle, and one to change the bulb").

The Concept of Type

Folklore is describable not only in terms of the genres of which folkloristic data are examples, but also on the basis of identifiable and distinguishable *types*. The songs "Babylon" and "Naomi Wise" discussed above can be identified generically as *ballads* because both are songs that have as their objective to tell a story, and singing is the means of telling the story in each. But each also tells a distinctive tale; and both are regarded as examples of folklore because each is known to have been sung by multiple individuals at multiple times and in multiple places. The title "Babylon" or "Naomi Wise," then, does not merely identify a song sung at one time and place by one individual to one particular audience. It is also the designator of a *type set*, the members of which can all be conceptualized as *versions* of the same *ballad type* because all tell what one can conceive to be the same story, and all do so in what one can judge to be essentially the same way. Therefore, all singings of a song one can identify as "Babylon" or as "Naomi Wise" because of the common story they tell and the comparable way they tell that story can be organized into a type set that is itself identifiable as "Babylon" or "Naomi Wise." Moreover, every member of the set can be regarded as a version of "Babylon" or "Naomi Wise" and hence as a version of the same ballad.

Students of traditional tales were the first to demonstrate the centrality of type sets in folkloristics. Pioneering researchers beginning with the Grimms discovered through their investigations that certain stories are communicated repeatedly, either orally or both orally and through writing. By calling attention to this fact, they laid the foundation for a conceptualization of each telling of a traditional tale as a *folkloristic datum*, on the one hand, and as a a *version of a distinctive tale type,* on the other.

A combination of generic and type sets serves as the basis for the principal classification scheme that folktale researchers employ. Finnish folklorist Antti Aarne (1867–1925) created the first tale-type index, *Verzeichnis der Märchentypen* (Index of Folktale Types), Folklore Fellows Communications 3 (Helsinki, 1910). In compiling it, Aarne sought to create a system in terms of which folklorists throughout the world could identify, classify, and locate versions of particular folktales. Acknowledging that the scheme he devised represented principally the range of folktales then known in Northern Europe, and that it was intended only as a practical research guide, Aarne divided folktales into three principal generic subsets: animal tales, ordinary folktales, and humorous tales. He also discerned subsets in each of these generic groupings, based on the identities of the principal characters or on the nature or selected aspects of a tale's content. He identified animal tale subsets, for example, by the kinds of animals involved in the action. He distinguished among ordinary folktales based on whether they are magical, religious, romantic, or concerned with the actions of stupid ogres. He differentiated among humorous tales according to who their principal characters are—numskulls, married couples, parsons, or liars.

While these generic groupings and subgroupings constitute the overall organizational scheme for Aarne's work, the foci of his index are the individual entries. Each entry is identified by a number and descriptive title—for example, Type 1, *The Theft of Fish,* and Type 300, *The Dragon-Slayer.* Furthermore, each entry identifies not only a particular story, but also multiple storytellings that can be brought together into a single type set and identified as versions of the same tale type because of the number and nature of similarities discernible in the plots of the tales told during each. As used by folklorists, then, *tale type* is a term that identifies a group of stories that are configurable into a set and identifiable in a common way because they share a common plot. To designate a story by a number and/or descriptive title from Aarne's index is to identify it as one of multiple tellings of a particular story and hence as one of multiple versions of the same tale type.

Aarne isolated and indexed 540 distinguishable tale types in his work. But he included 1,940 numbered slots, leaving a majority of them open so the index could be expanded and new types added. Aarne planned to enlarge his index, but died before he could do so. Finnish folklorist Kaarle Krohn (1863–1933) invited the American folktale scholar Stith Thompson (1885–1976) to revise and expand Aarne's work. Thompson did so twice: as *The Types of the Folk-Tale: Antti Aarne's Verzeichnis der Märchentypen,* Folklore Fellows Communications 74 (Helsinki, 1928), and *The Types of the Folktale: A Classification and Bibliography,* second revision, Folklore Fellows Communications 184 (Helsinki, 1961).

Thompson added two generic subsets (formula tales and unclassified tales) to Aarne's original three, and increased the number of type slots in the system from 1,940 to 2,499. In the 1961 revision, Thompson identifies, numbers, and characterizes the plots of 3,229 distinguishable tale types and subtypes. He also expands the geographical coverage to include the range of folktales found in all of Europe, Western Asia, and places settled by peoples from these areas.[38] An outline of Thompson's classification scheme with subgroupings and the ranges of tale-type numbers appears in Box 4–8.

Folklorists throughout the world utilize the 1961 revision of the tale-type index. They supplement it with complementary

BOX 4–8
Tale Classification Used in Stith Thompson, *The Types of the Folk-Tale,* 2d rev. (Helsinki, 1961)

I. Animal Tales

1 – 99	Wild Animals
100 – 149	Wild Animals and Domestic Animals
150 – 199	Man and Wild Animals
200 – 219	Domestic Animals
220 – 249	Birds
250 – 274	Fish
275 – 299	Other Animals and Objects

II. Ordinary Folktales

300 – 749	A. Tales of Magic
300 – 399	Supernatural Adversaries
400 – 459	Supernatural or Enchanted Husband (Wife) or Other Relatives
460 – 499	Supernatural Tasks
500 – 559	Supernatural Helpers
560 – 649	Magic Objects
650 – 699	Supernatural Power or Knowledge
700 – 749	Other Tales of the Supernatural
750 – 849	B. Religious Tales
850 – 999	C. Novelle (Romantic Tales)
1000 – 1199	D. Tales of the Stupid Ogre

III. Jokes and Anecdotes

1200 – 1349	Numskull Stories
1350 – 1439	Stories about Married Couples
1440 – 1524	Stories about a Woman (Girl)
1525 – 1574	Stories about a Man (Boy)
1525 – 1639	The Clever Man
1640 – 1674	Lucky Accidents
1675 – 1724	The Stupid Man
1725 – 1849	Jokes about Parsons and Religious Orders
1850 – 1874	Anecdotes about Other Groups of People
1875 – 1999	Tales of Lying

IV. Formula Tales

2000 – 2199	Cumulative Tales
2200 – 2249	Catch Tales
2250 – 2299	Unfinished Tales
2300 – 2399	Other Formula Tales

V. Unclassified Tales

2400 – 2499	Unclassified Tales

BOX 4–9
Sample Tale Type Entries

175 *The Tarbaby and the Rabbit.* The rabbit, who has been stealing fruit from a garden, is captured by means of a tarbaby, an image with tar. The rabbit tries to make the tarbaby talk and finally becomes so angry that he strikes it. He sticks to the tarbaby and is captured. Usually followed by the briar-patch punishment for the rabbit. Motifs: K741. Capture by tarbaby. K581.2. Briar-patch punishment for rabbit.
[Following are references to published studies and texts of the tale type and a listing of places from which versions have been reported, either in print or as being on file in archives. These include Argentina, Chile, Colombia, Cuba, France, India, Japan, Latvia, the Philippines, Spain, and Puerto Rico.]

*   *   *

366 *The Man from the Gallows.* A man steals the heart (liver, stomach, clothing) of one who has been hanged [Motifs E235.4, E236.1]. Gives it to his wife to eat. The ghost comes to claim his property and carries off the man.
[Following are references to other source references, studies, and published and ar-chival texts, indicating that versions of the tale type have been recorded in such countries as Denmark, England, France, Germany, Hungary, Norway, Russia, and the United States.]

indexes that use the Aarne-Thompson sys-tem and that focus on folktales from spe-cific countries (Japan and Ireland, for ex-ample) or regions (India, Pakistan, and Ceylon, for instance, and Cuba, Puerto Rico, the Dominican Republic, and Spanish South America).[39] Sample entries from Thompson's second revision of the tale-type index are presented in Box 4–9, with explanations of the kinds of information they provide.

Folklorists normally use the word *type* only in discussions and studies of folktales. But ordering folklore examples into type sets and identifying both the sets and indi-vidual members of them in common ways are fundamental tasks and regular practices in folkloristics, regardless of the forms or genres upon which researchers focus. To identify a song as "Child 274," for instance, is to note that it can be assigned to the type set to which Francis James Child gave the number 274 and the title "Our Goodman"

in *The English and Scottish Popular Bal-lads.* How this came to pass illustrates the processes by which researchers establish type sets.

Child got the name "Our Goodman" from the first line of a text of a song in-cluded in a late eighteenth century manu-script and published in a book of Scottish songs, both authored by David Herd.[40] In his work, Child includes under number 274 and title "Our Goodman" Herd's text and an undated broadside text titled "The Merry Cuckold and Kind Wife." In doing so, Child indicates that these two songs can be conceptualized and characterized as differ-ent versions of the same ballad, and that other songs he describes in the headnote to 274 are also versions of "Our Goodman," even when they have been identified by other names and reported from non–En-glish-speaking countries (Flemish Belgium, Germany, France, and Italy being among those Child mentions). Any song that folk-

lorists identify as a version of Child 274 or
"Our Goodman" (or both), then, is one they
regard as a member of a single type set, with
all members of the set being judged to tell
the same story in essentially the same way.
The two texts of "Our Goodman" presented in Box 4–10 illustrate the kinds of
similarities and differences commonly
found among versions of a single ballad
type.[41]

BOX 4–10
Two Versions of Child 274, "Our Goodman"

Version 1

1 Hame [home] came our goodman,
     And hame came he,
   And then he saw a saddle-horse.
     Where nae [no] horse should be.
2 "What's this now, goodwife?
     What's this I see?
   How came this horse here
     Without the leave o' me?"
Recitative. "A horse?" quo she.
     "Ay, a horse," quo he.
3 "Shame fa your cuckold face,
     Ill mat ye see [poorly do you
       see]!
   'T is naething but a broad sow
     [a pig that has a litter]
   My minnie [mother] sent to
       me."
   "A broad sow?" quo he.
     "Ay, a sow," quo she.
4 "Far hae I ridden,
     And farer hae I gane,
   But a saddle on a sow's back
     I never saw nane."
5 Hame came our goodman,
     And hame came he;
   He spy'd a pair of jack-boots,
     Where nae boots should be.
6 "What's this now, goodwife?
     What's this I see?
   How came these boots here,
     Without the leave o' me?"
   "Boots?" quo she.
     "Ay, boots," quo he.
7 "Shame fa your cuckold face,
     And ill mat ye see!
   It's but a pair of water-stoups
     [water buckets or pitchers]
   My minnie sent to me."

"Water-stoups?" quo he.
     "Ay, water-stoups," quo she.
8 "Far hae I ridden,
     And farer hae I gane,
   But silver stirrups on water-stoups
     I saw never nane."
9 Hame came our goodman,
     And hame came he,
   And he saw a sword,
     Whare a sword should na be.
10 "What's this now, goodwife?
     What's this I see?
   How came this sword here,
     Without the leave o me?"
   "A sword?" quo she.
     "Ay, a sword," quo he.
11 "Shame fa your cuckold face,
     Ill mat ye se!
   It's but a porridge-spurtle
     [stick for stirring porridge]
   My minnie sent to me."
   "A spurtle?" quo he.
     "Ay, a spurtle," quo she.
12 "Far hae I ridden,
     And farer hae I gane,
   But siller [silver]-handled spurtles
     I saw never nane."
13 Hame came our goodman,
     And hame came he;
   There he spy'd a powdered wig,
     Where nae wig should be.
14 "What's this now, goodwife?
     What's this I see?
   How came this wig here,
     Without the leave o' me?"
   "A wig?" quo she.
     "Ay, a wig," quo he.
15 "Shame fa your cuckold face,
     And ill mat you see!
   'T is naething but a clocken-hen
     [sitting hen]
   My minnie sent to me."
   "Clocken hen?" quo he.
     "Ay, clocken hen," quo she.
16 "Far hae I ridden,
     And farer hae I gane,
   But powder on a clocken hen
     I saw never nane."
17 Hame came our goodman,
     And hame came he,
   And there he saw a muckle coat
     [overcoat],
   Where nae coat should be.
18 "What's this now, goodwife?
     What's this I see?
   How came this coat here,
     Without the leave o' me?"

"A coat?" quo she.
"Ay, a coat," quo he.
19 "Shame fa your cuckold face,
        Ill mat ye see!
     It's but a pair o blankets,
        My minnie sent to me."
     "Blankets?" quo he.
     "Ay, blankets," quo she.
20 "Far hae I ridden,
        And farer hae I gane,
     But buttons upon blankets
        I saw never nane."
21 Ben [inside] went our goodman,
        And ben went he,
     And there he spy'd a sturdy man
        Where nae man should be.
22 "What's this now, goodwife?
        What's this I see?
     How came this man here,
        Without the leave o' me?"
     "A man?" quo she.
     "Ay, a man," quo he.
23 "Poor blind body,
        And blinder mat ye be!
     It's a new milking-maid,
        My mither sent to me."
     "A maid?" quo he.
     "Ay, a maid," quo she.
24 "Far hae I ridden,
        And farer hae I gane,
     But lang-bearded maidens
        I saw never nane."[42]

*   *   *

Version 2

First night when I came home as
    drunk as I could be,
I found a coat a-hanging on the rack
    where my coat ought to be.
Come here, my little wifie, explain
    this thing to me,
How come a coat a-hanging on the
    rack where my coat ought to be?
You blind fool, you crazy fool, can't
    you plainly see?
It's nothing but a bed-quilt your
    grandma sent to me.
I've traveled this world over a thou-
    sand miles or more,
But pockets upon a bed-quilt I never
    have seen before.

The second night that I come home as
    drunk as I could be,
I found a horse in the stable where my
    horse ought to be.

p I/M

Come here, my little wifie, 'n' explain
    this thing to me,
How come a horse in the stable where
    my horse ought to be?
You blind fool, you crazy fool, can't
    you plainly see?
It's nothing but a milk-cow your
    grandma sent to me.
I've traveled this world over a thou-
    sand miles or more,
But saddle on a milk-cow's back I
    never have seen before.

The third night that I came home as
    drunk as I could be,
I found a head on the pillow where my
    head ought to be.
Come here, my little wifie, 'n' explain
    this thing to me,
How come another head on the pillow
    where my head ought to be?
You blind fool, you crazy fool, can't
    you plainly see?
It's nothing but a cabbage-head your
    grandma sent to me.
I've traveled this world over a thou-
    sand miles or more,
But a mustache on a cabbage-head I
    never have seen before.[43]

Another type-set-based reference work is Archer Taylor's *English Riddles from Oral Tradition* (Berkeley and Los Angeles: University of California Press, 1951). Like Aarne-Thompson and Child, Taylor assigns numbers to riddles after first classifying them as distinguishable types. Each number thus designates not just one riddle, but a set of riddles, all of which can be regarded as versions of the same riddle type because they all characterize the same phenomena in identical or only slightly differing ways. Taylor distinguishes and identifies 1,749 riddle types, many of which are divisible into subsets. Among those that had been recorded and reported in notable numbers of versions by the time Taylor's work was published are 587, Summer and Winter Clothing ("In spring I am gay, / In handsome array; / In summer more clothing I wear; / When colder it grows, / I fling off my clothes; / And in winter quite naked appear"—answer, a tree), and 738, Cannot Put Humpty Dumpty Together Again ("Humpty Dumpty sat on a wall, / Humpty Dumpty had a great fall, / All the king's horses and all the king's men / Couldn't put Humpty Dumpty together again"—answer, egg).

Commenting on one frequently documented riddle type, Taylor writes, "English riddlers show a great liking for the personification of a bottle as a person whose head is chopped off, whose blood is drunk, and whose body is left standing."[44] He assigns the number 805 to the riddle and identifies it as "Take Off His Head; Drink His Blood: A Bottle." Taylor presents twenty-three texts of this riddle type, designating all versions by the number 805 and suffixing a different lower case letter to each to distinguish among them. Six of Taylor's twenty-three versions are presented in Box 4–11. They illustrate the kinds of similarities and differences one finds among members of riddle type sets.

The nature of the relationship described rather than the words used to characterize

---

BOX 4–11
Versions of the Riddle "Take Off His Head, Drink His Blood: A Bottle"

805b .
As I went along the river, / I met a man. / I chopped off his head, / I drank his blood. (Answer: a bottle of rum) (recorded in Bermuda)

805d.
When I was goin' 'cross London Bridge, / I met an old man on de way. / I brek his neck an' drank his blood, / An' t'rew his body away. (Answer: a bottle of liquor) (recorded in Virginia)

805h.
As I was walkin' down th' road / I met up with my very best friend, / I pulled off his head an' drinked his blood / And left his body stand! (Answer: a bottle of whiskey) (recorded in the Ozark Mountain region of the United States)

805n.
Around the rick, around the rick, / And there I found my uncle Dick; / I screwed his neck, I sucked his blood, / And left his body lying. / What was it? (Answer: a bottle of wine) (recorded in England)

805o.
As I was going over London Bridge, / I saw two men a-hanging, / I ate their flesh, and drunk their blood, / And left their bones a-hanging. (Answer: two bottles of wine) (recorded in England)

805u.
As I was going across London Bridge, / I met my sister Sally. / I bit off her head and sucked her blood, / And left her body standing. (Answer: bottle of wine) (recorded in Illinois)[45]

---

it is the basis for configuring examples of beliefs into type sets. This is exemplified in Wayland D. Hand, *Popular Beliefs and Superstitions from North Carolina*, The Frank C. Brown Collection of North Carolina Folklore, volumes 6 and 7 (Durham: Duke University Press, 1961, 1964). Hand configures the beliefs he focuses on into fourteen generic subsets, with members of each subset exhibiting differing and sometimes multiple similarities. These include such things as common concerns with life-cycle events (birth, marriage, death), natural phenomena (weather, the human body), and the supernatural (witchcraft, ghosts).

Hand numbers entries consecutively from 1 to 8569, with each number designating both a particular belief and the type set into which it is grouped with other belief statements that characterize the same relationship. Since wording is not a defining criterion for belief as a genre, Hand does not list and number separately the alternative ways of stating beliefs, as Taylor does for riddles. In the notes that follow each entry, however, Hand describes variations when differences in wording alter the specifics of the relationship the belief statement characterizes. Number 7024 in Hand's work, for instance, is "Lightning never strikes twice in the same place." Most examples of that belief type in Hand's data base were communicated in identical or inconsequentially different words, so he does not list each one, since doing so would be repetitious. Instead, he simply gives references to places from which and/or works in which the belief has been reported. However, he cites those alternatively worded versions that are notable variations—for instance, that *old people believed* that lightning would not strike in the same place twice" (recorded in Tennessee), or that *it is safe to stand under a tree that has once been struck by lightning*" because "lightning never strikes twice in the same place" (recorded in Alabama).[46]

For some belief types, noteworthy variation in wording occurs. This is the case, for instance, with 6658, "When cats wash their faces, it is the sign of rain." Hand's notes indicate that sometimes a person specifies what part of its face the cat must wash (jaws, the right ear); when the washing

must take place (before breakfast); how the cat must wash ("with dainty touches of her velvety paw"); and where or under what circumstances the washing must be done (in the parlor, while the cat is facing east). Despite these differences, Hand regards all these alternatives as versions of a common belief and hence as members of the same type set.

Even when they have not proposed or developed indexes of types, folklorists still configure their data into type sets and identify both the individual examples and the set in a common way. There is no type index of games, for instance. But designations such as "London Bridge," "Red Light, Green Light," and "Simon Says" are used to identify distinguishable game type sets as well as each member of those sets, and hence every playing and documented version of those games.[47] Similarly, while no one has yet devised a comprehensive index of legends, folklorists have come to identify these tales linguistically in specific ways (as "The Vanishing Hitchhiker," "The Kentucky Fried Rat," and "The Choking Doberman," for example), indicating that they order stories with similar plots into type sets and regard each member of each set as a version of a particular legend type.[48] The number and nature of similarities discernible in the two texts presented in Box 4–12 are the bases for identifying them as records of two tellings of the same story, and hence as two versions of a single legend type that folklorists identify as "The Death Car."

The discussion above reveals that phenomena are identifiable as folklore only when and because they can be configured with like phenomena into type sets. Every example of folklore is, by definition, a member of a type set and therefore a version of a specific type and one of multiple versions of a particular story, song, tune, dance, riddle, basket, belief, chair, etc. Therefore, when folklorists identify a phenomenon as an example of folklore because of its similari-

BOX 4–12
The Death Car

Version 1

A white fellow from around here [Mecosta, Michigan], named Demings, committed suicide in his car back in 1938. He had a 1929 Model-A Ford, painted all over with birds and fish; it would catch your eye right away. He was going with a girl who didn't care much for him, Nellie Boyers, and it seems they had a fight when he took her on a date to the Ionia State Fair. When he came back he pulled off the road into the brush, stuck a gas hose onto the tailpipe, turned the motor on, and sniffed the other end of the hose. He must have prepared for it, because he had the cracks under the seat and on the floorboards all chinked up with concrete, to keep the gas from escaping. He killed himself in August, and no one found him till October, in the hunting season. A guide kept going out to the spot where Demings had parked; he'd see the car and say, "That fellow's always hunting when I am." Finally he took a close-up look, and smelled the body.

A used-car dealer in Remus sold the car at a reduced price to Clifford Cross. Cliff did everything possible to get the smell out; he upholstered it, fumigated it, but nothing worked, and in the middle of the winter he would have to drive around with the window wide open. I said one time, "If I'm going to freeze to death driving with you I'd rather be out on my feet," and I got out. Another time a little white dog crawled inside while Cliff was getting gas, and started to bark from the back seat after he drove off. Cliff thought it was the dead man's ghost, and he stopped that car and shot out like the Devil was after him. Finally he give up trying to get the smell out, and turned the car in for junk.[49]

*   *   *

Version 2

You know that car dealer out on University Boulevard? Its specialty is repossessed cars. Well, they say they repossessed this red Corvette a few years ago. The owner had been murdered and hidden in the trunk. Well, this car dealer cleaned up the car, repainted it and re-carpeted the trunk, and about a week later they sold that car to some guy. But he returned the car after a week, said there was a bad smell in it that he couldn't get rid of. This happened a couple of more times with other people who bought the car, and now that dealer is stuck with the car. I think its going price is something like $100. But it serves them right. That place is a big clip joint anyway. I hope they never sell the car.[50]

ties to other phenomena documented through time and space, they invoke the concept of type set.

Conclusion

As illustrated throughout this chapter, folklore can be conceptualized and studied as a *describable entity*. Doing so involves ordering folklore examples into sets and subsets (for example, as genres, types, and subtypes), based on similarities that one discerns in them. Since the phenomena that folklorists document and study are numerous and diverse, folkloristic data can be grouped into a large number and variety of sets and subsets; and the similarities discernible among members of given sets are necessarily multiple and varied because all folklore examples are multifaceted and multicontextual. When folklorists take exception to one another's definition of a genre such as *Märchen*, myth, or legend, they often do so because they are emphasizing different facets or contexts or considering other criteria than are those whose characterizations they criticize.[51] Subjective judgment is always involved in deciding which characteristics are distinctive to a particular expressive form or what weight to give similarities and differences when determining how to classify a folklore example according to genre or type. But while differences and disputes about definition and categorization are inevitable among folklorists, as they are among scholars in all disciplines, the concepts of genre and type are fundamental in folkloristics; and the acts of configuring folklore examples into sets and distinguishing among generic and type sets are basic and essential tasks that every folklorist must carry out.

Notes

1. For filmic examples, see *On Being a Joines: A Life in the Brushy Mountains* (1980, Tom Davenport, Tom Davenport Films, color, 16mm. and VHS, 55 min.), which organizes an individual's stories (genre) into four categories, based on his experiences, and *Folk Housing in Kentucky* (1970, Lynwood Montell, narrator, Western Kentucky University, color, 16mm., 35 min.), which concerns house types.

2. Pioneering folklorists employed words in their investigations that were in common parlance among speakers of European languages at the time they were first used. These are sometimes called *emic* words, or terms for *native categories*, since they are specific to particular cultures. With time and usage, however, many of these words took on the status of technical terms and were used cross-culturally, implying that the genres they denote are universal (*etic* or analytical, as opposed to *emic* or "native," categories). Since the 1960s, some folklorists have made a point of documenting and eliciting cultural (*emic*) words

for genres and characterizing them from the point of view of people who use them. For a discussion of this distinction, see Dan Ben-Amos, "Analytical Categories and Ethnic Genres," *Genre* 2 (1969):273–301, reprinted in Dan Ben-Amos, ed., *Folklore Genres*, Publications of the American Folklore Society, Bibliographical and Special Series 26 (Austin: University of Texas Press, 1976), pp. 215–242. For additional discussion of the concept of genre in folkloristics, see Roger D. Abrahams, "Genre Theory and Folkloristics," Lauri Honko, "Genre Theory Revisited," and Dan-Ben-Amos, "The Concept of Genre in Folklore," all published in Juha Pentikäinen and Tuula Juurikka, eds., *Folk Narrative Research: Some Papers Presented at the VI Congress of the International Society for Folk Narrative Research*, Studia Fennica: Review of Finnish Linguistics and Ethnology 20 (Helsinki: Finnish Literature Society, 1976), pp. 13–43.

3. Only some, but not all, examples of every expressive form are identifiable as folklore. Since there is no expressive form/genre which consists solely of examples that are identifiable as examples of folklore, then there are no genres that are exclusively folkloristic. Therefore, although many folklorists do so, it is incorrect to speak of "folklore genres" as if such categories of phenomena actually exist. They do not.

4. Charles G. Zug, III, *Turners and Burners: The Folk Potters of North Carolina* (Chapel Hill: University of North Carolina Press, 1986). The quote is from p. 374.

5. For another example of research on material culture in which purpose is an important, although not the only, criterion for identifying and classifying objects, see John Michael Vlach, *The Afro-American Tradition in Decorative Arts* (Cleveland: Cleveland Museum of Art, 1978, reprinted by the University of Georgia Press, 1990).

6. The descriptions presented here come from the following sources: H. F. Raup, "The Fence in the Cultural Landscape," *Western Folklore* 6 (1947):1–12; Mamie Meredith, "The Nomenclature of American Pioneer Fences," *Southern Folklore Quarterly* 15 (1951):109–151; and Austin E. Fife, "Jack Fences of the Intermountain West," in D. K. Wilgus, ed., *Folklore International: Essays in Traditional Literature, Belief, and Custom in Honor of Wayland Debs Hand* (Hatboro, Pa.:

Folklore Associates, 1967), pp. 51–54. The Fife essay is reprinted in Austin E. Fife, *Exploring Western Americana,* ed. Alta Fife (Ann Arbor: UMI Press, 1988), pp. 159–166.

7. Fife, pp. 160–161.

8. Alan Dundes, "Brown County Superstitions," *Midwest Folklore* 11 (1961):25–56. The quote that follows is from p. 28. Dundes reprinted the interpretive section of the essay (pp. 25–33), but not the many pages of field data, with a new title ("The Structure of Superstition") in his book *Analytic Essays in Folklore* (The Hague: Mouton, 1975), pp. 88–94. Most of the examples of superstitions presented in the discussion that follows are taken from Dundes's work. Others are well known and cited frequently in books and essays, including such reference works as Wayland D. Hand, ed., *Popular Beliefs and Superstitions from North Carolina,* The Frank C. Brown Collection of North Carolina Folklore, vols. 6 and 7 (Durham: Duke University Press, 1961, 1964). Dundes undertook a structural analysis of superstitions because of his dissatisfaction with his predecessors' and peers' attempts to define superstitions on the basis of such other criteria as believableness or truthfulness. Such criteria are apparent in the alternative definitions of superstition presented in Box 4–1.

9. Because of the pejorative connotations *superstition* has in popular parlance, many folklorists today avoid using the word and instead identify examples such as those presented in this paragraph as *folk beliefs, popular beliefs, folk notions,* or *conventional wisdom.* See, for instance, Hand; Michael Owen Jones, "Folk Beliefs: Knowledge and Action," *Southern Folklore Quarterly* 31 (1967):304–309; Patrick B. Mullen, "The Function of Magic Folk Belief among Texas Coastal Fishermen," *Journal of American Folklore* 82 (1969):214–225; and Kenneth L. Ketner, "Superstitious Pigeons, Hydrophobia, and Conventional Wisdom," *Western Folklore* 30 (1971):1–17.

10. That utterances, however, are sometimes forced into these structures has long been realized. See, for example, the essay by Jones.

11. *Theoretical Anthropology* (New York: Columbia University Press, 1953), p. 294.

12. *The Psychology of Superstition* (London and Baltimore: Penguin Books, 1969), pp. 9–10.

13. *A Dictionary of Superstitions* (Oxford and New York: Oxford University Press, 1989), pp. v and viii.

14. Robert A. Georges and Alan Dundes, "Toward a Structural Definition of the Riddle," *Journal of American Folklore* 76 (1963):111–118. The quote that follows is from p. 113. Most of the riddles presented and discussed are cited in the Georges-Dundes essay and can be found in Archer Taylor, *English Riddles from Oral Tradition* (Berkeley and Los Angeles: University of California Press, 1951), a major riddle compilation. Another source of examples discussed is given in note 15.

15. The riddles with the answers *paddle, water lilies, mushroom,* and *eyelashes* were recorded in Zambia, Africa, in 1963, and are reported in D. F. Gowlett, "Some Lozi Riddles and Tongue-Twisters Annotated and Analysed," *African Studies Quarterly Journal* 25 (1966):139–158.

16. "The Riddle," *California Folklore Quarterly* 2 (1943):129.

17. "Riddles," in Richard M. Dorson, ed., *Folklore and Folklife: An Introduction* (Chicago: University of Chicago Press, 1972), p. 130.

18. "A Developmental Structural Account of Riddles," in Barbara Kirshenblatt-Gimblett, ed., *Speech Play: Research and Resources for Studying Linguistic Creativity* (Philadelphia: University of Pennsylvania Press, 1976), p. 118.

19. Murray B. Peppard, *Paths through the Forest: A Biography of the Brothers Grimm* (New York: Holt, Rinehart and Winston, 1971), pp. 40–41.

20. Propp's book has been translated into English with the title *Morphology of the Folktale,* 2d ed., trans. Laurence Scott and rev. and ed. by Louis A. Wagner, Publications of the American Folklore Society, Bibliographical and Special Series 9 (Austin: University of Texas Press, 1968). Quotes are from pp. 6 and 21.

21. The list provided here is derived from Propp's work and from Archer Taylor, "The Biographical Pattern in Traditional Narrative," *Journal of the Folklore Institute* 1 (1964):124–126. In the second edition of the

English translation of Propp's *Morphology* (1968), the 31 functions are characterized and discussed in detail on pp. 25–65.

22. Stith Thompson, *The Folktale* (New York: Dryden Press, 1946), p. 8.

23. *The Science of Folklore* (New York: W. W. Norton, 1964), p. 1 (originally published in 1929).

24. "The Forms of Folklore: Prose Narratives," *Journal of American Folklore* 78 (1965):4.

25. "A Two-Dimensional Scheme for the Classification of Narratives," *Journal of American Folklore* 78 (1965):23.

26. For examples on phonograph albums, see *Songs and Ballads of Newfoundland Sung by Ken Peacock* (Folkways FG 3505, 1956), and *Roger Abrahams: Make Me a Pallet on Your Floor and Other Folk Songs* (Prestige International 13034, n.d.).

27. Gordon Hall Gerould, *The Ballad of Tradition* (New York: Oxford University Press, 1932, reprinted as a Galaxy Book paperback in 1957), provides a multifaceted characterization and discussion of the traditional ballad. A complementary work that focuses on music (tunes) as well as words of traditional ballads is Bertrand Harris Bronson, *The Traditional Tunes of the Child Ballads and Their Texts, According to the Extant Records of Great Britain and America*, 4 vols. (Princeton: Princeton University Press, 1959–72). See also Bertrand Harris Bronson, *The Ballad as Song* (Berkeley and Los Angeles: University of California Press, 1969).

28. Maud Karpeles, *Folk Songs from Newfoundland* (London: Oxford University Press, 1934), vol. 2, p. 79, reprinted in Evelyn Kendrick Wells, *The Ballad Tree: A Study of British and American Ballads, Their Folklore, Verse, and Music* (New York: Ronald Press, 1950), pp. 104–105.

29. Ballads printed and distributed on broad sheets are called *broadside ballads*. Not all vulgar ballads are so disseminated, and not all broadsides are vulgar ballads. All kinds of ballads have been, and can be, printed on and transmitted by broad sheets. So the distinguishing criterion for the ballad subset called the *broadside ballad* is the print medium through which the ballads are disseminated, taught, and learned. Available book-length works on broadsides include Leslie Shepard, *The Broadside Ballad: A Study in Origins and Meaning* (London: Herbert Jenkins, 1962), and Claude Simpson, Jr., *The Broadside Ballad and Its Music* (New Brunswick, N.J.: Rutgers University Press, 1966).

30. For examples on phonograph albums, see the Archive of American Folk Song, *Folk Music of the United States, Album 12: Anglo-American Songs and Ballads* ("Naomi Wise," sung by Mrs. Lillian Short, 1941, recorded by Vance Randolph); *Doc Watson* (Vanguard VSD–79152, 1964); and *Old Time Music at Clarence Ashley's, Volume Two* (Folkways FA 2359, 1963), which includes a bibliography and discography. For more information about the ballad and events on which it was based, see Robert Roote, "The Historical Events behind the Celebrated Ballad 'Naomi Wise,'" *North Carolina Folklore Journal* 32 (1984):70–81.

31. D. K. Wilgus and Eleanor R. Long, "The Blues Ballad and the Genesis of Style in Traditional Narrative Song," in Carol L. Edwards and Kathleen E. B. Manley, eds., *Narrative Folksong, New Directions: Essays in Appreciation of W. Edson Richmond* (Boulder: Westview Press, 1985), pp. 437–482. Quotes and the ballad text are from the Wilgus-Long essay, pp. 437, 438, 440, and 441.

32. From H. M. Belden, *Ballads and Songs Collected by the Missouri Folk-Lore Society*, University of Missouri Studies 15 (Columbia, 1940), pp. 323–324.

33. "Arch and Gordon" sung by Mrs. Will Cline to D. K. Wilgus, Tape T7–1, Western Kentucky Folklore Archive, Bowling Green, Kentucky. For an example on a phonograph album in which the singer explains a song before singing it ("Stagolee"), see *The Immortal Mississippi John Hurt* (Vanguard VSD 79248, 1967).

34. The range and variety of subsets into which scholars configure ballads is readily apparent in tables of contents of, and introductions to, ballad anthologies, such as MacEdward Leach, ed., *The Ballad Book* (New York: Harper & Brothers, 1955, see "Introduction," pp. 1–44); Bartlett Jere Whiting, ed., *Traditional British Ballads* (New York: Appleton-Century-Crofts, 1955, see "Contents," pp. iii–iv, and "Introduction," pp. v–xii); and Albert B. Friedman, ed., *The Viking Book of Folk Ballads of the English-Speaking*

World (New York: Viking Press, 1956, Compass Books paperback edition 1963, see "Contents," pp. v–viii, and "Introduction," pp. ix–xxxv).

35. For example, "Fairy tales become myths, or animal tales, or local legends. As stories transcend differences of age or of place and move from the ancient world to ours, or from ours to a primitive society, they often undergo protean transformations in style and narrative purpose. For the plot structure of the tale is much more stable and more persistent than its form" (Thompson, p. 10).

36. Wilgus and Long, p. 438.

37. Thompson, p. 235.

38. Stith Thompson, *The Types of the Folktale: A Classification and Bibliography*, 2d rev., Folklore Fellows Communications 184 (Helsinki, 1961), p. 7.

39. Hiroko Ikeda, *A Type and Motif Index of Japanese Folk-Literature*, Folklore Fellows Communications 209 (Helsinki, 1961); Sean O'Súilleabháin and Reidar Th. Christiansen, *The Types of the Irish Folktale*, Folklore Fellows Communications 188 (Helsinki, 1963); Stith Thompson and Warren E. Roberts, *Types of Indic Oral Tales: India, Pakistan, and Ceylon*, Folklore Fellows Communications 223 (Helsinki, 1960); Terrence L. Hansen, *The Types of the Folktale in Cuba, Puerto Rico, the Dominican Republic, and Spanish South America*, University of California Folklore Series 8 (Berkeley and Los Angeles: University of California Press, 1957). For a bibliography of tale-type indexes, see David S. Azzolina, *Tale Type and Motif Indexes: An Annotated Bibliography*, Garland Folklore Bibliographies (New York: Garland, 1987).

40. David Herd, two-volume folio manuscript, 1776, British Museum; David Herd, *The Ancient and Modern Scots Songs, Heroic Ballads, etc., Now First Collected from Memory, Tradition, and Ancient Authors*, 2 vols. (Edinburgh, 1776).

41. Other works which classify ballads according to type sets are two books by G. Malcolm Laws, Jr.: *American Balladry from British Broadsides*, Publications of the American Folklore Society, Bibliographical and Special Series 8 (Philadelphia, 1957), and *Native American Balladry: A Descriptive Study and a Bibliographical Syllabus*, Publications of the American Folklore Society, Bibliographical and Special Series 1 (Philadelphia, 1950,

rev. ed., 1964). Works that use Child's indexing system and both supplement and complement his massive work are Tristram P. Coffin, *The British Traditional Ballad in North America*, rev. ed., Publications of the American Folklore Society, Bibliographical and Special Series 2 (Philadelphia, 1963), rev. and enl. by Roger deV. Renwick (Austin: University of Texas Press, 1977); and Bronson, *The Traditional Tunes of the Child Ballads*, which includes information in vol. I, pp. 100–119, about versions available on phonograph record, such as *Child Ballads Sung By Ewan MacColl* (Folkways FG 3509, 1961), and the Archive of American Folk Song, *Folk Music of the United States: Album 12—Anglo-American Songs and Ballads* ("Our Goodman" sung by Orrin Rice, 1943, recorded by Artus M. Moser).

42. From Francis James Child, *The English and Scottish Popular Ballads*, 5 vols. (Boston: Houghton Mifflin, 1882–98), "274. Our Goodman," Text A, vol. 5, pp. 91–92; reprinted from a 1776 work.

43. This version was sung by Dan Tate, Fancy Gap, Virginia, on June 1, 1962, and recorded by George Foss. Bronson got it from the Archive of American Folk Song recording No. 12,005 (A11) and printed it in his *The Traditional Tunes of the Child Ballads*, vol. 4, pp. 118–119.

44. Taylor, *English Riddles*, p. 290.

45. Taylor, *English Riddles*, pp. 291–293.

46. Hand, p. 361; emphasis added.

47. Numerous compilations of game descriptions have been published, often limited to games reported from specific countries or peoples and organized according to generic subsets. Examples include the following: Alice B. Gomme, *The Traditional Games of England, Scotland, and Ireland*, 2 vols. (London: Folk-Lore Society, 1894, 1898, reprint ed., New York: Dover Publications, 1964); William Wells Newell, *Games and Songs of American Children* (New York: Harper & Brothers, 1883, reprint ed., New York: Dover Publications, 1963); Stuart Culin, *Games of the North American Indians*, 24th Annual Report, Bureau of American Ethnology (Washington, D.C., 1907); Stuart Culin, *Korean Games, with Notes on the Corresponding Games of China and Japan* (Philadelphia, 1895, reprinted as *Games of the Orient: Korea, China, Japan*, Rutland, Vt.: Charles

Tuttle, 1958); Iona and Peter Opie, *Children's Games in Street and Playground* (Oxford: Oxford University Press, 1969); Paul G. Brewster, *American Nonsinging Games* (Norman: University of Oklahoma Press, 1953); and Brian Sutton-Smith, *The Games of New Zealand Children,* University of California Folklore Studies 12 (Berkeley and Los Angeles: University of California Press, 1959).

48. For examples and discussions of urban legends, see Jan Harold Brunvand, *The Vanishing Hitchhiker: American Urban Legends and Their Meanings* (New York: W. W. Norton, 1981), *The Choking Doberman and Other "New" Urban Legends* (New York: W. W. Norton, 1984), *Curses! Broiled Again! The Hottest Urban Legends Going* (New York: W. W. Norton, 1989); and Gary Alan Fine, *Manu-facturing Tales: Sex and Money in Contemporary Legends* (Knoxville: University of Tennessee Press, 1992).

49. From Richard M. Dorson, *Negro Folktales in Michigan* (Cambridge: Harvard University Press, 1956), p. 99.

50. Brunvand, *The Vanishing Hitchhiker,* p. 21.

51. For examples of such disagreements, see Dundes, "Brown County Superstitions," pp. 25–29, and Robert A. Georges, "The General Concept of Legend: Some Assumptions to be Reexamined and Reassessed," in Wayland D. Hand, ed., *American Folk Legend: A Symposium,* Publications of the UCLA Center for the Study of Comparative Folklore and Mythlogy 2 (Berkeley and Los Angeles: University of California Press, 1971), pp. 1–19.

5. The Dissemination of Folklore

Folklore type sets may be created, expanded, subdivided, redefined, merged, or eliminated. These processes occur as new examples of folklore are discerned, documented, and made available for study. Sometimes folklorists discover new data that require alterations in established type sets. On other occasions the phenomenon itself undergoes change as it is disseminated through time and space, thus requiring a reconceptualization. An example is an item of food—the pasty.

Yvonne R. Lockwood and William G. Lockwood trace the history of this food in one specific region.[1] The pasty (pronounced *páss-tee*) is a turnover with a pie-like crust filled with a variety of ingredients. It is the national dish of Cornwall. Cornish immigrants settled in Michigan's Upper Peninsula (U. P.) in the 1840s, working in the iron and copper industry. Finns, Italians, Slavs, and other newer immigrants to the area "looked upon the Cornish as representatives of American culture. They had status and their lifestyle was taken as a model of American life," write the Lockwoods.

These later immigrants who worked beside the Cornish and under their direction in the mines of the U. P. quickly adopted the pasty. "Some Finns were receptive to pasty because they had similar regional dishes—such as *piiraat* and *kukko*—which resemble pasty. These are dough-enveloped specialties of meat, fish, vegetables, rice, and so on, varying in size from individual turnovers to large loafs," write the Lockwoods; "many Finns came to believe the pasty was a Finnish food. In a similar way, some Italians in the U. P. also regard the pasty as Italian."

Although the Lockwoods do not use the term *type* or *subtype*, these constructs dominate their study. They write, "The content of the pasty, as it developed in the U. P., is a standardization of but one of the many Cornwall variants: a basic mixture of meat, potatoes, onion, rutabagas, and/or carrots. Although some variation still occurs, it cannot deviate far from this particular combination of ingredients and still qualify as pasty," that is, a particular type set.

Other aspects of pastymaking complicate the creation of a type set, at once

Figure 5–1: Maxine Tarvin, a former Upper Peninsula resident living in Ohio, in her kitchen with a tray of pasties (photo by Yvonne R. Lockwood).

suggesting the need for expansion or subdivision of the set. The crust, for example, may be either puff pastry or similar to American piecrust (although less flaky). Ingredients may be layered so that meat juices and seasonings percolate down through the vegetables. "Sealing the pasty is another area for variation," write the Lockwoods. Older "Cousin Jacks" and "Cousin Jennies" insist a "real" Cornish pasty is sealed by "making a rope," a method of tightly closing the dough across the top of the pasty. But many seal it like a pie, i.e., by pinching, folding, or crimping the edges. Some pasty makers (particularly those of Cornish descent) add initials indicating for whom the pasty is intended. These are formed from dough and baked on top of one end. Some insert toothpicks.

Some of the differences in ingredients and methods of preparation result from the association of the pasty with particular ethnic groups. For instance, write the Lockwoods, "rutabagas in pasty are said to be Cornish and carrots Finnish. Pasty accompanied by buttermilk is regarded as a Finnish ('bad') habit, especially by the Cornish. 'Chipping' rather than chopping the meat and rutabagas, closing with a 'rope,' and layering ingredients, are known as Cornish."

"Marked changes are now occurring in pasty; it is rediversifying," write the Lockwoods. While it was once possible to devise a pasty type set, or pasty subtypes based on variations in ingredients and techniques associated with ethnic groups, the differences have increased dramatically in number and relative importance. For example, people now include kidneys, peas, and a variety of other ingredients in pasty, or they prepare pasty with condensed onion or mushroom soup, or they serve pasty with gravy. Accompaniments and condiments have become highly variable, such as serving pasty with catsup, chowchow pickles, crisp vegetables, tea, and beer. "Originally

pasty was hand food," write the Lockwoods. "However, more and more Yoopers now eat pasty on plates with forks. . . . Once pasty rests on a plate, it lends itself to innovations that some regard as abuse: its crust is broken in the center, releasing its moisture and heat, and it is smothered with butter, gravy, or other substances." Furthermore, "Although the half-moon shape remains standard, a common family version has evolved known as 'pasty pie'"; others make an oversized half-moon shape that they cut in two on serving.

Commercialization has contributed to this diversification, write the Lockwoods. Health food stores offer a vegetarian version, often with whole wheat crust. Other restaurants make pasty with cheese, bacon, or chili topping. Some sell pizza pasty (with the ingredients enfolded in pizza dough, like calzone).

Normalform

Whatever the expansion, subdivision, merger, or redefintion of the type set, there still exists the notion of what the pasty is or should be. This concept is the *normalform*. It lies at the basis of configuring phenomena into type sets in folkloristics. Every researcher, like every other human being, develops an idea of what constitutes the normalform of a folklore type. Often this derives from the version of the type one learns first. It may also relate to one's having given a particular version a unique stylistic signature in performance. "'Barb'ry Allen' as I sing it has got seventeen verses," Berry Sutterfield of Marshall, Arkansas, told collector John Quincy Wolf; "and if you hear somebody sing it with more or less than seventeen verses, it ain't right."[2]

An example of developing a normalform in the process of constructing a type set is Archer Taylor's study "The Shanghai Gesture."[3] Taylor had been intrigued by the name for years, having seen it used as the title of a play by John Colton, published in 1926. In a preface to the play, John D. Williams describes the gesture, which consists of putting the thumb to the nose and extending the fingers, and emphasizes its use to scoff. He attempts to relate the name to the verb *to shanghai.*

Taylor rejects this connection of the Shanghai Gesture to a term referring to the use of trickery to secure sailors for voyages to the Orient. Instead, he suggests the name refers to the New Zealand and Australian word *shanghai,* meaning a beanshooter, catapult, or slingshot. "In the gesture the thumb and forefinger are spread like the letter Y and therefore resemble the arms of the toy," writes Taylor. "I have not learned why the toy is called a shanghai, but its shape is an adequate explanation of this name for the gesture." The gesture has also been called "Spanish fan," "to take a sight," and the like, which derive from a kindred comparison of the gesture to a familiar object.

In his preface to Colton's play, Williams says the right hand is used for the gesture. Examples Taylor documented indicate that "makers of the gesture may be indifferent about the choice of hands, but show a definite and perhaps significant preference for the left hand." Moreover, the "gesture may be made more conspicuous and emphatic by waving the hand back and forth or by wiggling the fingers." The gesture can be emphasized further by "joining the thumb of the second hand to the extended finger of the first hand and . . . by wiggling the fingers of both hands, waving the hand back and forth, or grinding an imaginary coffeemill with the outer hand." Taylor refers to variations using both hands as "the tandem gesture."

The use of the word *fan,* writes Taylor, may refer to the back-and-forth motion of the hands. However, a few references call

for placing the hands palm to palm and then unfolding them into the gesture as the thumb is brought into contact with the nose, which resembles the unfolding of a fan.

For Taylor, then, based on his early reading of a description of the gesture and perhaps from his own firsthand observation of someone making it, the normalform of the Shanghai Gesture consists of at least one hand, fingers extended and the thumb touching the nose. The purpose—an important aspect of the gesture's normalform—is to convey derision or insolence. The fingers may be wiggled, but they need not be. A variation is the tandem gesture in which the two hands are joined; they may be moved in various ways to add emphasis.

Taylor searched archaeological, archival, and bibliographical documentation for descriptions, depictions, and interpretations of gestures. He discounted some references because they only mentioned putting a finger near the nose or holding an open palm close to the face. He found nothing quite like the postulated form of the Shanghai Gesture—the normalform he had constructed as well as the type set he was developing—until the sixteenth century.

In Rabelais's *Pantagruel* (1532), Taylor discovered a passage describing a dispute in sign language between Panurge and an Englishman. Panurge lifted his right hand, put his thumb to his right nostril, shut his left eye, and made the other eye wink emphatically. He then raised his left hand, "with hard wringing and streching forth his four fingers and elevating his thumb, which he held in a line directly correspondent to the situation of his right hand, with a distance of a cubit and a half between them," i.e., a gap of two feet or more. He lowered his hands toward the ground and finally aimed them at the Englishman's nose.

The Englishman responded by lifting his open left hand into the air, "then instantly shut into his fist the four fingers thereof, and his thumb extended at length he placed upon the gristle of his nose." Next, "he lifted up his right hand all open," then lowered and bent it downwards, "putting the thumb thereof in the very place where the little finger of the left hand had been and did close in the fist, and the four right-hand fingers he softly moved in the air." Finally, "he did with the right hand what he had done with the left, and with the left what he had done with the right," reads the passage.

"Both Panurge and the Englishman have somewhat elaborated upon the usual form of the tandem gesture," writes Taylor, referring to the apparent deviation from his conception of the normalform. "Panurge adds, as not infrequently occurs elsewhere, motions of the eyes and eyelids and holds the two hands parallel" and at least two feet apart.

The earliest illustration of the Shanghai Gesture that Taylor located is a print of 1560 by Peter Bruegel titled "La Fête des fous" (the festival of fools). A fool makes the tandem gesture with the thumb of his left hand beneath the nose rather than at the tip. "This minor variation in form does not appear to be significant," writes Taylor. From this and other evidence Taylor infers

that "the Shanghai Gesture was known in both Rome and Antwerp in the last quarter of the sixteenth century."

Taylor found other examples of the gesture, in what he conceived to be both its usual and several unusual forms, in England and the United States in the nineteenth and twentieth centuries, including references in the writings of Washington Irving, Charles Dickens, and Mark Twain. However, the gesture was considered a novelty when it came into widespread English use in the early 1800s. This suggests, writes Taylor, "that it was invented anew, or was borrowed from abroad, or was revived." Moreover, the mid-nineteenth century examples in America seem to "express incredulity rather than an insult. They show no recollection of Washington Irving's use of the gesture" in 1809, thus departing from the normalform. Some references to putting the thumb on the nose or beside it, writes Taylor, may actually refer to the gesture of laying the finger beside the nose to express awareness or shrewd knowledge of a situation; hence, several writers may have mingled two different gestures.

Taylor provides a glossary of English names for the Shanghai Gesture. Among them are "to pull bacon" (used since mid-

Figure 5–2: A detail of Peter Bruegel's "La Fête des fous" (the Festival of Fools), 1560, showing the Shanghai gesture.

nineteenth century), "coffee-milling" (current from about 1830 to 1890), "to take a double sight" (mentioned by Charles Dickens in *Sketches by Boz*), "English snooks," "fan the nose," "to take a grinder," "to make a long nose" (which has equivalents in Dutch, Finnish, French, and German), "to thumb the nose" (appparently American in origin, as in F. Scott Fitzgerald's reference to it in *Tales of the Jazz Age* [1922]), "Queen Anne's fan," "to take a sight" (derived from the naval phrase "to take a sight with a sextant"), "to cock a snook" (a Briticism), and "Spanish fan." In other words, not only does the gesture vary in nature and even meaning from Taylor's conception of its normalform, but also its name differs through time and space.

When considering the Shanghai Gesture on the European continent, Taylor discovered that early German references are difficult to interpret. Idioms such as *einem eine lange Nase machen* and *mit einer langen Nase abziehen* (making a long nose or going away with a long nose) do not refer to the Shanghai Gesture, writes Taylor, but rather to the notion, in more idiomatic English, of a "long face" or "to be down in the mouth." In France the idiom *avoir un pied de nez*, to have a long nose (to be humiliated, rather than mocked), dating from at least 1608, is similar to the German gesture of the Long Nose. The French evidence "leads to the same conclusion as the German evidence, namely, that the gesture of the Long Nose occurs . . . both earlier and more abundantly than the Shanghai Gesture and that the name for the Shanghai Gesture is derived from the name for the Long Nose."

Allusions to other gestures further complicate the issue of developing a normalform or of ordering versions into a type set. One, according to Taylor, is the Devil's Horns, which consists of "stretching out the hand with the index and little fingers extended and the remaining fingers bent in"; it signifies mockery (particularly of a

cuckold, a man whose wife has been unfaithful). "The gesture of the Ass's Ears consists in placing the thumbs of one or both hands at the temples and waving the fingers." In addition, "the gesture implies that the one who mocks observes that the persons mocked have ass's ears, that is, have been disappointed or have exhibited their folly, or he expresses his wish that they may have them." Conjectures Taylor, "Waving or wiggling the fingers in the Shanghai Gesture may have been suggested by the Ass's Ears," although the motion "might be readily explained in both gestures as an obvious means of emphasis."

Taylor concludes his study by contending that "the notion of the Shanghai Gesture is derived ultimately from the Long Nose and means much the same as 'I see that you have a long nose' or 'I wish you may have a long nose.' The Shanghai Gesture calls attention to such an observation or wish, and wiggling the fingers adds emphasis" and whimsy. He continues: "The examples that have been cited from four centuries and a dozen or more countries are in complete agreement regarding its context and use," particularly that it is a gesture of derision to which no obscene connotations cling, at least not originally.

"As far as the available evidence goes, the Shanghai Gesture"—as Taylor has conceptualized its normalform and characterized it as a type with subtypes—"is a rather recent invention that has somewhat slowly found popular acceptance," he writes. "Rabelais may have known it in 1532. Bruegel used it in 1560. Mallery certainly knew it in 1594. Paul Scarron mentioned it several times around 1650. Goethe knew it in 1775." Taylor continues, "The Shanghai Gesture rests on a very natural and readily intelligible development from the Long Nose. The spark which may have set off this development is perhaps the military salute. In the two centuries and half [sic] between Rabelais and Goethe military procedures developed rapidly and became standardized," he writes. "I am therefore inclined to regard the Shanghai Gesture, which came into use in this period, as a parody of the military salute. Such a connotation clings to it. English and American writers have used it freely after Washington Irving mentioned it in 1809 and after it had been brought to popular notice as a streetboy's gesture in London about 1810."[4]

Taylor's analysis of the Shanghai Gesture illustrates how one's notion of a normalform of a folklore type set may develop and be reconsidered throughout research. It also indicates that type is the central construct in folkloristics. Researchers like Taylor focus on questions about the existence and nature of folklore as type.

Distribution of Types

A question raised because of our ability to group phenomena into folklore type sets is what the distribution of types and subtypes is. This leads to mapping, well illustrated by European folklife atlases that indicate the locations of types of buildings, foods, stories, songs, traditional expressions and terms, and even customs and rituals. In their essay "Hay Derricks of the Great Basin and Upper Snake River Valley," Austin E. Fife and James M. Fife illustrate the process of mapping the distribution of types and development of subtypes in one region of the United States.[5]

Fife and Fife documented approximately 1,500 examples of handmade hay derricks in Utah and Wyoming. These devices help the rancher or farmer to stack hay for feeding cattle during winter. On small farms the derrick may be within the barnyard and therefore need not be mobile. With increased acreage of alfalfa came the need for a derrick that could be moved around the field where several stacks could be built with the same device. "So it is that in the

Great Basin and upper Snake River Valley there are hay derricks of most varied design and efficiency, reflecting the alfalfa production of a particular community, or the acreage of alfalfa of particular farms, or representing survivals of earlier conditions," they write.

Although important, these facts ignore some peculiar circumstances, observe the authors. Miles of dry land and mountain ranges separate the valleys. "This fact would be of no interest in explaining the geographical distribution of quilt patterns, for example, since these are easily carried from one valley to another in complete defiance of natural barriers," they state. Because of their bulk, however, hay derricks usually remain behind when a farmer moves to another valley. "Upon arriving at his new farm he will build another derrick either like his former one . . . or a new type, copying a local model the design and operating principle of which may differ somewhat from the derrick to which he had been accustomed."

The Fifes organized hay derricks into six basic type sets, with from one to four subsets of each type. Residents described a simple derrick as consisting of a single upright mast in the ground anchored by several cables. Finding no existing examples, however, the Fifes concentrate on other types and their distribution and evolution, beginning with one they designate as type 2a. Derricks of this type are anchored like the single vertical mast of type 1 (or given greater rigidity, as in type 2c), but the kinds of booms vary. (The boom supports a large fork that picks up hay from a wagon and drops it on the ground to build a stack.) Specific communities, write the Fifes, "adhere to a particular subtype." Examples of type 2 seem to dominate where alfalfa is produced on a small scale and is stacked in the barnyard.

Type 3 differs from type 2 in having a triangular base, which eliminates the need

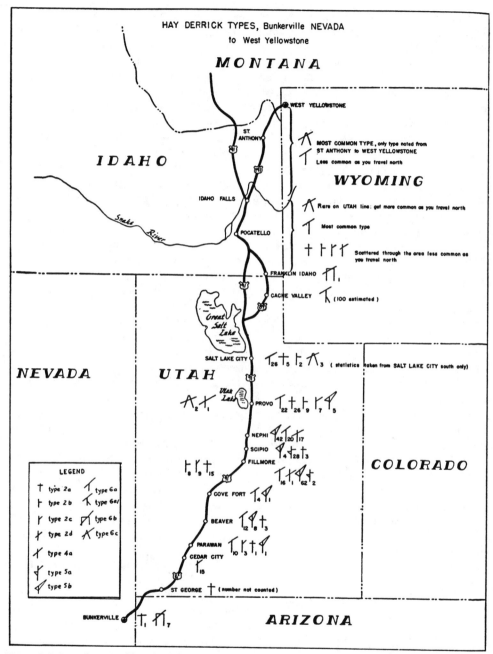

Figure 5–3: Distribution of hay derrick types (reprinted by permission of the California Folklore Society).

for costly cables for anchoring and gives the derrick mobility; with log chains attached to the base, horses or a tractor could drag it. This type proved suitable for farms with a moderate amount of alfalfa production, and sturdy enough to accommodate a fork with four tines. The later six-tine fork, however, tended to tip over the derrick because of the greater amount of hay it carried from load to stack.

Early experiments with derricks capable of being moved led to the development of types with a rectangular base (e.g., type 4). Since the derrick was then six to eight feet from the stack, the boom had to be lengthened to bring the loaded fork over the center of the stack. The derrick design became more complex (type 5). Subsequent developments simplified the design once again, thus producing a derrick that is "the most efficient, the most mobile, and the best suited to the requirements of alfalfa production on a large scale," write the Fifes. These modern stackers also "eliminated the use of costly materials from extracommunity sources."

Finally, the genesis of the derrick types in this region apparently occurred within the area itself without outside influence. "That the early settlers of this area had used hay derricks prior to pioneering the Rocky Mountain West seems doubtful," write the Fifes, "since the use of any kind of stacker must have awaited the discovery that, in a climate so cold in winter and so dry, hay may be properly stored without a permanent shelter."

Polygenesis

Besides motivating folklorists to determine the distribution of types and subtypes, configuring phenomena into folklore type sets also raises the question of why there *are* multiple examples of the phenomenon a given type set represents, and hence why there is more than one version of a distinguishable story, song, riddle, game, pot, or house, for example. Since this question can be answered in numerous ways, folklorists have responded to it by advancing alternative hypotheses.

One hypothesis is that the phenomenon represented by a given folklore type was created more than once, at different times and places by different human beings (*polygenesis*). However, these independently created phenomena are so strikingly similar in what they express and the way they do so that they can all be grouped into a single set and regarded as versions of one phenomenon. Folklorists present several hypotheses as to why this occurs.

One explanation for polygenesis is that all human societies go through the same stages of intellectual and cultural development. People, therefore, are programmed or predisposed to express the same things in the same kinds of ways because they are all products of the same evolutionary processes. Another hypothesis is that the nature and operation of the psyche are the same in all human beings, and that universal psychic states and psychological processes manifest themselves expressively in the same forms and ways in all individuals. A third interpretation is that human beings characterize or symbolize similar experiences in similar ways, making comparable expressive representations of comparable experiences configurable into the same type sets.

We discussed cultural evolutionism in chapter 2. Later, in the section on folklore as behavior (chapter 8), we examine psychologically oriented studies. Suffice it to illustrate the third hypothesis (that folklore originates polygenetically because of similar responses to similar experiences) by reference to an essay by Gary Alan Fine titled "Cokelore and Coke Law: Urban Belief Tales and the Problem of Multiple Origins."[6]

Figure 5–4: Construction of hay derrick types 2a to 5a (reprinted by permission of the California Folklore Society).

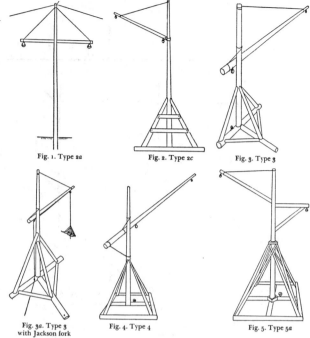

Fig. 1. Type 2a   Fig. 2. Type 2c   Fig. 3. Type 3

Fig. 3a. Type 3
with Jackson fork   Fig. 4. Type 4   Fig. 5. Type 5a

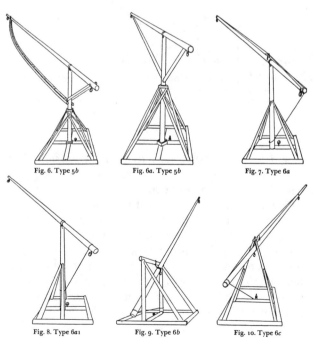

Fig. 6. Type 5b   Fig. 6a. Type 5b   Fig. 7. Type 6a

Fig. 8. Type 6a1   Fig. 9. Type 6b   Fig. 10. Type 6c

Figure 5–5: Construction of hay derrick types 5b to 6c (reprinted by permission of the California Folklore Society).

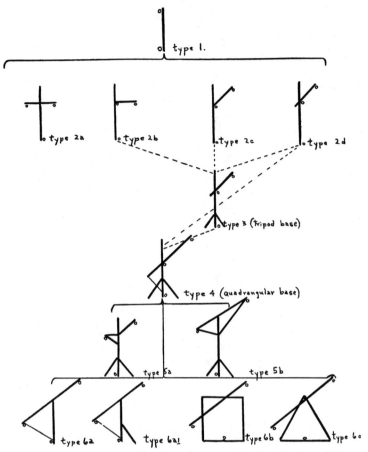

Figure 5–6: The generic development of hay derrick types of the Great Basin and Upper Snake River Valley (reprinted by permission of the California Folklore Society).

"If numerous similar events occur (of the type that potentially provokes legends), then it follows that parallel legends may develop independently," contends Fine. He considers the contamination of soft drinks by decomposed mice (and other things) "a common urban belief tale, which is said to 'reflect some of the basic anxieties of our time.'" Accounts have been collected in many states. About 20 to 30 percent of college students have heard of it, reports Fine. Some versions are told as personal experience narratives, that is, as something that happened to the teller of the story.

Fine wondered if these reports all had a single origin, or if they originated in multiple places. Court records would provide evidence of whether or not suits were ever filed, thus indicating that the experience of purchasing and consuming a contaminated soft drink had occurred more than once. Unfortunately, many suits are dropped or settled out of court; also, lower court records are not preserved. Records of deci-

Clevis made from wagon axle used to join boom and mast to derricks of types 6a and 6b prior to use of the modern ball-and-socket joint

Type 6a   A very early and primitive specimen

Type 6b

Type 6c

Figure 8   Photographs of Hay Derricks

Figure 5–7: Photographs of hay derricks (from Austin E. Fife, Exploring Western Americana, *UMI Research Press, 1988, p. 152, by permission of Alta Fife).*

sions of state appellate courts for cases involving appeal are available, however, and Fine examined these.

The earliest case was in 1914, in Mississippi. Harry Chapman, who found a mouse drowned in a bottle of Coca-Cola, sued Jackson Coca-Cola Bottling Co. and won. The local franchise of Coca-Cola appealed; the lower court ruling was affirmed. For the period 1914 to 1976, Fine discovered a total of 45 cases in which mice were found in soft-drink bottles. The 1950s had a particularly large number of cases (15). Twenty-five of the victims were males and 20 were females; 41 were adults and four were minors. Cases occurred in 23 states and the District of Columbia, with 21 instances in the 11 southern states. Of the 45 cases, 30 were decided on appeal for the original plaintiff, eight required a new trial, and seven involved a directed verdict for the defendant. Damages ranged from $50 to $20,000.

In all these cases it was not denied that a mouse or other object was in the drink. Other contaminants included roaches, maggots, worms, putrid peanuts, cigarette butts, concrete, kerosene, glass, hairpins, safety pins, paint, etc. Mice were also discovered in milk cartons, beer bottles, pies, and dishes served at some restaurants.

For each case appealed in Minnesota in 1976, 412 cases were heard at the county or district level, writes Fine. By extrapolation, there may have been as many as 18,000 instances of mice in soft-drink bottles. "One account suggests that for every ten claims brought to Coke's attention only one ends up in court. This provides the astounding figure of 180,000 bottled mice," suggests Fine. "Finally, if each of these individuals told twenty acquaintances about this remarkable, startling, and horrifying event, there may be as many as 3,600,000 people who either heard a personal experience story from a victim or were victims themselves."

Whatever the actual number of bottled mice, many Americans experienced this unpleasant surprise or know someone who did. "Because of the dramatic, horrifying qualities of the event, along with its functional value for expressing real fears about the industrialization of America, each of these versions is likely to be widely diffused," writes Fine. "Thus, multiple creation [i.e., polygenesis] and diffusion are likely to support each other in this instance. As the stories are spread by people who did not experience the events personally, they may be systematically altered to produce a better story. Similarly, when two of these conduits intersect, the future teller may combine elements from both versions, possibly assuming that they are accounts of the same event," he contends. "As new cases are diffused, stories currently circulating will be altered to fit the new facts, as the continued diffusion is given impetus by personal experiences—spread orally or through the print media."

Monogenesis

An alternative to polygenesis is the proposition that a specific story, song, ritual, game, etc., has a single origin (monogenesis)—that is, the phenomenon the type set represents was created only once and at a particular time and place by some particular person(s). Its creator and/or some other human being then reproduces it. This results in the creation of versions of the original, each of which can in turn serve as a model for the creation of additional versions. Implicit in this hypothesis are the assumptions that (1) all versions of a type are manifestations of the interactions of human beings, and (2) all versions of a type are related to each other by virtue of their descent from a common single original. The authors of most studies of folklore involving fairy tales, ballads, food (the pasty), gestures (the Shanghai Gesture), handcrafted implements (hay derricks), and other complex forms assume monogenesis rather than multiple origins.[7]

Stith Thompson, for instance, assumes there was a single origin for the tale type that is the subject of his essay "The Star Husband Tale."[8] Eighty-six versions make up the type set upon which Thompson focuses, all of them recorded from North American Indians, the only peoples from among whom the story has been reported. Thompson describes what he calls the "simplest form" of the story as follows:

> Two girls are sleeping in the open at night and see two stars. They make wishes that they may be married to these stars. In the morning they find themselves in the upper world, each married to a star—one of them a young man and the other an old man. The women are usually warned against digging but eventually disobey and make a hole in the sky through which they see their old home below. They are seized with longing to return and secure help in making a long rope. On this they eventually succeed in reaching home.

This is the normalform of the tale type "on the Pacific coast from Southern Alaska to Central California, in the Western Plateau and Plains from the Arizona and New Mexico border north far into Canada; then in the Great Lakes area and east to Nova Scotia." Thompson adds that versions with this plot are also found "in Oklahoma, Texas, and Louisiana," but that it "has not been reported in the Southwest among Pueblos or the Navaho or Apache."

Thompson states that there is variation "at some fourteen different points," each of which he identifies and treats as a *trait*. By analyzing the 86 versions of the type set with particular attention to the specifics of and variations among these traits (e.g., number of women, method of ascent to the upper world, identity of husband), notes Thompson, "it is possible to establish without room for reasonable doubt the affinities

of nearly all the versions." He proceeds to do this after summarizing the plots and giving sources by culture area and tribe for each version. On the basis of this trait analysis, Thompson reconstructs the *archetype* or hypothetical original form of the tale "from which all other versions were produced by some individual or group changes."

> Two girls (65%) sleeping out (85%) make wishes for stars as husbands (90%). They are taken to the sky in their sleep (82%) and find themselves married to stars (87%), a young man and an old, corresponding to the brilliance or size of the stars (55%). The women disregard the warning not to dig (90%) and accidentally open up a hole in the sky (76%). Unaided (52%) they descend on a rope (88%) and arrive home safely (76%).

The similarity between the earlier quoted normalform of the tale and the archetype as Thompson here describes it is obvious. Readily apparent, too, is the part that statistical data play in reconstructing the hypothetical original form, for the figures presented parenthetically throughout Thompson's description of the archetype indicate the percentages of the 86 versions in which each trait can be found.

In addition to reconstructing the archetype, Thompson also hypothesizes from his analysis that the Star Husband Tale was probably created in the Central Plains area of North America and diffused in all directions from its place of origin. He states that it is "impossible to tell just when this tale began to be told," though it obviously was created long before the late nineteenth century, when researchers first began to document and report versions of it. Furthermore, Thompson states that six distinguishable subtypes of the tale type developed as it was disseminated across the North American continent.

The most frequently reported and widely known of these he calls "the porcupine redaction." In the normalform of this sub-

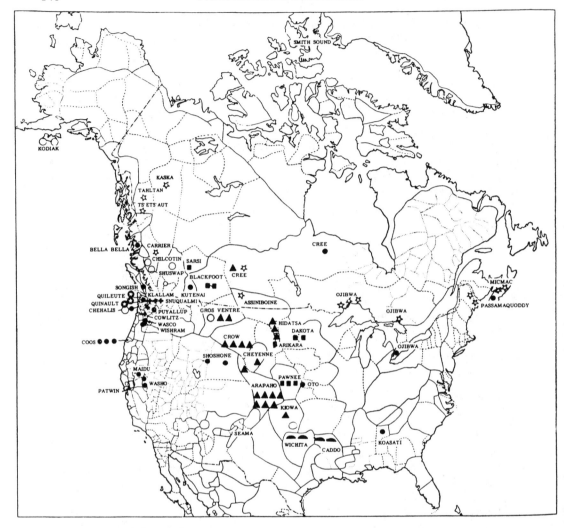

TYPES OF THE STAR HUSBAND

●	Type I.	The Basic Tale (complete and incomplete)
▲	Type II.	The Porcupine redaction
■	Type IIa.	Intermediate Versions
☆	Type III.	Trickster Animals Under the Tree
✛	Type IV.	Origin of the Transformer
✪	Type V.	The Sky War
◗	Type VI.	The Bird Rescuer
○	Fragmentary Versions	

Figure 5–8: Distribution of types of the "Star Husband" tale (by permission of Scandinavian University Press/Universitetsforlaget).

type, Thompson indicates, a girl chases a porcupine up a tree. As she climbs it, the tree stretches, and she finds herself in the upper world. The porcupine is transformed into a young man, who is the personification of a heavenly body (moon, sun, or star). The girl and young man marry, and she later gives birth to a son. As time passes, she disobeys a taboo not to dig and discovers a skyhole through which she can see the earth. With son in hand, she tries to reach earth on a sinew rope, but it is too short. Her husband discovers her and sends down a rock that kills his wife but spares the son, who safely reaches earth, experiences numerous adventures, and sometimes becomes a tribal culture hero.

The other five subtypes, Thompson indicates, differ only slightly from the reconstructed archetype. "Intermediate versions" constitute a type subset that includes tales which follow the archetype in most details but either switch as the story progresses from a focus on two girls to one or conclude with the kind of Star Boy adventure sequence usually found only in versions of the porcupine subtype. The "animal tricksters under the tree" subtype similarly follows the plot of the archetype, but depicts the two girls as being lodged in a treetop after their descent by rope from the upper world. They appeal to passing animals to rescue them, promising to become their wives in return. When an animal responds to their request, they trick him and escape, thus avoiding the promised marriage. Versions of the "origin of the transformer" subtype begin with two girls digging for roots and being taken up to the sky magically by a gust of wind, and they end with the surviving son becoming a transformer and culture hero who orders the universe as it has existed ever since. In the "sky war" subtype, the action follows that of the archetype, but serves as a prelude to the story of a war between Sky and Earth People. Finally, in the "bird rescuer"

subtype, the girl is saved by a bird (eagle or buzzard) when she is unable to reach earth because the rope she is descending from heaven on is too short. Unlike the porcupine redaction, these other five subtypes occur in only small numbers of versions and have limited geographical and cultural distribution.

The Historic-
Geographic Method

Thompson's essay on the Star Husband tale type exemplifies a study of folklore type sets according to the *historic-geographic method*, a complex of investigative procedures and analytical techniques that folklorists evolved slowly during the course of the nineteenth century.[9] Also identified as the *Finnish method* because Finnish folklorists Julius Krohn (1835–88), Kaarle Krohn (1863–1933), and Antti Aarne (1867–1925) were the first to systematize and employ it consciously in the late 1800s and early 1900s, this means of study has as its objective to determine the "life history" of a type. Employing the method entails assuming that the phenomenon the type set represents had a single origin and that it is possible for one to (1) reconstruct the original by analyzing the traits discernible in all available versions, (2) hypothesize when and where the initial version of the type was created, and (3) determine the extent to which and ways in which the type has both remained stable and varied as versions of the phenomenon the type set represents have been disseminated through time and space.[10]

In his essay "The Proverbial Three Wise Monkeys," Wolfgang Mieder, like Stith Thompson, has as his objectives to pose and answer questions about the life history of a folklore type.[11] How did the saying "Hear no evil, see no evil, speak no evil" originate, wondered Mieder, and how and why did it

become associated with three monkeys?
Mieder's search for answers to these questions led him to two existing proverb type
sets, both of which, he hypothesizes, served
as sources for the saying on which he focuses, a saying that also evolved into a
distinguishable proverb type once it became widely known and used.

Mieder discovered reference to "Audi,
vide, tace, si vis vivere in pace" in the Latin
Gesta Romanorum (Roman Stories), published in England in the fourteenth century.
This expression, which means "Hear, see,
and be silent if you would live in peace,"
appears in Tale 68, "Of Maintaining Truth
to the Last." In this story about adultery by
a soldier's wife, a rooster escapes death by
not revealing the affair. Refusing to utter
the truth to a handmaid who can interpret
its crowing, the rooster says, "Hear, see,
and say nothing if you would live in peace."

Because the expression does not appear
in collections of classical Latin, Mieder
assumes it originated in the Latin of the
Middle Ages. The proverb, he writes, spread
to other European languages "as a loan
translation" from the *Gesta*, appearing in
English as early as 1430 and French even
earlier. The proverb in French is "Pour
vivre en paix il faut être aveugle, sourd et
muet," which appeared in a ballad of that
title written in 1392 by Eustache Des-
champs:

> He who would live peacefully
> Without bodily danger
> Should have a mouth like an elephant
> Eyes as blind as a mole
> And hear only as much as a smoked herring
> If he wants to preserve his body and goods
> And act as if he were dead
> Without seeing, hearing and speaking.

The proverb was translated from Latin
and accepted into the major European
vulgate languages and became part of an
international stock of proverbs, observes
Mieder. "Nowhere, however, are there any
animals directly connected with this Euro-

*Figure 5–9: The "Three Wise Monkeys" in the
form of wood figures, purchased in December,
1978, in Detroit, Michigan, by Mr. and Mrs.
George Schumm (photo by Wolfgang Mieder).*

Figure 5–10: From Proverbi Figurati di Guiseppe
Maria Mitelli, *Testo di Lorenzo Marinese e Nota
di Alberto Manfredi sull'arte incidere (Milano:
Casa Editric Cerastico, 1963, ill. 4) (photo by
Wolfgang Mieder).*

pean proverb, and the three monkeys associated with today's saying have to come from another culture since monkeys were not indigenous to Europe."

"There is no reason why polygenesis should not be possible with proverbs," continues Mieder. "Giving advice for living a careful and secluded life by shutting off one's communicative means surely might have inspired people independently of one another to formulate a rather similar expression based on the triad of hearing, seeing and speaking. But how about the association with the three monkeys?" The answer seems to lie in complex religious traditions in Asia. Monkeys are associated with the Koshin cult in China. And in Japan, "a Koshin deity became associated with three monkeys that were believed to act as its attendants. . . . Koshin stones were erected at crossroads beginning in the sixteenth century in Japan. The Koshin symbol on the stones usually was accompanied by three monkeys covering their ears, eyes, and mouth carved on the pedestal of the stone." Koshin stones in the precinct of Tokyo reveal three seated monkeys as described above. According to Mieder, they "represent the Japanese expression 'mi-

zaru, kiki-zaru, iwa-zaru,' or 'not seeing, not hearing, not speaking,' in which the Japanese word 'zaru' meaning 'not' can also easily be associated with the word for monkey 'saru,' giving us perhaps a linguistic clue to why three gesturing monkeys are being portrayed on these stones." He continues that "to this can also be added the fact that Koshin is a deification of that day of the month that corresponds to the Day of the Monkey in Chinese tradition."

Apparently, then, there were two independent proverb types involving the precept of not seeing, hearing, or speaking, one in the West and one in the East. There is still the question of how today's English form of three monkeys representing "Hear no evil, see no evil, speak no evil" developed.

"Audi, vide, tace" disappeared from use in the nineteenth century, according to Mieder. Moreover, the three monkeys expression was not documented in Western sources before 1875. Most likely, writes Mieder, when Europeans and Americans finally came in contact with the Japanese culture in the late nineteenth century, "they must have been attracted to these curious carvings of the three monkeys,

Figure 5–11: Koshin stones from Miwa Zennosuke, Koshin-machi to Koshin-to *(Tokyo, 1935, plate 5) (photo by Wolfgang Mieder).*

bringing them back to their homelands as souvenirs and thereby making an international phenomenon out of them."

"Audi, vide, tace" only forbids speaking, whereas the Japanese expression negates hearing and seeing as well as speaking. There is no particular order to the arrangement, although the contemporary English proverb usually begins with "Hear no evil." Finally, neither of these expressions refers to evil.

The first English reference to the three monkeys proverb appeared in 1884 in an English travelers' handbook to Japan; it also contains the first mention of "evil." The editors state that the three monkeys press their hands on eyes, mouth, and ears indicating that they will not see, say, or hear anything evil. "What is important is that the word 'evil' is brought into currency in the English verbalization of the three monkeys message," writes Mieder, "one that was bound to catch on due to the popularity of such early travelers' guides." A reference in the British *Army & Navy Stores Catalogue* (1926) to the three wise monkeys demonstrates that carvings were being commercially marketed. Florence Boyce Davis (1873–1938), a Vermont poet, published a four-stanza didactic poem about the three monkeys with an illustration in a children's magazine (1922), reprinted five years later in a popular anthology.

Since the Second World War, artifacts depicting the new proverb have proliferated. Cartoonists have often used the expression to satirize politicians and public figures. Sometimes they add a fourth figure (monkey or human) as contrast to criticize the philosophy of the monkey proverb.

"Due to its vivid imagery of the three monkeys to which the proverb 'Not hearing, not seeing, not speaking' was attached in the Far East, it quickly replaced the similar European proverb of '*Audi, vide, tace*' when communication between the cultures of East and West was increased in the second half of the nineteenth century," writes Mieder about the contemporary expression. "The three monkeys and their wisdom were quickly accepted and became known in English as 'Hear no evil, see no evil, speak no evil.'" He continues: "At first, it was taken as a serious bit of folk wisdom, but as the monkey group became more and more popular through modern merchandizing efforts, people also began to put into question the philosophy of passivity expressed therein." While small statues of the traditional three monkeys still abound, there has also been an increase in humorous cartoons, advertisements, T-shirts, wall plaques, and even poems. Mieder concludes: "The three sacred and wise little monkeys have lost their innocence and have become almost a negative symbol—perhaps one of the most fascinating expressions of life's ambivalence."

Automigration

Addressing questions about the origin of the phenomenon a folklore type set represents and about the existence, nature, and distribution of multiple versions of a type necessarily raises questions about the diffusion of folklore through time and space. Folklorists conceptualize and characterize folklore as being diffused in two contrasting but complementary ways: either without or with the movement or migration of people. The former is sometimes called *automigration*; there is no special term in English for the latter.

As noted earlier, folklore has been, and can be, conceptualized as artifact and hence as a phenomenon that is passed on from person to person and handed down from members of one generation to those of the next. People everywhere learn most of their folklore directly from those with whom they interact regularly and most intimately, thus requiring no movement or migration

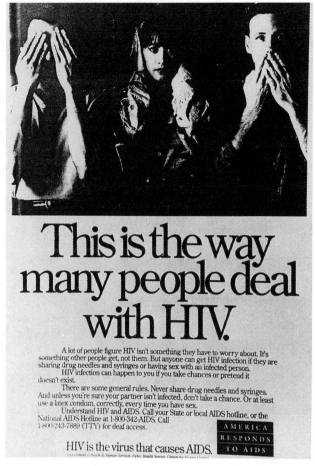

Figure 5–12: From the UCLA Daily Bruin *(by permission of Department of Health & Human Services, Public Health Service, Centers for Disease Control and UCLA* Daily Bruin*).*

for folklore to be diffused through time and space. As Fine points out in his study of Cokelore mentioned earlier in this chapter, if each of the 180,000 individuals on record who found a dead rodent or other contaminant in a soft-drink bottle "told twenty acquaintances about this remarkable, startling, and horrifying event, there may be as many as 3,600,000 people who either heard a personal experience story from a victim or were victims themselves." Furthermore, as Fine implies, these victims did not have to venture away from their usual environments or interact with people other than those with whom they regularly associate in order for the stories of their experiences to become widely known by intimates and strangers alike. As Kaarle Krohn noted in 1926 with regard to the transmission of traditions among European peasants, folklore can be diffused orally "from farm to farm, village to village, parish to parish, in a continuous chain of neighborly contacts. Like coins passing from hand to hand," he continues, folklore passing "from mouth to mouth" can be disseminated over great distances while people merely follow their daily routines.[12]

Folklore is also diffusible through time and space by automigration because versions of types can be transmitted indirectly via such phenomena as books, newspapers, magazines, radio, phonograph records, compact disks, television, videotape, film, computers, photographs, photocopies, fax machines, and three-dimensional likenesses. In order to reconstruct the history of the Three Wise Monkeys (discussed above), Mieder relies on printed versions and material representations of the proverb type. Amy Kitchener's study of joke types generated by the 1991 Persian Gulf War between United Nations Coalition and Iraqi forces illustrates how diverse and complex automigration can be as a consequence of the widespread availability and use in today's world of multiple media.

Kitchener documented multiple tellings of 129 verbal and 17 visual jokes about the war.[13] Most individuals heard and told them while interacting face-to-face with other people. For example, an undergraduate man reported having heard the joke "What can you do to stop an Iraqi bingo game? Yell out B–52," during a round of joketelling in a Los Angeles cafe. "Did you hear they [the Coalition Forces] caught Saddam Hussein? They caught him at a pay phone dialing 911" was reported by an undergraduate student who overheard her stepfather tell it to a waiter in a restaurant. A woman graduate student heard the following in two different joketelling sessions: "Did you hear they captured Saddam Hussein's son? And tomorrow they're going to Baghdad" (a pun on the colloquial expression "to bag Dad," meaning "to capture the father"). Another student reported a similar version, indicating she had heard it told by a history professor who claimed to have heard it on the news.

Yet other examples were diffused through print. For instance, "The Iraqis have a new calendar. They've dated it from January 1 to January 15. They've decided to blow off the rest of the year." This joke was reported in a graduate student publication

as having been published in the Los Angeles Times "View" section two days before the war began. Newsweek (February 18, 1991) printed a joke told by American soldiers stationed in the Persian Gulf. The Washington Post (January 26, 1991) reported the following joke: "How many gears do Iraqi tanks have? Five. One forward and four in reverse."

Television comedians and nightclub comics told Gulf War jokes, thus contributing to their diffusion. For example, Mark Russell asked, "What do Eastern Airlines [at the time recently bankrupted and grounded] and the Iraqi Air Force have in common? Departure times." Jay Leno, Johnny Carson, comedians on "Saturday Night Live," and a host of stand-up comics in clubs in Las Vegas, San Francisco, New York, Los Angeles, and other cities told jokes about the war, most of which were or subsequently became traditional.

Radio stations also disseminated Gulf War jokes. Rick Deeze on 102.7 KIIS-FM in Los Angeles reported several. One was, "How many Iraqis does it take to launch a SCUD missile? Three. One to aim the missile, one to launch the missile, and one to watch CNN [Cable News Network] to see where it landed." Some people included jokes in letters they mailed to friends and acquaintances, such as "What's the Iraqi national anthem? Duck!" Others photocopied visual jokes and handed them out. Many sent both verbal and visual jokes via fax machines. Yet others told Gulf War jokes to friends they telephoned; this included calls between the United States and Israel. For example, "Why isn't Saddam Hussein going out and getting drunk with his friends? Because he's getting bombed at home."

Finally, the computer served as an important medium of transmission. One of the jokes that appeared on computer at the University of Arizona was, "Arizona's ailing economy got you down? No problem!

I'm heading to Baghdad. I hear it's a real boom town." Another asked: "Isn't war a gas? Not yet." A third reported the following joke, crediting it to Herb Caen's column in the *San Francisco Chronicle* (February 22, 1991): "How many members of the coalition forces does it take to screw in a light bulb? We are not prepared to comment on specific numbers at this time."

Many, like the last one, use earlier joke cycles as models to frame a question. A large number are scurrilous, depicting not only Saddam Hussein but also Iraqi people in the worst possible light, demeaning women, debasing dress and customs, and mocking Iraqi technology. A few implicitly criticize the American government for not reporting enough information, while several censure CNN and other news media for reporting too much (especially the locations hit by Iraqi SCUD missiles). Whatever their rhetoric, the jokes demonstrate that examples of folklore sometimes seem to gush forth and flow rapidly through numerous channels without requiring any movement of people.[14]

Diffusion

People *do* move about and migrate from place to place, however; and when they do, they don't forget what they know, including folklore. Historical and contemporary examples of human movement and migration include travel by adventurers and explorers, religious pilgrimages, military expeditions, the forced relocation of indentured servants or slaves, the customary wandering of families or groups (e.g., the Irish tinkers and certain Gypsy populations), colonization, employment away from home (e.g., in lumbering camps, on board ships, or as nannies taking care of children), itinerant occupations (traveling salespersons, circuit preachers, skilled craftsworkers), corporate relocation to other areas, immigration to another country, migration from one region to another, and tourism. Examining the temporal and spatial distribution of versions of folklore types in conjunction with information about human movements and migrations enables folklorists to test and generate hypotheses about the nature and consequences of the mobility and adaptability of members of the human species. A study by Anna Birgitta Rooth provides an example.

In her essay "The Creation Myths of the North American Indians," Rooth reports that 250 of 300 North American Indian creation stories she analyzed can be configured into eight distinguishable "myth-types," normalforms of each of which she sketches.[15] The *Earth-Diver* characterizes the creation of the earth through the magical expansion of a small amount of sand or mud retrieved from the bottom of primeval or flood waters by a bird or swimming animal. *World-Parents* describes the creation of inhabitants of and things on the earth through a union of Sky-father and Earth-mother. The *Emergence Myth* details the emergence of humans and other living beings from their home within the earth to its surface and their subsequent migration and settlement. Spider is depicted as the being that weaves "an umbrella-like foundation for the earth" or who "fastens with his web or thread the rushes which will be the earth" in the *Spider as Creator* tale. The *Creation of the World through Struggle and Robbery* is a tale type that portrays a figure who "shapes the world and gives it its character by Theft or Robbery of the sun, fire or water; or he struggles with these 'giants' or keepers of fish or of weather." The *Ymir Type* is distinguished by its depiction of the world as being "created from the corpse of a dead giant or a dead man or woman." The *Two Creators*, as the designator of the myth-type implies, describes two beings (e.g., brothers, father and son, uncle and nephew) who jointly create the world, usually as a consequence of their competing with each other to display their relative strength, ability, endurance, or skill. Two beings are also involved competitively as creators in the *Blind Brother* myth, in which one of two brothers is blinded when the other tricks him into opening his eyes before reaching the surface while emerging from the depths of the ocean.

Versions of seven of these eight myth-types, Rooth notes, have been reported from parts of Eurasia as well as from native North America. The World-Parents, Emergence Myth, and Spider as Creator or First Being are found in South and East Asia and islands of the Pacific, as well as being reported from an area of southern North America that forms "the northern part of the Meso-American tradition-area," which "includes southern California, Arizona, New Mexico, and Texas, with some offshoots in the Plains." For four of the other five myth-types she identifies—Earth-Diver, Creation or Formation of the World through Struggle and Robbery, Ymir Type, and Two Creators—versions have been reported from throughout North America, as well as from East and North Asia and as far west as Northern and Eastern Europe. On the basis of her grouping stories with comparable plots into eight distinctive myth-type sets and determining their geographical distribution, Rooth concludes that "there is a relationship between the Meso-American tradition area and the Pacific Islands, East, and South Asia, on the one hand, and between North America and East and North Asia on the other, thus showing two channels of cultural contact between Eurasia and America."

From these remarks and others made throughout her essay, one can infer that Rooth hypothesizes that each of the seven myth-types she focuses on had a single origin at some unspecified time and place in Europe or Asia and that versions of each were brought to the New World by people migrating to North America via northeastern Asia and Alaska, on the one hand, and from Southeast Asia by way of Pacific islands to Meso-America, on the other. Rooth's data and conclusions thus provide corroborating evidence for the two hypotheses that scholars have advanced to explain how people identifiable as *Indians* or *Native Americans* got from the Old to the New World: by sea or across a hypothetical land bridge connecting Siberia and Alaska, or by sea across the Pacific Ocean.

Rooth's study of the distribution of seven creation myth-types over vast areas in the Old and New Worlds illustrates that stories are diffused through space whenever human beings migrate. Furthermore, regardless of where they settle, migrants remember and tell tales they learn in their homelands. Many such stories are diffused and perpetuated intergenerationally as well. But folklore types can also be diffused through involuntary relocation and interpersonal and intergroup contacts. A study by Alan Dundes illustrates these processes by focusing on the borrowing by American Indians in the southeastern United States of African tales diffused in historical times through slavery and the African diaspora.

In "African Tales among the North American Indians," Dundes first notes the large number of parallels between American Negro (i.e., African American) folktales characterized in Joel Chandler Harris's "Uncle Remus" compilations and stories collected from the Cherokee and the Creek Indians.[16] He cites research from the late nineteenth century suggesting that "Negro tales with African or European analogs could hardly have originated with American Indians. The direction of migration was clearly from the Old to the New World and not the other way around," for "it is hard to imagine that an American Indian tale diffused to many parts of Africa by those few American Negroes who returned to Africa." The "extensive contact and intermarriage between Negroes and Indians in the southeast and elsewhere," which is well documented historically, likely brought about the diffusion of tales from Africans to Native Americans, writes Dundes.

Dundes compares tale types found among American Indians with those reported from Western Europe and Africa. This establishes several tests regarding possible directions of diffusion, such as whether or not particular "Negro-Indian parallels" are "European tale types," whether or not allegedly American Indian tales are "found among American Indian peoples other than the Cherokee and Creek Indians," and whether or not the tales are "African tale types." He then examines what he conceives to be the normalforms of several American Indian tale types found in the southeastern United States.

Eight versions have been documented, mostly from the Creek, of the tale type in which a trickster dupes two animals in a tug-of-war in which each animal believes he is pulling against the trickster. This "tale is not reported from other American Indian groups" outside the Southeast. "It is not a European tale type. From the list of references in the *Motif-Index* under K22, Deceptive tug-of-war, one can easily ascertain the African origin of this tale," writes Dundes. He cites Kenneth Clarke's doctoral dissertation, "A Motif-Index of the Folktales of Culture Area V, West Africa" (1958), which lists 11 references, along with other documentation not reported by Clarke.

Dundes discusses parallels for other types as well. He concludes with mention of the rabbit-trickster dispute among earlier researchers, citing the contention by James Mooney in 1888 (which continues to be accepted) that the Cherokee rabbit trickster could not have been a borrowing from African Americans. Dundes insists that "the rabbit does *not* figure as a trickster in most North American Indian folklore rep-

ertoires." Moreover, in East Africa, which was a source for slaves along with West Africa, the hare is the principal trickster figure. "Therefore since the rabbit is not a trickster figure outside the southeast in American Indian folklore and since there can be no question that African narrative elements were introduced into American Indian tales, one can plausibly argue that the rabbit trickster figure so popular in American Negro tradition is African, not American Indian," contends Dundes.

On the basis of inventorying, comparing, and considering the geographical distribution of versions of selected tale types and motifs reported from African Americans and Native Americans in the Southeast, Dundes implies two things. First, Africans who were brought to the United States as slaves remembered and told versions of stories they had learned in their homelands, with many tale types having been perpetuated intergenerationally for more than two centuries among the slaves' descendants. Second, through their long and close interactions with African Americans (including intermarriage), Native Americans (particularly Creeks and Cherokees) learned versions of some of these African-based tale types and subsequently told them with sufficient frequency that the types became traditional among their own peoples. Dundes's essay thus illustrates two ways that folklore can be diffused: through the involuntary relocation of people (in this case, by enslavement), and through a process of "borrowing" that often results when people interact.

Whether folklore is diffused because of or without the movement or migration of people, the fact that it *is* transmissible raises questions about the relative stability of the phenomena folklore type sets represent. Since similarities among phenomena constitute the bases for ordering them into folklore type sets, similarities must always be and remain qualitatively greater than differences for a phenomenon to be regarded as a member of a type set and hence as a version of a type and as an example of folklore. But as Thompson's study of the Star Husband Tale (discussed above) indicates, variation does occur; and often the number and/or nature of differences leads the folklorist to group some members of a type set into subsets and to construct normalforms of both. Since subsets of type sets are definable only in terms of and in conjunction with types, the two always coexist. But differing criteria are used to define subsets.

Sometimes the versions of a type that are configurable into a subset are widely distributed geographically. This is the case, for instance, with what Thompson calls the "porcupine redaction" of the Star Husband Tale. Although versions of it have not been reported from as extensive an area as have versions of the archetype, the porcupine redaction is nevertheless widely known and told in North America. Subsets of types that are not limited in their geographical distribution are usually called *subtypes* by folklorists.

Versions of type subsets are not always boundlessly distributed, however. Sometimes the versions that constitute the subset of a tale, song, proverb, riddle, or other kind of folklore type are found only in a particular country, region, or language-speaking area (e.g., Israel, the Balkans, among speakers of Celtic languages). Noting that folklore, like plants, must often be adapted to specific places in order for it to survive, Swedish folklorist Carl Wilhelm von Sydow borrowed the word *oicotype* from botany to identify subsets of types that are delimited geographically, culturally, or linguistically.[17] Von Sydow exemplifies this concept by noting, for instance, that in the Slavic oicotype of Tale Type 530, *The Princess on the Glass Mountain*, the sought-after princess is in a high tower rather than atop a glass mountain, and that in the Indian oicotype she is on a "high palisade."[18] According to von Sydow, oicotypification usually occurs when an "active tradition bearer" or "traditor" moves to a different community and discovers that the traditional tales he or she knows are not completely compatible with those of the new environment. The traditor may decide to tell the tales anyway, changing them as necessary to make them meaningful to their new audience members and conformable with their storytelling norms. Eventually, a tale may become "fully acclimatised; but then it develops by degrees into an oicotype separate from that of the country of origin." However, states von Sydow, "oicotypification also takes place . . . if a people is divided up into separate cultural spheres, or further, gives birth to new, separate peoples, so long as they had, before the division, common traditions that afterwards survived."[19]

Versions of types are sometimes also grouped into subsets on the basis of the development of distinctive normalforms within individual communities. This may occur as a consequence of a process of *localization*, with community members using local place or proper names in their versions of stories or songs, for example, or eliminating or adding obscene references or supernatural elements in narratives to create a normalform of the type that is compatible with community norms and distinctive to that locality. The process by means of which such normalforms of types are constructed is also sometimes identified as *communal re-creation*, since the evolution of the local normalform requires a transformation of the normalform of a type and usually involves multiple members of a community instead of a single individual.[20]

Subsets of types may also be temporally rather than spatially bounded. Tristram P. Coffin hypothesizes, for example, that more recently reported versions of many Anglo-

BOX 5–1
"Mary Hamilton"

Version 1 (1824)

1 Word's gane to the kitchen,
    And word's gane to the ha,
    That Marie Hamilton gangs wi
        bairn
        [is with child]
    To the hichest [highest] Stewart of
        a'.

2 He's courted her in the kitchen,
    He's courted her in the ha,
    He's courted her in the laigh [low]
        cellar,
    And that was warst of a'.

3 She's tyed it [the baby] in her
        apron
    And she's thrown it in the sea;
    Says, "Sink ye, swim ye, bonny
        wee babe!
    You'll neer get mair o me."

4 Down then cam the auld queen,
    Gould tassels tying her hair:
    "O Marie, where's the bonny wee
        babe
    That I heard greet sae sair
        [crying so lamentably]?"

5 "There was never a babe intill my
        room,
    As little designs to be;
    It was but a touch o my sair side,
    Come oer my fair bodie."

6 "O Marie, put on your robes o
        black,
    Or else your robes o brown,
    For ye maun gang [must go] wi me
        the night,
    To see fair Edinbro town."

7 "I winna put on my robes o black,
    Nor yet my robes o brown;
    But I'll put on my robes o white,
    To shine through Edinbro
        town."

8 When she gaed [went] up the
        Cannogate,
    She laughd loud laughters three;
    But whan she cam down the
        Cannogate
    The tear blinded her ee [eye].

9 When she gaed up the Parliament
        stair,
    The heel cam aff her shee [shoe];
    And lang or she cam down again
        She was condemned to dee [die].

10 When she cam down the
        Cannogate
    The Cannogate sae free,
    Many a ladie lookd oer her win-
        dow,
    Weeping for this ladie.

11 "Ye need nae weep for me," she
        says,
    "Ye need nae weep for me;
    For had I not slain mine own sweet
        babe,
    This death I wadna dee
        [wouldn't die]."

12 "Bring me a bottle of wine," she
        says,
    "The best that eer ye hae,
    That I may drink to my weil-wish-
        ers,
    And they may drink to me."

13 "Here's a health to the jolly sail-
        ors,
    That sail upon the main;
    Let them never let on to my father
        and mother
    But what I'm coming hame
        [home]."

14 "There's a health to the jolly sail-
        ors,
    That sail upon the sea;
    Let them never let on to my father
        and mother
    That I cam here to dee."

15 "Oh little did my mother think,
    The day she cradled me,
    What lands I was to travel through,
    What death I was to dee.

16 "Oh little did my father think,
    The day he held up me,
    What lands I was to travel through,
    What death I was to dee.

17 "Last night I washd the queen's
        feet,
    And gently laid her down;
    And a' the thanks I've gotten the
        nicht
    To be hangd in Edinbro town!

18 "Last nicht there was four Maries,
    The nicht there'l be but three;
    There was Marie Seton, and Marie
        Beton,
    And Marie Carmichael, and
        me."[21]

        *   *   *

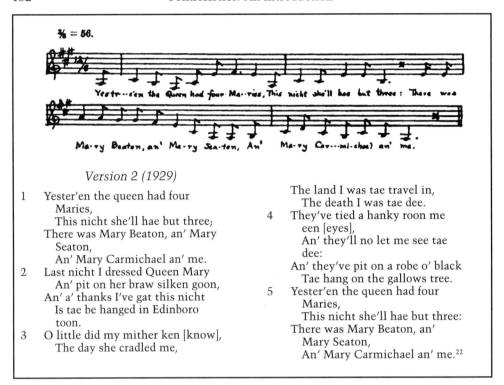

Version 2 (1929)

1   Yester'en the queen had four
        Maries,
        This nicht she'll hae but three;
        There was Mary Beaton, an' Mary
        Seaton,
        An' Mary Carmichael an' me.
2   Last nicht I dressed Queen Mary
        An' pit on her braw silken goon,
        An' a' thanks I've gat this nicht
        Is tae be hanged in Edinboro
        toon.
3   O little did my mither ken [know],
        The day she cradled me,

The land I was tae travel in,
    The death I was tae dee.
4   They've tied a hanky roon me
        een [eyes],
        An' they'll no let me see tae
        dee:
        An' they've pit on a robe o' black
        Tae hang on the gallows tree.
5   Yester'en the queen had four
        Maries,
        This nicht she'll hae but three:
        There was Mary Beaton, an'
        Mary Seaton,
        An' Mary Carmichael an' me.[22]

American ballad types are more lyrical than narrative. These versions can be configured into subsets of ballad types, members of which share only the retention of what Coffin calls the "emotional core" of the type. He presents and illustrates his thesis in a discussion of the Anglo-American ballad "Mary Hamilton."[23]

The normalform of "Mary Hamilton" (Child 173), according to Coffin, is exemplified by Child's version A. In it, the first five stanzas focus on maid-in-waiting Mary Hamilton's affair with the husband of Mary, Queen of Scots; her resulting pregnancy; her murdering the baby; and the queen's discovery of the affair. The next five describe her trial and conviction for infanticide. Stanzas 11 to 18 dwell on her feelings as she stands on the gallows waiting to die (see box 5–1). The "ballad draws to its end

in four heart-rending stanzas," writes Coffin, referring to stanzas 15 to 18. "This is the essence of the story: the beauty and youth of a girl snuffed out by law."

Over time, notes Coffin, versions of the ballad have become abbreviated, losing much of the background information and action. What remains stable is that the girl is identified as one of the Queen's favored maidens who is about to die. "The basic thing is that 'Mary Hamilton' as it is found today is almost always a lyric and that the tendency to preserve the core and not the plot of the song is typical," writes Coffin. Furthermore, he implies that the normalform of this subset has become the American oicotype of the ballad type, for the "full plot" has been "lost forever"; and what remains is "a fine blend of plot residue and universal emotion." The same kind of transformation, he contends, has occurred in such other familiar ballad types as "Charles Guiteau," "Twa Corbies," "Sir Patrick Spens," "Edward," and "Lord Randal."

Conclusion

The fact that versions of particular folklore types exist through space as well as through time motivates folklorists to want to map a given type's geographical distribution and to determine the nature of and reasons for its stability and variability. Conceptualizing folklore as being describable and transmissible predisposes folklorists to focus on folklore types in their multiple versions. It also makes questions relating to the history of given types in time and space central in scholarly inquiry. But folklore is not a superorganic phenomenon that exists in isolation, as viewing folklore as describable and transmissible entity might seem to imply. It is both a part and manifestation of what we call *culture*; and the ways it is related to other aspects of culture provide insights into the part it plays in the everyday lives of social collectivities and individuals. Conceptualizing folklore as culture is the third perspective to be discussed in this work and is the subject of the next two chapters.

Notes

1. Yvonne R. Lockwood and William G. Lockwood, "Pasties in Michigan's Upper Peninsula: Foodways, Interethnic Relations, and Regionalism," in Stephen Stern and John Allan Cicala, eds., *Creative Ethnicity: Symbols and Strategies of Contemporary Ethnic Life* (Logan: Utah State University Press, 1991), pp. 3–20. Quotes are from pp. 5, 6, 7, 8, 9, and 10.

2. Sutterfield is quoted by John Quincy Wolf in "Folksingers and the Re-Creation of Folksong," *Western Folklore* 26 (1967):106.

3. Archer Taylor, *The Shanghai Gesture*, Folklore Fellows Communications 166 (Helsinki, 1956). Quotes are from pp. 5, 6, 10, 15, 20, 22, 34, 36, 37, 38, 39, 58, and 60.

4. Coauthor of this book Robert A. Georges recalls a traditional children's rhyme-and-gesture trick popular in the Pittsburgh, Pennsylvania, area during the late 1930s and early 1940s. An individual makes the military salute, saying, "I'm the captain of the ship." He or she then moves the hand from brow to nose, resting the thumb on the tip of the nose and extending the four fingers to create the Shanghai Gesture, and says, "Pardon, sir, my hand slipped." Children delighted both in the rhyme and in the transformation of the gesture from one of respect to one of disrespect.

5. Austin E. Fife and James M. Fife, "Hay Derricks of the Great Basin and Upper Snake River Valley," *Western Folklore* 7 (1948):225–239. Quotes are from pp. 226, 228, 230, 231, 235, and 236. The essay is reprinted in Austin E. Fife, *Exploring Western Americana*, ed. Alta Fife (Ann Arbor: UMI Press, 1988), pp. 141–157.

6. Gary Alan Fine, "Cokelore and Coke Law: Urban Belief Tales and the Problem of Multiple Origins," *Journal of American Folklore* 92 (1979):477–482. Quotes are from pp. 478 and 481. The essay is reprinted in Gary Alan Fine, *Manufacturing Tales: Sex and Money in Contemporary Legends* (Knoxville: University of Tennessee Press, 1992), pp. 79–85.

7. For an example of a diffusion study of a folksong on phonograph album, see *The Unfortunate Rake, A Study in the Evolution of a Ballad*, notes by Kenneth S. Goldstein (Folkways FS 3805, 1960). For a filmic account of children's games that emphasizes monogenesis, see *Pizza, Pizza, Daddy-O* (1969, Bess Lomax Hawes, Extension Media Center, University of California, Berkeley, black and white, 16mm. and VHS, 18 min.).

8. Stith Thompson, "The Star Husband Tale," *Studia Septentrionalia* 4 (1953):93–163; reprinted in Alan Dundes, ed., *The Study of Folklore* (Englewood Cliffs, N.J.: Prentice-Hall, 1965), pp. 414–474. Quotes are from the reprinted version, pp. 419, 449, 451, 452, 453, 454, and 455.

9. For a discussion of the evolution of the historic-geographic method, see Archer Taylor, "Precursors of the Finnish Method," *Modern Philology* 25 (1928):481–491, and Stith Thompson, *The Folktale* (New York: Dryden Press, 1946), pp. 428–448.

10. Julius Krohn was the first to employ the procedures and techniques of historic-geographic method, in his studies of the Finnish epic the *Kalevala*, particularly *Kalevalan toisinnot* (The Variants of the Kalevala) (Helsinki, 1888). Kaarle Krohn was the first to utilize the historic-geographic method to study folktales—in his works *Bär (Wolf) und Fuchs* (Bear [Wolf] and Fox) (Helsinki, 1883) and *Mann und Fuchs* (Man and Fox) (Helsinki, 1891). Antti Aarne authored numerous historic-geographic studies of folktales, including *Die Tiere auf der Wanderschaft* (The Animals in Night Quarters), Folklore Fellows Communications 11 (Hamina, 1913); *Der reiche Mann und sein Schwiegersohn* (The Rich Man and His Son-in-Law), Folklore Fellows Communications 23 (Helsinki, 1916); and *Die magische Flucht: eine Märchenstudie* (The Magic Flight: A Folktale Study), Folklore Fellows Communications 92 (Helsinki, 1930). Procedures for conducting historic-geographic studies are described and codified in Kaarle Krohn, *Die folkloristische Arbeitsmethode* (Folklore Methodology) (Oslo, 1926), translated into English as *Folklore Methodology*, trans. Roger L. Welsch, Publications of the American Folklore Society, Bibliographical and Special Series 21 (Austin: University of Texas Press, 1971). A brief characterization of the method also appears in Thompson, *The Folktale*, pp. 428–448. Other published studies that employ and illustrate the historic-geographic method include the following: Walter Anderson, *Kaiser und Abt* (The King and the Abbot), Folklore Fellows Communications 42 (Helsinki, 1923); Warren E. Roberts, *The Tale of the Kind and the Unkind Girls* (Berlin, 1958); Holger Olof Nygard, *The Ballad of Heer Halewijn, Its Form and Variations in Western Europe: A Study of the History and Nature of a Ballad Tradition*, Folklore Fellows Communications 169 (Helsinki, 1958); and Elsa Enäjärvi Haavio, *The Game of Rich and Poor: A Comparative Study in Traditional Singing Games*, Folklore Fellows Communications 100 (Helsinki, 1932).

11. Wolfgang Mieder, "The Proverbial Three Wise Monkeys," *Midwestern Journal of Language and Folklore* 7 (1981):5–38. Quotes are from pp. 7, 8, 9, 10, 11, and 20.

12. Krohn, *Folklore Methodology*, p. 59.

13. Amy Kitchener, "Explosive Jokes: A Collection of Persian Gulf War Humor," unpublished manuscript. See also Alan Dundes and Carl Pagter, "The Mobile SCUD Missile Launcher and Other Persian Gulf Warlore: An American Folk Image of Saddam Hussein's Iraq," *Western Folklore* 50 (1991):303–322.

14. Discussions of the role audio and electronic media play in the diffusion of folklore include the following: Archie Green, "Hillbilly Music: Source and Symbol," *Journal of American Folklore* 78 (1965):204–228; Ed Kahn, "Hillbilly Music: Source and Resource," *Journal of American Folklore* 78 (1965):257–266; and John Dorst, "Tags and Burners, Cycles and Networks: Folklore in the Telectronic Age," *Journal of Folklore Research* 27 (1990):179–190. See also Linda Dégh, *American Folklore and the Mass Media* (Bloomington: Indiana University Press, 1994).

15. Anna Birgitta Rooth, "The Creation Myths of the North American Indians," *Anthropos* 52 (1957):497–508. Quotes are from pp. 498, 499, 500, 501, 502, 503, 504, 505, 506, 507, and 508.

16. Alan Dundes, "African Tales among the North American Indians," *Southern Folklore Quarterly* 29 (1965):207–219. Quotes are from pp. 208, 210, 212, 213, and 218. Compilations of the "Uncle Remus" tales by Joel Chandler Harris (1849–1908) were published between 1880 and 1948 and have been compiled into and issued as a single volume, *The Complete Tales of Uncle Remus*, comp. by Richard Chase (Boston: Houghton Mifflin, 1955).

17. For a discussion of this point, see Carl Wilhelm von Sydow, "Geography and Folk-Tale Oicotypes," in *Selected Papers on Folklore*, ed. Laurits Bødker (Copenhagen, 1948), pp. 44–59.

18. Von Sydow, p. 57.

19. Von Sydow, pp. 52 and 55.

20. The term *communal re-creation* is most often associated with American ballad scholar Phillips Barry (1880–1937). He discusses the concept in "The Part of the Folk Singer in the Making of Folk Balladry," in MacEdward Leach and Tristram P. Coffin, eds., *The Critics and the Ballad: Readings* (Carbondale: South-

ern Illinois University Press, 1961), pp. 59–76.

21. From Francis James Child, *The English and Scottish Popular Ballads*, 5 vols. in 10 pts. (Boston: Houghton Mifflin, 1882–98), vol. 3, pp. 384–385.

22. From Phillips Barry, Fannie Hardy Eckstorm, and Mary Winslow Smyth, *British Ballads from Maine: The Development of Popular Songs, with Texts and Airs* (New Haven: Yale University Press, 1929), pp. 258–259.

23. Tristram P. Coffin, "Mary Hamilton and the Anglo-American Ballad as an Art Form," *Journal of American Folklore* 70 (1957):208–214, reprinted in Leach and Coffin, pp. 245–256. Quotes are from the reprinted version, pp. 254, 255, and 256. See also Carlos Drake, "'Mary Hamilton' in Tradition," *Southern Folklore Quarterly* 33 (1969):39–47, which synthesizes scholarship on this ballad and attempts to refine Coffin's notion of "emotional core." For an example on phonograph album, see the Archive of American Folk Song, *Folk Music of the United States: Album 7—Anglo-American Ballads* ("The Four Marys," sung by Mrs. Texas Gladden, 1941, recorded by Alan Lomax).

Folklore as Culture

6. Folklore in Cultural Contexts

Viewing folklore examples as artifacts and as entities that are configurable into generic and type sets and transmissible through space makes similarities and differences among individual examples of folklore the foci of inquiry. Since the beginnings of their field in the early nineteenth century, however, folklorists have also been aware that the phenomena they study are integral parts of a complex of creations and conventions which are fundamental to the existence, perpetuation, and survival of humans as social beings. This complex of interrelated behaviors that human beings create, learn from, and teach each other and that serve as bases for collective social identification is what is commonly called *culture*.

Conceiving of folklore examples as cultural phenomena began long before Edward B. Tylor defined the word *culture* in 1871 as "that complex whole which includes knowledge, belief, art, morals, law, custom, and any other capabilities and habits acquired by man as a member of society."[1] Early Greek writers such as Hesiod and Herodotus were aware that the myths they characterized were not instinctive phenomena, but rather stories that individual human beings create and others subsequently learn, repeat, and live by. In the foreword to their collection of German legends (*Deutsche Sagen*, 2 vols., 1816, 1818), the Grimms indicate that these narratives are part of a larger whole that embodies and reveals the character of a nation (see Box 6–1).

By creating the *Kalevala* from songs and poems he learned mostly at first hand from rural Finns, Elias Lönnrot constructed an epic he felt symbolized not only the historical development, but also the shared spiritual values and democratic and humanistic orientations of his people.[2] In urging readers of *The Athenaeum* in 1846 to collect examples of those "manners, customs, observances, superstitions, ballads, proverbs, etc.," which he proposed be called *folklore*, William John Thoms notes that such a seeming "mass of minute facts, many of which, when separately considered, appear trifling and insignificant," actually "assume a value that he who first recorded them never dreamed of attributing to them" until they are "taken in connection with *the system*" of which they all are part (emphasis added).[3]

Those who pioneered in documenting and studying folklore, then, were also pioneering students of culture. By the time Tylor penned his often-quoted definition in 1871 and anthropology emerged subsequently as the discipline that appropriated

---

BOX 6–1
From the Foreword by Jakob and Wilhelm Grimm to Their *Deutsche Sagen* (German Legends), Volume I, 1816

We recommend our book to devotees of German poesie, history, and language and hope that it will be welcome to all as purely German fare. For it is our firm belief that nothing is as edifying or as likely to bring more joy than the products of the Fatherland. Indeed, an apparently insignificant, self-occasioning discovery and endeavor in the study of our own indigenous culture can in the end bring more fruit than the most brilliant discovery and cultivation of foreign fields.[4]

culture as its central construct, folklorists had, for more than half a century, been conceptualizing examples of folklore as aspects of culture and discerning and discussing relationships between folklore and other cultural phenomena.

Folklore as an Aspect of Culture

Since the inception of their discipline, folklorists have been aware that the phenomena they study are related to other aspects of the cultures of which they are a part, and therefore that folklore serves as an important source of cultural knowledge and understanding. "There is no subject of inquiry relating to the history of a people more interesting than its popular mythology and superstitions," wrote Thomas Wright in 1846.[5] "In these we trace the early formation of nations, their identity or analogy, their changes, as well as *the inner texture of the national character*, more deeply than in any other circumstances, even in language itself" (emphasis added). Concerned with the history and consequences of the Christianization of "the Teutonic tribes" beginning in the fourth century, Wright notes that missionaries succeeded in destroying everywhere "the worship of Woden," but failed to overturn "the belief in the airy spirits of the popular creed." These fairies, elves, nymphs, and other supernaturals constituted a "much larger class of beings of the popular belief" than did the deities. And they were beings "with whom the people supposed they had a nearer connection, and whose influence, good or evil, they believed themselves to be daily experiencing." The "popular belief in these things and their effects," Wright asserts, "was so intimately interwoven in the *national character*" that the people "held by it like the language, with which, also, they had a strong tie" (emphasis added).

Wright emphasizes the ongoing importance of these pagan beliefs and the practices based on them:

> The common ceremonies of life, at every minute bore allusions to them; things so difficult to eradicate, that now, after so many centuries of successive improvement and refinement, in our salutations [greetings], in our eating and drinking, even in our children's games, we are perpetually, though unwittingly, doing the same things which our forefathers did in honour or in fear of the elves and nymphs of the heathen creed.

J. F. Campbell similarly recognizes that folklore reflects other aspects of culture. In the preface to his *Popular Tales of the West Highlands*,[6] Campbell explains what the stories he collected in Scotland in 1859 and 1860 "can teach us . . . about the people, their origin, and their habits, past and present." Campbell states that

> the manners [of the characters in the stories] are generally those of the day. . . . Kings live in cottages, and sit on low stools. When they have coaches, they open the door themselves. The queen saddles the king's horse. The king goes to his own stable when he hears a noise there. Sportsmen use guns. The fire is on the floor. . . . The king's mother puts on the fire, and sleeps in the common room, as a peasant does. The cock sleeps on the rafters, the sheep on the floor, the bull behind the door. A ladder is a pole, with pegs stuck through it. Horses put their noses "into" bridles. When all Ireland passes in review before the princess, they go in at the front door and out at the back, as they would through a bothy [hut]; and even that unexplained personage, the daughter of the king of the skies, has maids who chatter to her as freely as maids do to Highland mistresses. When the prince is at death's door for love of the beautiful lady in the swan's down robe, and the queen mother is in despair, she goes to the kitchen to talk over the matter.

> The tales represent the actual every-day life of those who tell them, with great fidelity. They have done the same, in all likelihood,

time out of time, and that which is not true of the present is, in all probability, true of the past; and therefore something may be learned of forgotten ways of life.

In describing ways that folklore mirrors both contemporary and "forgotten ways of life," nineteenth-century folklorists established a methodological precedent that their twentieth-century successors have followed and refined. Specifically, they demonstrated that correlations exist between folklore and other aspects of culture, and that discerning and analyzing these correlations provide insights into the part folklore plays in social life. A sampling of selected studies suggests the variety of interrelationships between folklore examples and other cultural phenomena and the functional implications of them.

Relationships between Folklore and Other Cultural Phenomena

Writing about hooked rugs in Newfoundland, Canada, Gerald L. Pocius attempts to unravel a mystery.[7] According to some researchers, folk art styles bear a relationship to social stratification. Egalitarian societies supposedly create styles characterized by repetition of simple, symmetrical elements. Hierarchical societies allegedly produce asymmetrical, nonrepetitive styles. Many hooked rugs made in Newfoundland incorporate traditional, symmetrical patterns which often are so widely spread that they are named and have a geographical and temporal distribution, writes Pocius. In contrast to these geometrical designs, other hooked rugs are individualistic, and sometimes asymmetrical, in design. Often a woman makes rugs in both styles. Is Newfoundland simultaneously an egalitarian and hierarchical society?

Pocius hypothesizes that the rugs do indeed relate to social stratification. Until recently, he writes, an "almost feudal economic system existed whereby one community resident, the merchant, supplied all the community's manufactured goods and much of its food, while providing the only outlet for the sale of fish." The merchant class holds a privileged status. So do the clergy. The fishermen and their families, who constitute the vast majority of residents, possess lower status. Local communities are hierarchical in regard to a tiny minority, but egalitarian in terms of the majority. "This social pattern is integrally connected to the use of specific hooked-rug styles within the home," contends Pocius.

Almost all social activity in these outport communities occurs in the kitchen: wakes, wedding receptions, and visiting, for example. Family members and neighbors interact as equals. When the merchant or clergyman calls, however, deference to

Figure 6–1: Mary Margaret O'Brien of Cape Broyle, Newfoundland, hooking a rug in a block design (photo by Gerald L. Pocius).

Figure 6–2: Geometric pattern hooked rug, from Cape Broyle, Newfoundland (photo by Gerald L. Pocius).

status requires entertaining these privileged residents "away from the noise and smell of the kitchen." Individualistic and often asymmetrical rugs lie on the floor of the parlor where interaction is hierarchically based. The symmetrical, geometrically repetitious rugs—which are traditional, and have antecedents in the community—welcome friends and neighbors into the kitchen. Differences in hooked rug styles, then, seem to correlate with where rugs are used, which in turn reflects social relationships. "Like individuality and social stratification, the innovative rug kept in the front room was rarely seen, although its existence was acknowledged." Found in the kitchen, the tradition-based, geometrical rug "provided a clearer pattern of the intricate social cooperation" in the Newfoundland communities, concludes Pocius.

While Pocius focuses on social class distinctions expressed through material culture in a Canadian province, Satu Apo examines texts of 235 magic tales recorded during the nineteenth century in five rural parishes in Southwest Finland.[8] Her objective is to determine what "picture" they

Figure 6–3: Pastoral scene on a hooked rug with textured sky and trees using various shades of blue and green, from Bay Bulls, Newfoundland (photo by Gerald L. Pocius).

provide of "relationships between different social classes."

Some 60 percent of the tales, Apo reports, depict "the rise of a young main character of low birth [usually a peasant] via marriage to a person at the top of the social hierarchy." Story characters dramatize the status differences. For example, royalty, the clergy, and rich freeholders appear as repugnant or hateful villains. They threaten to kill their lowly servants if these underlings cannot accomplish impossible tasks (e.g., mow in a single day a meadow so huge that it normally "took five men five weeks to mow it"). They also take advantage of women, forcing them to engage in sexual intercourse while their powerless husbands are made to watch. But these higher-ups are also frequently degraded, particularly "by means of sex, anal comedy and violence." A clever shepherd tricks a king into having intercourse with a horse or goat, for example. A priest is tied to a tree and forced to dance as he dangles in midair while a shepherd boy plays a magic fiddle whose tunes no hearer can resist.

The social criticism and aggression expressed in the stories, Apo states, are "not merely a reflection of social situations prevailing at the time the material was collected." Instead, they are manifestations of "pressures built up over the centuries by the social hierarchy." Apo concludes that "the protest manifest in the folktales of Southwest Finland is in the nature of kicking against prevailing conditions and does not aim at social change." Hence, "The socio-psychological function of the texts was, we may assume, to let off steam." Apo thus sees the Finnish magic tales she examines as mirroring a society whose structure privileges the few at the expense of many. But not all that the stories depict is reflective of an actual reality. They also project an alternative in which statuses are inverted when the underprivileged get the upper hand, if only symbolically.

Figure 6–4: Ruth Benedict (courtesy Columbiana Collection, Low Memorial Library, Columbia University).

While Apo focuses on relationships between social stratification as it is portrayed in folktales and as it existed in reality in the nineteenth century, Ruth Benedict explores multiple ways that folklore can "tally" with other aspects of culture. In her 1935 study of Zuni myths,[9] Benedict echoes the kinds of views expressed by such earlier researchers as Campbell (quoted above) when she writes, "The agreement between the conduct of contemporary life and the picture of life in the folktales is very close. The roles of men and women in Zuni life, the role of the priesthoods, the conduct of sex life, the concern with witchcraft, are all faithfully indicated." (See Box 6–2 for an example.)

But Benedict also finds instances of stories that do not "tally with culture" in what they depict, challenging the view that folklore is always a "mirror" that reflects and reinforces present everyday behaviors.

BOX 6-2
The Pitfall: A Zuni Tale

They were living at Matsaka. An old man and an old woman lived alone a little distance to the east from the rest of the village. When the spring came, this old man planted a corn field and his wife a garden of squash and pumpkins. They worked hard in their fields, but as the sprouts came up, the crows ate them. The old man and the old woman were very sad. They said, "We will give prayer meal to our fathers." They dug a little hole, and standing over it, they prayed that nothing should eat their tender plants. They scattered the meal in the hole and covered it over.

The next morning they came to see if any plants had been spared. A few were growing nicely. Every morning for four days they came to look at their fields. The fourth day the man found that all were growing up, and his wife's squash and pumpkins too. They worked very hard and they had the best field anywhere about. Every morning they prayed and put down the meal, and their crops grew and ripened.

The witches in Matsaka were jealous of the old people's fields. The head witch man went out to the Place of the Burnt Wood and gave the witches' coyote cry. When he had done this four times, the witches gathered one by one. In the village one witch would go to the house of another and say, "Don't you want to come to the kiva to smoke?" So they came out together, and gathered at the witch's council room. When they had all come together, the head witch took his hoop and banked the dirt on either side so that it stood upright. He jumped through it first and the next one and the next followed him, and each as he went through turned into a coyote.

The head witch said, "What do you say to eating up the field of the old man?" Every one said, "We will be glad to eat his field. It was in our minds to suggest this when you spoke." All together the coyotes went out to the field, and they ate every growing thing.

Next morning the old man went out and he saw that everything was gone. He thought it was real coyotes that had eaten it. He came home and told his wife what had happened to their corn and squash and pumpkins. They were very sad. He told his

wife he would stay in the field all the next night and watch.

When evening came, he went to his shelter and lay down without a fire, so that the coyotes might not know he was there. Where the corn was short, he went to sleep. At midnight the coyotes came. The old man waked up and listened. He still thought they were really coyotes. At last he saw one of them drop a mouthful of food, and another said, "Don't be so careless. Chew it all up, and spit it out if it's too much." The old man exclaimed, "What, are you talking!" He was frightened, and ran home to tell his wife.

His wife said, "Tomorrow we shall go to our field and dig a pit, and cover it with sunflower stalks. On top of this we shall put sand and dirt." They went next morning to the field, and dug the pit and placed the sunflower stalks above it. When evening came they took their sheepskins to sleep on and went to their shelter.

The coyotes thought that the man was well frightened and would not return to his field, so the next night they went again. The head witch went first. At the Place of the Burnt Wood they all met together and they said to the head witch, "You shall go ahead." When he had reached the field he saw no one, so he went into the field and began to eat. As he ate he came to the pit which had been covered with stalks. He stepped upon it and the stalks broke under him, and he fell into the hole. Immediately he cried out, and all the witches thought he was calling them. They sent the second witch and he also came to the pit. He said, "What are you doing down there?" And the witch chief whispered from the bottom of the pit, "Come down here, there are lots of beautiful girls here; I am beating the drum while they are grinding. Come also; we shall enjoy all these girls." When he heard this, the second witch jumped into the pit.

Presently the witches sent a third coyote to see what had become of their brothers. The coyotes in the pit whispered to him, "Oh, our brother, come on in; down here there are lots of girls. They are grinding while we beat the drum. Come down and play with them." When he heard this, the third witch jumped into the pit. When he did not return, the witches sent a fourth man into the field, and when he had come to the pit and called down into it, again they whispered, "Come down here, there is lots of fun. We have all the pretty girls, and we are beating the drum for them while they grind." Thereupon the fourth witch jumped into the pit.

When none of the witches returned, all the coyotes went together. They came to the pit, and when they had heard the good fortune of their brothers, they all jumped in. When all of the coyotes were in the bottom of the pit, the old man and the old woman came out of the shelter, and they took wood and cedar bark, and threw it into the hole, and dropped fire upon it, and burned up all the coyotes. All those witches were killed, but they did not really die; they came back in different bodies, and that is why there are witches with us today, and they are always jealous of anybody's success.[10]

Sometimes the realities portrayed in folklore prevailed in the past, but not today. This is the case, for instance, with characterizations of people entering their houses "by means of a ladder to the roof and down another ladder from the hatchway," which had been common in Zuni society until doors replaced ladders in all but ceremonial structures by 1888. Ordinary store-bought knives displaced stone knives except for ceremonial use; yet references in myths are to knives made of stone. "At present sheep herding occupies much of the life of Zuni men," reports Benedict, "and hunting is in abeyance. In the tales, however, all heroes are hunters, and there is no mention of sheep herding except in tales recognized as Mexican." Benedict attributes these differences to "cultural lag," noting that myths sometimes "perpetuate traditional forms"

and reflect past rather than present realities.

Benedict indicates that, in addition, folklore sometimes does not mirror the behavior of the Zuni of either the present or the past, making cultural lag an unacceptable explanation for the noncorrelations. "The most striking instance," she states, "is that of the constant recurrence of polygamy in the tales"—striking because "Zuni institutions are thoroughly monogamous." Concludes Benedict: "Marriage with many wives is a Zuni fantasy of the same order as raising the dead or traveling with seven-league boots in other bodies of folklore." It plays "a fairy-tale role in Zuni mythology." Another noncorrespondence appears in stories depicting the abandonment, neglect, or abuse of children when in actuality "[a]ll men and women, not only the parents, give children the fondest care." (See Box 6–3 for an example.)

Some tales describe violence "based on secret enmity" in a society in which "homicide occurs with such extraordinary rarity that instances are not even remembered." Other narratives portray individuals arranging their own murders and those of their adulterous spouses in a society in which "suicide is unknown and even inconceivable to the Zuni mind," and "violence is culturally taboo." These recurrent themes in Zuni tales, notes Benedict, do not mirror other aspects of culture, for they do not reflect the actual realities of the Zuni way of life as it existed either when Benedict was doing her field research or at any time before that, according to available information. But they do "tally with culture," nevertheless, for they are "folkloristic daydreams" that have "a psychological significance" because they reflect and reveal collective anxieties that result from culturally imposed behavioral norms and expectations.

For Benedict, the noncorrelations between folklore and other aspects of culture

BOX 6–3
The Girl Who Would Not Get Water: A Zuni Tale

A woman was living at Owl Spring. She had one daughter. Every day the little girl worked all day long. She ground flour and baked corn-cakes. One night she was tired. Her mother said to her, "There is no water. Go fetch a jar of water." The little girl cried; she was so tired she could not go for water. Her mother scolded her. Poor girl, she went down into the cellar and sat down on the floor and cried. After dark Black Moth came out. He heard the little girl crying and he said, "Who is crying here?" The little girl said, "I am a little girl. I was tired with cooking and grinding and I could not go for water. My mother scolded me and I have nowhere to go." "Come with me. I will carry you on my back to my home." The little girl went up out of the cellar and got on Moth's back. He flew up with her to the mountains.

Her mother looked everywhere for her. She went to the cellar but she could not find her there. She cried all night long. She thought to herself, "Oh alas, I asked too much of my daughter." In the morning she got up and went to the spring for water and she saw the big rock where her little girl used to set down her jar while she dipped the water with her gourd. She cried and cried. For four days she cried for her daughter. She took her jar and went down to the river thinking she might see her daughter there. Black Moth flew down to the stream. He said to the mother, "Why are you crying?" "Oh alas, my daughter was tired and would not go to fetch water. I whipped her and she went into the cellar and never came up again." Black Moth said, "I found your daughter crying in the cellar and took her to my house. Do you want your little girl back again?" The mother sobbed, "Yes, oh yes." "When she comes you must not cry. Go back to your home and wait. Get everything ready. Have all the people waiting to receive her."

The mother went back to the pueblo and told the priest to make a proclamation that all the people should be ready to welcome her little girl. Next day everybody prepared all kinds of food for the feast. In Moth's house, Moth made the little girl ready to go to her own home. Moth's mother washed her head and dressed her in her best clothes. She told her, "When you get to the village everybody will be waiting for you. They will be lined up in two rows and you will walk between them. At the far end your mother will be standing at her own door. If she is crying, spread your wings and fly away. But if she does not cry, go in and stay with her."

Black Moth took the little girl on his back and flew until they came near the village. She got off his back and walked in. Everything was just as Moth had said. All the people of the village were lined up in two rows and she walked down the center. The first people that she passed were not crying. Down at the far end her mother was standing by her own door and the tears were running down her cheeks. As soon as the little girl saw her mother's tears she became an owl and flew away into the air. Poor mother, she cried and cried. All the people cried. Because the little girl became an owl there, we still call it Owl Spring.[11]

result either from cultural lag following technological change or from folklore as an expression of fantasy. In a study of the "Kentucky Fried Rat" legend, Gary Alan Fine hypothesizes that this story reflects major changes in American society. For Fine, the legend also expresses anxieties and fears over these changes and their consequences.[12]

Fine mentions several changes since the 1940s. One is the demise of small towns and the swelling of urban and suburban areas. Residence affects social life. Anonymity, impersonal settings, fleeting brushes with transients and strangers—these are the backdrop of stories that folklorists often call *contemporary* or *urban legends*. Writes Fine: "What could better serve as a metaphor for the city as a jungle than the belief that the New York sewer system is filled with albino alligators, which swim through toilet pipes and bite victims in public washrooms?" Suburban malls become a breeding ground for many crime victim stories, including the account of the mutilated shopper in a department store dressing room, her fingers severed and rings stolen (see Box 6–4).

In addition, nationwide chains have pushed aside many mom-and-pop grocery stores, hardware emporiums, and local eateries. Communities have become less self-sufficient and more dependent on impersonal corporations. Alienation follows. "Horror" stories implicate the outside agencies in various machinations. "The accounts of McDonald's hamburger meat being composed of worms or snakes found in imported sweaters sold in discount store

chains are responses to this loss of community control," writes Fine. Beliefs that fast-food corporations willingly contaminate their food with worms (Wendy's, to explain its burgers' juiciness), buckshot (Arby's Roast Beef), or dog food (Pizza Hut) criticize the industry. So do accounts charging that "decomposed mice are found in Coke bottles, that Bubble Yum bubble gum is made from spider eggs, and that children have died from Pop Rocks."

Values, too, have changed in recent decades, writes Fine, with greater emphasis on, for example, consumption, play, and leisure as opposed to work, sexuality, and equality in family roles. Altering basic mores generates feelings of ambivalence. "This ambivalence, often not talked about openly, is expressed indirectly through folklore which disguises the threat through the projection of the fear to a 'real' occurrence," writes Fine. "Stories about corporations which manufacture bathing suits that become transparent in water indicate a fear of the effects of overt sexuality," he contends. "Rumors about Ray Kroc, the owner of McDonald's, being a member of the Church of Satan, the rock group KISS standing for Knights in Satan's Service, or Procter and Gamble being owned by Rev. Moon's Unification Church reflect threats to traditional religion."

In light of these structural changes in American society, Fine examines two subtypes of the Kentucky Fried Rat story. The first, drawn from the UCLA Folklore Archives, dwells on the experiences of a young man and his date who purchase a bucket of fried chicken from a fast-food chain before going to the movies. While munching on the food in the darkened theater, the woman complains her chicken is "rubbery." She becomes so ill that the man rushes her to the hospital, where she is diagnosed as having been poisoned. What caused it? The man runs to his car, rummages through the remains of fried chicken,

BOX 6–4
The Mutilated Shopper at the Mall

Well, I work in Jordan's and I heard from another salesgirl about a problem that [they] had at Sears on a Friday or a Saturday night. A lady was there shopping. Her husband had left her off. And she was trying on dresses or sportswear. It was at the end of the day, possibly an hour before closing time. The husband went outside to wait for her to come out. And she didn't arrive when the store closed. So, he called security.

And security went into the store looking for her. And they found her in a fitting room. And evidently she had been mugged and her finger had been cut off and her diamonds cut off her finger. And she was unconscious. This is what I heard.[13]

and discovers that the batter-encrusted, deep-fat-fried, half-eaten piece of his date's food is a rat. It died of strychnine poisoning. So does the woman.

In a second subtype, documented in the University of Minnesota Folklore Archives, a woman is eating Kentucky Fried Chicken while watching television in her living room. Because of the extra crispy coating, it is not until after a few bites that she realizes she is chewing on a rat. An employee at the Kentucky Fried Chicken franchise where she had bought the bucket of crispy chicken had fried the rat as a prank.

Fine isolates themes in this legend, interpreting them in terms of changes in the fabric of American life. That the contaminant is a rat or mouse seems appropriate, for these rodents often symbolize urban decay and the decline of community and morality. Why the reference to a fast-food chain? "The target for our fears [generated by social changes] has shifted to corporations, which, like foreigners, are outsiders to the local community . . . and have not adopted moral injunctions," writes Fine.

In one instance contamination results from unsanitary conditions. The corporate kitchen contrasts with the one at home. "Anxiety and guilt arise from the change from eating personally prepared food to eating what profit-making enterprises serve; these emotions have been projected onto the commercial establishment, and transformed into fear," writes Fine. The other subtype of the legend implies deliberate sabotage and human malice. "Because of the impersonality of large institutions, workers do not feel morally attached to their supervisors or to those served," suggests Fine.

Eating the chicken "in the dark" may have symbolic significance as well as explain why the rat goes undetected for several bites. "It acknowledges the change of eating habits produced by contemporary time schedules. The family dinner, once a focal component of American cultural tradition, has been replaced by eating as a hurried secondary activity," writes Fine. One account explicitly blames the wife for not performing her homemaking role. It states that "a wife who didn't have anything ready for supper for her husband" quickly purchased a basket of chicken, lit candles for dinner, and only on eating the allegedly home-cooked meal did she discover that she had served fried rat. "While the primary culprit is the national chain," writes Fine, "implicit blame accrues to the decline of family eating traditions."

In the 63 cases that identify the victim's sex, 51 (or 81%) point to the female. Fine hypothesizes two reasons. "First, women are perceived as more vulnerable to attack than men," and second, "if these legends do represent the longing for a lost community life, the woman as victim is symbolically proper. The woman by neglecting her traditional role as food preparer helps to destroy the family by permitting the transfer of control from the home to amoral profit-making corporations. Thus, the receipt of a rat is appropriate symbolic punishment."

According to Fine, 76 percent of the people he sampled believe the event definitely or probably happened. Often people tell the legend while eating (frequently at fast-food restaurants) or while deciding where to eat.

"This set of Kentucky Fried Rat legends indicates that contemporary folklore content is responsive to environmental change and the psychological effects that are concomitant with this change," Fine concludes. The legend, he states, "depicts the harm which comes from a lack of personal control" engendered by the breakdown of community, the dominance of outside agencies, and the change in lifestyle and eating habits. "Massive social structural changes do not just happen in isolation but produce a myriad of cultural effects . . . ," Fine contends. Some folklore examples like the Kentucky Fried Rat legend create a concrete target for anxieties resulting from social changes and cultural challenges. These examples provide specifics regarding conditions, causes, or consequences that render the diffuse changes and abstract reasons more understandable.

Folklore in National and Tribal Contexts

Studies such as those by Pocius, Apo, Benedict, and Fine emphasize one-to-one correlations and noncorrelations between folklore examples and other aspects of culture. Other research concerns ways that multiple and differing kinds of folklore examples reveal and relate to cultural preoccupations of given peoples. "It is difficult to look at a basket and not perceive the great number of other ideas, designs, uses, and implications that must attach to it," writes Barre Toelken in "The Basket Imperative."[14] "Not only do baskets . . . *parallel* the patterns, repetitions, and assumptions of oral literature, tribal dance, philosophy, and religion, and not only are they integrated utilitarian expressions of practical survival for many people, they are as well *symbolic* of these areas," he contends.

Several Native American tribes used baskets as containers for babies as well as food, observes Toelken. Some food baskets resembled the human breast so closely "that the implied connection of nurturing would have been difficult to overlook." Materials used for baskets had other uses in houses, clothing, and boats in addition to food or medicine. Several Northwest Coast tribes utilized cedar bark "not only for baskets but also for fishing line and for hats which ranged in usage from protective to ceremonial," serving as sun shields, life preservers, markers of social position and clan, and displays of "public legal documentations of personal relationships."

Figure 6–5: Mildred Youngblood, a Cherokee in Woodbury, Tennessee, making a basket, 1980 (photo by James Bassler).

Particular colors "reflected cultural values." In some tribes, baskets had special uses in marriage ceremonies. Often women made certain baskets while men constructed others (e.g., eel traps and clam baskets). Some tribes sang to the plants that gave them fibers with which to make baskets; others prayed. "Thus the basket was not only a utilitarian object," writes Toelken, "but suggestive and reminiscent of relationships between the sexes, cultural roles, and restrictions or taboos which grew out of very strict concepts of interaction between humans and nature."

Many tribes also told stories concerning the proper ways to employ baskets in order to dramatize "delicately poised relationships, ideals and concepts which would have been otherwise very abstract." For

Figure 6–6: Finished basket by Mildred Youngblood (photo by James Bassler).

instance, the Lummi in northwest Washington recount an incident involving several young girls who picked berries in the woods. Finding the task easy, they ate first one basketful and then another. In so doing they violated a norm in many tribal societies. Gatherers and hunters should bring the food back and share it with others. According to the story, each time the girls emptied the baskets they knocked them against their thighs several times to clean them of stems and leaves. The fifth time they wanted to clean and eat berries, they could not stop knocking the baskets. The intensity of the motion caused them to take flight. Sometimes Lummi children are told that when they hear birds flying overhead this should remind them of the selfish girls who ate berries in the woods. Birds are noted for bringing food back to their children. Ironically, "selfish girls who eat their berries in the woods are transformed into another life where they are obliged by nature to share every berry." This is "clearly a symbolic story in which baskets and food and taboos are so closely interlaced in a memorable system which ensures that everyone will share and eat," Toelken writes.

In a number of tribal stories the spirits of dead people are transported in baskets. When Coyote loses patience while carrying the spirits of his wife or children, he drops the basket or stamps his foot, "upon which the delicate soul immediately flees back to the land of death." Such "culturally based expression" as these stories may communicate several abstractions like decorum or the relationships posited by tribal religion. Often "the role of the basket in this set of relationships is so central as to be in and of itself unmistakably symbolic."

Alan Dundes also focuses on how different kinds of folklore relate to cultural preoccupations of a people.[15] He explores ways that folklore reflects the alleged "future orientation in American worldview." By worldview he means "a cognitive set by means of which people perceive, consciously or unconsciously, relationships between self, others, cosmos, and the day-to-day living of life."

Dundes notes that worldview is usually "implicit rather than explicit." However, "it is frequently the case that in folklore implicit worldview principles and themes are made explicit." Dundes indicates that a "futuristic orientation" is "an attribute of American worldview." This is clearly revealed in examples of American folk speech, specifically in "proverbs, folk metaphors, and other traditional linguistic clichés and formulas . . . found throughout the United States."

"What's up?" "What's new?" "What's happening?" and similar greeting formulas reveal a future orientation. So do leave-taking expressions like "See you later," "See you around," and "You all come back and see us." An emphasis on ends also indicates American future orientation, as suggested by the popularity of such traditional sayings as "Tall oaks from little acorns grow," "The early bird catches the worm," and "A stitch in time saves nine." Writes Dundes, "The positive attitude towards ends is revealed by such phrases as to be the 'end' or the 'living end' or to be 'endsville' or to refer to something as the 'be and end all.'"

The preference for what is yet to come over what has been is also revealed by "the penchant for the new." Manufacturers constantly "replace their products . . . with *new*, improved versions." And "the newcomer, the newlyweds, the tenderfoot, the freshman, and, in acting, the 'new faces' . . . attract the greatest interest." Expressions such as "Better luck next time" and "There's always tomorrow" indicate the feeling that the future is more important than the present, as do "You ain't seen nothin' yet" and "The best is yet to come." Americans, states Dundes, admire a "man who knows where he's going" but have no time for one who "doesn't know where his next meal is coming from." According to Dundes, even "negative judgments" and outright warnings "express the same futurity," as illustrated by "That remains to be seen" and "That'll be the day," on the one hand, and "You'll be singing a different tune" and "You're going to get yours," on the other.

The "future-orientation in American folk speech," Dundes insists, "does not exist in a cultural vacuum. The penchant for valuing the future highly may well be correlated with a tendency to denigrate or ignore the past." Dundes notes that "one might find past orientation in the United States, but not to the extent that one can find it in tradition-bound areas of Europe." Conversely, "one might find future orientation in Europe, but not always in as intensified a form as in the United States." What is important, then, is the occurrence and frequency of occurrence of indicators of future orientation. These, Dundes insists, are numerous and pervasive in American life, as examples of folk speech clearly attest.

Folklore in Social Subgroups and Communities

Studies such as those characterized above focus on folklore as aspects and manifestations of the cultures of national or tribal societies. Others concern the part folklore plays in cultures of subgroups and communities based on, for example, gender, age, occupation, provenience, religious affiliation, club membership, or recreational preferences.[16] Both kinds of studies involve conceptualizing folklore as a part of culture and exploring relationships between folklore examples and other cultural phenomena common to people identifiable in a common way. Therefore, both concern behaviors that appear to be normative for members of the social collectivity under consideration. Some degree of homogeneity is thus assumed for group members; similarities are given priority over differences; and behaviors that group members appear to share receive greater emphasis than do those that seem to be anomalous or idiosyncratic.[17]

Elliott Oring's study of the folksongs sung by English and American whalers during the nineteenth and early twentieth century illustrates the similarities between nation- or tribal-focused and subgroup-oriented studies of folklore as culture.[18] "The society I have chosen to study," writes Oring, "is based on an occupational consciousness of kind, that is, the members of this society recognize themselves as a distinct group on the basis of their occupation." Singing is a well-documented tradition among members of this occupational subgroup; and songs about whaling, notes Oring, "could only have originated among men engaged in the profession" and were "perpetuated almost exclusively among men who had engaged in the whaling enterprise."

Overall, "the culture of the whalemen"

is "realistically reflected" in the songs, "sometimes in minute detail," Oring reports. Inexperienced men made up the majority of the crew members on most ships, for instance; and the songs realistically portray experiences and treatment of these "greenies." Agents recruited crews and outfitted them for journeys, often romanticizing a physically demanding job that usually lasted much longer than the recruits were led to believe (see Box 6–5).

Once they had signed up and set sail, greenhands had to master their jobs quickly, from rigging ropes to standing watch and looking for whales from a 100-foot-high masthead (see Box 6–6). Songs highlight whale sightings and describe the actions taken after one occurs (Box 6–7).

"The boats are lowered away and they spread out to cover a large area and wait for the whale to rise," Oring reports. The songs detail the competition among boat crews to be the ones to make the strike. The whale is harpooned when it surfaces, and the harpoon line is let out. As the wounded whale tires, the crew pulls the line in; and the boats move alongside the floundering ani-

---

BOX 6–6
Whale Watch at the Masthead: Song Excerpt

It's now to the masthead
All of us must go
And when you see those sperm whales
Sing out there she blows.

But that is not all to his sorrow he will
    find
Two hours to the mast head he must go.
He descends to the deck with head dizzy
    and sick
And for his life he would not give a
    damn.[20]

BOX 6–7
Excerpt from Song Describing Whale Sighting

Next morning at daybreak
About five o'clock
The man at the masthead
Cried yonder she spouts.

Where away does she lay
And the answer from aloft
Two points on our lee bow
And about three miles off.

Then it's call up all hands
And it's be of good cheer
Put your tubs in your boats
Have your bow lines all clear.

Away up your boats now
Jump in you boat's crew
Lower away now lower away
My brave fellows do.[21]

BOX 6–5
Whaleman's Song Excerpt

'Tis advertised in Boston
New York, and Albany
Five hundred young Americans
Are wanted for the sea.

They take you down to Bedford
That famous whaling port
And give you to some landsharks
To board and fit you out.

It's then that they will show you
Their fine clipper ships
They say you'll have five hundred sperm
    [whales]
Before you're six months out.[19]

---

mal. "The officer of the boat then plunges a six foot lance into the whale's lungs several times in order to kill it," writes Oring. As the dying whale struggles, the water "becomes extremely bloody"; and when the whale dies, "it rolls over on its side with its dorsal fin projecting above the water." This final phase of the struggle is repeatedly dramatized in whalemen's songs (see Box 6–8). Moreover, in songs describing the killing of a whale, comments Oring, the scene "is depicted realistically with little exaggeration or idealization. The literary conventions accurately describe whaling customs."

"Why did the whalemen sing songs which described their profession, often in the minutest detail?" asks Oring. The answer, he states, is that singing about "the capture of the whale" was a way of symbolizing the whalemen's "wish to return home," an act that could not occur until the ship's crew had accomplished its mission. "Whaling voyages lasting three or four years were not considered excessive," Oring reports, adding that trips of both forty-seven months and eleven years are on record. Therefore, the killing of each whale not only brought the crew a step closer to achieving its goal, but also shortened the amount of time remaining before the ship returned to its home port. On "long voyages to capture the sperm whale there would be weeks and months of bad luck during which no whales would be sighted, let alone taken," Oring informs his readers. Singing songs about success in whale hunting "during these long periods of ill luck, when the wish to return home was undoubtedly at its peak," was obviously a way for the whalemen to enjoy vicariously the kinds of experiences that were essential before their wish to return home could become a reality.

To further support his hypothesis that singing songs about capturing whales served a wish-fulfilling function, Oring describes another traditional activity in which whalemen engaged during long and idle periods at sea. Many of these sailors etched graphic images onto the teeth and bones of whales, creating a distinctive art form known as *scrimshaw*. Whaling scenes such as those described in songs predominate in scrimshaw art. However, whalemen also frequently etched figures of women. There were no women on the ships, of course; but they obviously were very much in the artists' thoughts. Furthermore, some pieces of scrimshaw called *busk* were made specifically for the creator's wife or sweetheart, to be worn next to her heart. This offers further evidence, contends Oring, that while it was demanding and often exciting, the whaleman's life was also a lonely one. Thoughts of and longing for loved ones and home manifested themselves expressively in both verbal and material art that made life a bit more bearable for the whalemen as they dreamed of and waited for return and reunion.

Rosan A. Jordan combines cultural and sexual identity in her study of Mexican-American women's traditional narratives. She postulates that these accounts reveal differences between male and female ethos and worldview.[23]

"The Hispanic ideal of modest and submissive behavior for women and dominant, aggressive behavior for males is a familiar one," writes Jordan. Within the family, the male commands authority. The woman nurtures others while sacrificing herself. Men engage in extramarital affairs; father-

---

BOX 6-8
Song Excerpt Describing the Death of a Whale

Spout spout spout
The waves are purling all about
Every billow on its head
Strangely wears a crest of red

See her lash the foaming main
In her flurry and her pain
Take good heed my hearts of oak
Lest her flukes as she lies

Swiftly hurl you to the skies
But lo her giant strength is broke
Now she turns a mass of lead
The mighty mountain whale is dead.[22]

Figure 6–7: An example of scrimshaw or whale ivory that has been etched, the incised lines darkened with ink; it portrays a longboat approaching a harpooned whale (photo by Louis S. Martel, courtesy Mystic Seaport Museum Collection, Mystic, Connecticut).

ing children, whether legitimate or not, proves virility. Females must remain chaste. According to Jordan, the folklore of women reveals how they "actually view their culturally assigned roles and how they respond to cultural pressures," at least in symbolic form if not in individual actions.

For example, Jordan collected a number of stories in Texas from three sisters of Mexican heritage. The "vaginal serpent" theme dominates. Narratives describe snakes or lizards pursuing and sexually assaulting women. One of the women, Mary, reported:

> This is about the things that old ladies talk about, you know, when they're out in the country. And they said that before there was any outhouses and you had to go to the bathroom behind the bushes, you had to be very careful because there was kinds of animals that liked women and would get inside.
>
> And there was this girl that was real young, and some kind of animal got inside of her, and so she got pregnant; and she was *like* she was pregnant. She had morning sickness and she started getting fat, so her parents thought that she had been running around with a boy, you know, that somebody had gotten her pregnant. They used to beat her up and try to get her to tell who the boy was that was responsible for her condition. But she

didn't know what they were talking about, because, you know, in those days they would never tell their children about the facts of life or anything.

> So this went on for some time, a few months, and so one day they went out to town or someplace and they locked her in the house, and when they came back—they were gone I guess a couple of days or so—and when they came back they found it, that she had given birth to a whole bunch of little animals, and they were eating her up. And she was dead.

Mary also told of an incident involving a snake that people in West Texas call *chirrionera*. It "grows real long and likes women. And they whistle, you know, like regular men—wolf whistle, you know. They whistle to women as they go by." A group of families lived in the same area. The men worked in the fields. The women stayed at home with the children, but at a certain hour they took their husbands lunch. When they walked through the woods the *chirrionera* whistled at them. Their husbands advised, "Well, stay together and he won't bother you."

Because she was pregnant, one woman couldn't maintain the others' pace. When the group emerged from the woods she was not among them. The husband went in search of her. He found her lying at the base of the tree where the *chirrionera* whistled at the women. "And so when he got there," said Mary, "the baby had been born, and the snake had choked the baby, was wrapped around the baby. And she [the mother] was dead."

Mary's sister, Betty, described to Rosan Jordan several incidents that had occurred in the family. One time their great-grand-mother was walking in the field. "She was having her period and he [a *chirrionera*] could smell that. And he got in her skirt and she couldn't get him out, and finally she had to take off her skirt and leave it there. She came home in her pettiskirt. Yeah, they can smell it when a woman is having her period, and they like it, and they try to get up there."

In another account, Betty told of the time her grandmother was nursing Cosme. When she awoke each morning, "she was dry. And she wouldn't have nothing to give Cosme. She had blisters around her nipples, and she was dry." One night she lay awake. Just before dawn "she felt it get on top of the covers. And Tio Neo got up and killed it." Once the *chirrionera* was gone the blisters disappeared. "This really happened. I mean, some of the things may be made up, but I know that to be true." According to Jordan, Mary stressed "the discomfort, helplessness, and humiliation of the woman" in one story. "And Betty grouped the tale with others that emphasize women's vulnerability to physical assault." The women in these narratives "exist in a world where their sexuality makes them constantly vulnerable. They are liable to sexual assault by snakes or lizards and are mistreated by their families, who wish to restrict their sexual activities. They suffer, are humiliated, and are vindicated only in dying," writes Jordan. "Demonstrations of female sexuality such as pregnancy or menstruation make them even more vulnerable. They die giving birth; snakes steal their mother's milk.

In several of the stories, other women turn their backs on the suffering of the victim." Women learn early in life to fear sexual violation and not to enjoy sex. "Thus, in addition to portraying women as abused and misused by others, the narratives . . . also reveal a certain degree of self-hatred in women and a distrust of their own sexuality."

Jordan continues: "The women's narratives . . . show women to be not so much passive and submissive as helpless and vulnerable, and not so much modest and pure as fearful and self-loathing where sexuality is concerned." The vaginal serpent cycle also "reflects anxieties related to bearing children as well as sexual anxieties."

Other stories provide insight into attitudes toward maternal activities and attendant conflicts and stresses. For instance, many accounts have been recorded about La Llorona, or the Weeping Woman, who wanders grief-stricken in search of her "lost" children (usually killed by her). Many Mexican-American women, who are expected to have numerous children as proof of their husbands' masculinity, fear the dangers of childbearing; "they are also aware of the difficulties poor women face in giving their children adequate care," adds Jordan. "It is likely that the La Llorona tradition serves as an expression of some of the fears and apprehensions they feel about being mothers and caring for children." Sometimes, too, the frightening figure may be intended "as a cultural reinforcement to encourage conscientious maternal behavior." (See Box 6–9 for examples of stories about La Llorona.)

Yet other lore expresses women's resentment against cultural norms that define their role as women, against male domination and treachery, and against overprotectiveness. "Women's folklore can be an important means of indicating differences in male and female ethos and worldview and exposing ideologies that have been ac-

BOX 6–9
Examples of La Llorona Stories

In the dead of the night, the country folk say, a sad voice calls for the attention of passersby. A beautiful country girl, it is said, was taken into service, brought to the capital, and there seduced by a young reprobate of the aristocracy. The girl returned home to have her baby. She drowned the infant in a creek and soon afterward went mad. Her cry is heard at night as she searches creeks and branches for her lost child.[24]

*   *   *

A long time ago there was a woman who had two children. She did not love them; so she mistreated and neglected them. The children were always hungry and cold because their mother was too busy going to parties and dances to take care of them.

Finally one of the children died and later the other died too. The woman felt no remorse. She continued to lead a very gay life. When she died, she had not confessed her sins or repented of her ill-treatment of the children. Now she appears in the east and southeast parts of Austin [Texas] grieving for her children. Her soul is doing penance for her sins.[25]

*   *   *

My brother had a very good friend who was a shoemaker. The two were heavy drinkers, and they liked to go out together to eat and drink.

Well, one night my brother went to see his friend about twelve-thirty and prevailed on him to go out to drink with him.

Shortly after the two had started out for their favorite saloon, they noticed that a very attractive woman was walking just ahead of them. They decided to follow her. The two followed for a long time, but they couldn't catch up with her. When it seemed that they were coming up even with the woman, she suddenly seemed to get about half a block ahead of them. Finally, my brother and his friend decided to turn back, but as a parting gesture they said, "Good-by, my dear!"

At the same time that the two said, "Good-by, my dear!" the attractive woman whom they had followed turned around. She had the face of a horse, her fingernails were shiny and tin-like, and she gave a long, piercing cry. It was La Llorona.

My brother would have run, but his friend had fainted, and he had to revive him. The two reformed after that encounter with La Llorona.[26]

*   *   *

The weeping woman was a young Mexican woman who had an illegitimate baby. The father of the child took it away from her and drowned it in a small lake. This caused the young woman to go crazy, and she drowned herself in the same lake. She now appears during the summer months in the lake not far from the shore, weeping and wailing. When a man goes in to save her, she drifts towards the middle of the lake just out of his reach. When they get to the middle of the lake, the man is exhausted. He at last reaches her and grabs her so he can bring her back to shore. But she hugs him and starts to laugh, and they both go down together.[27]

Figure 6–8: Concerned about the threat of nuclear war, on August 4, 1985, more than 20,000 people encircled the Pentagon and other buildings (the Lincoln Memorial is in the background) with a 15-mile long ribbon of fabric panels depicting "What I cannot bear to think of as lost forever in a nuclear war" (photographer unknown; courtesy Linda Pershing).

cepted as representing the total culture as reflecting only a male ideal," writes Jordan. The male ideal of a woman is that she is submissive, suffers in silence, represses sexual needs, and serves as a symbol of purity. In women's folklore, Jordan concludes, one can see "reflections of the fears and anxieties that women experience because of these ideals" and catch "glimpses of women's resentment of the repressive role given them."

Rather than just venting feelings of resentment against cultural norms, sometimes a group uses folklore actively for social and political critique in attempts to alter institutions, values, and policies dominating their lives. According to Linda Pershing's research, this is what occurred in 1985 when more than 20,000 women marched on Washington, D.C., to surround the Pentagon with a ribbon of panels they had sewn in protest of nuclear armament.[28]

The ribbon was the brainchild in 1982 of Justine Merritt, a 69-year-old former high school teacher in Denver, Colorado, who learned needlework from her grandmother and mother. She spent more than 700 hours on a yard-long panel, creating a rainbow collage of embroidered names of people dear to her: "What I cannot bear to think of as lost forever in a nuclear war." A plan began to emerge among a group of close friends to encircle the Pentagon with a ribbon of panels on August 4, 1985, to commemorate the fortieth anniversary of the atomic bombing of Hiroshima and Nagasaki. As news of the idea spread, thousands of women made panels. Motifs ranged from family portraits to butterflies, abstract designs, and, especially, children. Themes dwelt on a concern for wholeness and relatedness (between nature and humanity, among peoples of different races and ethnicities, and between the personal and the political). "The imagery is startling and compelling," writes Pershing. "Think of it—a ribbon around the Pentagon—lengths of colorful fabric stitched by women and ceremonially wrapped around an impenetrable, stone building that symbolizes the nation's military might."

For the women involved, "the making of Ribbon panels became an affirmation of life and an act of self-actualization and empowerment, choosing to create a thing of beauty and value in the face of despair over the

Figure 6–9: Ribbon panel by Alexandra Genetti of Woodacre, California, called "History of the World in One Yard," which depicts the creation and evolution of life on the earth including amoebae, dinosaur, hieroglyph, Egypt along the Nile, the Great Wall of China, the Hag Sofia, the modern skyline of San Francisco, and her two children's faces along with ancient goddesses and the Virgin Mary; embroidered in small letters across the top is "Continue Goddess, Goddess breast, Breast Milk, Milk Flow, Flow life, Life Pass, Pass time, Time Continue" (photo by Linda Pershing).

possibility of future annihilation." Ribbon panels disclosed flaws in the fabric of American culture, "metaphorically accentuating what needs to be done to repair the damage." Further, writes Pershing, "By encircling the Pentagon, an unmistakable symbol of national militarism, panel makers were commenting on the continuing escalation of nuclear weaponry that many feared would lead to the destruction of all they cherished." In addition, "The Ribbon represents the voices of those who are often trivialized or ignored by legislators and policymakers. With their appliquéd diapers and embroidered flower gardens panel makers suggested that the details of their personal lives—details overlooked by 'the powers that be'—were what led them to participate in a public demonstration and that these details were, in fact, the essence of their protest."

Like Rosan Jordan and Linda Pershing,

Herminia Q. Meñez explores the folklore of a sex-based group.[29] In this case it is males in a particular occupation at a certain social level; the lore is an aspect of material culture. Referring to the jeepney, with its painted scenes and provocative sayings, Meñez writes that most researchers have incorrectly interpreted this vehicle in the Philippines as a unique expression of Filipino identity. "The emphasis heretofore on the jeepney as a visual encapsulation of Filipino culture has obscured the significance of the lower class, urban, male, occupational subculture of jeepney drivers in the interpretation of their folk art and inscriptions." After all, it is these men who usually paint and inscribe the vehicles. What are they attempting to communicate, and why?

Dominant themes in the vehicle's ornaments include love and sex, driving speed, economic success, religion, and family. A

Figure 6–10: Jeepney drivers in the Philippines often proclaim sexual prowess (photo by Hermenia Meñez, courtesy UCLA Folklore and Mythology Archives).

Figure 6–11: The text at the bottom of the vehicle, Kapantay ay Langit, means "Heaven's Equal," referring to the quality of the ride (photo by Hermenia Meñez, courtesy UCLA Folklore and Mythology Archives).

radio and cassette tape player, and even a small television set, blare out to attract the commuter and impress upon the public the driver's financial success. Paintings of rural scenes and crocheted curtains are reminiscent of village homes. Objects such as rosary beads, holy pictures, and miniature altars speak of religious interests.

Inscriptions on jeepneys reveal the same themes. Of 264 signs documented, 27 percent concerned love and sex, 13 percent economic success, 12 percent driving speed, 8 percent religion, and 8 percent the family. The remainder were devoted to titles of popular shows and songs (7%), a desire to emigrate (7%), memos to riders (3%),

ethnicity and nationalism (6%), and a miscellany (7%).

Inscriptions feature linguistic play enriched by the multilingual resources of the city, including English, Tagalog, and Taglish or "mix-mix." Drivers exploit language, transposing syllables or superimposing native and foreign words on one another. They produce double or triple entendres, such as "CHICKSeater." According to Meñez, the term "chicks may be American slang for girls, or it may refer to *balut* (chicken or duck egg embryo)," a favorite delicacy said to increase male potency. "Reading both meanings simultaneously creates a highly erotic metaphor," writes Meñez. "At the same time, the sign can be interpreted as an innocent play on 'two-seater'." The decorated vehicles "reflect the flamboyance, earthy humor, satiric wit, and daredevil driving style of their creators," Meñez observes. They originate as competitive strategies for achieving power and status. "The use of elegant titles is another manifestation of the competition for social status," like the extensively painted scenes and the bold inscriptions. Some of the names suggest playful attempts to affiliate with royalty: "Jeepney King II," "Road Emperor," "Jason the King," "Prince William," and "Denis D'Great." Others allege a privileged childhood. Some are sexually suggestive: "Lady Killer," "Chick Hunter," and "Baby Maker." Such hyperbole and boastfulness contribute to the jeepney driver's image as "a model of machismo for many lower class urbanites."

In sum, "Jeepney inscriptions are rhetorical devices for attaining social and material gains," writes Meñez. The lavish ornamentation and the mottoes, prayers, proverbs, captions, and one-liners are intended to entice the commuter and to "provide entertainment for the duration of the ride." For the drivers, aggressive language and images help "relieve some of the tensions generated by the frenetic pace of urban life," the tropic heat, and the noxious fumes. "As city dwellers—drivers and passengers—battle with the impossible traffic in Manila's congested streets, jeepney folk art and inscriptions provide a relief from what would otherwise be a grim battlefield." Although originating in fierce competition for financial gain and status—and being a product of a lower class, urban male, occupational subculture—the jeepney is a welcome sight for commuters of varied backgrounds.

What is the relationship between folklore and other aspects of culture in a female occupational group—particularly in a modern, organizational setting? If the lore seems "deviant," is it invariably harmful to self, the work subculture, or the organization as a whole? Patricia Atkinson Wells addresses such questions in a study of the "paradox of functional dysfunction" in the behavior of staff personnel at a Girl Scout camp held each summer on Catalina Island in California.[30]

The official image of the Girl Scouts is that of young women who are proper and decorous. "A Girl Scout is clean in thought, word, and deed; a Girl Scout is a friend to all and a sister to every other Girl Scout; a Girl Scout is kind to animals," etc. It is difficult for staff to live up to the image, policies, and professed values of the organization, however, "in a work environment that is isolated, stressful, and often hostile, and in which there is intense confinement and enforced communalism," writes Wells. Some respond by engaging in activities that violate the image and proscribed codes of conduct. They cope "through jokes and joking relationships, eccentric behavior, and/or ridicule or rejection of the Girl Scout image."

One summer, for example, a group of staffers spoke to each other with lisps. During another season they adopted spurious Southern accents. Several defaced (or personalized) the camp uniform of white blouse, green shorts, and green knee socks by recutting the shorts, adding decorative braid or ribbon, or wearing badges and buttons conveying various philosophical or political beliefs. Some wore boxer shorts or 1950s-style house-dresses. Many sang parodies of camp songs, whether "obscene, scatological, or merely silly," Wells writes. For instance, "Girl Scouts together, happy are we" became "Girl Scouts together, *sappy* are we."

The staff members developed sayings and catchphrases setting a tone for the season or expressing attitudes toward work. "Just when you thought it was safe to go back to the water"—derived from an advertisement for the film *Jaws II*—jokingly conveyed the serious threat of operating an oceanfront camp. "Another day, another dime" commented on the unrelenting sameness of daily tasks as well as staff members' remuneration. "Miller Time"—a beer slogan—expressed both pride in completing an arduous task and the need for a well-earned break. Camp-owned sailing craft carried names for popular alcoholic drinks, such as *Daiquiri, Margarita,* and *Harvey W.* (for "Wallbanger").

"Status boundaries, power, and interpersonal relations assume looming importance in this kind of enforced community life," Wells observes. "Pranks aimed at undermining or ridiculing authority or the organizationally sanctioned hierarchy were common." For example, staff members frequently stole the 100-pound bell sounded for wake-up or meals. Administrators' underwear often flew from the flagpole and had to be publicly reclaimed during the formal flag-raising. The special table for high-ranking staff sometimes wound up on the dining hall roof, completely set for a meal. Feared or despised personnel had their cabins wrapped in toilet paper while they slept inside.

Much of this folklore might appear to management to be dysfunctional, because it goes against the organizational image and policy, and since it does not further particular organizational objectives. "Such behavior does, however, function for members of the work group as survival tools, aesthetic outlets, and expressions of group identity, community, and solidarity," writes Wells. This expressive behavior makes it possible for people to do their work, and "it may help in achieving *other* organizational objectives—a paradox of 'functional dysfunction.'" That is, such behavior aids in achieving in a "perverse" sort of way exactly those skills, values, and qualities most cherished and taught to campers: imagination, initiative, problem solving, and teamwork. Thus,

Figure 6–12: *A portion of one wall of Girl Scout counselors' cabin at a summer camp on Catalina; alcoholic beverages are prohibited (photo by Patricia A. Wells and Teri Brewer, courtesy UCLA Folklore and Mythology Archives).*

Figure 6–13: *"A Dime a Dozen" conveys the feelings of overworked, underpaid counselors in a Girl Scout camp (photo by Patricia A. Wells and Teri Brewer, courtesy UCLA Folklore and Mythology Archives).*

the behavior which seemingly deviates from cultural norms may be functional for the individual, the occupational subgroup, and even the larger organization. This is not always the case, however, as a study of a children's joke seems to indicate.

C. W. Sullivan, III, examines the relationship between a joke and other aspects of culture in an age-based group.[31] He cites "an unusually long text which includes in one tale all of the major motifs that occur in most of the versions collected" (normalform). Called "Johnny Says His ABCs," the joke is "very popular among elementary schoolers and retains its popularity into the early junior high school years" (see Box 6–10).

That this is a historical document is evident by the joke's having been collected in the United States and England for at least 30 years, according to Sullivan. He notes that one might approach the joke in terms of genre concerns, placing it within a larger group of "dirty jokes" or "joking narratives" in general. Or one could identify motifs or perhaps establish a tale type from the set of versions. "But this sort of categorization establishes what the joke is without attempting to explain why it is so consistently popular among children," writes Sullivan. He opts for a "contextual" approach that relates the joke to culture.

From this perspective, the joke seems to have several possible meanings or to serve multiple functions in the lives of schoolchildren. "That 'Johnny Says His ABCs' quite accurately depicts the dehumanization inherent" in school as an institution is likely, but it is "only one clue to the joke's continued popularity," he contends. Like many other jokes and songs among children, this narrative mocks the school and teachers. The "teacher comes out on the losing end in an exchange with a student," a theme in stories about teachers arriving late and being locked out, or in the examples of correct but inappropriate responses by students. For example, a teacher yells, "Order, children, order!" at an unruly class. A student in the back replies, "I'll have a hamburger and fries." "'Johnny Says His ABCs,'" writes Sullivan, seems not

---

BOX 6–10
"Johnny Says His ABCs"

There's this kid, Johnny, an' he's always sayin' bad words, right in class, in front of the teacher, an' everything. Well, one day, the teacher's havin' everybody say the alphabet, an' Johnny's raisin' his hand like he wants to say it. The teacher figures there's no way Johnny can say bad words when he's sayin' the alphabet, so she tells him, "Go ahead."

Johnny says he doesn't want to say the alphabet; he wants to go to the bathroom. The teacher says bathroom time was a half hour ago an' why didn't he go then? He says he didn't have to go *then*; he has to go *now*.

The teacher says he can't go now, an' he'll have to wait for the next bathroom time. Then she asks, "Who'll say the alphabet?" Johnny waves his hand around, but the teacher says he can't go to the bathroom now. Johnny says he doesn't have to go anymore, an' he wants to say the alphabet.

The teacher says, "Go ahead."

Johnny says, "A, B, C, D, E, F, G, H, I, J, K, L, M, N, O, Q, R, S, T, U, V, W, X, Y, Z!"

The teacher says, "Where's the P?"

Johnny says, "It's runnin' down my leg!"[32]

merely to make the teacher a victim of a student's clever answer, but to assault the entire institution of school. "Ultimately it is the lesson that is disrupted by Johnny's accident and triumph." (See Box 6–11 for examples of common parodies of the song "The Battle Hymn of the Republic" that express children's views about school authorities.)

Sullivan adds: "There are still other reasons why 'Johnny Says His ABCs' has a strong appeal to elementary school children. Its scatological nature links it with numerous other items of children's folklore about body parts and bodily functions." The joke permits the child to utter a word, even making a pun, that might otherwise be prohibited. (See Box 6–12 for some examples.)

"In addition," notes Sullivan, "this joke may be popular precisely because it deals with a common elementary schooler's anxi-ety, the fear of not being able to 'hold it' until bathroom time." Thus, "'Johnny Says His ABCs' turns the potentially embarrassing situation into a triumph for the student; it is the teacher who is defeated. A child might feel a bit less anxious knowing that the teacher might actually be at fault."

Sullivan concludes: "Ultimately, however, the specific motifs of this joke, as well as the context in which the narrative is transmitted and enjoyed, suggest that the primary focus of 'Johnny Says His ABCs' is the 'hidden' curriculum of the elementary school," that of schools as institutions going beyond academic purposes to practice dominance and subordination, regimenting children and enforcing discipline. Hence, "the children who tell this joke are responding (on the conscious or the unconscious level) to the social as well as the academic nature of the school experience," contends Sullivan.

BOX 6–11

Children's Parodies of "The Battle Hymn of the Republic"

Mine eyes have seen the glory
  of the burning of the school
We have tortured every teacher
  and we've broken every rule
His truth is marching on.

Glory, glory hallelujah,
  teacher hit me with a ruler
Met her at the door
  with a Colt .44
The truth is marching on.

* * *

My eyes have seen the glory
  of the burning of the school
We have tortured every teacher,
  we have broken every rule
We have stood in every corner
  of that cotton-pickin' school
Our fame is marching on.

Glory, glory hallelujah,
  teacher hit me with a ruler
I stood behind the door
  with a loaded forty-four
And that teacher don't teach no more.

* * *

Mine eyes have seen the glory
  of the burning of the school
We have tortured every teacher
  and have broken every rule
We have hung [principal's name]
  on the flagpole of the school
As the brats go marching on.

Glory, glory hallelujah,
  teacher hit me with a ruler
I hit her on the bean
  with a rotten tangerine
As the brats go marching on.[33]

BOX 6-12
Children's "Naughty" Folklore

Ladies and gentlemen,
Take my advice,
Pull down your pants
And slide on the ice.

⋆   ⋆   ⋆

A bug and a flea
Went out to sea
Upon a reel of cotton;
The flea was drowned
But the bug was found
Biting a lady's bottom.[34]

⋆   ⋆   ⋆

Teacher, teacher, I declare.
I see someone's underwear.
They're not white. They're not blue.
They're not pink, but they sure do stink!

⋆   ⋆   ⋆

Jesus loves me, this I know,
For the Bible tells me so.
I am Jesus' little lamb.
Yes, you're goddamned right, I am.

⋆   ⋆   ⋆

Jack and Jill went up the hill
Riding on an elephant.
Jill got off to help Jack off the elephant.[35]

William A. Wilson's investigation of Mormon missionary folklore illustrates how a culturally oriented analysis of members of a religious and occupational subgroup can reveal broader human processes and concerns.[36] Wilson begins his essay by stating that, like all human beings, individuals who serve as Mormon missionaries are identifiable in multiple ways. Using himself as an example, Wilson writes, "I am a Mormon; but I am also a father, a teacher, a Democrat, an Idahoan, a tennis fan, a photography nut, and so on." In some situations, Wilson implies, his identity as a Mormon is irrelevant; but at other times it becomes dominant. When this is the case, Wilson states, "I will think and act in traditionally prescribed ways, in ways somewhat similar to those in which other Mormons will think and act when their Mormon identities are dominant."

Mormons who serve as missionaries are also "composite[s] of . . . identities," Wilson notes; yet "for the most part, from the time they are called to the [mission] field until they are released two years later, these young people [most between the ages of nineteen and twenty-three] are engaged full

tilt in missionary activity." Furthermore, "Even in those moments when they are not directly involved in proselyting efforts," adds Wilson, "they must at all times, day and night, be accompanied by at least one other missionary companion, a circumstance that reminds them constantly of their missionary role." Hence, Mormon missionaries' "shared identity persists for a sustained period," and "it is possible to identify a missionary lifestyle that has produced a common folklore."

One aspect of this lifestyle is the social status distinction between experienced and inexperienced missionaries. The latter, commonly referred to as *greenies*, are made more aware of the obvious when, shortly after arriving at their posts, they become victims of seasoned missionaries' pranks. Sometimes the initiates are instructed to follow absurd, though purportedly "official," rules, such as saving stubs of bus tickets for a supposed eventual rebate, or learning a numbering system so they can save time by referring to prayers by numbers rather than actually reciting them (see Box 6–13).

Initiation into Mormon missionary cul-

BOX 6–13
Mormon Missionary Stories of Praying by Numbers

[In Texas a senior companion instructed his new junior companion how prayers were to be offered in the mission.]

"Now, Elder [addressing an inexperienced missionary], out here we pray an awful lot. If we had to repeat these prayers all the time we'd spend most of our time on our knees and never have time to do the Lord's work. Instead, we have all the prayers numbered." With that the two slid to their knees and the senior volunteered to say the prayer.

"Number 73," he prayed, and jumped into bed, leaving the new missionary in a crumpled mass on the floor.

*   *   *

[In Spain greenies and senior missionaries prepared to eat a first dinner together.]

The zone leader asked one of the older elders to say the blessing on the food. They all bowed their heads, and the elder very seriously said, "Number nine. Amen." While the poor new missionaries were still recovering from that, the zone leader looked at the elder who had said the prayer and just as seriously retorted, "Elder, you always say the same prayer."[37]

---

ture involves not only surviving pranks but also mastering a specialized vocabulary. Writes Wilson:

> A greenie newly arrived in the field will often hear his companions speaking a language he does not understand. A junior companion is not just a junior companion—he is "little brother," "the young one," "boy," "the slave." The senior companion, on the other hand, is "the boss," "the pope," "the chief," "sir." The girl back home is "the wife," "the lady in waiting." The rejection letter from this girl is "the Dear John," "suitable for framing," "the acquittal," "the Big X." The mission home is "the zoo," "the Kangaroo court." Investigators are "gators," "our people." Good investigators are "goldies," "dry Mormons." Investigators who are not interested in the message but like to talk to missionaries are "professionals," "gummers," "lunchy," "the punch and cookie route." The Book of Mormon is a "bomb" (BOM). Baptisms are "tisms," "dunks," "splashes," "payday." Tracting is "bonking on doors," "self-torture." The tracting area is "the beat," "the jungle," "the war zone." Good missionaries are "spiritual giants," "rocks," "nails." Aspiring missionaries are "straight-arrow Sams," "cliff climbers," "pharisees." Bad missionaries are "screws," "hurters," "leaks," "liberals." The mission president is "the man," "Big Roy," "the head rhino." A returned missionary is "a reactivated makeout," "an octopus with a testimony."

Wilson notes, "No missionary will know all of these terms. But almost all will know some of them or others like them." When Wilson and co-researcher John B. Harris asked individuals "why they used the language," they were told most often that "it creates a feeling of self-identification with other missionaries." Wilson continues: "It contributes, in other words, to that sense of community the initiation pranks help to establish. Once a greenie learns it he no longer is a greenie, an outsider. He is now a missionary. He belongs. He speaks the language." Knowing and using the missionary slang is also "a means of letting off steam," according to Wilson. "A missionary who can laugh at his beat-up bicycle ('the meat grinder'), at his food ('green slop'), at his apartment ('the cave'), and even at chafing rules is likely to be much more effective than one who broods over these circumstances."

Learning and using slang is not the only way for Mormon missionaries "to cope with the pressures resulting from submitting to a way of life and to the sometimes nagging rules prescribed by mission authorities," Wilson asserts. Storytelling often functions in this way, too. The stories Wilson and Harris have recorded most frequently are versions of a tale type that describes the clever but unsuccessful efforts of a pair of missionaries to deceive their superiors into thinking they are proselytizing while they instead sneak off to relax, see the local sights, or travel. (See Box 6–14 for an example.)

Wilson describes the kinds of variations that occur among the multiple versions of

this "mixed-up-report narrative" that he and Harris have collected over the years.

The details can change. The landlady can send all the reports in at once to save money. The place the elders visit will depend on the mission; from Brazil they go to Argentina, from Chile to the Easter Islands, from Italy to Egypt, from Norway to Scotland, from Germany to Yugoslavia, from Okinawa to Hong Kong, and from parts of the United States to other parts of the United States. In all cases, however, the structure is the same: the missionaries prepare activity reports for several weeks in advance and leave them with the landlady; the missionaries take an unauthorized trip; the landlady sends the reports in out of sequence (or all at once); the missionaries are caught.

In discussing the story, one Mormon informant said that he enjoyed it "because missionaries don't do that kind of thing, and these guys did." Stated another, "Those of us who were straight, who kept the rules, had to tell stories like these to survive." Noted a third, "You would always like to do something like that yourself, and you kinda admire someone who had the guts to do it."

Storytelling among Mormon missionaries thus serves to reinforce the importance of adhering to norms of behavior by recounting experiences illustrating what happens to those who break the rules. But while the mixed-up-report narrative is generally considered humorous, usually evoking smiles or laughter from tellers and listeners, other tales are more serious and sobering. "One widely known story, recounted throughout the mission system," writes Wilson, "tells of elders who . . . are struck dead for testing their priesthood power by attempting to ordain a post or a coke bottle or an animal." Another tells about a missionary whose praying to the Devil results in the appearance of a black figure on a horse and the missionary's subsequent punishment. Sometimes he dies or leaps from an upstairs window to his death;

BOX 6–14
Mormon Missionary Mixed-Up-Report Story

Two missionaries were stationed in Zambia (formerly Northern Rhodesia) and were doing their normal missionary work. After a while they decided to split and take off into the Congo. Their chapel was only forty miles from the Congo, and Leopoldville, where all the revolutionary excitement was going on, was not much further away. So they devised a plan—to make out their weekly reports to mission headquarters two weeks in advance and give them to their landlady, who in turn would send one in each week at an appointed time. By this means, the missionaries would have two free weeks to venture into the wilds of the Congo. All this would have gone well, except the stupid landlady sent the report for the second week in first and the report for the first week second. That spilled the tomatoes, and the mission president caught them.[38]

or he may be found "suspended in air, his hair sometimes as white as an old man's"; "slammed against the wall"; pinned to the ceiling, dead; or burned to death in his bed, sometimes with only "the shell of a body" remaining with "cooked out" insides. Other stories portray the torment or death of missionaries for breaking such other rules as "experimenting with spiritualism, playing the ouija board, swimming, boating, dating a girl, playing rock music, arguing with companions, not staying with companions, or sometimes simply not working hard enough." Such stories, Wilson writes, "have an emotional impact" that is impossible to characterize. They are frightening as well as didactic; and those who tell and hear such tales "will not lightly violate mission rules."

Mormon missionary stories are not all concerned with the consequences of violating behavioral norms, however. Many also depict "a generous God" who rewards "those who do his will." Some such tales concern dutiful missionaries being miraculously rescued during a severe storm, or winning a convert because they survive after eating poisoned food the person had earlier served them (see Box 6–15).

Others illustrate ways that missionaries emerge victorious during confrontations (see Box 6–16) and depict dedicated elders finding willing converts by knocking at just one more door at the end of a long and unsuccessful day. These stories portray "the very real dangers missionaries face on the highways and at the hands of the frequently hostile people they must try to convert," writes Wilson; and they illustrate the rewards that can come from keeping the faith and persevering.

Wilson's study demonstrates that folklore is an integral aspect of Mormon missionary culture and that it serves multiple functions. Playing and being made the butt of initiatory pranks, together with learning and using a specialized lexicon, serve as

---

BOX 6–15
A Mormon Missionary Poison Story

There were two elders who were tracting, and one woman invited them into her home and said she was looking for a true church. And she fed them. They made an appointment to come back and teach her some time later. As soon as they came back, and she saw who they were at the door, she invited them in and said, "I want to be baptized," without even talking to them. And they asked her why, and she said that she had read that the true servants of the Lord could eat poison things and they would not be harmed. And then she told them that what she had fed them last week had been poison.[39]

---

major means of enculturating individuals and making them feel that they are truly a part of a distinctive subgroup or community. Sharing traditional humorous anecdotes and didactic tales that recount the successes and failures of others teaches and reinforces norms of behavior that missionaries are expected to uphold. Language use and storytelling also provide means for missionaries to deal with job-created stress and enable them to break rules vicariously through fantasizing. Concludes Wilson:

The problems faced by missionaries are not just missionary problems; they are human problems. A missionary who tells a new junior companion to save worthless bus-ticket stubs is not much different from a boy scout who sends a tenderfoot on a snipe hunt or a logger who crams a greenhorn's lunch bucket full of grasshoppers. The world is full of greenies who, to function adequately, must first be initiated. Other people besides missionaries, then, must develop a sense of community, must deal with pressures imposed by the systems they live under, must encourage proper behavior, and must come at last to believe they can subdue the world. . . . From

BOX 6-16
Mormon Missionary Confrontation Stories

A jokester says, "I hear you guys believe in baptism by immersion," and throws a bucket of water on the elders, one replies, "Yeah, and we also believe in the laying on of hands," and then he "cools him." When a nosy lady snickers, "I hear you Mormons wear secret underwear," a sharp elder responds, "Well, isn't *your* underwear secret?" Or "Ma'am, there's nothing secret about our underwear. If you'll show us your underwear, we'll show you ours." When a redheaded Norwegian woman fumes, "I know what you guys do. You come over here to get all the women and you take them back to Salt Lake City and sell them," the missionary replies, "That's right. We just sent a shipment off last week. In fact, we had ten with red hair, and lost one dollar a piece on them." When a woman asks the missionaries at her door if it is true that all Mormons have horns, the new junior companion replies: "Yeah, as a matter of fact I just had mine clipped in Salt Lake just before I came out here." And she says, "Really?" and he says, "Yeah, you can feel the little bumps right here on my forehead." And so she put her hand on his forehead, "Well, I don't feel anything." And he said, "Not even a little bit silly?"[40]

Figure 6–14: Unknown to the administrators, young Mormon missionaries decorated the backs of ceiling tiles in the training center at Provo, Utah, with images and comments expressing their feelings and expectations about their forthcoming missions (photo by James B. Allen, courtesy William A. Wilson).

studying the folklore of missionaries, or railroaders, or college professors, we will, to be sure, discover what it means to be a missionary, a railroader, or a college professor. But if we learn to look, we will discover also what it means to be human.

Implicit in this quotation from Wilson's essay is the view that while folklore is culturally coded, describing and referring to experiences and symbols that are distinctive to individual groups and subgroups, it actually functions in the same ways for members of all social collectivities. Wilson further implies that one can generalize about the number and nature of functions of folklore, irrespective of its specific content or of the shared social identity that serves as the criterion for defining the membership of any given group whose folklore one might scrutinize.

William Bascom presents and supports this position explicitly.[41] Convinced that "the folklore of a people can be fully understood only through a thorough knowledge of their culture," Bascom surveys selected works whose authors conceptualize and analyze folklore in sociocultural contexts. On the basis of these studies, he concludes that one can speak about what folklore does for people in terms of four functions it repeatedly fulfills.

First, folklore enables human beings to "escape in fantasy from repressions imposed upon [them] by society, whether these repressions be sexual or otherwise and whether they result from taboos on incest or polygamy, or from a taboo on laughing at a person afflicted by yaws." Moreover, "folklore also reveals man's attempts to escape in fantasy from the conditions of his geographical environment and from his own biological limitations as a member of the genus and species *Homo sapiens.*" Zuni tales about violence and child abandonment that Benedict describes function in this way, as do those Finnish stories analyzed by Apo in which social status is inverted when exploiters become the exploited and vice versa. Telling and listening to narratives about nonconforming Mormon missionaries also function as ways of coping with repressions resulting from social pressures to adhere to demanding behavioral rules.

A second function of folklore, Bascom states, is to validate culture, "justifying its rituals and institutions to those who perform and observe them." For example, mythologies explain how things came to be the way they are and why phenomena behave or operate as they do. Hence, myths are told to justify, legitimize, and defend the status quo, usually as a reminder and reinforcer, but sometimes in response to skeptics' criticisms or malcontents' claims.

Examples of folklore can also serve as "pedagogic devices" and hence as means of educating people. Adults tell children scary stories to discipline them, notes Bascom; and they sing lullabies "to put them in a good humor." Fables and proverbs teach and reinforce morals and values, while riddling "sharpen[s] the wits of young children." In many societies, "folklore appears to be the principal feature in the general education of the child."

"In the fourth place," Bascom indicates, "folklore fulfills the important but often overlooked function of maintaining conformity to the accepted patterns of behavior." He explains how this differs from validating culture and enculturating or educating individuals: "More than simply serving to validate or justify institutions, beliefs, and attitudes, some forms of folklore are important as means of applying social pressure and exercising social control." Folklore is used instrumentally throughout life "to express disapproval" of behavior, on the one hand, and "to express social approval of those who conform," on the other. Proverbs, for instance, can be "highly effective in exercising social control." As Wilson's Mormon missionary data effectively illustrate, so can storytelling.

Bascom admits that the four functions he describes are not mutually exclusive and that he oversimplifies "the varied functions of folklore in order to stress certain important ones." He also states that to talk of "four functions of folklore" is to speak "loosely," since different folklore examples and the generic sets to which they belong have functions that "are to some extent distinctive and must be analyzed separately." But Bascom contends that the four functions he characterizes are important because they "can be grouped together under the single function of maintaining the stability of culture." This, Bascom concludes, is what is most important about folklore; and the multiple ways it contributes to the maintenance of cultural stability account for folklore's durability and pervasiveness.

> [Folklore] is used to inculcate the customs and ethical standards in the young, and as an adult to reward him with praise when he conforms, to punish him with ridicule or criticism when he deviates, to provide him with rationalizations when the institutions and conventions are challenged or questioned, to suggest that he be content with things as they are, and to provide him with a compensatory escape from "the hardships, the inequalities, the injustices" of everyday life. Here, indeed, is the basic paradox of folklore, that while it plays a vital role in transmitting and maintaining the institutions of a culture and in forcing the individual to conform to them, at the same time it provides socially approved outlets for the repressions which these same institutions impose upon him.[42]

Notes

1. Edward B. Tylor, *Primitive Culture: Researches into the Development of Mythology, Philosophy, Religion, Language, Art, and Custom*, 7th ed., 2 vols. in 1 (New York: Brentano's Publishers, 1924), p. 1.

2. Kai Laitinen, "The *Kalevala:* The Finnish National Epic," in Michael Owen Jones, ed., *The World of the Kalevala: Essays in Celebration of the 150 Year Jubilee of the Publication of the Finnish National Epic* (Los Angeles: UCLA Folklore and Mythology Publications, 1987), p. 33.

3. William John Thoms, letter in *The Athenaeum*, No. 982 (August 22, 1846), p. 862; reprinted in Richard M. Dorson, ed., *Peasant Customs and Savage Myths: Selections from the British Folklorists* (Chicago: University of Chicago Press, 1968), vol. 1, pp. 52–55. The quote is from the reprinted version, p. 53.

4. From Donald Ward, ed. and trans., *The German Legends of the Brothers Grimm* (Philadelphia: Institute for the Study of Human Issues, 1981), vol. 1, p. 11.

5. Thomas Wright, "On Dr. Grimm's German Mythology," in *Essays on Subjects Connected with the Literature, Popular Superstitions, and History of England in the Middle Ages*, 2 vols. (London: John Russell Smith, 1846), vol. 1, pp. 237–252; reprinted in Dorson, vol. 1, pp. 41–51. Quotes are from the reprinted version, pp. 41 and 43.

6. J. F. Campbell, *Popular Tales of the West Highlands*, 4 vols. (new edition, London: Alexander Gardner, 1890–93). Quotes are from vol. 1, pp. lxi–lxii.

7. Gerald L. Pocius, "Hooked Rugs in Newfoundland: The Representation of Social Structure in Design," *Journal of American Folklore* 92 (1979):273–284. Quotes are from pp. 282, 283, and 284. For other treatments of how spatial arrangements express values, see Kenneth L. Ames, "Meaning in Artifacts: Hall Furnishings in Victorian America," *Journal of Interdisciplinary History* 9 (1978):19–46; Dell Upton, "White and Black Landscapes in Eighteenth-Century Virginia," *Places* 2 (1985):59–72; and Gerald L. Pocius, *A Place to Belong: Community Order and Everyday Space in Calvert, Newfoundland* (Athens: University of Georgia Press, 1991).

8. Satu Apo, "Class Relations as Reflected in Southwest Finnish Magic Tales," in Anna-Leena Siikala, ed., *Studies in Oral Narrative*, Studia Fennica: Review of Finnish Linguistics and Ethnology 33 (1989):200–209. Quotes are from pp. 200, 202, 203, and 207.

9. Benedict's study was published originally as *Zuni Mythology*, Columbia University Contributions to Anthropology, 2 vols. (New York: Columbia University Press, 1935). The introductory essay to the work is reprinted in Robert A. Georges, ed., *Studies on Mythology* (Homewood, Ill.: Dorsey Press, 1968), pp. 102–136. Quotes are from the reprinted version, pp. 106, 107, 108, 110, 112, and 113.

10. From Benedict, vol. 2, pp. 160–162.

11. From Benedict, vol. 2, pp. 40–41.

12. Gary Alan Fine, "The Kentucky Fried Rat: Legends and Modern Society," *Journal of the Folklore Institute* 17 (1980):222–243. Quotes are from pp. 224, 226, 227, 228, 231, 232, 233, 234, 236, 237, and 238. The essay is reprinted in Gary Alan Fine, *Manufacturing Tales: Sex and Money in Contemporary Legend* (Knoxville: University of Tennessee Press, 1992), pp. 120–137.

13. From Eleanor Wachs, "The Mutilated Shopper at the Mall: A Legend of Urban Vio-

lence," in Gillian Bennett and Paul Smith, eds., *A Nest of Vipers: Perspectives on Contemporary Legend V* (Sheffield: Sheffield Academic Press, 1990), p. 143.

14. Barre Toelken, "The Basket Imperative," in Suzi Jones, ed., *Pacific Basketmakers: A Living Tradition* (Fairbanks: University of Alaska Museum for the Consortium for Pacific Arts and Cultures, Honolulu, Hawai`i, 1982), pp. 25–36. Quotes are from pp. 26, 27, 28, and 29.

15. Alan Dundes, "Thinking Ahead: A Folkloristic Reflection of the Future Orientation in American Worldview," *Anthropological Quarterly* 42 (1969):53–71; reprinted in Alan Dundes, *Interpreting Folklore* (Bloomington: Indiana University Press, 1980), pp. 69–85. Quotes are from the reprinted version, pp. 69, 70, 71, 72, 74, 75, 76, and 82.

16. Numerous films and videotapes concern examples of folklore of subgroups and explore their relationships to other aspects of culture and as indicators of group identity. For regional ethnic traditions, see, for example, *Chulas Fronteras (Beautiful Borders)* (1976, Chris Strachwitz and Les Blank, Flower Films, color, 16mm., 60 min.), which documents the work and celebrations of the people of Musica Nortena, a border region known for its unique Mexican-American music; *Yeah You Rite!* (1984, Louis Alvarez and Andrew Kolker, Center for New American Media, color, 16mm. and VHS, 25 min.), which concerns dialect use in New Orleans; and *Zydeco: Creole Music and Culture in Rural Louisiana* (1984, Nicholas R. Spitzer, Office of Folklife Programs, Smithsonian Institution, color, VHS, 56 min.).

17. Jennie A. Chinn criticizes such assumptions in "African American Quiltmaking Traditions: Some Assumptions Reviewed," in Barbara Brackman et al., *Kansas Quilts and Quiltmakers* (Lawrence: University Press of Kansas, 1993), pp. 157–175.

18. Elliott Oring, "Whalemen and Their Songs: A Study of Folklore and Culture," *New York Folklore Quarterly* 27 (1971):130–152. Quotes are from pp. 130, 132, 133, 136, 138, 145, 146, and 147. "The Coast of Peru," excerpted in Box 8, can be heard on such phonograph albums as *Sea Chanteys and Sailor Songs at Mystic Seaport* (Folkways FTS 37300, 1978); A. L. Lloyd and Ewan MacColl, *Haul on the Bowlin' and Other Chanties and Foc'sle Songs, Volume I* (Stinson SLP 80, 1962); and

Musical Score from the Film Whaler Out of New Bedford (Folkways FS 3850, 1962).

19. Cited in Oring, p. 133.
20. Cited in Oring, p. 135.
21. Cited in Oring, pp. 135–136.
22. Cited in Oring, p. 137.
23. Rosan A. Jordan, "The Vaginal Serpent and Other Themes from Mexican-American Women's Lore," in Rosan A. Jordan and Susan J. Kalčik, eds., *Women's Folklore, Women's Culture* (Philadelphia: University of Pennsylvania Press, 1985), pp. 26–44. Quotes are from pp. 26, 27, 28, 29, 30, 33, 35, 36, 39, 42, and 43.

24. Cited in Bacil F. Kirtley, "'La Llorona' and Related Themes," *Western Folklore* 19 (1960):156–157.

25. From Soledad Pérez, "Mexican Folklore from Austin, Texas," in Wilson M. Hudson, ed., *The Healer of Los Olmos and Other Mexican Lore*, Publications of the Texas Folklore Society, 24 (Dallas: Southern Methodist University Press, 1951), p. 74.

26. From Pérez, p. 76.
27. From Robert A. Barakat, "Wailing Women of Folklore," *Journal of American Folklore* 82 (1969):271.

28. Linda Pershing, "Peace Work Out of Piecework: Feminist Needlework Metaphors and the Ribbon around the Pentagon," in Susan Tower Hollis, Linda Pershing, and M. Jane Young, eds., *Feminist Theory and the Study of Folklore* (Urbana: University of Illinois Press, 1993), pp. 327–357. Quotes are from pp. 329, 343, and 344.

29. Herminia Q. Meñez, "Jeeprox: The Art and Language of Manila's Jeepney Drivers," *Western Folklore* 47 (1988):38–47; for illlustrations, see Meñez, "Kings of the Road: Machismo and Manila's Jeepney Drivers," *The World & I* (August 1991):657–665. Quotes are from the 1988 essay, pp. 39, 43, 45, 46, and 47.

30. Patricia Atkinson Wells, "The Paradox of Functional Dysfunction in a Girl Scout Camp: Implications of Cultural Diversity for Achieving Organizational Goals," in Michael Owen Jones, Michael Dane Moore, and Richard Christopher Snyder, eds., *Inside Organizations: Understanding the Human Dimension* (Newbury Park, Calif.: Sage Publications, 1988), pp. 109–117. Quotes are from pp. 112, 113, and 114. For filmic examples of women's folklore in work settings, see *Beauty Knows No Pain* (1973, Elliott Erwitt, Benchmark

Films, color, 16mm., 25 min.), which concerns the ritualized training and testing of young women wanting to be College Rangerettes in Kilgore, Texas; *Clotheslines* (1981, Roberta Cantow, Buffalo Rose Productions, color and black and white, 16mm., 3/4" video, and VHS, 32 min.), about women's work at home; and *The Pink Panther* (1977, CBS Productions; color, 3/4" video, 14 min.), which dwells on the ceremony and ritual of an annual convention of Mary Kay Cosmetics saleswomen.

31. C. W. Sullivan, III, "Johnny Says His ABCs," *Western Folklore* 46 (1987):36–41. Quotes are from pp. 37, 39, 40, and 41.

32. From Sullivan, pp. 36–37.

33. From Simon J. Bronner, comp. and ed., *American Children's Folklore* (Little Rock, Ark.: August House, 1988), pp. 97–98.

34. From Iona and Peter Opie, *The Lore and Language of Schoolchildren* (Oxford: Clarendon Press, 1959), pp. 97 and 19 respectively.

35. From Barbara Kirshenblatt-Gimblett, ed., *Speech Play: Research and Resources for Studying Linguistic Creativity* (Philadelphia: University of Pennsylvania Press, 1976), pp. 103 and 104.

36. William A. Wilson, "On Being Human: The Folklore of Mormon Missionaries," 64th Faculty Honor Lecture, Utah State University (Logan: Utah State University Press, 1981). Quotes are from pp. 3, 4, 7, 10, 11, 12, 13, 14, 15, 16, 17, 21, and 22. See also William A. Wilson, "Dealing with Organizational Stress: Lessons from the Folklore of Mormon Missionaries," in Jones et al., pp. 271–279.

37. Wilson, "On Being Human," p. 8. People tell similar stories about narrators (including folklorists) whose storytellings consist of citing numbers rather than actually narrating. For examples, see Robert A. Georges, "Using Storytelling in University Instruction," *Southern Folklore* 50 (1992), pp. 7–8 and p. 16, n. 2.

38. Wilson, "On Being Human," p. 12.

39. Wilson, "On Being Human," p. 16.

40. Wilson, "On Being Human," pp. 18–19.

41. William R. Bascom, "Four Functions of Folklore," *Journal of American Folklore* 67 (1954):333–349. Quotes are from pp. 338 and 343–349 passim. For a modification of this view, particularly in studies of women's folklore that examine coding strategies by which group members challenge cultural norms or appropriate power, see essays in Susan Tower Hollis, Linda Pershing, and M. Jane Young, ed., *Feminist Theory and the Study of Folklore* (Urbana: University of Illinois Press, 1993), and Joan Newlon Radner, ed., *Feminist Messages: Coding in Women's Folk Culture* (Urbana: University of Illinois Press, 1993).

42. For a critique of functional analyses of folklore, including the Bascom essay characterized here, see Elliott Oring, "Three Functions of Folklore: Traditional Functionalism as Explanation in Folkloristics," *Journal of American Folklore* 89 (1976):67–80.

7. Folklore in the Culture of Groups in Contact

Each work discussed in the preceding chapter characterizes folklore as an aspect and manifestation of the culture of a single social group. Implicit in the studies surveyed are the assumptions (1) that the group under consideration has a culture; (2) that folklore is an integral and essential part of the culture of that group; and (3) that the culture (including the folklore) of any given group can be discerned, described, and analyzed independently of the cultures of other groups.

Historically, researchers have made the cultures (including folklore) of national or tribal societies the foci of their inquiries. As we noted in chapters 2 and 6, folklorists as the pioneering students of culture were initially interested in folklore because they correctly hypothesized that documenting and studying it had the potential to provide insights into the historical roots, cultural distinctiveness, and/or national character of individual European countries. When folklore research commenced in other parts of the world in the second half of the nineteenth century, investigators also first documented and described national and tribal societies.

As the study of culture evolved and the data base expanded, however, it became increasingly apparent that it was not defensible to conceptualize and characterize national or tribal societies and their cultures solely or simply as autonomous, homogeneous, and/or indivisible entities. All societies, researchers discovered, are heterogeneous as well as homogeneous. Furthermore, all are made up of multiple social groups whose cultures are sometimes compatible and sometimes in conflict with each other and with the cultures of other societies and groups within them. This discovery made scholars realize that while groups can be regarded as autonomous and their cultures distinctive for selected inquiries, they must also be conceptualized and studied in terms of their relationships to and effects upon each other, since groups do not exist in isolation. The ways intergroup contacts affect and are reflected in folklore are the concerns of this chapter.

National/Tribal Cultures in Contact

One obvious site for intergroup contacts is along national borders. Because political boundaries separate peoples from each other, they also predispose individuals to draw distinctions and to focus on differences between groups that regularly interact. Furthermore, the process of differentiating often gives rise to or intensifies feelings of competitiveness that manifest themselves and find expression in folklore. Susan Gordon discovered this to be the case in northern Costa Rica, where Costa Ricans frequently denigrate their Nicaraguan neighbors by portraying them negatively in stereotypes, gossip, and jokes.[1]

Costa Ricans living along their northern border, Gordon reports, use numerous negative descriptors stereotypically to identify *los Nicas*, as they commonly and often pejoratively call Nicaraguans. These include "*analfabetos* (illiterate); *audaces* (daring); *fachentos* (bragging, show-off); *viciosos* (full of vice); *machistas* (super-male); *malcriados* (bad mannered); *pelean a machetazos* (machete-fighters); *supersticiosos* (superstitious); *incultos* (uncouth); *campesinón* (earthy, unpolished); [and] *violentos* (violent)."

Gossip reinforces the widely held views that Nicaraguans are also disease-ridden and ignorant about good hygiene. During an outbreak of colds and flu in the northwestern Costa Rican town of Liberia in 1983, for instance, the customers of a beauty salon Gordon patronized agreed that "the Nicas were to blame, not only for the colds and flu, but also for the increase in venereal disease." Nicaraguans are frequently said to cause damage and destruction in Costa Rica as well. During Gordon's 1983 visit to the border area, the citizenry and journalists both blamed an anonymous group of "three Nicas" for many serious crimes, including setting a fire that destroyed several buildings in the town of Upala.

Costa Ricans react negatively to their northern neighbors in part because Nicaraguans regularly cross the border into their country looking for work, refuge, and aid. The Costa Ricans regard these "others" as intruders who threaten their economic security and democratic way of life. An informant exemplified this dissatisfaction with the Nicaraguans' intrusion by telling Gordon a tale about a confrontation between a "Tico" (Costa Rican) and a bird, a story he called alternately a *chile* and a *chiste* (joke) (see Box 7–1).

The narrator told Gordon when he concluded that the bird in the tale is like a Nicaraguan: "Even though the Tico [Costa Rican] couldn't kill him, at least he sent the bird back to his own country."

Gordon states that "a nationally based dichotomy" between Costa Ricans and Nicaraguans is longstanding and ongoing. It is discernible "in historical records, archival data, correspondence, newspaper reports and commentaries, and individuals' interpretive characterizations of past events." Furthermore, it has been reinforced over

---

BOX 7–1
The Tico and the Bird

Well, there's this Tico [Costa Rican] shooting at a bird in San Jose [the capital city of Costa Rica], in Central Park. And bang! nothing. And the bird jumped, and he came toward this way, and the individual followed him, and another shot, bam! nothing, and the bird jumped and kept jumping, and the guy after him, walking and walking until he arrived in Canas. And he looked back and once again, bam! He tried to hit the bird and no luck. The bird kept jumping further ahead.

Then he said, "What rotten luck. I've wasted so many shots and haven't been able to kill this damned bird." And the little bird let out a few whistles, "Yiii iii," he whistled, and the guy, good and mad.

Ok, he arrived in Liberia, and the fellow, blam! and nothing. And the bird still walking, followed along the highway, until, at last, he arrives at the border, and once more, bam! and nothing, and by now the bird is standing on the other side of the border and starts to dance on a branch.

Then, he says, "Good. It's all right that I didn't shoot you, but I sent you back to your country, you scoundrel."[2]

---

the years by major historical, economic, and political changes in Nicaragua, of which a majority of Costa Ricans disapprove.

But the attitude is not the same in the two countries, Gordon reports. When she extended her research to the Nicaraguan side of the border in 1985, she found little antagonism among citizens of that country for their Costa Rican neighbors. "For the most part," Gordon writes, the Nicaraguans she interviewed "seemed genuinely bewildered at Costa Rica's continued negativity toward Nicaragua." While some people made sarcastic remarks about Costa Ricans—that they are snobbish, for instance, or that the men are *maricones* (effeminate)—"Nicaraguans tend to voice little of the personal hostility toward a stereotypical Costa Rican."

Gordon's findings indicate that both Costa Ricans and Nicaraguans make qualitative distinctions between their cultures. They distinguish on the basis of many and varied criteria, such as industriousness and political preferences and alliances. But both judge Costa Rica to be better insofar as the standard of living and economic well being are concerned, as the folklore examples and remarks Gordon quotes and discusses clearly reveal.

The expectation that the grass is always greener across a border often motivates individuals to want to relocate, even when doing so involves taking risks or breaking laws. The desire to reap anticipated benefits of living "on the other side," and the nature and consequences of attempts to do so, have been sources and subjects for the past 130 years of *corridos* (ballads) and *canciones* (songs) of Mexicans who aspire to immigrate to the United States, according to Maria Herrera-Sobek's research findings.[3]

On the basis of 3,000 ballads and other songs she collected and/or analyzed between 1976 and 1989, Herrera-Sobek identifies three recurrent themes relating to Mexicans' experiences in trying to become American immigrants: the "quest for a *mica*, a legal border-crossing card (also called a green card); conflict and tension between *la migra* (the border patrol) and the immigrant; and the role of *coyotes* or guides, who serve as mediators (for a fee they smuggle undocumented persons into the United States)." Herrera-Sobek writes that "the songs symbolically reflect the struggles of aspiring immigrants by objectifying and parodying situations and persons with whom immigrants come into daily

contact." By doing so, they contemporize events "to make them meaningful to continuing immigrant experiences," often satirizing them, venting negative feelings, and symbolically transforming "hardship into victory through parodying the immigrants' plight."

Many songs dwell on the lack of, or attempts to obtain, a "green card," the resident identifier or work permit issued by the United States Immigration and Naturalization Service (INS). In Spanish the laminated card is metonymically called *mica*, by analogy with the mineral that crystalizes in thin, translucent layers. The quickest and surest way to gain permanent residency is to marry a U.S. citizen, the theme of the song "La Bracera," in which a man's search for a prospective mate backfires. Having no legal papers, the singer finds a girl to whom he immediately proposes, hoping through marriage to obtain a visa and passport. After the wedding ceremony he reveals that he is one of the illegal aliens (*mojados*, "wetbacks"; also *ilegales*, "illegals," *alambristas*, "wire jumpers," *indocumentados* or *sin documentos*, "without green cards or legal documents," and *braceros*, "field hand"). She responds that he is out of luck; she too is undocumented and married him for the same reason, to be able to cross the border legally.

Mexicans traveling from the interior of their country do not know border crossing rules and procedures, so the *coyote* becomes an indispensable, although often distrusted and despised, middleperson. The *coyote* has a reputation for being wily, sly, sneaky, and clever at deceptions. He or she charges high fees, sometimes taking advantage of the *pollos* (chickens), those who are innocent and naively expect the *coyote* to transport them across the border safely and even help them obtain jobs. But undocumented workers are relieved when they "learn the safest routes to take and no longer need the services of the *coyotes*," as apparent in such songs as "No necesito coyote" (I Don't Need a Coyote):

> Con esta van cuatro veces
> que he visitado Tijuana
> la ciudad más visitada
> de mei tierra mexicana
> porque es la puerta de entrada
> a la Unión Americana.
> Por Tijuana, Mexicali
> Nogales y Piedras Megras
> no necesito coyote
> para cruzar la frontera
> Yo no tengo pasaporte
> y paso cuando yo quiero.

> (This makes the fourth time
> I have visited Tijuana
> The city most visited
> In my Mexican homeland
> Because it is the gateway
> To the United States.
> Through Tijuana, Mexicali
> Nogales and Piedras Negras
> I don't need a coyote
> To cross the border
> I don't have a passport
> And I cross whenever I please.)

The illegal aliens must also contend with the INS. "Contemporary *corridos* continue the literary tradition of incorporating within their lyrics formidable heroes who challenge and battle the foe," writes Herrera-Sobek. "In the latter part of the nineteenth century, the Texas Rangers ("*Rinches de Tejas*") served as the forces of evil in constant pursuit of the Mexican hero," she states. Later "the Rangers found their counterpart in the *Federales* (federal soldiers) who fought against Mexican rebel guerrilla fighters." More recently, it has become the border patrol, the *migra,* who is "the villain" and "portrayed in *corrido* lore as the arch-enemy of the undocumented worker." Many jokes and stories evince the Stupid American motif. "The Anglo is portrayed as clumsy, dim-witted, and easily duped by the sharp-witted Mexican," notes Herrera-Sobek. "In ballads sung in the 1960s and 1970s," however, "the role of the border patrol changes from 'Stupid American' to villain; the patrol is viewed as vindictive, their actions hypocritical." INS officials are described as acting like *perros* (dogs), and vans used to transport undocumented workers are called *perreras* (dogcatcher vans).

"The final stage in the process of reducing the pain of illegal immigration," Herrera-Sobek indicates, is to portray those identified as or with Anglos as *indocumentados.* One popular song that does this is "Superman *es ilegal*" (Superman Is an Illegal Alien). The singer asks, "Is it a bird, an airplane? No man, it's a wetback."

The song reveals that Superman has arrived from Krypton and is "just another undocumented worker like me." He appears fair-skinned and blue-eyed like Americans, but he is not really white because Kryptonites are yellow-green. Superman does not serve in the military or pay taxes; he is a journalist but does not have a green card. By assailing Americans' most cherished comic-book hero, the song incorporates several grievances, particularly the specter of racism and unequal treatment under the law (see Box 7–2).

"The *corrido* in the nineteenth and early twentieth centuries was used to denounce injustices suffered at the hands of the Mexican *federales*, the Texas Rangers, and the *patrons* (bosses)," Herrera-Sobek asserts. During the 1970s and '80s it "continued to serve as a vehicle for airing grievances," giving the plight of the illegal immigrant greater attention. The "affirmation of self" through the composing and singing of *corridos* and *canciones* "transforms the [illegal] immigrant from low social status into a figure of heroic and epic proportions. Viewed in this light," she concludes, "it is easy to comprehend the great popularity and lasting appeal of *corridos* and *canciones.*"

BOX 7–2

"Superman es ilegal"

Hablado:
¿Es un pájaro, es un avión?
No hombre, es un mojado.
Cantado:
Llegó del cielo
y no es avión.
Viene en su nave
desde Kryptón.
Y por lo visto
no es americano;
sino otro igual
como yo indocumentado.
Así que migra
él no debe trabajar,
porque aunque duela
Superman es ilegal.
Es periodista
También yo soy
Y no "jue" al army
¡A que camión!
Aquel es güero,
ojos azules,
bien formado;
y yo prietito
gordiflón y muy chaparro.
Pero yo al menos
en mi patria ya marché
Con el coyote que pagué
cuando crucé.
No cumplió con el
servicio militar.
No paga impuestos
y le hace al judicial.
No tiene mica
ni permiso pa' volar;
y les apuesto que ni
seguro social.
Hay que echar a Superman
de esta nación.
Y si se puede
regresarlo pa' Krypton.
¿A cúal borraron
cuando llegó?
De un colorcito
verde limón.
Y no era hierba
ni tampoco un agripao
más bien agüita
d'esa que hace reparao.
Y que yo sepa
no lo multan por volar
sino al contrario
lo declaran Superman.
Hay que echar a Superman
de esta nación.
Y si se puede
regresarlo pa' Krypton.
¿Dónde está es autoridad
de immigración
¿Qué hay de nuevo
Don Racismo en la Nación?

Spoken:
Is it a bird, an airplane?
No man, it's a wetback.
Sung:
He came from the sky
And he is not an airplane.
He arrived in his spaceship
From Krypton.
And anyone can see
He is not an American;
He is just another
Undocumented [worker] like me.
So, border patrol,
He should not be allowed to work,
Because even though it hurts
Superman is an illegal alien.
He is a journalist
So am I
And he did not serve in the army
What a bastard!
He is fair-skinned,
Blue-eyed,
And has a great physique;
And I am dark-skinned,
Fat, and very short.
But at least I served
in my country's army
With the smuggler whom
I paid when I came.
He did not do his
Military service.
He does not pay taxes
And practices law.
He does not have his green card
Nor a permit to fly;
And I bet he does not
Even have a social security card.
We have to kick Superman
Out of this country.
And if we can
Send him back to Krypton.
Whose skin did they whiten up
When he arrived on earth?
Wiping out his native
Lemon-green color from Krypton.
He wasn't a green-colored plant
Nor was he sick
It was probably water
Firewater, that is!
And as far as I know
They don't fine him for flying;
On the contrary
They declare him Superman.
We have to kick Superman
Out of the country.
And if we can
Send him back to Krypton.
Where are you now
Border patrolmen?
What's new in the
Nation, Mr. Racism?[4]

Just as the nature and results of inter-group contacts along political boundaries become sources and subjects of folklore, so do those that occur when members of one group either consciously try to change or inadvertently influence the behavior of those from another society. Adrienne L. Kaeppler discusses changes that occurred in Tongan traditional dances principally as a result of the influence that Christian missionaries had after they arrived and set up shop on the Tongans' island home.[5] Historically, according to Kaeppler, traditional Tongan dance "was performed on formal occasions to show allegiance to the chiefs, to commemorate life crises, such as funerals or puberty rites of the chiefs, and to entertain visiting dignitaries." The coming of Christian Europeans changed many things. "Methodism became almost a State Religion, and the old dances were considered 'heathen' and not in keeping with the precepts of Christianity." Hence, they were banned (see Box 7–3). Catholicism, however, permitted dances but required certain changes.

Three dance types, claimed locally to be entirely new inventions or introductions

from Samoa, are really "evolved forms of indigenous dance types with new names and new music," writes Kaeppler. If the Tongans were to dance openly, their dances had to appear to be new to the missionaries. But the missionaries did not dance, so the Tongans had no new dance models to borrow. Sometimes a "new" dance, therefore, "simply consisted of recombining dance movements already known to them," and accompanying a new piece of sung poetry. "From the Tongan point of view, if the sung poetry was of a new kind (e.g., in Western style patterned after hymn singing), this would constitute a new dance type," writes Kaeppler. "From the missionary point of view it would also constitute a new dance type because if the music was new, the dance must also be new," she continues. "It was in this mutually happy atmosphere that Tongan dance has flourished ever since."

Kaeppler describes four dances in the early literature of Tonga. These include "1) the *me'etu'upaki*, a men's standing dance in which paddles (*paki*) are used; 2) the *me'elaufola*, a group dance done by either men or women; 3) the *'otuhaka*, a sitting group dance; and 4) *ula*, a standing dance performed by young women."

Of these four dances, the first, *me'etu'-upaki* (see Box 7–4), "has come down to us virtually unchanged in movement, poetry, and music," writes Kaeppler, although the function has changed from a formal dance "to a conspicuous display separating the descendants of the sacred line of chiefs from the rest of the society." The second dance, *me'elaufola* (Box 7–5), also described and depicted by Captain James Cook in his voyages in the late eighteenth century, fell into disuse owing to missionary influence; it reappeared later in the same form but with a new name, *lakalaka*.

A third traditional dance type, the *'otuhaka*, evolved into a new dance—*ma'ulu'-ulu*—with identical seated position, move-

---

BOX 7–3
Westerners' Response to Tongan Traditional Dances

"Anyone engaging in any heathen dance . . . shall be fined five dollars," warned the Tonga Gazette on March 7, 1888. And on December 6, 1882, an act regulating the schools announced: "It shall be with the Schoolmasters to regulate the native dances, as the Lakalaka and the Otuhaka, and it is not lawful for the children to engage in these in different places and at different times, but as arranged by the Schoolmaster; should any child break the regulation, he or she shall on conviction be fined in the sum of one dollar."[6]

BOX 7–4
The Tongan Dance *Me'etu'upaki*, 1777

It was performed by men; and one hundred and five persons bore their parts in it. Each of them had in his hand an instrument neatly made, shaped somewhat like a paddle, of two feet and a half in length, with a small handle, and a thin blade; so that they were very light. With these instruments they made many and various flourishes, each of which was accompanied with a different attitude of the body, or a different movement. At first, the performers ranged themselves in three lines; and, by various evolutions, each man changed his station in such a manner, that those who had been in the rear, came into the front. Nor did they remain long in the same position; but these changes were made by pretty quick transitions. At one time they extended themselves in one line; they, then, formed into a semicircle; and lastly, into two square columns.

They made a great many different motions; such as pointing them (*paki*) toward the ground on one side, at the same time inclining their bodies that way, from which they are shifted to the opposite side in the same manner, then passing them quickly from one hand to the other, and twirling them about very dexterously.

The musical instruments consisted of two drums, or rather two hollow logs of wood, from which some varied notes were produced, by beating on them with two sticks. It did not, however, appear to me, that the dancers were much assisted or directed by these sounds, but by a chorus of vocal music, in which all the performers joined at the same time. Their song was not destitute of pleasing melody; and all their corresponding motions were executed with so much skill, that the numerous body of dancers seemed to act, as if they were one great machine.[7]

BOX 7–5
The Tongan Dance *Me'elaufola*, 1777

The women accompanied their song with several very graceful motions of their hands toward their faces, and in other directions, at the same time, making constantly a step forward, and then back again, with one foot, while the other was fixed. They then turned their faces to the assembly, sung some time, and retreated slowly in a body, to that part of the circle which was opposite the hut where the principal spectators sat. After this, one of them advanced from each side meeting and passing each other in the front, and continuing their progress round, till they came to rest. Their manner of dancing was now changed to a quicker measure, in which they made a kind of half turn by leaping, and clapping their hands, and snapping their fingers, repeating some words in conjunction with the chorus. Toward the end, the quickness of the music increased, their gestures and attitudes were varied with wonderful vigor and dexterity.[8]

ments, and structure (the first section accompanied by drum, the second by poetry in song). Its music and instrumentation changed, however, from bamboos rolled in a mat to a skin drum. Tongan oral tradition reports that the *ma'ulu'ulu* came from Samoa in the late 1800s. It is in fact the name of a Samoan dance, and older Tongans recall traveling troupes of Samoan dancers per-

forming it. "This was said to stimulate the creation of a new dance type, which is simply a revitalized *'otuhaka* with a new name and new drum accompaniment," writes Kaeppler.

Finally, the older *ula*, a standing dance performed by one to eight women, was succeeded by a new dance type, *tau'olunga*, "again said to have come from Samoa about the turn of the century" and taught to local Tongans by a Samoan visitor. It uses the same movements of *ula* but differs in the enthusiasm of motion, the instrumentation (highly Westernized, with the accompaniment of guitars and ukuleles), and the music (Western-harmonized poetry). Like its predecessor, the *tau'olunga* can be performed at any informal gathering or follow a seated dance on a formal occasion in display of the grace and beauty of high chiefly women.

"*Tau'olunga* is an amalgam of many elements. Its music is adapted from Western music traditions. Its name and manner of performance are borrowed from Samoa. Its movements and role are Tongan." Kaeppler concludes that "change in Tongan dance has taken place but . . . the change was largely evolutionary rather than by invention or new introductions." However, the development of dance types does reveal the influence of the diffusion of song or poetry styles, musical instruments, and bodily movement patterns through such human population movements as colonialism, tourism, and traveling dance troupes.

Sometimes intergroup contact results in the creation of folklore that serves as a "cognitive device to analyze and evaluate alien cultural introductions." Elli Köngäs Maranda proposes this thesis based on a study of riddling among the Lau of Malaita in the British Solomon Islands.[9]

Riddling is a popular pastime among the Lau, and anyone may engage in it at any time. By contrast with Lau myths, which are "agents of conservatism" that "support the social and religious hierarchy," riddles among the Lau "question the order of society" and "seem to reach for the new." Through riddling the Lau "cope with external cultural pressures" that occur because of the introduction of new "goods and procedures" to which they have been exposed via contacts and interactions with "Chinese tradespeople, Christian missionaries,

[and] British colonial government officials."

The Lau, notes Köngäs Maranda, value their traditional culture and don't readily accept innovations suggested by foreign models. When considering change, they "gather together to discuss the new thing, to express opinions, to offer explanations, and to work it through together." New phenomena are the topic of discussion at these informal gatherings, called *rebolaa* or "chattings." They also become subjects for riddling.

These "riddles of modernization," as Köngäs Maranda calls them, sometimes "give unconditional support to Western technology, which is seen as effective and superior to traditional Lau technology." They "recommend Western objects," usually taking "one function of the object and point[ing] out its effectiveness." Two riddles that exemplify this function are "A man when he speaks, all villages here hear" (a radio), and "A man, if you say a word to him and he hears, even after a year, he says it" (a tape recorder). (See Box 7–6 for additional examples.)

Other riddles have as their purposes to expand and cultivate knowledge. The Lau have never seen a camel, Köngäs Maranda states; yet they pose riddles that are metaphorical descriptions of that animal. These include "Riddle, a riddle. A man eats for a year and drinks for a year," and "A man if he drinks today, he will wait six months; when the sixth month comes, he will drink again." When Köngäs Maranda asked the Lau how they knew about camels, she learned that someone had seen one on an American soldier's pack of Camel cigarettes during World War II.

Lau riddles also demonstrate how Western technology requires more technology to make it work, as in the following:

"A thing, only when his food arrives, he cries. If it does not arrive, he never cries" (an engine).

BOX 7–6
Some Lau Riddles Illustrating the Effectiveness of Western Technology

1. Riddle, a riddle.
   A thing, even if a tree is hard, it eats it all up today (an ax).
2. A leaf, when the wind blows, and even when it rains and you are cold, if you cover your body with it, you won't be cold (a blanket).
3. A small child carries a big man (a chair).
4. Even if a thing goes into the surf, into the wind, it does not sink (a ship).
5. Eight men who speak with four different accents (a mandolin).
6. A ship arrives. If we step into it, our feet won't be dirty (boots).
7. A small child comes and sometimes gives us to eat from his mouth (a spoon).
8. A thing, even when it is far away, when it is sent, it arrives, it does not speak, and we understand it (a letter).[10]

culture . . . by working new things into the system."

When one people colonizes the country of another, some of the beliefs, experiences, and feelings of both the colonizers and the colonized are understandably manifested in folklore. Francis A. de Caro and Rosan A. Jordan explore correlations between folklore and other aspects of cultures of the dominant and subordinate groups in a study of stories, rituals, and the sun helmet as a symbol among the British in India under colonial rule.[11]

The sun helmet has become a familiar object, one that appears in countless movies, comic strips, and advertisements. To many it signifies the explorer, the big game hunter, or the white man in the tropics. Invented in India (where it was called a *topi*), the sun helmet evolved from a large, cumbersome toadstool shape to smaller, lighter, and more graceful forms like the Napier *topi*. The term *topi* derives from the Hindi, meaning "a hat." By the end of the eighteenth century, the natives referred to Europeans in India as *topi-wallahs*, that is,

"A man, if his food does not arrive, it is impossible for him to speak with us" (a radio).
"A man must stand in the sea to live; if his foot is dry, he dies" (a lantern).

Other riddles illustrate that things made in the Western world don't last and can sometimes even be dangerous:

"A big men's house, very many men live in it. If they come out, they die" (matches).
"A thing, when it hits a man, he dies" (a truck).

"The important consideration is not whether Lau riddles recommend change or point out its disadvantages," writes Köngäs Maranda, "but, rather, that riddles serve as a form that discusses new phenomena and makes people familiar with their different properties." Because they fulfill these objectives, riddles "insure the viability of the

THE TOADSTOOL TOPEE.

Figure 7–1: The toadstool topi or sun helmet worn by the British in India in the 1820s or 1830s (courtesy Francis A. de Caro and Rosan A. Jordan).

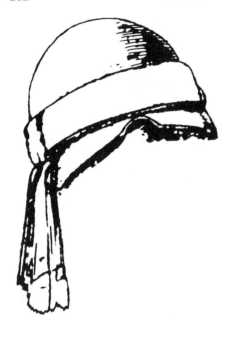

THE NAPIER TOPEE.

Figure 7–2: By the 1850s, the small, light, graceful Napier topi had become popular with many Anglo-Indians as well as English planters (courtesy Francis A. de Caro and Rosan A. Jordan).

wearers of hats rather than turbans. By the middle of the nineteenth century, *topi* meant a particular kind of hat, the sun helmet. It is stiff and relatively light in weight (often being constructed of pith, or *sola*). It has a high crown and a wide brim that slopes downward. And it is ventilated.

Loyalty to this headgear derived in part from beliefs that the Indian sun posed a threat to Europeans. Exposed areas on the top and back of the head, the temples, and the neck invited penetration of the sun's rays into the skull. A sloping, wide brim protected the temple and neck, and holes allowed for circulation of cooling air. That some physicians argued sunstrokes resulted from a rise in general body temperature rather than direct exposure to the sun, that Indian men got along quite well with a cloth turban, and that Indian women and children survived with no headgear at all suggest the *topi* served other purposes than merely shading its wearer's head. According to de Caro and Jordan, "it reassured people with real fears about the tropical sun, and hence relieved their anxiety and helped them to function more effectively." In addition, "the *topi* also served as a powerful community symbol associated with a sense of Anglo-Indian identity."

Figure 7–3: The English chaplain to the Anglo-Indian community is depicted in George F. Atkinson's 1860 novel Curry and Rice *as wearing a rather smart topi (courtesy Francis A. de Caro and Rosan A. Jordan).*

Two rituals of passage developed among the British to emphasize a transition from one important state to another. Upon reaching the Suez Canal on the voyage out, those going to India for the first time would don a *topi*—one purchased either earlier in England or at a shop ashore, such as the famous emporium of Simon Artz. In a public ritual on the voyage of return home from India, passengers removed their sun helmets and tossed them overboard as the ship steamed out of Port Said at the northern end of the Suez Canal and into the Mediterranean. "Whichever direction one was going, then," write de Caro and Jordan, "Port Said was the geographical location that marked the beginning of wearing or ceasing to wear a sun helmet. Port Said was also where the East began, our informants almost universally agreed."

Their informants, British nationals who had been in India from the 1920s through the 1940s, also told a similar personal anecdote. They "recalled that they, going out to India for the first time . . . acquired the 'wrong' *topi*, one which was thought by seasoned Anglo-Indians to be inappropriate, usually because it was of a style out of date; sometimes it was pointed out that only missionaries still wore this style of helmet." Once in India and made aware of the mistake, the would-be sahib or memsahib quickly acquired the proper *topi* (see Box 7–7). Not only did this experience recur in personal narratives, but it also became the topic of a joke. In one version, two women shop for *topis* in a London store. An army officer insists that their choice is unsuitable. "I assure you," he says, "nobody wears those except missionaries." They reply, "Oh, but we *are* missionaries."

De Caro and Jordan write: "In one sense the wearing of a *topi* was an assertion of Britishness." Indeed, in India's Eurasian community, persons of mixed European and Indian ancestry "wore *topis* with even

---

BOX 7–7
Anecdotes about the Wrong Topi

You sort of absorbed a lot of the Indian lore before you got there. . . . There were various ceremonial things really, or semi-ceremonial things. . . . You always used to stop at Port Said . . . and go to a shop called Simon Artz. . . . And you bought your *topi*, your *sola topi*, which, having bought, when you got to India you found quite useless because it was of the wrong design.

* * *

I must have looked the most awful ass. I went out [from England to India] with an old fashioned type of *topi* that nobody wore at all. My mother advised me; she gave me the wrong name. I got one of those cork *topis*. Everyone wore the "Bombay bowler."[12]

---

greater zeal than the English themselves, as a badge of the European identity that they preferred to emphasize. There were in fact jokes about Eurasians wearing pith helmets at inappropriate times, such as at night or with pajamas."

The researchers contend that "the *topi* was not a symbol of England but of Anglo-India, Britishness on only one side of Suez. Anglo-India was a colonial subculture, and the British in India, though temporary sojourners, saw themselves as somewhat different from other Englishmen, as having been conditioned by this Indian experience." Consequently, British newcomers confronted suspicion. Would they fit in or not? Would they buck established Anglo-Indian ways? Would they "go native"? Members of the colonial group dubbed newcomers *griffin*, and referred to behavior out of keeping with Anglo-Indian standards as *griffish* (perhaps derived from the mythological creature's nature as being half one thing and half another).

De Caro and Jordan write that in their judgment "the wrong-*topi* stories are expressions of the critical social need to make outsiders insiders, to bring newcomers into the group, and of the fact that this process of initiation is not to be taken for granted." The Englishman in India had to be enculturated, learning the ways of Anglo-India. "His first *topi* is 'wrong' because it came from outsiders, not insiders." It was purchased from a London outfitter or in a shop in Port Said. "Only in Anglo-India itself can one obtain the correct version of the essential community symbol; only Anglo-Indians can confer the knowledge necessary to make the transition to becoming one of them," write the authors about self-conceptions and concerns of British society in India.

Contacts between Immigrant Groups and Host Societies

Awareness of and judgments about differences between the cultures of contact groups also affect and are reflected in the folklore of immigrant groups and the societies to which they immigrate. Sometimes immigrants judge folklore and other culturally based behaviors learned in their homelands to be inferior to or incompatible with those of the host society. When this occurs, they frequently discontinue or suppress their native ways or substitute newly acquired alternatives for them.

As we discussed in chapter 3, this was the case with Mrs. Fannie Jurva, who remembered vividly historical-supernatural legends she had learned in her Finnish homeland. But she did not share them with anyone for 43 years after she had immigrated to the United States because she felt they had no relevance in her adopted country.[13] Japanese immigrants similarly found their native supernatural beliefs and traditional cures to be incompatible with their

new life in America until they were interned in relocation camps during World War II. As Marvin K. Opler's study of Tule Lake internees (discussed in chapter 3) reveals, the *issei* (immigrants) not only found these folklore examples to be relevant to their existence once again, but they also shared them for the first time with their American-born children (*nisei*).[14] Hence, homeland folklore persists only in individuals' memories when they judge it to be in conflict with or out of place in a society to which they immigrate. When immigrants judge their homeland folklore to be relevant to or compatible with their new social environment, however, folklore continues to have meaning for them and to be evident in their behavior and shared with others.

Sometimes conditions in places to which individuals immigrate are so similar to those in their native land that the immigrants do not need to modify their behavior, including their folklore, in any appreciable way. This was the case, for instance, with sponge fishermen and their families who emigrated from their Greek island homes during the first decade of the twentieth century to settle in Tarpon Springs, Florida.[15]

Tarpon Springs became the center of the American sponge fishing industry when the outbreak of the Spanish-American War in 1898 forced the Key West–based fleet to find a new home port. The nature of the industry also changed shortly thereafter, for deep-sea diving replaced shoreline pole hooking as the principal means of harvesting sponges. Since mechanized diving was commonly used in the early twentieth century by Greeks on the Dodecanese Islands, Tarpon Springs businessmen imported from Greece a properly outfitted boat and experienced diver and crew.

Initial sponge fishing expeditions by this boat and crew in 1905 into the deep waters of the Gulf of Mexico yielded such abundant catches that Tarpon Springs leaders immediately sent to Greece for additional equipment and personnel. By 1907, 800 Greeks from six islands were manning 50 diving boats and 55 smaller hook boats based in Tarpon Springs. Wives and families from Greece soon joined the fishermen; and they organized a religious community and built their first church by the end of that year.

Unlike their countrymen who settled in other parts of the United States, the Greeks of Tarpon Springs had to make few immediate concessions in their new environment. The Florida climate was comparable to that of their home islands. Because of their numbers, they could continue to speak Greek, practice the Greek Orthodox religion, maintain their family structure, and perpetuate familiar dietary habits and modes of dress. The men engaged in the same occupation as they had in Greece and used the same technology in their work. Theirs was virtually a life transplanted.

The spongers found traditional native beliefs and customs to be relevant in and compatible with their new social environment. The most tenacious were bound up with Greek Orthodoxy. Fishermen continued to believe that Saint Nicholas, the patron of all Greek seamen, looked after and protected them in America as he had in their homeland. His presence continued to be attested by the raging tempest he caused at sea each year on his December 6 name day, just as he had done in Greece. Saint Nicholas was also responsible, the spongers said, for the fact that Tarpon Springs was never hit by hurricanes or other destructive storms that regularly struck and often devastated other Gulf port cities.

Petitioning the saint during inclement weather by offering prayers and making promises before his icon (displayed prominently in the cabin of every sponge boat) invariably lessened the danger from raging winds and damage from choppy seas. To show their appreciation to Saint Nicholas for his protection, Tarpon Springs spongers, like their homeland counterparts, regularly contributed to their religious community a percentage of the proceeds from the sale of each trip's harvest and/or from the last day's catch.

As they did in their homeland, the fishermen claimed that other saints could also be counted on to help them in times of trouble and need. Captains frequently carried icons of family patron saints on their boats, placed next to the likeness of Saint Nicholas. The belief in the efficacy of prayer and the wondrous power of these saints was illustrated and reinforced by frequently told personal experience stories exemplifying saintly intercession and miraculous assistance. (See Box 7–8 for an example.)

After that incident, Captain Gonatos promised to his patron saint the earnings from the last day's sponge catch on each trip. He sent the money to a monastery named for Saint Catherine on Calymnos, his native island. He told the men who worked on his boat that even if they found *gold* on the last day of each trip at sea, it would be given to Saint Catherine's monastery in appreciation for the miracle that had been performed for him. No crewman ever refused to work for Gonatos because of this stipulation, for all knew that the wonder had indeed occurred.

Other folk beliefs also continued to be relevant and meaningful for the Greek sponge fishermen after they immigrated to Tarpon Springs. They honored the taboo against sailing on unblessed waters by not leaving port from the end of December until Epiphany (January 6), when priests blessed the sea and fleet for the new year. In addition, prior to every sailing, a priest blessed with holy water each boat and its deck, diving equipment, sail, mast, bunks, motor, and individual crew members, to protect the men and vessel from danger and

---

BOX 7–8
A Sponge Fisherman's Tale

My father was a great captain here [in Tarpon Springs, Florida]. He came from the old country as a diver. Well, he had at times three and four boats. Each boat had six men. And he was a great sponge diver. And he named one of his boats *Saint Catherine.*

Well, at high seas one night when a storm was arriving (before they had weather reports at all), there was a hurricane. And he lost his rudder—he lost the steering of the boat, which is a big piece of wood about six inches thick, two feet wide, and, let's say, about ten feet long. It sets on the back of the boat. And that came *off!* And it was *lost.* And they were just bouncing on the seas. . . .

Now, my father always had Saint Catherine's icon in his boat. So he got on *his knees.* (Now, you can picture a great captain getting on his *knees* and praying to be *saved!*) Well, no sooner was he finished with his prayer (now, this was in the middle of the night; the whole boat was bouncing, and everybody was ready to jump overboard and drown, expecting the worst). And they heard that rudder bouncing on the side of the boat—*beating* on it. And he jumped up, he looked over, and he saw that. Now, that weighs about three or four hundred pounds—a heavy, heavy object. And my father reached down from the side of the boat and picked it up with his own strength. He picked it up by *himself,* you see. Well, now, you can imagine the impact it had on *him* for *Saint Catherine!*[16]

---

to insure an abundant sponge harvest. Furthermore, boats would not set sail on Tuesday, a bad luck day, since it was on that day of the week that the city of Constantinople fell to the Turks in 1453. The spongers also continued to observe the taboo against setting sail when a priest or woman in black mourning clothes appeared along the docks on the day of a planned departure, since both foreshadowed ill luck. Additional traditional precautions included wearing gold crosses or amulets to ward off evil and insure safety, and avoiding whistling when a diver was under water to prevent mishap or injury to him.

The immigrant sponge fishermen's adherence to and perpetuation of these and other homeland beliefs and customs continued for the fifty years or so that the American sponge industry thrived and Greeks dominated its operations in and from the port of Tarpon Springs. However, as members of the immigrant generation age and die, as their American-born progeny work in jobs outside the sponge business, and as social and environmental changes and a decreasing demand for natural sponges contribute to the industry's decline, the relevance of the Greek sponge fishermen's homeland folklore to, and its compatibility with, the changing Tarpon Springs community and needs of its members also diminish.

Homeland folklore may not only remain relevant in the place to which individuals immigrate and be compatible with the culture of that society. It may also take on new meanings, serve additional functions, and affect members of the host society as well. This is the case in Los Angeles, according to Mary MacGregor-Villarreal, with Catholic Mexican-Americans' reenactment each Christmas season of Mary and Joseph's journey to Bethlehem and their search for shelter the night before Jesus Christ's birth.[17]

Las posadas, as this annual dramatization is called, is celebrated in homes every evening from the 16th through the 24th of December. On each of the nine nights, either individuals selected to portray Mary and Joseph or all the participants in a candlelight procession request and are refused

Figure 7–4: Houseowners turn Mary and Joseph away when they request shelter during the Pico Adobe posadas (photo by Mary MacGregor-Villarreal, courtesy Chicano Heritage Project, UCLA Folklore and Mythology Archives).

follows the dramatization. Children break a *piñata*, and participants visit socially with one another and partake of special holiday foods, such as *tamales* (cornhusk-wrapped and seasoned meat–stuffed cornmeal dumplings) and *buñuelos* (deep-fried flat cinnamon and sugar–topped pastries). Each night, a different family offers shelter to the lodging seekers and hosts the social gathering. Family members, friends, and neighbors are the only participants in these home *posadas*, which serve social as well as religious functions for those involved.

lodging at house after house, until they arrive at a predesignated home into which they are welcomed. Participants sometimes also sing, either with or without musical accompaniment; and the words exchanged at each stop may either be recited or sung or spoken in verse. Participants may also carry "a litter with small figures of Joseph and Mary." On "*la noche buena* or Christmas Eve," the last night of the *posadas*, "the *nacimiento* or birth of the Christ child is reenacted."

On each of the nine nights, a celebration

In Los Angeles, *las posadas* has, over the years, come to be celebrated publicly as well as in homes. Public celebrations are held at such varied places as a church (San Gabriel Mission), a historical monument (Pico Adobe in Mission Hills), a cultural center (Plaza de la Raza in Lincoln Heights), and a historic tourist and commercial site (Olvera Street in downtown Los Angeles). Like their home counterparts, these public *posadas* consist of both the dramatization of the Holy Couple's search for lodging and a festive gathering. Therefore, they fulfill both religious and social functions for most of the participants.

In addition to the similarities, there are notable differences among the public

Figure 7–5: Children dressed as angels observe the nacimiento (manger scene) at Pico Adobe (photo by Mary MacGregor-Villarreal, courtesy Chicano Heritage Project, UCLA Folklore and Mythology Archives).

Figure 7–6: Figures of the Holy Family atop the andas (litter) at Olvera Street (photo by Mary MacGregor-Villarreal, courtesy Chicano Heritage Project, UCLA Folklore and Mythology Archives).

seph wear biblical costumes, as do those accompanying them who play the parts of angels, the three wise men, and other religious personages. These "stars" of the procession also rehearse in advance for their "performance." Live animals sometimes parade in the procession as well, and on occasion a child is used in place of a doll as a living representation of baby Jesus.

Activities besides those typical of home *posadas* also occur between the time the procession ends and eating and drinking begin. At the San Gabriel Mission, participants sing carols in Spanish and English, and the priest explains the meaning of Christmas and emphasizes the importance of perpetuating traditions such as *los posadas*. Musicians and dancers perform after group singing at Pico Adobe, and a priest celebrates mass and delivers a brief sermon at Plaza de la Raza. Assorted pastries (*pan dulce*) and hot chocolate are the standard fare at San Gabriel Mission and Pico Adobe, while a variety of foods is available for purchase from booths and stores at the other two public sites. "One of the most obvious results of presenting *las posadas* publicly to large audiences," writes Mac-Gregor-Villarreal, "is the expansion and elaboration of the *fiesta* portion of the event," with the organizers including "activities which will appeal to the audience and maintain its interest while still conforming to the motives for performing the celebration in public."

posadas and between them and *posadas* celebrated in homes. At Olvera Street *posadas* are presented on nine consecutive nights, as they are in homes, while those at the other three public sites are held only one night annually. All four public *posadas* attract sizable and heterogeneous crowds, in contrast to the small, intimate gatherings that typify their home counterparts. The large numbers of participants at public *posadas,* moreover, demand and justify additions and adjustments to the traditional celebration. Public address systems are used at Olvera Street and Plaza de la Raza; and a master of ceremonies presides at three of the four sites to inform participants of what is happening, to control the crowds, and to usher people from one activity to the next. Printed programs distributed at Plaza de la Raza provide transcriptions of lyrics so those who don't know the songs may also join in the singing.

Going public has had other effects on the way *posadas* are celebrated. At three of the sites, individuals portraying Mary and Jo-

In addition to details and procedures, public *posadas* are also similar to and different from those in homes in their objectives and functions. Like hosts of home *posadas*, those in charge of public celebrations recognize the combined religious and social significance of the event. But they have other goals as well. Organizers of the San Gabriel Mission and Pico Adobe celebrations aspire to preserve a custom traditionally celebrated by pioneering Spanish or *Californio* families and "to make others aware of the rich California heritage from the Hispanic era." Cultural preservation is also a goal of the Olvera Street *posada*, together with the desire to make the general population of Los Angeles more aware of Mexican culture and to support businesses on the famous street by attracting larger-than-usual crowds of prospective customers over the nine-night period. Publicly displaying and reinforcing Mexican/Chicano identity and instilling in participants "a pride in Mexican culture" are the principal objectives of organizers of the Plaza de la Raza *posada*, at which the majority of attendees are people of Mexican birth or descent.

The Los Angeles public *posadas* are obviously modeled after home celebrations. They thus constitute both a continuation and a transformation of a tradition with a long history and an ongoing cultural significance. Celebrating *las posadas* publicly can be either an alternative to home celebrations or an additional way to commemorate the Christ child's birth. It is also a means for individuals of diverse ethnic backgrounds to learn about an aspect of Spanish/Mexican culture and to participate in it.

Contact between immigrants and members of the host society has the potential not only to increase individuals' awareness of each others' culture and to affect each others' behavior through folklore. It often stimulates them to create new folklore as well. Florence E. Baer found this to be the case in Stockton, California, where an immigrant population inadvertently triggered tensions that led to the creation by and circulation among members of the host society of rumors, legends, and jokes that stereotyped and denigrated refugees from Southeast Asia who were resettled in their community.[18]

According to a legend that began in 1980, a woman in North Stockton discovered that her expensive pet dog was missing. A neighborhood youth allegedly had seen a Vietnamese family down the street eating the dog, and reported this to the owner. Supposedly the garbage collector later found the dog's head and fur in the trash.

Other stories spread quickly. Some teenagers told of an immigrant who had skinned two cats and started to boil them. They were identifiable by their tails hanging over the sides of the pot. Because the man could not speak English and no interpreter could be found, the policeman were unable to read him his rights and, therefore, could not arrest him. (According to Baer, police deny any such incident.) While "teenagers repeating this story assure their listeners it is true," writes Baer about the gruesome accounts, "they really seem more interested in 'grossing out' one another than in compelling belief in the story."

A supermarket sits next to an apartment complex occupied almost exclusively by Indochinese. The interdiction "Don't shop at Fry's!" precedes several stories that tell of immigrants opening the lids of mayonnaise, pickle, and peanut butter jars, tasting the food, then replacing the lid and putting the container back on the shelf. They treat boxes of cereals, crackers, and cookies similarly.

"A former Laotian army officer, Baccum Kham, now with Catholic Charities, affirmed the truth of the stories," writes Baer. "He explained that at home on the Indochinese peninsula all foodstuffs are in open bins, and it is customary to taste before you buy. . . . Catholic Charities has posted signs in Vietnamese, Laotian, and Cambodian throughout several stores in the area warning against opening packages and jars. Baccum said the practice has stopped, but the stories proliferate," observes Baer. She also reports a frequently told story about an immigrant shopper who removes a clean Pamper disposable diaper from its box and replaces it with a soiled diaper changed in the store, putting the box back on the shelf.

Baer cites several jokes. One asks

whether or not the listener has seen a new Vietnamese cookbook; it's called *How to Wok Your Dog*. Another states that the television program "That's Incredible" will feature a Vietnamese family with a dog over a year old. A bumper sticker reads: "Save a Dog—Eat a Refugee." Finally, Baer mentions the prevalence of the epithet "fish heads." The jokes and name-calling, writes Baer, "clearly reflect and help reinforce the community's shared feelings about the Vietnamese."

In 1980, about 3,000 Southeast Asians—"boat people"—arrived in Stockton. They came from Laos, Cambodia, and Vietnam, but locals lumped them together as Vietnamese. Ignorant of the local social structure, refugees moved into apartment buildings in North Stockton (home to the affluent, largely white residents) rather than South Stockton (where lower income minority groups dwell). Moreover, Stockton's unemployment rate had surged to over 19 percent at about this time. Rumors about the refugees began almost at once among resident Americans, with the belief emerging that "they" eat dogs and cats. "According to the students [at the local college where Baer teaches], the practice was widespread; animal heads, often in plastic bags, were to be found outside apartment houses wherever Vietnamese were living." The local newspaper carried accounts as rumor, rather than as fact, and also reported meetings at which the county board of supervisors and the city council discussed the matter.

One councilman appears largely responsible for having elevated the first rumors to the status of fact. He collected and repeated stories, which gained credibility because of his official position and his publicized demand for an ordinance banning the eating of dogs and cats, with a reward for information about those doing so. The City Council Legislative Committee refused to enact such a law, however, since there was no evidence of purloined pets and because such an ordinance would inflame public sentiment. The newspaper carried the headline: "Council Nixes Ordinance to Ban Eating of Pets."

Baer notes various attitudes and feelings among resident Americans. In 1982, faculty at the local college, some of whom seemed to accept the stories as true, instead of "feeling dismay or disgust . . . , believed that dog-eating was a condition the refugees had been reduced to in their homelands and that they would abandon the practice once they realized it was not approved here." These tellers did not express open animosity toward the refugees. "Students like a gruesome story; their academic elders saw the stories as a kind of initiation to which each new wave of immigrants is subjected."

A vocal and influential group in town opposed the relocation of Southeast Asians in North Stockton, contends Baer. They threatened violence. Targets included refugees, the United States government, and Catholic Charities. "Also this year [1982] a Vietnamese family that chose to live in an apartment house in which there were no other Vietnamese was quickly made the scapegoat of the complex, being blamed for all ills from cockroaches to impetigo." Most anti-refugee lore concentrates on bizarre eating habits, however.

According to Baer, "the Indochinese refugees are regarded as unwelcome competition by other minority members and as an economic burden by the rest of the community." In addition, "the stories of Vietnamese eating pets function specifically to support the belief that the refugees are consuming—using up—our share of this world's goods." In general,

> folklore about the newest wave of immigrants concentrates on their consumption of *our* goods and belongings, on their depriving us of what is rightfully ours. They eat our pets. They take food out of jars and packages, leaving us short of our full share when we

unsuspectingly buy the product. By using school tennis nets for fishing, they prevent our children from playing tennis and deny our sport fishermen a fair share of the available fish. They take our seats on the school grounds. They receive large welfare checks and considerable medical benefits and make heavy use of educational facilities, thus increasing our taxes and depriving our own (suddenly) deserving poor of governmental largesse.

In sum, writes Baer, "Underlying the folklore . . . is a view of America as a place where there is no longer enough to go around and where anything acquired by one group is acquired at the expense of everyone else. This view seems to reflect the principle of limited good."

The contact between immigrants and members of a host society often stimulates the creation of new folklore within the immigrant group.[19] An example is the Hmong who, a century and a half ago, left China to settle in the north of Vietnam and Laos. Following the withdrawal of United States forces in the 1970s, thousands of these tribal people who had fought against communist forces fled to Thailand, with many refugees being resettled by sponsors in France, the U.S., and other countries. At one time referring to themselves as *M'peo,* "embroidery people," the Hmong were noted for an elaborate textile tradition called *paj ntaub,* "flower cloth." Women created embroidered, batiked, or appliqued items such as backpacks, toy mobiles, funeral pillows and burial clothing, and belts in bright colors and precise, geometrically symmetrical designs.

According to research by Sally Peterson and by Marsha MacDowell, changes came with displacement of the Hmong. In the refugee camps in Thailand, many craftspeople encountered different versions of their own village traditions, and expanded their repertoires of designs. They also developed a new form and style. No longer

able to farm, they were encouraged by relief administrators to produce a pictorial art in thread. The name *paj ntaub dab needj,* meaning flower cloth of people, customs, and traditions, is usually translated as "story cloths." Appearing in the U.S. in the late 1970s, these textiles differed in being representational, not geometric; eventually they were produced in blues, beiges, and pastel and earth tones in order to match popular colors in American home interiors which contrasts sharply with the bright color combinations preferred by the Hmong. Story cloths depict Hmong folktales, everyday life, customs, rites of passage, and the escape from Laos. At first they were sold to non-Hmong, but more recently Hmong have displayed pieces in their own homes and cultural centers, writes MacDowell, "as visual props which help explain their history and traditions." Like their Western pictorial counterpart in easel paintings, story cloths are hung on the wall as "art" to look at. But, writes Peterson, they also serve as "pedagogic tools for teaching children about their heritage."

Other Intergroup Contacts within Societies

Intergroup contacts within societies obviously are not limited to interactions between immigrants and host society members. They can occur between any groups, regardless of the criteria used to define and distinguish them. Furthermore, any intrasocietal intergroup contact can be reflected in and affected by folklore; and the folklore of any group, like other aspects of its culture, can be affected by intergroup contact as well.

As we noted in chapter 5, one consequence of contacts between groups within a society (like those between societies) is that one group may "borrow" folklore from another, adapting it as necessary to suit its

Figure 7–7: Detail of Paj ntaub, *or "story cloth," 1988, a new pictorial textile art form by Hmong refugees depicting customs and daily activities in Laos (photo by M. O. Jones).*

needs, and making the other group's folklore a part of its own culture. In his comparative study of African American and Native American folktales recorded in the southeastern United States (discussed in chapter 5), Alan Dundes concludes that striking similarities in the tale types of the two groups are due to longtime and close contact (including intermarriage). Dundes hypothesizes that the Native Americans borrowed tales from the African Americans, making African-based stories a part of their own group's folklore.[20]

Also in chapter 5 we referred to pasties in Michigan's Upper Peninsula.[21] Cornish immigrants introduced this turnover filled with meat and vegetables. Finnish, Italian, and Slavic immigrants had somewhat similar dough-enveloped specialties whose nature affected, and in turn was affected by, the Cornish pasty in America. The pasty further diversified through the influence of vegetarians, and also as a result of attempts by commercial establishments to appeal to tourists by adding cheese, bacon, or chili topping or by using pizza dough. According to Yoopers (Upper Peninsula residents), "violations" in pasties abound. They blame specific groups. For example, dousing pasty with gravy is said to be French Canadian (by

others), Cornish (by Finns), Mennonite (by the owner of a pasty shop who learned pasty making from Finns), eaten only in the eastern U. P. (by those in the western region), or eaten only by non-Yoopers. But despite different conceptions of what its normal form is or should be, the pasty has evolved from a Cornish to a multiethnic to a regional food and symbol; and it has become a part of the folklore and hence of the culture of all these groups.

Individuals borrow folklore when they judge it to be potentially useful and meaningful for members of a group of which they are a part. But frequently they simply note or acknowledge the folklore of other groups, or they highlight it in order to emphasize group distinctiveness. According to Richard Bauman, this was the case with seventeenth-century Quakers, who distinguished themselves from others in part by their nonparticipation in and condemnation of traditional festivals and festive behavior.[22]

"As one might expect," writes Bauman, "the early Quakers shared the well-known Puritan antipathy toward festivity." William Penn and others invoked economic rationales, declaring festivals wasteful and in opposition to the desired goal of accumulating wealth. Furthermore, festival participants' excessive eating and drinking were seen as "injurious to the health" and as spiritually harmful, Bauman asserts. The Quakers felt that the gluttony apparent during festivals was morally unacceptable, for "to bring injury on oneself by intemperance is to sin against God."

Some Quakers viewed erecting Maypoles and the festivities associated with them as idolatrous displays. They saw morris-dancing as "savage," rooted in heathen practice. They attacked athletic contests as displays of fleshly pride. Some decried the singing of "corrupt and vain harvest songs," which they considered "filthy and abominable" and tending to subvert modesty and chastity.

Religious values and economic concerns thus entwined. "From bawdy songs to sexual license, it was feared, was but a small step," writes Bauman. "A rationally organized industrial economy," moreover, such as was emerging, required an evenness of time and a predictable uniformity and standardization. To many Quakers, the licentious behavior in evidence during scheduled festivals was consistent with the ways non-Quakers behaved generally. Festive events, including those held on holy days, simply provided people who participated in them with "an additional excuse for indulging in sinful practices that characterized their lives at all times" anyway.

Having established an image of sinful people and activities, "the Quakers then used it as a basis to define themselves, their own moral way of life, by opposition," writes Bauman. He concludes that "because of this Puritan legacy and the concomitant rational economic ideology that dominates modern life, it still remains difficult to reconcile participation in festivals with being a 'serious' person."

Folklore and individuals' use of it are also bases for distinguishing between the two sexes. In her study of Zuni mythology (discussed in chapter 6), Ruth Benedict characterizes briefly some of the differences between stories told by men and women.[23] "Men tell the tales which feature extended accounts of the stick races, of gambling, and of hunting," writes Benedict. "Women tell those which detail cooking techniques." Zuni women's narratives are detailed; men's are not. Furthermore, there is a correlation between the sex of the narrator and attitudes toward the characters in tales. In telling a story Benedict identifies as "The Deserted Husband," for instance, a woman narrator provides justification for the female protagonist's adultery by describing her husband's failure to be communicative and to show gratitude to his wife for all she does for him. A man's telling of the same tale, by contrast, indicates that the wife commits adultery because she is promiscuous. The husband is portrayed as blameless and wronged, justifying his subsequent vengeful actions.

Differences between the folklore of the two sexes is also the focus of Carol A. Mitchell's research on male and female joketelling.[24] Mitchell sought to "discover and delineate the differences in male and female joke-telling in a single community," that of the Colorado State University campus at Fort Collins. She studied how such differences seem to affect the appreciation and interpretation of jokes.

"In determining the degree of appreciation of jokes," Mitchell writes, "the sex of the performer and the audience is probably as important as the content of the joke itself." While men and women often enjoy the same jokes, especially sexual ones, "men appreciate the joke for one set of reasons and women appreciate the joke for a somewhat different set of reasons."

Consider the following anecdote of which Mitchell collected three variants, all from women.

> A guy and a girl were in the front seat of a car adjusting themselves after a quicky. The guy looks a little uncomfortable and says to

the girl, "If I'd known you were a virgin, I would have taken more time."

The girl looks back at him and says, "If I'd known you weren't in such a hurry, I'd have taken off my pantyhose."

According to Mitchell's research, men and women seem to enjoy the joke about equally. "The element that makes it particularly humorous to females is the idea that the man in his rush to have intercourse does not even realize she has on pantyhose." Some of the women Mitchell interviewed told her that in their dating experience the joke was not farfetched, given the inconvenience of pantyhose in sexual situations as well as their dates' lust. "The men, on the other hand, thought it was 'pretty unrealistic, but still kind of funny.' Thus women enjoy not only the male who is a sexual fool, but also the problem of the pantyhose; while men seemed to focus on the male fool and be relatively unaware of the problem of pantyhose."

Certain kinds of rape jokes are more popular among women than among men. These include an entire cycle about Mary Jane, who is so naive that she does not realize she is being assaulted. Along with another joke that Mitchell collected which concerns having been "reaped," these narratives (see Box 7–9) "are a kind of 'whistling in the dark' for women, an easing of the tension they feel because of the fear of rape." Since the jokes do not treat rape at all realistically, women can enjoy them.

By contrast, "Rape jokes that males tend to enjoy often condone the action," writes Mitchell. An example features a Texan who must drink a quart of whiskey, rape an Eskimo girl, and kill a polar bear. Confused from intoxication, he mixes up the latter two challenges and suffers accordingly (see Box 7–10).[25]

Mitchell collected this joke only from men, not women. When informed of the joke, some women found it amusing; but

---

BOX 7–9

Jokes Appreciated More by Women Than by Men

Mary Jane is walking down this alley and a man came up and told her to take all her clothes off. Mary Jane just laughed and laughed because she knew her clothes wouldn't fit him.

*   *   *

Mary Jane was taking a bath one night when a man jumped in through the window. Mary Jane wasn't worried though. She knew she had the soap.

*   *   *

Mary Jane was walking along the street one night when a man came up and ripped off her blouse. Mary Jane just laughed and laughed because she knew her money was in her shoe.

*   *   *

Okay, this is a story about a little mousey girl and a little mousey boy. Little mousey boy asked little mousey girl for a date. So she fixed her little mousey hair and put on a nice mousey dress and fixed her little mousey face, put on her little mousey eyelashes. Well, after she was all fixed up, her date didn't come and she was waiting and waiting and she ran out, all in her little mousey dress, to look for him, and along came this big machine [a combine, or reaping machine, used to harvest grain] that just cut her up when she was looking for him. Just tore her little mousey dress and messed up her little mousey eyelashes. All her little mousey mascara ran, and finally her boyfriend came along and said, "What is wrong with you?"

And she said, "I've been reaped."[26]

BOX 7-10

A Joke Appreciated More by Men Than by Women

About the time Alaska became a state, this Texan, still wanting to be from the largest state, decided to move there. After his arrival in Alaska he sauntered into a bar and up to a couple of Alaskans that were there. In a loud voice he asked, "How do I become an Alaskan?"

The two Alaskans looked at the Texan, all dressed in fancy cowboy boots and ten gallon hat, then at each other, and finally back at the Texan. One of them said to the Texan, "If you want to become a real Alaskan, here's what you have to do. Drink a quart of whiskey, rape an Eskimo girl, and kill a polar bear."

The Texan ordered a quart of whiskey and drank it down, then he staggered out of the bar.

A couple of days later the same two Alaskans were sitting in the same bar when the Texan came staggering in again. The Texan was all scratched and torn, his clothes little more than rags. He stumbled up to the two Alaskans and asked, "Now where's that Eskimo girl I'm supposed to kill?"[27]

---

the rape joke series. It concerns male exhibitionism, which often provokes a fear reaction in women.

There was this man who was an exhibitionist. And he was going to take a trip on this airplane. And there was this stewardess who was waiting at the top of the stairs that go onto the plane, and she was collecting tickets. So when this man got to the top of the stairs, he opened his coat and exposed himself. And the stewardess said, "I'm sorry sir. You have to show your ticket here, not your stub."

"Without exception, women who answered the questionnaire and who were interviewed indicated that they enjoyed this joke," writes Mitchell. Indeed, 80 percent of the women rated it very funny. "Comments indicated that they identified with the stewardess in the joke whom they admired for her calmness and quick wit." Many of the women "indicated that the man in the joke," who in their opinion deserved what he got, "symbolized male aggressiveness in our society." Moreover, writes Mitchell, "Of the fourteen jokes used on the questionnaire, this joke elicited the most comments indicating female resentment and hostility toward male sexual aggressiveness."

Men generally reacted positively to the joke, but they did not consider it as funny as women did. "While the men often enjoyed the stewardess's witty 'put down,' none of them mentioned that the exhibitionist 'got what he deserved,' as women had," observes Mitchell. Several men explained that the flight attendant remained cool because stewardesses are supposedly promiscuous and therefore not easily shocked. (By contrast, the women had seen the joke as a denial of the promiscuity of stewardesses.) "Men also focused on the fact that the stewardess has insulted the exhibitionist for his small penis size, while very few women even mentioned the content of the insult."

most "objected to the idea that rape could be part of an initiation rite." It was humorous to women only because "the intended rapist was fool enough to rape a polar bear and has been suitably punished in the process rather than getting away with it." The men tended to ignore the fact that the Texan appeared willing to murder the Eskimo woman. They "seemed to be laughing more at the way the man failed to live up to the whole super masculine image of the drinker, hunter and womanizer," writes Mitchell. "Some felt that this masculine image was foolish in the first place, and others particularly liked to see a Texan fail in the masculine role."

Mitchell includes one other example in

The theme of violence done to a male by a female characterized a small number of jokes that women appreciate more than men. The women's comments about such jokes, "like the comments about the exhibitionist joke, indicated a good deal of hostility toward men." Women who enjoyed such jokes focused on "the man not listening to a woman—as they felt often happened in our culture—and consequently being punished."

Mitchell's research suggests that there are three categories of jokes that women tell and appreciate more than men do. The largest consists of jokes relating to the female experience, such as women's apparel, menstruation, pregnancy, and the fear of rape. A small number concern violence to men by a woman or her agent. And a few make the man appear disgusting.

Men, on the other hand, "appreciate jokes dealing with topics that are particularly related to the male experience," such as comparisons of penis size, injury to the testicles, or threat of castration. But men prefer to have other men tell these jokes, just as women prefer having rape jokes told to them by other women. "When told in same-sex situations, the fears about rape and castration can be laughed at and tensions relieved; however, when a female tells a male a castration joke, often the joke seems hostile, and the man may feel that the woman is showing hostility toward him."

One of the most popular jokes told by men concerns plans to capture a gorilla that has escaped to a housetop. The zoo keeper's assistant explains to the homeowner that he intends to climb to the roof, where he will knock the gorilla off the house with a club. A dog stationed below will grab the gorilla by the testicles and drag him to a cage. Then the homeowner will slam the cage door shut. When the homeowner asks why he brought a rifle along with the club, dog, and cage, the man replies, "Well, just in case the gorilla knocks me off first, you shoot the dog."

Eighty-three percent of the male interviewees gave this joke a 1 or 2 rating on a scale of 1 to 4 with 4 lowest. Although women thought it amusing, they rated the joke lower, with 93 percent rating it as a 2 or 3. Men often made comments such as, "I guess I think it's funny because of the feeling I get in my own mind of what it would be like if the dog were to bite me. I think most males can really identify with the guy from the zoo." Women, on the other hand, tended to sympathize with the gorilla. Several indicated that they did not understand the joke or that it took so long for them "to get it" that it was not funny. Likewise, few women managed to grasp the meaning of, and therefore did not find very amusing, the following anecdote: "Do you know what a no-no bird is? A bird with one inch legs and [testicles] the size of basketballs. And every time it goes to land it goes, 'No! No!'"

Not surprisingly, jokes told by men that degraded women or that pictured the female body as repulsive (e.g., sexual organs as dirty, enormously oversized, sickening) tended to offend women. Many women felt insulted and became angry when apprised of such jokes.

"Men and women often react differently to the same jokes, with men enjoying certain kinds of jokes more than women and vice versa," writes Mitchell. Furthermore, "oftentimes with jokes that are enjoyed particularly by one sex, any humor in the joke for the other sex lies in a somewhat different interpretation of the joke or in the emphasis of another aspect of the joke."

Men and women seem to enjoy some jokes equally and even to interpret them similarly. But sometimes, as with the following anecdote, men and women emphasize different aspects of the joke. The story tells of a priest and nun playing golf. The priest tees off on the first hole and puts the ball in the sandtrap. "God damn it, I missed." The nun admonishes him, "Oh, Father, you shouldn't say that, or a thunderbolt from heaven will strike you dead." On the second hole the priest puts the ball in the woods. He curses again. The nun repeats her warning. On the eighteenth hole he fails to hit the ball at all. "God damn it, I missed again," exclaims the priest. Suddenly a thunderbolt strikes the nun dead. A booming voice from the heavens says, "God damn it, I missed again."

Mitchell writes: "Both men and women enjoy the unexpected image of a fallible God in one of the most popular jokes collected." Not only does God miss the priest with the thunderbolt, but He also swears, breaking the First Commandment by using His own name in vain. "Thus God himself is brought down to the human level. Both sexes also enjoy the irony of the situation in which righteousness is punished and blasphemy goes unpunished, and the joke is seen as a criticism of social morality which indicates that good will be rewarded and wickedness punished." However, according to Mitchell, "men often mentioned that the 'nagging nun' got what she deserved, while women more often focused on the irony of the nun being in the right but still not being rewarded," a reflection of women in society who lose even though they behave as they have been taught. "While women do not particularly like the nun in the joke, they feel more sympathy for her than do the men."

Mitchell also examined differences between men and women in regard to the kinds of jokes told by each sex and the situations in which, and the audiences to whom, each tells jokes.[28] Between the winter of 1972 and the fall of 1975, she collected 1,507 jokes, along with the name, age, sex, ethnic origin or race, religion, and occupation of the informant plus information about the setting in which the jokes were told. She coded the data, classifying jokes according to form, plot, character, theme, and sometimes setting.

"The differences in the male and female joke-telling traditions are similar to and derive from the different roles that men and women have been expected to play in our [i.e., American] society. And in turn the joke-telling traditions continue to help in the maintenance of those separate roles," writes Mitchell. More male jokes, for example, seem openly hostile and aggressive. Female aggressiveness in male jokes appears in a negative light (as nagging or promiscuity, for example), and male characters punish women in some way for this trait.

In Mitchell's study, men's jokes tend to be longer, more narrative in form; women's jokes are shorter, often in brief question-and-answer form (and women also told more humorous personal experience stories rather than jokes per se). "Men told higher percentages of obscene jokes, religious jokes, ethnic and racial jokes, jokes about death, and jokes about drinking." On the other hand, women told a greater number of absurd jokes, Polack jokes, morbid jokes, jokes about authority figures, and jokes involving a play on words.

In addition, according to Mitchell's research men seem to enjoy competitive joke-telling sessions; women do not, feeling that the competitive nature of the event will cause hurt feelings and hostility. Men enjoy telling jokes to larger audiences and even to casual acquaintances, often in public places such as bars and business settings, whereas women prefer telling their jokes to small groups of close friends. Women tend to tell jokes to audiences of the same sex; men appear more willing to tell their jokes to opposite-sex audiences and to audiences of both sexes.

"And finally," writes Mitchell, "male tellers are more likely to use jokes sometimes to deride someone whom they dislike, while women rarely do this; and men are more likely than women to tell jokes that they think might be offensive to some members of the audience." Indeed, men seem to use jokes to "keep friendships from becoming too intimate, while women tend to use jokes as a way of sharing pleasure, and they attempt to make even formal jokes seem like intimate communications." Mitchell concludes: "Many, if not most, of these differences occur because of our society's views of what is masculine and what is feminine, and joke-telling is one of the institutional structures that have evolved to reinforce the appropriate kinds of behavior in males and females."

Although groups of males and females in society are constantly in contact, Mitchell implies, their folklore distinguishes them from each other, whether or not they are aware of this. Sometimes, however, individuals consciously use folklore ambiguously, frequently to conceal and often to selectively reveal or reinforce an identity about which they want or are forced to be ambivalent. Joseph P. Goodwin details such a situation in his study of gay men's folklore in Middle America.[29]

According to Goodwin, homosexuals "tend to divide their time between the gay subculture and the larger, more visible straight culture." When interacting with each other, gay men are able to make their sexual orientation explicit. However, when interacting with straights or in mixed company, individuals tend to conceal their gay identity because of their awareness of social stigmatization and likely rejection. Consequently, gays make use of an ever-evolving and changing body of folklore that functions in part to characterize and comment on the behaviors they have in common, and in part to enable them "to recognize and communicate with one another without being discovered."

Gay communication strategies include drawing on a lexicon of words, expressions, and nonverbal signals that are semantically ambiguous, making it possible for one to use them in gay or mixed company. To call someone *active*, for instance, might be interpreted by a nongay as someone who is energetic or productive; to gays, however, the word "describes a man who takes the inserter role in oral or anal intercourse," as opposed to the insertee or *passive*. The word *switch-hitter*, usually associated with the game of baseball, denotes a bisexual man in gay parlance, as does the expression *AC/DC*. A preference for *French* over *Greek* reveals a desire to engage in oral (rather than anal) intercourse, as does wearing a light blue (rather than a navy blue) bandana. A black bandana or black leather signals a desire to engage in sadomasochistic acts; a white bandana indicates an interest in masturbating another (when worn on the right) or being masturbated (when worn on the left). One unfamiliar with these words, expressions, objects, and actions might well ascribe other meanings or no significance at all to them. But according to Goodwin, learning them is a step in a process through which male homosexuals become a part of and learn to operate in the gay community.

Humor similarly is an integral part of the gay community's folklore. Sometimes individuals tell selected jokes to give others hints that they are gay so they can infer from others' reactions whether they are gay as well. In telling the following joke, Goodwin states, "the narrator was saying, in effect, 'I'm gay (as you can tell, since I understand this joke), and I think you may be gay too.'

> A Greek, an Italian, and a Jew were walking down the beach and found a lamp. They picked it up and rubbed it, and a genie came out and said, "I'm going to grant you each a wish, but there's one condition: you can't do anything ethnic for twenty-four hours. If you do you'll vanish."
> So they were walking down the street and passed a restaurant. They could smell the spaghetti, and the lasagna, and all the pasta,

and the Italian said, "I'm hungry. I'm going in and have something to eat." And the Greek and the Jew said, "No! You can't do that! That's ethnic!" And he said, "Oh, that's ridiculous; everybody's got to eat." So he went in. And just as he stepped through the door—poof!—he vanished.

So the Greek and the Jew went on down the street, and they saw a five-dollar bill lying on the sidewalk. And the Jew said, "Look! Somebody dropped some money. I'm going to pick it up." And the Greek said, "No, you can't do that! That's ethnic!" And the Jew said, "Nonsense. Everybody needs money." And he bent over to pick up the five-dollar bill and—poof!—they both vanished.

"This joke draws its humor from a number of stereotypes," Goodwin states: "the Italian's fondness of pasta, the Jew's thriftiness (or even miserliness), and the Greek's predilection for anal intercourse." He continues, "The implied pedication of the Jew by the Greek is too esoteric a reference for most straights to understand." Therefore, if the narrator determined that the listener "understood the joke," he "would have been encouraged to explore the matter further."

Humor also enables gays interacting with each other to comment on and make light of stereotypical and typical homosexual behavior. Sometimes humor has as its *raison d'être* simply to make "homoerotic references," as in the following:

Did you hear about the original hard-luck guy? He crossed a bloodsucker with a cockroach and got a bloodroach.

*   *   *

Do you know how to get four gay men on a barstool? Turn it upside-down.

*   *   *

What do you get when you put two gay men named Bob together? Oral Roberts.

Other jokes depict gays putting straights in their places, expressing gay power, and laughing at homophobia (see Box 7–11).

Not all gay folklore is esoteric or humorous, Goodwin emphasizes. The experience of "coming out" (making one's homosexuality known) is "a continuous process" that can be "quite traumatic and imbued with fear and apprehension." Hence, it is not surprising that stories about individuals' personal experiences in coming out "make up one of the major subdivisions" of the narrative folklore that circulates among gays. Other kinds of personal experience stories that Goodwin exemplifies and discusses are those that have as their sources and subjects love affairs, sexual "exploits and misadventures," threatening and dangerous events, and "female impersonation." Furthermore, the outbreak and consequences of AIDS and its rapid spread among homosexuals have "brought new fears to the gay world." According to Goodwin, jokes about AIDS circulate continuously among straights; but they "seem never to have been popular in the gay community." Nevertheless, many of these jokes are familiar and of concern to homosexuals because they denigrate gays, implying that they alone are responsible for the outbreak and spread of the disease. The following are illustrative.

Do you know what *gay* stands for? Got AIDS yet?

*   *   *

What do you call a gay man in a wheelchair? Roll-AIDS.

*   *   *

Do you know how AIDS got to California? In an old Hudson.

*   *   *

Do you know how to keep from getting AIDS? Sit on your ass and keep your mouth shut.

Writes Goodwin, "AIDS has become one more burden with which gay men must deal, one more source of stress making them turn to their subculture for support."

BOX 7–11
Three Gay Jokes

This was about 1906 and this little fairy walks into this bar in San Francisco and he sits way at the end of the bar. And he, the bartender comes up to him and he says, "I'd like a martini." And the bartender comes up to him. He says, "We don't serve fairies or faggots in this place." So the little fairy is just infuriated and he just sits there with his legs crossed an' there at the bar and glares at the bartender. Just about that time the earthquake hits. My God, chandeliers falling, bottles falling behind the bar. Oh, it's complete chaos, people screaming. Then everybody clears out. Everybody's running out an' the bartender's behind the bar all shook up you know, just shaking and he looks over across the bar and here the little fairy's still sittin' there glarin' at him. The little fairy says, "Now are you gonna serve me that martini or shall I do it again?"

        *   *   *

Two gay men are sitting on the bank of the Ohio River down near Cincinnati, and this big ship comes by, loaded with cars and trucks. One of the guys says, "What's that?"
And the other one says, "That's a ferry boat."
The first one says, "Well, I *knew* we were organized, but I damn sure didn't know we had a navy!"

        *   *   *

This traveling salesman is looking for a place to stay because he's really tired and it's getting late. So he stops at this house and asks if they can give him a place to stay and something to eat. And the farmer says he's sorry, but he doesn't have any room. "But if you go on up the road about half a mile, I'm sure you can stay at Farmer Jones's, but I'd better warn you, he's sort of strange." The salesman said that didn't matter, he was so tired.
So he went to Farmer Jones's and Farmer Jones said sure, he could stay there. But they had just one rule: no one talked during supper. The first person to talk had to do the dishes. So they sat down and ate. Then they just sat there; and finally after forty-five minutes the salesman couldn't take it any longer. He jumped up, grabbed the farmer's beautiful daughter, and ravished her right there on the dining room floor. Nobody said anything. So they got up and sat down. About forty-five minutes later the salesman grabbed the farmer's wife, 'cause she wasn't too bad looking either, and pulled her down on the floor and ravished her. Nobody said anything. So they got up and as the salesman started to sit down he knocked over the candle and burned his arm. He ran up the stairs to the bathroom screaming. He yelled down, "Where's the Vaseline?" The farmer said, "Never mind. I give up. I'll do the dishes."[30]

Goodwin's study demonstrates that folklore is a fundamental means for individuals to conceal and reveal their gay identity. One may use or avoid using the words, expressions, intonations, and gestures and wear or not wear the articles of clothing and jewelry that are traditional signs or symbols of gayness. One may tell or not tell the humorous and serious stories that portray or comment on gay men's experiences and lifestyles. Because folklore is an integral and fundamental part of the gay subculture, it enables gays to hide their identity, on the one hand, and to communicate esoterically in mixed company and explicitly among themselves, on the other.

Folklore is not only a means for individuals to selectively reveal or conceal who they are. It is also a way for them to identify vicariously with groups for which they do not qualify for membership. This was the case during the ethnic revival movement of the 1950s in the United States. "To be considered culturally literate, many Americans felt the need to learn about the histories and cultures of American nationality groups, and to sample their folklore as well," writes R. J. Evanchuk.[31] Many who felt they had no unique ethnic ancestry themselves "'adopted' single cultural communities," taking part in their activities as if they too belonged to those groups.

Folk dance enthusiasts from American mainstream society formed loose federations which promoted the concept that doing dances from various countries deepened one's understanding of peoples of the world. This seemed "the American way of doing things," although Evanchuk recalls that regular visitors to these dance events included members of the Federal Bureau of Investigation (FBI) or Central Intelligence Agency (CIA), perhaps because of Cold War fears that such dances were associated with the Soviet Union and its allies.

In 1956, a Balkan troupe called Kolo (the name for the national dance of Yugoslavia) toured the U.S. It "not only changed the lives of many individuals in the United States, but also irreversibly altered the nature of international folk dancing and the personal lives of many of its participants," writes Evanchuk. Supporters became Balkanophiles, adopting a surrogate ethnic identity through devotion to the dance. Based on interviews with many participants, Evanchuk analyzes how and why this transformation occurred.

Contrasted with typical American folk dance troupes concerned with how an "ideal performer" should look, "the Macedonians came in a multitude of sizes, shapes and costumes." Reflecting years later on their first impressions, devotees commented on how "different" it all was from what they had experienced previously. Perhaps it was not so much difference, writes Evanchuk, "but similarity, a marked similarity to themselves." Besides observing that Kolo performers' shapes ranged from thin and willowy to frankly fat, some in the audience likened several Yugoslavian dancers to their own friends. Said one interviewee, "These were real people." Writes Evanchuk: "Noting these similarities among Yugoslavian performers and their own friends and acquaintances appears to have been one of the first major steps in the bonding process between the primarily non-Yugoslavian folk dancers and the ethnic culture itself."

Familiarity with the music and dance also contributed to the growing sense of identity with the Balkan troupe. That they perceived the dances and music as simpler than what a professional dance troupe would perform also appealed to some audience members. Moreover, the typical circle or line dances permitted a greater degree of participation of less-skilled individuals. One interviewee recalled that after seeing the performances the phrase "we can do that" was "on everyone's lips or on their mind."

The following summer, large numbers of Americans departed for Yugoslavia and other Balkan countries, making the journey a pilgrimage to the wellspring of culture to purchase authentic Balkan folklore. "This group of people went into towns and cities and expropriated costumes, folk art, instruments, and dance directions from entire neighborhoods," writes Evanchuk. Having discovered that many Balkan women wore long, thick braids under their elaborate headdresses, a number of Americans haunted shops back in the States in search of false hair to cover their permanents. Others drove to Mexico or sent to New York City for boots. Some hunted for coin necklaces and embroidered trim from Eastern Europe.

By the end of the fall of 1957 quite a few Americans had established a regime for learning and performing Balkan dances. Evanchuk quotes one man's typical week: "Monday after work was Serbo-Croatian language practice; Tuesday night, the singing group met; Wednesday, the dance group practiced; Thursday was usually a night at a Yugoslav cafe, eating, dancing, practic[ing] the language and listening to the orchestra; Friday was dancing, and Saturday and Sunday more of the same with sewing of costumes, attending an ethnic picnic or seeing a Yugoslavian movie if there was one around."

Another individual recalled efforts at this time to learn Serbo-Croatian. The only language aids available were distributed by the U.S. Armed Forces. In order to learn grammar and sentence construction the dancers had to work with such examples as "Do you have a gun?" "Raise your hands above your head," and "Take me to the railroad station."

Members of local Yugoslav and Bulgarian communities began to request that folk dance devotees teach them the dances of their own province or country. Thus, writes Evanchuk, "the folk dancers helped to make Balkan dance an object of appreciation for the ethnic communities, instilling in those members a more positive sense of their own Balkan ethnic identities."

In sum, "The folk dancers used Balkan folklore to shape a new identity of sorts for themselves." They developed a surrogate ethnic identity, feeling compelled to do so after having visualized and compared "their supposedly dull lifeless mainstream culture to that of the Balkan one," writes Evanchuk. They "began to lead a double existence, with job, home, and family on one side and their Balkan world on the other." Eventually "the Balkan identity began to project itself into other aspects of their lives." Enthusiastic participation of mainstream Americans in the Balkan eth-

nic experience derived in part, then, from identification with the ethnic performers who were physically similar to themselves and to "a dissatisfaction with the supposed dullness of their own majority culture." So great was the impact of the Balkan dance movement on his life that, 30 years later, one person said, "By God, when I die I hope I have a heart attack while dancing Ucest Kolo!"

As discussed by Evanchuk, another group's folklore brought together a disparate audience who, by adopting and behaving in accordance with the other group's traditions, developed an identity in common with that group. The folklore was clearly labeled as belonging to "the other." Performing it provided participants with a surrogate identity and a sense of community with an other that they felt lacking in their prior experiences.

Sometimes, however, folklore may spontaneously unite a gathering of people, bonding them together by giving them a common voice. A sense of community, of oneness, results. The film *"We Shall Overcome"* describes several situations that exemplify this.[32]

The exact origins and early development of the forerunner to the song "We Shall Overcome" have not been traced. Undoubtedly influenced by both European-American and African American traditions, "I Shall Overcome" was sung by plantation slaves. In the film *"We Shall Overcome"* members of the Moving Star Hall Singers of John's Island, South Carolina, sing "I Shall Overcome" in the "shout" style typical of slavery days. They clap hands as accompaniment while they sing the old words: "I'll be all right . . . I'll be like Him . . . I'll wear the crown . . . I will overcome." According to one of the church members, Janie Hunter, singing the song as they toiled long hours in the fields helped the slaves endure. By the end of the nineteenth century, "I Shall Overcome" or "I'll Be All Right" was often sung in African American churches, its melody having evolved to resemble more closely the versions of "We Shall Overcome" sung today.

In 1945, striking members of the Negro Textile Union sang "I Will Overcome" on the picket line in Charleston, South Carolina. This marked the first time that the song was adapted for use in social protest. Delphine Brown and other striking workers had experienced the song in gospel style, sung rapidly and shouted. On the picket line, however, they sang slowly. They also added words and verses, perhaps most important of which was "We'll win our rights some day." According to Corrine Chisholm, "Well . . . I'll be frank with you. When we first started singing it I thought it was kinda silly. But as the strike went along, and we continued singing, it gave me a whole lot of encouragement in believing that we would overcome, and it made me stick that much closer to the strike—fight that much harder—and we did overcome. We won it."

A year later some of these striking workers introduced the song to the Highlander Folk School in Montego, Tennessee, a training center for labor organizers. Verses changed. Eventually performers associated with the folksong revival learned the song; some altered the timing and added new verses.

The song became associated with the civil rights movement. According to Bernard Lafayette, Guy Carawan from California (who became music director of the Highlander Folk School in 1959) introduced it at a mass meeting in Nashville. "The song really caught on, because it was dynamic. We could add verses to it, verses relevant to our own movement." Charles Neblett, a member of the Freedom Singers who helped through their music to bring the civil rights movement to national attention, commented: "I believe that the music was the glue that held it all together. That no matter . . . how hard a situation

was, if we could all get together and sing—it was a spiritual kind of thing. It gave us more power, more strength to go on even further."

At one point in the film, Janila Jones recounts an experience at the Highlander Folk School. She had been a teenager at the time. "One night at Highlander—I can remember that we were watching a movie when some men came in with guns and billy clubs. And the power was turned off, and we were in complete darkness. There we were, some of us barely knowing each other.

"And unknowing of what it was that was happening and going on," she continues. "So there was a lot of fear in the room. But as the men walked around between us—with their guns and their billy clubs—somebody decided to sing 'We Shall Overcome.'"

In a separate interview Guy Carawan remarks, "She's the one who got the idea. She started humming 'We Shall Overcome' and that got everybody humming together, and then they just started singing, and for about two hours—that actually quieted some of the terror and fear that people had about what some of these deputized thugs were doing."

Janila Jones says, "There seemed to be a need to say to the men . . . ," and then she sings the words "We are not afraid." She adds: "And those lines helped convince us that we were not afraid."

Guy Carawan explains, "Janila was a wonderful singer . . . , in her early teens, and that night when they raided Highlander she sat there in the dark and made up the verse on the spot, 'We are not afraid,' and helped about 50 people there sing in the dark, 'We are not afraid,' and sing 'We Shall Overcome' just to keep their spirits up while the deputized thugs went around and ransacked everybody's luggage."

Janila Jones says, "It unnerved them. One of the men turned to me with his flashlight. As he shone it in my face, he said—*very* nervously—'If you have to sing, do you have to sing so loud?' And that statement just raised my voice even higher," she says and then sings, "We are not afraid today."

She continues: "And everybody—just seemed like nature came into that room: the water on the outside and even the trees just picked up and we were a part of that nature, in tune to what was happening. So much so that it unnerved them [the intruders], and they began to back up even though they . . . [had arrested some people on trumped up charges]; they retreated, very nervously, and had to leave."

In sum, a courageous teenager in a room of 50 frightened people who scarcely knew one another began humming a tune familiar to some. Composing her own words on the spot—"We are not afraid"—and adding them to other verses of "We Shall Overcome," Janila Jones helped unite friends and strangers into a single community, in the process unnerving the intruders who had sought to terrorize them.

Elsewhere in the film Willie Peacock refers to an incident at a mass meeting in Sunflower County, Mississippi, home to one of the most racist senators in Congress. Members of the Ku Klux Klan patrolled the event, spreading fear through the group. Protesters began singing "We Shall Overcome." After half an hour of singing, "there was no fear—nobody was afraid of anything." As he explains about singing such a song, "It puts you in touch with a larger self that couldn't be killed."

Dorothy Cotton elaborates: "'We Shall Overcome' is a song that helped us realize our connectedness whether that was in a small group in a workshop or in a neighborhood in a community. It made me feel connected. 'We Shall Overcome' was a way to instill hope in people who had no hope."

Charles Sherrod says, "When you have a .45 pointed at your face saying, 'Nigger, get out of town.' . . . When we have dreams that

we fight for, the best way that we have found to put that energy where we can reach for it when we need it is song, and there's no greater song than 'We Shall Overcome.' It's there to sustain us. That's the real meaning of 'We Shall Overcome.'"

According to Andrew Young, "In the Poor People's Campaign, Martin Luther King brought together poor whites from Appalachia, Cesar Chavez and the Hispanics from California, people from big cities in the North, some of our Asian minorities, and *everybody* sang 'We Shall Overcome.'"

At the end of the film, Pete Seeger, who often sang the song on his worldwide tours, reminisces about one occasion when he performed for 2,000 Lutheran church members and was asked who is referred to in the song as "we." At first he suggests it is Blacks in the South. But then he says, "I confess that when I sing it I think of the whole human race. We're either going to make it together or we're not going to make it at all. But I think we have a chance. 'We'—that's the important word—*we* will overcome."

"We Shall Overcome" has been adapted for use in social movements in places as far apart as South Korea, Sweden, Thailand, Lebanon, South Africa, and the Soviet Union. It has served antiwar protest and expressed international peace and disarmament sentiments. The women's movement adopted it as its theme song, as did the Irish nonviolent movement in Northern Ireland. Striking workers from schoolteachers to coal miners and supporters of various social programs continue to sing "We Shall Overcome," thereby uniting themselves into common cause and emphasizing their sameness while minimizing their differences.

Conclusion

In this chapter we have demonstrated that intergroup contacts affect and are reflected in folklore. Peoples living along international boundaries often differentiate themselves and express this distinction through folklore. Folklore is also rooted in and indicative of the nature and results of intergroup contacts resulting from exploration, colonization, proselytizing, and immigration. Within societies, groups demarcate boundaries between themselves and others, the bases for and consequences of which are often expressed and symbolized in folklore. Finally, folklore also brings people together by serving as the expressive basis for communal identity and collective action. As an aspect of culture, folklore is a human creation that embodies and memorializes people's shared and unique experiences. As a mirror of culture, folklore documents and reveals the many similar and different ways that human beings behave in order to satisfy common needs, achieve common goals, and solve the problems of everyday life.

Notes

1. Susan Judith Gordon, "Characterizing 'The Other': Costa Ricans' Ambivalent Attitudes Expressed Traditionally about Each Other and Their Nicaraguan Neighbors" (Ph.D. diss., University of California, Los Angeles, 1986). Quotes are from pp. 27, 28, 31, 64, 66, 77, 81, 82, 83, 126, 127, and 128.

2. From Gordon, p. 127.

3. Maria Herrera-Sobek, "*Corridos* and *Canciones* of *Mica, Migra,* and *Coyotes*: A Commentary on Undocumented Immigration," in Stephen Stern and John Allan Cicala, eds., *Creative Ethnicity: Symbols and Strategies of Contemporary Ethnic Life* (Logan: Utah State University Press, 1991), pp. 87–104. Quotes are from pp. 87, 88, 96, 97, 98, 102, and 103. For other studies of folklore along and/or relating to the United States-Mexico border, see Américo Paredes, *"With His Pistol in His Hand": A Border Ballad and Its Hero* (Austin: University of Texas Press, 1958), and "The Problem of Identity in a Changing Culture: Popular Expressions of

Culture Conflict Along the Lower Rio Grande Border," in Stanley R. Ross, ed., *Views Across the Border: The United States and Mexico* (Albuquerque: University of New Mexico Press, 1978), pp. 68–94; José Limón, "Folklore, Social Conflict, and the United States-Mexico Border," in Richard M. Dorson, ed., *Handbook of American Folklore* (Bloomington: Indiana University Press, 1983), pp. 216–226; James S. Griffith, "El Tiradito and Juan Soldado: Two Victim-Intercessors of the Western Borderlands," *International Folklore Review* 5 (1987):75–81; and Maria Herrera-Sobek, *Northward Bound: The Mexican Immigrant Experience in Ballad and Song* (Bloomington: Indiana University Press, 1993).

4. From Herrera-Sobek, pp. 99–100.

5. Adrienne L. Kaeppler, "Tongan Dance: A Study in Cultural Change," *Ethnomusicology* 14 (1970):266–277. Quotes are from pp. 266, 267, 269, 273, 275, and 276. For a filmic treatment of the contact between Western and tribal people (within the context of organized "travel adventure tours"), see *Cannibal Tours* (1987, Dennis O'Rourke, Direct Cinema Limited, color, 16mm. and VHS, 70 min.).

6. Cited in Kaeppler, p. 266.

7. James Cook, *A Voyage to the Pacific Ocean . . . in the Years 1776, 1777, 1778, 1779, and 1780* (London: Straham, 1784), vol. 1, pp. 247, 248, and 293.

8. Cook, pp. 250–251.

9. Elli Köngäs Maranda, "Folklore and Culture Change: Lau Riddles of Modernization," in Richard M. Dorson, ed., *Folklore in the Modern World* (The Hague: Mouton Publishers, 1978), pp. 207–218. Quotes are from pp. 207, 208, 209, 213, 214, 215, 216, and 217.

10. From Köngäs Maranda, pp. 210–212.

11. Francis A. de Caro and Rosan A. Jordan, "The Wrong *Topi*: Personal Narratives, Ritual, and the Sun Helmet as a Symbol," *Western Folklore* 43 (1984):233–248. Quotes are from pp. 238, 239, 240, 241, and 243.

12. De Caro and Jordan, pp. 240–241.

13. Elli Kaija Köngäs, "Immigrant Folklore: Survival or Living Tradition?" *Midwest Folklore* 10 (1960):117–123.

14. Marvin K. Opler, "Japanese Folk Beliefs and Practices, Tule Lake, California," *Journal of American Folklore* 63 (1950):385–397.

15. Robert A. Georges, "The Greeks of Tarpon Springs: An American Folk Group," *Southern Folklore Quarterly* 29 (1965):129–

141, and *Greek-American Folk Beliefs and Narratives* (New York: Arno Press, 1980), pp. 31–33 and 60–74. For a video about beliefs and customs of Florida fishermen, see *Fishing All My Days: Florida Shrimping Traditions* (1986, Alan Saperstein, Peggy Bulger, and Eric Larsen, Florida Folklife Program, color, VHS, 29 min.). For other films on immigrant traditions, see *Between Two Worlds: The Hmong Shaman in America* (1985, Siegel Productions, color, VHS, 30 min.); *Silk Sarongs and City Streets* (1987, Eric Van Schrader, The International Institute, St. Louis, Missouri, color, 3/4" and VHS, 28 min.); and *Moving Mountains: The Story of the Yiu Mien* (1990, Elaine Velazquez, The Media Project, Portland, Oregon, color, 16mm. and VHS, 58 min.).

16. Georges, p. 133. John Gonatos told this story to Georges in Tarpon Springs, Florida, in the summer of 1961.

17. Mary MacGregor-Villarreal, "Celebrating *las posadas* in Los Angeles," *Western Folklore* 39 (1980):71–105. Quotes are from pp. 72, 73, 74, 75, 77, 86, 87, 88, and 94.

18. Florence E. Baer, "'Give me . . . your huddled masses': Anti-Vietnamese Refugee Lore and the 'Image of Limited Good,'" *Western Folklore* 41 (1982):275–291. Quotes are from pp. 279, 282, 285, 289, and 291.

19. For an overview of new meanings to old forms and the recent creation of folklore within one ethnic group, see Yvonne Hiipakka Lockwood, "Immigrant to Ethnic: Symbols of Identity among Finnish-Americans," in Alan Jabbour and James Hardin, eds., *Folklore Annual 1986* (Washington, D.C.: Library of Congress, 1987), pp. 92–107. For both continuities and changes in folk art, including the creation of new forms and the use of new materials, see Marsha MacDowell, "Hmong Textiles and Cultural Conservation," in Thomas Vennum, Jr., ed., *Festival of American Folklife Program Book* (Washington, D.C.: Smithsonian Institution, 1986), pp. 91–93; Sally Peterson, "Translating Experience and the Reading of a Story Cloth," *Journal of American Folklore* 101 (1988):6–22; and Sally Peterson, "Plastic Strap Baskets: Containers for a Changing Context," in James Hardin and Alan Jabbour, eds., *Folklife Annual 1988–89* (Washington, D.C.: Library of Congress, 1989), pp. 138–147. Quotes are from MacDowell, p. 92, and Peterson, "Translating Experience," p. 20.

20. Alan Dundes, "African Tales among the North American Indians," *Southern Folklore Quarterly* 29 (1965):207–219.

21. Yvonne R. Lockwood and William G. Lockwood, "Pasties in Michigan's Upper Peninsula: Foodways, Interethnic Relations, and Regionalism," in Stern and Cicala, pp. 3–20.

22. Richard Bauman, "Observations on the Place of Festival in the Worldview of the Seventeenth-Century Quakers," *Western Folklore* 43 (1984):133–138. Quotes are from pp. 133, 134, 135, 136, 137, and 138.

23. Ruth Benedict, "Introduction to Zuni Mythology," in *Zuni Mythology*, Columbia University Contributions to Anthropology, 2 volumes (New York: Columbia University Press, 1935). Benedict's introductory essay to the work is reprinted in Robert A. Georges, ed., *Studies on Mythology* (Homewood, Ill.: Dorsey Press, 1968), pp. 102–136. Quotes are from the reprinted version, p. 133.

24. Carol A. Mitchell, "The Sexual Perspective in the Appreciation and Interpretation of Jokes," *Western Folklore* 26 (1977):303–329. Quotes are from pp. 305, 307, 308, 309, 310, 311, 312, 314, 317, 322, 323, 326, 328, and 329.

25. For a fuller discussion of this joke, see Carol A. Mitchell, "The Difference between Male and Female Joke Telling as Exemplified in a College Community," 2 vols. (Ph.D. diss., Indiana University, 1976), vol. 1, pp. 15–53.

26. From Mitchell, pp. 308–309. The second Mary Jane joke is from Mitchell's essay "Some Differences in Male and Female Joke-Telling," in Rosan A. Jordan and Susan J. Kalčik, eds., *Women's Folklore/Women's Culture* (Philadelphia: University of Pennsylvania Press, 1985), p. 165.

27. Mitchell, "The Sexual Perspective in the Appreciation and Interpretation of Jokes," p. 309.

28. Quotes are from Mitchell, "Some Differences in Male and Female Joke-Telling," pp. 166, 167, 169, and 185.

29. Joseph P. Goodwin, *More Man Than You'll Ever Be: Gay Folklore and Acculturation in Middle America* (Bloomington: Indiana University Press, 1989). Quotes are from pp. 1, 13, 17, 20, 21, 22, 27, 36, 37, 38, 51, 63, 80, 82, 83, and 85.

30. From Goodwin, pp. 36, 37, and 38.

31. R. J. Evanchuk, "Inside, Outside, Upside-Down: The Role of Mainstream Society Participants in the Ethnic Dance Movement," *Folklore and Mythology Studies* 11–12 (1987–

88):115–129. Quotes are from pp. 115, 116, 118, 119, 121, 123, 126, 127, and 128.

32. *"We Shall Overcome,"* a 58-minute videotape (1988), is produced by Jim Brown, Ginger Brown, Harold Leventhal, and George Stoney; directed by Jim Brown; edited by Ken Lewis; and narrated by Harry Belafonte. It is available from Resolution Inc./California Newsreel, 149 Ninth Street/420, San Francisco, CA 94103. See also the reviews by Arthur Gribben in *Western Folklore* 49 (1990):422–423, and Michael Owen Jones in *Folklore in Use* 1 (1993):95–98. *Ethnic Notions* (1986, Marlon Riggs, California Newsreel, color, video, 56 min.), on the other hand, traces deeply rooted stereotypes in America that have fueled anti–African American prejudice. See the review of this film (and *Hearts and Hands*) by Sharon R. Sherman, "Double-Edged Power: Historical Records of Gender and Race," *Western Folklore* 47 (1988):217–223.

Folklore as Behavior

8. Folklore and Human Psychology

Implicit in studies of folklore as artifact, describable and transmissible entity, and culture is the assumption that while it can be defensibly conceptualized in any one or combination of these ways, folklore is first and foremost a behavioral phenomenon. It originates in the brains of human beings, and it exists and persists because of and through human actions. Individuals create the stories, songs, tunes, games, sayings, objects, events, etc., that become folklore. Phenomena become folklore because other individuals besides their creators find them meaningful and subsequently behave in ways that enable them to generate those phenomena anew.

As we have noted and illustrated, narrating, singing, dancing, playing, object-making, etc., are processes by means of which peoples of all cultural backgrounds and eras express themselves. The fact that expressive processes are limited in number and cross-cultural in distribution makes questions about the behavioral bases and nature of folklore fundamental. It also requires folklorists to answer those questions in terms of conceptual schemes that focus on and attempt to explain behaviors known or presumed to be panhuman, or at least multicultural. Those studying folklore from a behavioral perspective, then, are concerned with how and why individuals as members of a single biological species, rather than as members of a variety of social collectivities (e.g., of distinctive tribes, countries, groups), behave. It makes our common identification as human beings the focus of inquiry and is therefore concerned with behaviors that are species, rather than culturally, shared and specific.

Folklorists have addressed behavioral questions since the early nineteenth century, often indirectly and without so identifying them. Among these are those having to do with learning. In repeatedly characterizing folklore as "oral tradition," researchers imply that learning and perpetuating folklore are dependent on individuals' stimulating and responding to each other face to face in one-on-one encounters or small-group gatherings. Such frequently made statements as those that certain folktales have been handed down from mother to daughter, or that an individual learned traditional fiddle tunes from his grandfather, are usually factual assertions, not clichés. Such statements embody a basic truth: that despite widespread literacy and media influence, human beings learn folklore mostly at first hand and usually from family members, friends, neighbors, peers, colleagues, and acquaintances. And folklore comprises much of each individual's behavior.

Hugh Miller captured the essence of this learning process when he wrote in 1835, "Old grey-headed men, and especially old women, became my books." Miller notes that these living teachers from whom he learned face to face were individuals who had not "been preoccupied by that artificial kind of learning, which is the result of [formal, institutionalized] education." Instead, their minds "had gradually filled, as they passed through life, with *the knowledge of what was occurring around them,* and with the information derived from *people of a similar cast with themselves,* who had been born half an age earlier" (emphasis added).[1] Dan Ben-Amos expressed it somewhat differently 136 years later, when he defined folklore in 1971 as "artistic communication *in small groups*" and indicated: "For the folkloric act to happen, two social conditions are necessary: both the performers and the audience have to be in the same situation and be *part of the same reference group.* This implies that folklore communication takes place in a situation in which *people confront each other face to face and relate to each other directly*" (emphasis added).[2]

As Miller's and Ben-Amos's statements imply, people interacting one-on-one or in small groups with familiar others generate a social environment that fosters and facilitates a more intimate and potentially more enduring kind of learning than that which occurs in the classroom. This "informal learning," as folklorists often call it, is frequently characterized as learning by a process akin to osmosis. Albert B. Lord's comments are typical. In discussing aspiring South Slavic epic singers in Yugoslavia, Lord notes that they learn by listening to other performers, "*imbibing* the rhythm of the singing and to an extent also the rhythm of the thoughts as they are expressed in song" (emphasis added). Furthermore, "oft-repeated phrases which we call formulas are being *absorbed*" (emphasis added).[3] While folklorists have been unable to characterize this kind of learning precisely, they recognize that it is a distinctive process, the nature and understanding of which are fundamental issues for ongoing discussion and analysis by those in their discipline.[4]

Dealing with folklore's durability also entails concerning oneself with behavior and exploring conceptual schemes that enable one to account for its continuity. The evolutionism and cultural determinism discussed in chapters 2 and 3 provide means of explaining folklore's existence over time. As noted earlier, those employing these schemes assume that folklore is a manifestation of an equilibrious lifestyle, associative thinking, and/or a retrospective world-view usually associated with particular stages of intellectual and social evolution. Historically, however, folklorists have both supplemented and challenged such notions by contending that phenomena must satisfy fundamental human needs to become folklore, and that folklore examples persist as long as people find them meaningful—and hence as long as they are reinforced.

Reinforcement

The concept of reinforcement evolved from experimental psychologists' research on learning. It is relevant to behaviors over which organisms have control (as opposed to those that are instinctual or biologically determined). Psychologist B. F. Skinner characterizes this *operant behavior* as behavior that is emitted, in the sense that "it *operates* upon the environment to generate consequences" (Skinner's emphasis).[5] Behaviors whose effects on the environment are beneficial to the emitting organism are said to be reinforcing and are likely to occur again. Most behaviors receive only intermittent reinforcement; but behavior reinforced intermittently "is remarkably stable and shows great resistance to extinction." Without reinforcement, behavior undergoes extinction. However, "An extinguished response is not forgotten," states Skinner. "It is simply not emitted in the circumstances in which it has been extinguished. This may be shown by changing the circumstances." Skinner provides a pertinent example. "Thus, we may no longer be reinforced for an outworn story, and it may seem to disappear entirely from our repertoire, only to be revived by a new audience, or by a moderate aversive pressure of such a question as *What was that story you used to tell?*" (Skinner's emphasis).[6]

In addressing the question of why ancient myths and rituals persist throughout the modern world and seem so resistant to

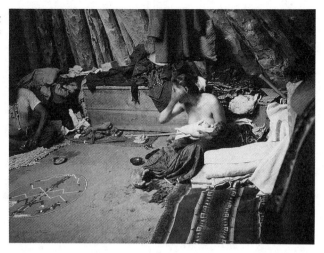

Figure 8–1: Navaho mother holding sick child near sand painting while tribal doctor chants (Neg. #2A 3646, courtesy Department of Library Services, American Museum of Natural History).

challenge or change, Clyde Kluckhohn finds that the principle of reinforcement provides a meaningful answer.[7] "If a Navaho gets a bad case of snow-blindness and recovers after being sung over" during a traditional healing ceremonial, writes Kluckhohn, "his disposition to go to a singer in the event of a recurrence will be strongly reinforced. And, by the principle of generalization, he is likely to go even if the ailment is quite different." But the ceremonial to which Kluckhohn refers involves and has consequences for more than just the patient. Others are also affected. "Likewise, the reinforcement will be reciprocal," he adds, for "the singer's confidence in his powers will also be reinforced." Furthermore, "there will [also] be some reinforcement for spectators and for all who hear of the recovery." (See Box 8–1 for a description of a Navaho healing ceremonial.)

Kenneth L. Ketner similarly finds the concept of reinforcement, as developed and articulated by Skinner, to be relevant for understanding and explaining a complex of beliefs and practices involving madstones.[8] These small calculi, found in the stomachs and other internal organs of dead ruminating animals such as deer and cows, have

come to be used traditionally over the years to counteract the effects on human beings of certain animal bites. Madstones are considered so valuable that they are sometimes bequeathed to heirs in wills.

Underlying madstone use is the belief that when a poisonous snake or rabid animal bites a person, a potentially lethal substance is injected into the victim's bloodstream, requiring immediate action if she or he is to survive. One way to deal with the dilemma is to apply a madstone directly to the bite, first making a cut if the wound is not bleeding, to be certain the madstone makes direct contact with the victim's blood.

When first applied, the madstone will not adhere if there is no poisonous substance in the bloodstream. If the madstone sticks to the wound, however, the victim has, indeed, been poisoned; and the madstone is left attached to the wound to suck the deadly substance from the person's body. When it falls off, the madstone is boiled in milk, which turns green as the poison pollutes it. The madstone is reapplied, boiled again in milk, and reapplied anew, as many times as necessary. When the madstone no longer sticks to the

---

BOX 8-1
Traditional Navaho Healing

In the hospital a Navaho is lonely and homesick, living by a strange routine and eating unfamiliar foods. Illness often gives the sufferer the suspicion that he is disliked or unprotected. During the chant [in a traditional healing ceremony] the patient feels himself personally (rather than impersonally) being succored and loved, for his relatives are spending their substance to get him cured, and they are rallying round to aid in the ceremonial.

Then there is the prestige and authority of the Singer assuring the patient that he will recover. In his capacity as Singer, gifted with the learning of the Holy People, he is more than a mortal and at times becomes identified with the supernaturals, speaking in their voices and telling the hearers that all is well. The prestige, mysticism, and power of the ceremonial itself are active, coming directly from the supernatural powers that build up the growing earth in spring, drench it with rain, or tear it apart with lightning. In the height of the chant the patient himself becomes one of the Holy People, puts his feet in their moccasins, and breathes in the strength of the sun. He comes into complete harmony with the universe and must of course be free of all ills and evil. Finally, it is very likely that he has seen the ceremonial work with others and may have had it before himself; in this case there will be an upswing of reawakened memories, like old melodies bearing him on emotional waves to feelings of security.

As well as this powerful reassurance, occupation and diversion are supplied to the patient. He has the sense of doing something about a misfortune which otherwise might leave him in the misery of feeling completely helpless. Although he does not himself actually carry out most of the necessary preparations, his mind is full of the things that have to be done. Arrangements must be made for paying the Singer and getting the food supplies together to feed all who come. Ritual material has to be gathered and people have to be found who will do it. During the actual ceremonial the patient's thoughts are busy following the Singer's instructions, pondering over the implications in the songs and prayers, the speeches and side remarks of the Singer. The period of four days of being quiet and aloof after the ceremonial is a splendid opportunity for rumination and for development of the conviction that the purposes of the chant have been achieved, or are starting to be achieved.

—Clyde Kluckhohn and Dorothea Leighton[9]

---

wound, the patient is free of poison; and the "curative episode," as Ketner calls it, ends.

Because of the reputation or appearance of an animal that bites him or her (such as a dog frothing at the mouth), "the victim is convinced that he [or she] has been exposed to a horrible illness," Ketner contends. Consequently, her or his "level of activity rises because of the aversive stimulus under which [she or] he suffers." If the victim has had positive past experience with madstones or has heard stories of others who have, she or he might be motivated to seek out the owner of a stone and follow the

prescribed procedures for using it. Seeing the madstone stick to a wound and the milk turn green as the stone boils in it provides perceptible evidence of its curative properties and reinforces belief in its efficacy. The curative episode concludes, Ketner states, "with the patient's release from [the] anxiety" generated when the victim first thinks that the animal which has bitten her or him must be poisonous or rabid, even though not all suspected animals are, in fact, rabid. The transmission of the disease from animal to human occurs in only 10 to 15 percent of cases.

Figure 8–2: A madstone cut in half to reveal interior composition of hair and calcium deposits (courtesy UCLA Folklore and Mythology Archives).

Intermittent reinforcement from one's firsthand experiences (including perceptible evidence) or from stories about others' positive experiences suffices to condition and perpetuate belief in the effectiveness of madstone use, Ketner indicates. Stories of "death from hydrophobia of a beneficiary of madstone treatment" aren't as plentiful as are those of successful curings; and tales about unsuccessful madstone use evoke rationalizations, such as the insistence that the curative episode was not carried out properly. Similarly, reports of individuals who have survived bites from poisonous or rabid animals without using a madstone or undergoing any other kind of treatment are often discounted by the assertion that the attacking animal must not really have been poisonous or infected. (See Box 8–2 for stories of individuals' experiences with madstones.)

Psychoanalytically Oriented Studies

Kluckhohn and Ketner account for the persistence of folklore in terms of models that have their origins in the research of experimental psychologists. Other folklorists find psychoanalytically oriented schemes more meaningful. Drawing principally on the work of Sigmund Freud and C. G. Jung, these investigators assume that folklore is a manifestation of the nature and workings of the human psyche. Their goal is to explain why folklore exists and endures by determining and describing what unconscious states, processes, and principles specific examples of folklore symbolize.

Alan Dundes's study of the earth-diver creation myth is one of his many published works that exemplify a Freudian approach to folklore.[10] Focusing on a tale type found in societies throughout much of the world, Dundes posits that such "recurrent myths" must "have similar meaning irrespective of specific cultural context." Accepting the view that there are "human universals," Dundes contends, "does not preclude the possibility that one myth found in many cultures may have as many meanings as there are cultural contexts." But it is its "universal meaning" that accounts for a myth's "widespread distribution," he insists.

Figure 8–3: Joseph D. Clark surrounded by madstone owners and enthusiasts at his home in Raleigh, North Carolina, on July 13, 1975 (courtesy News and Observer Publishing Company/N. C. Division of Archives and History).

Dundes uses as his normalform of the earth-diver myth the following plot summary, constructed by anthropologist Erminie Wheeler-Voegelin on the basis of Native North American versions of the tale type with which she was familiar:

> In North American Indian myths of the origin of the world, the culture hero has a succession of animals dive into the primeval waters, or flood of waters, to secure bits of mud or sand from which the earth is to be formed. Various animals, birds, and aquatic creatures are sent down into the waters that cover the earth. One after another animal fails; the last one succeeds, however, and floats to the surface half dead, with a little sand or dirt in his claws. Sometimes it is Muskrat, sometimes Beaver, Hell-diver, Crawfish, Mink who succeeds after various other animals have failed, in bringing up the tiny bit of mud which is then put on the surface of the water and magically expands to become the world of the present time.

According to Dundes, the "interesting features" of the myth are "the creation from mud or dirt" and "the magical expansion of the bit of mud." Just "how did the idea of creating the earth from a particle of dirt small enough to be contained beneath a claw or fingernail develop," Dundes asks, "and what is there in this cosmogonic myth

that has caused it to thrive so in a variety of cultures not only in aboriginal North America but in the rest of the world as well?"

In responding to these questions, Dundes relies on what he calls "two key assumptions." One is that there is a universal notion that birth occurs through the anus (what Dundes calls "the cloacal theory of birth"). The other is that men feel insufficient because of their inability to procreate as women do, resulting in a universal "male pregnancy envy." Freud identified the first of these "as one of the common sexual theories of children," Dundes notes. Because of ignorance of the nature of sexual intercourse, conception, and birth, the child "assumes that the lump in the pregnant woman's abdomen leaves her body in the only way he can imagine material leaving the body, namely via the anus." The second notion exists because men everywhere "would like to be able to produce or create valuable material from within their bodies as women do." The earth-diver myth is both a manifestation and symbol of the universally held concepts of cloacal birth and male pregnancy envy, Dundes posits, accounting for the story's popularity and cross-cultural distribution.

Dundes regards the dirt or mud of which

BOX 8-2
Experiences with Madstones

Our madstone is about as big around as a silver dollar, and I should say about a little better than a fourth of an inch thick. If you looked at it through a powerful magnifying glass, you will see that it is full of little holes, and it looks like hairs are in there. It is very polished. The Pawnees said that they have seen them in various sizes.

* * *

We are happy to learn that Mr. Elijah Pope, Sr., of this county, whose residence is near Dawson's Cross Roads, has succeeded in procuring a Mad-stone, or Stone, that will cure any poisonous bite—either Mad Dog, Snake, or Spider. Mr. Pope has been called upon several times to apply the stone since it has been in his possession, and has been successful in every case. Such as may be so unfortunate as to be poisoned by the bite or sting of anything, would do well to call on Mr. Pope.

* * *

I would like to give you a true account of an incident that happened in our family at Jim Town, Indian Territory, in 1895. . . . A big, black, shaggy Shepherd came galloping along the road dragging a section of heavy chain and frothing at the mouth. . . . The kids jumped up . . . hollering, "Mad dog."

My brother Joe jumped up and looked in the wrong direction and the dog whirled to one side and bit him in several places on his back. The rabid dog followed the road for a couple of miles into the Red River bottom where a man by the name of Tom Patton and another man were riding after cattle. . . . The dog turned on [Tom] and bit him several times on the leg.

My stepfather, H. B. Tucker, put Joe behind him on a horse and headed for Gainesville, Texas, which was about thirty miles to the south across Red River. He had heard that there was a madstone located there. On their arrival, the stone was placed on the wounds but failed to adhere (or stick, as we called it). My stepfather returned home convinced that the dog was not rabid and went back to plowing corn.

He had not much more than got his team [of horses] hitched to the plow when here came a rider with a message from Tom Patton who had also gone across the river into Texas to a madstone that he had heard of. He said that the madstone was sticking and to bring Joe on over at once. My stepfather unhitched the team from the plow and hitched them to a covered wagon and loaded the family into it. With the messenger as a guide he lost no time getting to the madstone. It was still sticking to Tom's wounds, there being several and each having to be treated separately.

When applied to a fresh wound it would stick for a while before it would fall off. Then the attendant would place it in sweet milk over a fire in the fireplace as they did not have a cookstove, and boil it for a few minutes until the milk turned a yellow-green and became slimy. After this, it would be re-applied to the wound. Each time it would stick to the wound. Each time it would stick for a shorter period of time until eventually it would not stick at all. Then it would be placed on another wound. On Joe, it adhered tightly for several hours before it came loose. . . .

My honest opinion is that had Brother [Joe] not received treatment by the madstone he would have gone raving mad within a few days.[11]

the world is created in the earth-diver myth as a symbol for excrement. He points out that many myths reported throughout the world portray feces, as well as mud and dirt, as the material from which humans and other phenomena are created. Clinical records reveal patients' preoccupation with excrement and other sticky or smelly body wastes (e.g., mucus, dirt accumulation between the toes). They also provide reports of men fantasizing about "excreting the world" and expelling the universe through their anuses. Male creator figures similarly abound. According to the Bible, Eve was "created from a substance taken from the body of Adam"; and it is usually males who are portrayed as creator figures in the world's mythologies. "Whether a male creator spins material, molds clay, lays an egg, fabricates from mucus or epidermal tissue, or dives for fecal mud, the psychological motivation is much the same," Dundes asserts. The creator figure in the earth-diver myth, he assumes, is necessarily male. Moreover, that figure symbolizes all members of his sex and compensates through his creative actions for a gender-based deficiency.

Other assumptions and concepts from Freudian psychology serve as a basis of Willie Smyth's explanation for the creation and popularity of jokes about the explosion 73 seconds after its nationally televised launching of the American space shuttle *Challenger VII* on January 28, 1986.[12] All seven people aboard were killed. Jokes about this major newsmaking event "appeared almost simultaneously" with the *Challenger*'s explosion and "quickly became omnipresent." Among those circulating widely in the United States five weeks after the disaster were the following.

> What does NASA [National Aeronautics and Space Administration] stand for?
> Need another seven astronauts (or not another soul alive).

* * *

> Why do they drink Pepsi at NASA?
> Because they can't get 7-up.

* * *

> Why didn't they put showers on the *Challenger*?
> Because they knew that everyone would wash up on shore.

* * *

> How do we know that Christa McAuliffe [the civilian schoolteacher aboard the spacecraft] wasn't a good teacher?
> Because good teachers don't blow up in front of their class.

* * *

> What were the last words said on the *Challenger*?
> I want a Light . . . no, no, a Bud Light!

Smyth points out that the *Challenger* jokes have a traditional question-and-answer or riddle format and are related to "cruel or sick jokes" that contain "graphic images of death or deformation." Like other jokes about "figures or events that dominate the media airways," they are also topical; and they "spread extremely rapidly in oral folk tradition" and may have multiple origins. (See Box 8–3 for examples.)

Smyth then poses and addresses the question, "Why are these jokes popular and considered to be funny?" He finds an answer in Sigmund Freud's discussion of tendentious jokes. He writes, "Challenger jokes, according to Freudian theory, allow some tellers and auditors to defuse psychic energy associated with that event through the evasion of restrictions (taboos) and through the opening of sources of pleasures that have become inaccessible." One feature of the *Challenger* jokes, Smyth notes, "is their potentially offensive character." While people call the jokes "horrible," "gross," and "disgusting," he reports, they also laugh at them and tell them to others.

BOX 8-3
Sick and Topical Jokes

How do you make a dead baby float?
Add root beer and a scoop of ice cream.

*   *   *

"Mommy, Mommy, why do I keep going
  around in circles?"
"Shut up or I'll nail your other foot to
  the floor."

*   *   *

[The following jokes circulated shortly
after Leon Klinghoffer, a wheelchair-
bound passenger aboard the cruise ship
Achille Lauro, was shot and pushed
overboard by terrorists off the coast of
Italy in 1985.]
What is a Leon?
Two shots and a splash.

*   *   *

What do the fish call Leon?
Meals on wheels.

*   *   *

[The following was one of the jokes
popular after the beheading of actor Vic
Morrow by a helicopter during a movie
shoot in 1982.]
Why did Vic Morrow get dandruff?
He lost his head and shoulders.[13]

This illustrates that the telling of such
jokes is an aggressive act that enables
people to express "inhibited impulses about
taboo subjects" without "psychic censor-
ship."

Like many disaster jokes, those about
the fate of the *Challenger* crew deal with
death. Furthermore, "Media bring awareness of the tragic death of renowned persons or abhorrent murders, creating crises
across entire nations." According to Freud,
"people can never imagine their own death
. . . and in their unconscious" they "are
convinced of their own immortality." Humor provides a means for them to ward off

"threats to this sense of immortality." It
enables them "to defuse, by means of laughter or groans, anxieties about and conse-
quent hostility toward thoughts of death
and dismemberment." This "defusion of
anxiety," according to Smyth, "works on
two levels. On [the] one hand the abstract
concept of death is presented in such a
manner that it can be laughed at," he states;
"and, on the other hand, the specific graphic
depiction of the details of death is robbed of
its anxiety-provoking power through em-
bedding the most graphic images of death
and dismemberment within a humorous
structure." Through joking, "the graphic
reality of tragedies can be reduced to the
realm of the unreal."

Like Freud, Carl Gustav Jung felt that
the kinds of phenomena folklorists document and study are manifestations of, and
can provide potentially important insights
into, the workings of the human psyche.
This is exemplified in Jung's discussion of
the trickster figure as depicted in a cycle of
orally told tales published by Paul Radin.[14]

The trickster cycle that Radin presents
and Jung analyzes is "found among the
Siouan-speaking Winnebago of central Wisconsin and eastern Nebraska." It consists of
49 stories that portray the multiple and
often conflicting ways Trickster behaves.
Radin notes that

> Trickster is at one and the same time creator
> and destroyer, giver and negator, he who
> dupes others and he who is always duped
> himself. He wills nothing consciously. At all
> times he is constrained to behave as he does
> from impulses over which he has no control.
> He knows neither good nor evil yet he is
> responsible for both. He possesses no values,
> moral or social, is at the mercy of his passions
> and appetites, yet through his actions all
> values come into being. But not only he, so
> our myth tells us, possesses these traits. So,
> likewise, do the other figures of the plot
> connected with him: the animals, the various
> supernatural beings and monsters, and man.

The story cycle begins with tales of Trickster's violating Winnebago taboos. Contrary to custom, he cohabits with a woman before going on the warpath, then discourages others from accompanying him and goes it alone. His naiveté is illustrated early on by his inability to find the shore as he swims alongside it and by his mistaking a tree trunk with a protruding branch for a person pointing. He captures some ducks by trickery, commands his anus to guard them as they cook and he naps, and punishes his anus for its failure to awaken him when foxes steal and eat the roasting ducks, leaving him nothing to eat but bones (see Box 8–4).

Because of its huge size, Trickster carries his penis on his back coiled up in a box. Upon seeing a group of women bathing on the other side of a lake, he dispatches his penis across the water, where it lodges in the vagina of a chief's daughter. Only an old wise woman's repeated stabbings with an awl bring about the dislodging of the giant penis. Trickster laughs as he watches the scene from across the lake, but regrets the old woman's interference. "Why is she doing this when I am trying to have intercourse?" he asks. "Now, she has spoiled all the pleasure." In a later tale, he sends his penis in pursuit of a taunting chipmunk, probing for it in the hollowed out part of a tree. When he pulls his penis out, he discovers that the chipmunk has bitten off pieces and reduced it in size. Trickster captures the culprit, finds the bitten off and partially chewed penis pieces, and transforms them into such useful things for humankind as potatoes, turnips, artichokes, and rice.

At the end of the story cycle, Trickster performs other good deeds, such as removing obstacles from the Mississippi River. He also "killed and ate all those beings that were molesting the people." After enjoying a last earthly meal, Trickster "left and went first into the ocean and then up to the heavens," where he remains in charge of a realm beneath and just like "the world where Earthmaker lives."

In his discussion and analysis, C. G. Jung places the Winnebago Trickster in a broad, comparative context. He notes similarities between Trickster's behavior and that of the medicine man or shaman, who "often plays malicious jokes on people, only to fall victim in his turn to the vengeance of those whom he has injured." Participants in medieval European secular and quasireligious celebrations similarly acted foolishly and unpredictably, engaging in masquerades and "pointless orgies of destruction" reminiscent of "the ancient saturnalia." Trickster's pervasiveness, Jung states, is everywhere apparent. "In picaresque tales, in carnivals and revels, in sacred and magical rites, in man's religious fears and exaltations, this phantom of the trickster haunts the mythology of all ages, sometimes in quite unmistakable form, sometimes in strangely modulated guise."

Like all mythical figures, according to Jung, Trickster corresponds "to inner psychic experiences and originally sprang from them." He is "an archetypal psychic structure of extreme antiquity," a "collective shadow figure" that "gradually breaks up under the impact of civilization, leaving traces in folklore which are difficult to recognize." The Winnebago Trickster "preserves the shadow in its pristine mythological form," notes Jung, and "points back to a very much earlier stage of consciousness which existed before the birth of the myth, when the Indian was still groping about in a similar mental darkness."

The trickster figure is not a mere "historical remnant," however, for it "continues to make its influence felt on the highest level of civilization." Trickster's ambivalence has its counterpart in "experiences of split or double personality." Moreover, the appeal of stories about Trickster is their "therapeutic effect." The Trickster myth, according to Jung, "holds the earlier low

BOX 8-4

Trickster Punishes His Anus and Eats His Own Intestines

After a while Trickster awoke, "My O my!" he exclaimed joyfully, "the things I had put on to roast must be cooked crisp now." So he went over, felt around, and pulled out a leg. To his dismay it was but a bare bone, completely devoid of meat. "How terrible! But this is the way they generally are when they are cooked too much!" So he felt around again and pulled out another one. But this leg also had nothing on it. "How terrible! These, likewise, must have been roasted too much! However, I told my younger brother, anus, to watch the meat roasting. He is a good cook indeed!" He pulled out one piece after the other. They were all the same. Finally he sat up and looked around. To his astonishment, the pieces of meat on the roasting sticks were gone! "Ah, ha, now I understand! It must have been those covetous friends of mine who have done me this injury!" he exclaimed. Then he poked around the fire again and again but found only bones. "Alas! Alas! They have caused my appetite to be disappointed, those covetous fellows! And you, too, you despicable object, what about your behaviour? Did I not tell you to watch this fire? You shall remember this! As a punishment for your remissness, I will burn your mouth so that you will not be able to use it!"

Thereupon he took a burning piece of wood and burnt the mouth of his anus. He was, of course, burning himself and, as he applied the fire, he exclaimed, "Ouch! Ouch! This is too much! I have made my skin smart. Is it not for such things that they call me Trickster? They have indeed talked me into doing this just as if I had been doing something wrong!"

Trickster had burnt his anus. He had applied a burning piece of wood to it. Then he went away.

As he walked along the road he felt certain that someone must have passed along it before for he was on what appeared to be a trail. Indeed, suddenly, he came upon a piece of fat that must have come from someone's body. "Someone has been packing an animal he had killed," he thought to himself. Then he picked up a piece of fat and ate it. It had a delicious taste. "My, my, how delicious it is to eat this!" As he proceeded however, much to his surprise he discovered that it was a part of himself, part of his own intestines, that he was eating. After burning his anus, his intestines had contracted and fallen off, piece by piece, and these pieces were the things he was picking up. "My, my! Correctly, indeed, am I named Foolish One, Trickster! By their calling me thus, they have at last actually turned me into a Foolish One, a Trickster!" Then he tied his intestines together. A large part, however, had been lost. In tying it, he pulled it together so that wrinkles and ridges were formed. That is the reason why the anus of human beings has its present shape.[15]

intellectual and moral level before the eyes of the more highly developed individual, so that he shall not forget how things looked yesterday." We desire "to get out of the earlier condition" through which we have presumably evolved; yet we cannot "forget it," for "nothing is ever lost." Writes Jung: "Outwardly people are more or less civilized but inwardly they are still primitives. Something in man is profoundly disinclined to give up his beginnings, and something else believes it has long since got beyond all that." Therefore, the Winnebago tales Radin documents and Jung analyzes fulfill an important function, for the trickster figure they portray "is a faithful copy of an absolutely undifferentiated human consciousness, corresponding to a psyche that has hardly left the animal level." Radin's concluding remarks capture the essence of the Trickster, echoing in many respects the views that Jung also expresses:

The symbol which Trickster embodies is not a static one. It contains within itself the promise of differentiation, the promise of god and man. For this reason every generation occupies itself with interpreting Trickster anew. No generation understands him fully but no generation can do without him. Each had to include him in all its theologies, in all its cosmogonies, despite the fact that it realized that he did not fit properly into any of them, for he represents not only the undifferentiated and distant past, but likewise the undifferentiated present within every individual. This constitutes his universal and persistent attraction. And so he became and remained everything to every man—god, animal, human being, hero, buffoon, he who was before good and evil, denier, affirmer, destroyer and creator. If we laugh at him, he grins at us. What happens to him happens to us.

Radin's reference to Trickster as undifferentiated and as representing both an undifferentiated human past and an individual's present derives from the fundamental goal of Jungian psychotherapy: to achieve psychic wholeness by reconciling the different aspects of the patient's personality, a process that Jung called *individuation*. Jung believed that all human beings strive toward the end of individuation, largely unconsciously.

Moreover, in Jung's view, according to Carlos Drake, a folklorist trained in Jungian psychoanalysis, unconsciousness consists of two parts: "a personal unconscious, containing all repressed and forgotten experiences of the individual's life, and a collective unconscious, linking him to the psychic life of human beings everywhere, past and present."[16] Jung came to this conception of a universal unconscious from experiences with psychotic patients whose ramblings revealed elements of ancient myths and motifs from fairy tales that they could not possibly have known about. Some of these were recognizable in the dreams and fantasies of ordinary people as well. Such images seemed to Jung "to be products of a kind of master mold out of which all human possibilities come into being; they are, in short, archetypal," writes Drake. These archetypal images may appear in individuals' dreams; particular archetypal figures and symbols can influence waking activities by being projected into some situations or onto a person or object. They also crop up in myths and folktales.

Drake elaborates on the notion of archetype in narratives, illustrating his points by referring to Type 1640, *The Brave Tailor*, in which an unlikely hero wins a king's daughter through several clever tactics. At the beginning of the story, the young man is a tailor of small stature who just happens to kill a number of flies at a single blow. "Convinced of his prowess," writes Drake, "he fashions something (a sign on his belt or a placard) to proclaim to the world his special ability, taking care to suggest rather than state he has killed many men at one blow."[17]

Drake infers that the story involves a persona-anima framework. The persona is the mask a person wears before the world. While most people's persona and role in life coincide, occasionally something goes wrong, such as confusing the role one plays with one's whole personality and suffering an inflation of the ego.

The anima, writes Drake, is the unconscious complement of the conscious persona; it is the feminine principle in men, with "the animus being the corresponding male principle in women. This archetype involves man's ages-long experience of woman, and is shaped in the individual by the projections he makes on the women in his life, beginning most importantly with his mother (or with the father, in the case of a woman)." Like other archetypes, it has both negative and positive aspects. "The anima is often responsible for man's weakness, moodiness, indecision, pettishness; it is also his push to creative activity," Drake writes.

For Jung, the anima mediates between the conscious and the unconscious, providing a way for unconscious contents necessary to compensate the conscious attitude to enter consciousness. Imbalances of the personality show up in dreams and in folktales like "The Brave Tailor," which Drake interprets as "an example of the development of a persona and a test of its strength by the anima." The tailor makes clothes. Clothing is often part of an individual's persona and is associated, like a uniform, with his or her role. In this folktale, "the hero's occupation in itself is insufficient for his persona; he needs something more," Drake writes. Seemingly random details set in motion a change in his personality. "He haggles with an old woman about jam; he feels himself a hero for having killed some flies. The old woman, a mother figure, supplies the necessary energy (in the form of jam) to initiate the change; the jam attracts the flies he kills." A second female figure, the princess, represents the anima. "To win her he must test the strength of his persona, and even after winning her he must deal with her destructive side," states Drake. "The series of encounters he has in order to satisfy her father's conditions suggests overcoming dangers from the unconscious, symbolized by giants and beasts."

By outwitting the giants and causing them to kill each other, and also by capturing a unicorn and a boar, the brave tailor demonstrates that his cleverness can master brute strength and animal instincts. According to Drake, the unicorn "may suggest the hero's ability to handle intrusions from the deepest level of the unconscious." All of the encounters take place in the woods, "often a symbol of the unconscious itself."[18]

"Some archetypes appear in recognizable ways," writes Drake, but often they are discernible only because of the relationship they bear to one another in a particular telling of a story. Hence, the kind of archetypal framework Drake infers to be present in the version of Type 1640 that he chooses as the normalform may not correspond to what others would identify in another version. While archetypal images may differ from one individual to another and from culture to culture, contends Drake, nevertheless some aspects of their representations are similar through time and space because archetypes are universal and timeless.

Developmental Psychology

In addition to drawing on experimental psychology and psychoanalytically oriented frameworks, some folklorists incorporate into their analyses elements from developmental and social psychology. Influenced by the writings of Jean Piaget, Erik Erikson, and others, these researchers examine the folklore of children and adolescents to determine how it reflects or is affected by the development of motor and cognitive skills, language acquisition and manipulation, and the learning of behavior appropriate to different social and gender-based roles. They seek to explain the nature and persistence of folklore by ascertaining stages and processes of human development universally or in particular groups.

A study by Dorothy Mills Howard of ball-bouncing rhythms and rhymes illustrates research on the relationship between folklore and levels of increasing physical dexterity in children.[19] "Very young children learning to bounce the ball use simple actions and rhythms: the bounce, catch, bounce, catch," writes Howard. "As their bodies develop coordinating ability, they adopt more difficult movement such as the bounce, pat (with the hand); the leg-over actions where the legs, first the right, then the left, are thrown over the bouncing ball; the toss to the sky; and the pantomimic gestures such as 'take a dive,' 'touch the floor,' which involve the knee-bend, waist-bend, neck-bend and coordinating movements of all parts of the body." Moreover, "certain rhymes usually accompany and call for certain body movements."

Howard organizes her collection of rhymes "to demonstrate the progressive intimacy of the rhythm patterns in the dramatic activity of ball-bouncing" as observable among contemporary American children. The first group, for instance, consists of jingles that accompany the simple movements of younger children: bounce, catch, bounce, catch.

> Hello, Bill
> Where you going, Bill
> Down town, Bill
> What for, Bill
> To pay my gas bill.

The child bounces the ball on the first syllable of each of the first four lines, and catches it on the last syllable of each line. On the fifth line the child bounces the ball on "pay" with "To" spoken as an unvoiced "t" and slurred into "pay" (i.e., "t-pay"), and then catches it on "bill."

Rhymes in the second group accompany not only bouncing, but also patting, a ball. In the third group, the rhymes correlate with leg movements and pantomimic gestures as well as with ball bouncing, catching, and patting. The fourth group involves rhymes associated with ball-bouncing games played by two people.

"All the child's movements are sensuous. Movement is the outward show of his [or her] awareness of self," writes Howard. "The voice is employed in many ways to make a rhyme fit the desired action," doing "unaccountable tricks with words." For instance, children adjust syllables to meet

ball and body movements; "they also give sound effects to please their unappraised and unconscious needs for melody and euphony." In the following rhyme, the child pronounces the word "plum" as "p-lum" with the "p" unvoiced:

> One, eat a plum
> Two, eat a peach
> Three, eat a plum
> Four, eat a peach
> Five, eat a plum
> And you will go
> P-lum, p-lum, p-lum
> (and on until the bouncer misses).

"The unvoiced 'p' accompanies and sounds like the hand pat," writes Howard. "The 'lum,' voiced, accompanies and sounds like the bouncing ball. Thus onomatopeia, one of the oldest tricks known to language and poetry, is employed unconsciously by children in a folk art which is a part of the cultural inheritance of children the world over."

Children chant rhymes not only when bouncing balls of course, but also when clapping, patting hands together, jumping rope, taunting others, or taking pleasure in the sounds of words and in manipulating language. In their research on children's speech play, Mary Sanches and Barbara Kirshenblatt-Gimblett place language ac-

Figure 8–4: Rhymed hand-clapping game (photo by Simon J. Bronner).

quisition and manipulation in a developmental scheme, from playing with sounds initially to playing with meaning as a child develops linguistic knowledge and understanding.[20] Doing so reveals that children's "verbal productions" tend to increase in size and complexity as they grow older, and that they differ from adults' "verbal art" in several ways, including the use of certain stylistic devices. In children's lore the rhyming couplet, for instance, dominates over more complex rhyme schemes and stanzaic structures, as the following illustrates:

Mabel, Mabel, strong and able,
Get your elbows off the table.
We've told you once, we've told you twice,
We'd never tell you more than thrice.

The presence of concatenations and expansion also tend to differentiate children's speech play forms from adult verbal art. Examples include the jumprope rhymes ending with "How many [doctors, kisses] did it take?" followed by "1, 2, 3, 4 . . ."; "It happened on: Monday, Tuesday, . . ."; and "And this is where I went: London, Paris, Saigon, ..."

Children are more involved with the sounds of words than with semantics and syntax. Hence, they play with homonyms (words that sound alike but have different meanings), as illustrated by another version of the "Hello, Bill" rhyme cited above from Howard's study:

Hello, Bill.
Where you going, Bill?
Downtown, Bill.
What for, Bill?
To pay my gas bill.
How much, Bill?
A ten dollar bill.
So long, Bill.

"To an adult, this verse seems rather simple," write Sanches and Kirshenblatt-Gimblett. "To a child, however, it may be hilarious. Its appeal stems from the con-

junction of (a) the homonymity involved and what this represents to the child and (b) the final position of the homonymous lexemes in the phrases." The child "finds it an enticing puzzle" to sort out "Bill" as a personal name from "bill" as an account and "bill" as a form of currency.

"In the development of a child's repertoire of speech play forms," write the authors, "the child gradually adds verses to his [or her] repertoire until about the age of eleven at which point interest in many of these kinds of productions drops off sharply and other kinds of verbal art . . . [e.g., prose narratives] appear to be of greater interest." In addition, "there are principles of selectivity whereby the older children reject some verses as 'babyish' and refuse to recite them. . . ." For children ages five to seven, "most of the instances of speech play are simple verses which are fairly short, none being more than five lines long," such as:

A skunk sat on a stump.
The stump said,
"The skunk stunk."
The skunk said,
"The stump stunk."

"The eight-year-olds, while still focusing on simple verses," write the authors, "start to play with social rules," as in the following:

My eyes have seen the glory
of the burning of the school.
We have tortured all the teachers.
We have broken all the rules.
We will try to kill the principal
tomorrow afternoon.
His truth is marching on.

"This trend continues until about eleven when we find some play with semantic relations, especially antithesis, and much longer utterances," for example:

Ladies and jelly-beans, hobos and tramps,
Cross-eyed mosquitos and bow-legged ants.
I come before ye to stand behind ye

To tell ye something I know nothing
    about. . . .

Also at about this time children recite
parody-rhymes based on sex themes, such
as

Violets are blue
And I turned red
As soon as I saw you
Nude in bed.

The authors contend that speech play in
children "is instrumental to the acquisition of adult verbal art." This is indicated
partly by the fact that children's speech
play exhibits many of the rhetorical figures
of adult eloquence that have been codified
in rhetoric handbooks (see Box 8–5).

Children's riddles (or children's conceptions and examples of what constitutes a
riddle) also differ from those of adults, and
from those of other children of different
ages. Influenced in part by the observations
of Jean Piaget that children show competence in problems of verbal classification at
about the age when riddles peak (the third
grade), Brian Sutton-Smith hypothesizes "a
developmental structural account" of
riddles among children.[21] He collected 316
riddles and 455 joke responses from a
sample of 623 children in small towns in
northwestern Ohio in the early 1960s. He
organizes these according to such categories as pre-riddles, implicit reclassifications, riddle parodies, and so on; their prevalence corresponds to children's ages and
cognitive development. A pre-riddle, for
example, is

Why did the man chop down the chimney?
He needed the bricks.

"These non-riddles actually constitute
about a third of all responses in the first two
grades," observes Sutton-Smith. They comprise as much as 80 percent of the responses
of four-year-old children. All employ a
question and answer, presenting a puzzle.
The answer, however, is arbitrary and de-

BOX 8-5
Rhetorical Patterns in Children's Rhymes

gradatio (linking repetition of words
    leading to a climax):

I went downtown
To see Mrs. Brown.
She gave me a nickle
To buy a pickle.
The pickle was sour,
She gave me a flower.
The flower was dead,
She gave me a thread.
The thread was thin,
She gave me a pin.
The pin was sharp,
She gave me a harp.
The harp began to sing,
"Minnie and a minnie and a ha ha ha."

conversio (repetition of the last word[s]
    in successive phrases):

I scream
You scream
We all scream
For ice cream.

similiter desinens (repetition of word
    endings):

Lift the nozzle
To your muzzle.
And let it swizzle
Down the guzzle.

similiter desinens and articulus (stac-
    cato effect achieved by single words
    set apart by pauses—also called a
    comma):

Did you eever, iver, over,
In your leef, life, loaf,
See the deevel, divel, dovel,
Kiss his weef, wife, woaf?
No, I neever, niver, nover,
In my leef, life, loaf,
Saw the deevel, divel, dovel,
Kiss his weef, wife, woaf.

complexio (repetition of both the first
   and last words of successive phrases):

Are you the guy
That told the guy
That I'm the guy
That gave the guy
The black eye?

No, I'm not the guy
That told the guy
That you're the guy
That gave the guy
The black eye.

repetitio (repetition of the initial word
   in successive phrases):

Some write for pleasure
Some write for fame,
But I write only
To sign my name.

conduplicatio (repetition of one or more
   words for the purpose of amplifica-
   tion or appeal to pity):

Needles and pins, needles and pins,
When you get married your trouble begins.

contentio (antithesis: opposite ideas jux-
   taposed):

Ladies and jelly spoons:
I come before you
To stand behind you
To tell you something
I know nothing about.
Last Thursday
Which was Good Friday
There'll be a mother's meeting
For fathers only.
Wear your best clothes
If you haven't any,
And if you can come
Please stay at home.

The admission is free
So pay at the door,
Pull up a chair
And sit on the floor.
It makes no difference
Where you sit
The man in the gallery
Is sure to spit.
We thank you for your unkind attention.
The next meeting will be held
At the four corners of the round table.

commutatio (two discrepant thoughts so
   expressed by transposition that the
   latter follows the former although
   contradictory to it):

Algy met a bear
The bear was bulgy,
The bulge was Algy.

adnominatio (pun or wordplay):

Do you carrot all for me?
My heart beets for you,
With your turnip nose
And your radish face.
You are a peach
If we cantaloupe,
Lettuce marry;
Weed make a swell pear.

translatio (metaphor):

Margaret, Margaret, has big eyes,
Spread all over the skies.

distributio (itemizing or assigning specific roles among a number of things
   or persons [typical of dandling
   rhymes for the fingers and toes]):

One for the money,
Two for the show,
Three to get ready,
And four to go.[22]

pends on the riddler's idiosyncratic experience.

An example of implicit reclassifications (homonymic riddles) is as follows:

> Why did the dog run out into the sun?
> He wanted to be a hot dog.

More than 60 percent of the examples in Sutton-Smith's collection consist of this kind of presentation of a word or term in one way, followed by an implicit reclassification so as to produce an anticlimax. The riddle is a puzzling question, but the answer reclassifies the significance of the question's terminology to show that the term has two meanings.

The following examples illustrate a third category, riddle parodies:

> Why did the chicken cross the road?
> He wanted to get to the other side.

and

> How much dirt in a hole 5 by 3 by 3 feet?
> None.

Riddle parodies defeat the expectation of verbal logic. "Instead of a complicated answer, we get a direct one. What seems like a riddle turns out to be an 'obvious question,'" writes Sutton-Smith.

A fourth type of alleged riddle—or response given by children who were asked for examples of riddles—constituting about 10 percent of his collection, involves inverted relationships, as in the following:

> What does one flea say to another as they go strolling?
> Shall we walk or take a dog?

Such a "riddle" upsets the conventional expectation (that dogs have fleas) and inverts the part-whole relationship between flea and dog (fleas have dogs).

Explicit reclassifications (homonymic oppositional riddles) take the form of:

> What has an ear but cannot hear?
> Corn.

This kind of riddle (4% of the corpus) presents a classification but then denies a criterial attribute. A homonym also figures in this example (the ear that hears and the ear of corn are different ears).

A sixth type (2%) involves classifications on the basis of noncriterial attributes, such as:

> White inside and red outside?
> An apple.

In this instance, two contrasted features provide the basis for the classification, and yet they are not criterial attributes because they do not distinguish "apple" from other things that also are white inside and red outside. Sometimes the classification is literal, but other times it is metaphorical.

Sutton-Smith notes that although examples in these last two types given to him by children who were asked for riddles constitute only 6 percent of his collection, they comprise the bulk of most other collections of traditional riddles and exemplify what Archer Taylor calls "true riddles."

Sutton-Smith's final category consists of multiple classifications, such as:

> What is the difference between a teacher and an engineer?
> One trains the mind, the other minds the train.

Known as conundrums, these constitute only 1 percent of Sutton-Smith's collection.[23]

"Developmentally speaking," writes Sutton-Smith, "we . . . find that riddles told by six- to eight-year-olds demonstrate a shift from a stage of pure incongruity (the pre-riddle) to a stage of resolvable incongruity. Pre-riddles are a third of the jokes in the first two grades," he continues. "By the third grade, the riddles of implicit reclassification are dominant and they remain so throughout this collection to the eighth grade." By the fourth grade, "the noncriterial riddles which have more to do with part-whole relationships and expected behavior patterns come into play," he writes. "Also, by the fourth grade and clearly thereafter, riddles give way to other joke forms in which questions of human relationships dominate over questions of the lexicon and classification." While younger children think in unidimensional ways, by the third grade children recognize two dimensions or meanings (and also, one infers from Sutton-Smith's data, by this age they have formed an intuitive understanding of what a true riddle is); and by the fifth grade they become interested in ambiguities focusing on behavioral expectations.

Besides studying children's play, rhymes, and riddles, researchers also have analyzed within a developmental framework the folklore of adolescents, including customs. An example is Julia Woodbridge Oxrieder's study of the slumber party as an event that marks and mirrors the transition from childhood to adulthood.[24]

A social custom, the slumber party involves several young females invited to one or another's home to "sleep over." They stay up late at night, discuss various topics (e.g., school, boys, relationships with parents), tell jokes, pose riddles, sing songs, play pranks, have pillow fights, tell ghost stories, and even delve into occult practices like seances.

While each activity has its own form and history, "as the sum of its parts, the slumber party as we know it today is a product of the twentieth century," writes Oxrieder. It exhibits the acquisition of numerous developmental tasks which a person learns in order to be judged reasonably happy and successful, Oxrieder contends. These developmental tasks appear at different periods in life, with achievement of them leading to success with later tasks, while failure results in difficulty with those tasks, unhappiness in the individual, and disapproval by the society.

For instance, when young girls ages six to ten play games at a slumber party, participate in pillow fights, or take flying leaps into a stack of sleeping bags, they avail themselves of "an opportunity to grow in muscular coordination within a non-threatening environment," writes Oxrieder. Games of strategy develop inductive and deductive reasoning skills. Participating in riddling increases a girl's awareness of abstract concepts. Moreover, at the slumber party a girl can express "normally inhibited sexual and aggressive feelings in socially sanctioned suggestive jokes," contends the author. "While the slumber party does hold many attractions, none is of greater significance than the feeling of acting grown-up and being away from parental control."

According to an 11-year-old girl, parents "aren't in there every second telling you what to do." Writes Oxrieder: "Attending slumber parties is one important and frequent way of establishing emotional and social autonomy from one's parents." Older girls begin to transfer feelings of tenderness and affection from parents to age mates. Sometimes young people sneak a drink of alcohol, both as a representation of adult behavior and as a rejection of parental control.

Seeking identity and reinforcing peer relationships seem dominant concerns when girls sleep over. Much of their talk focuses on appearance and self-improvement (weight, posture, mannerisms). The first girl to fall asleep becomes the object of pranks because the girls equate a late bedtime with adulthood. Punishment may include smearing the offender's face with makeup, putting peanut butter or toothpaste in her ears, tying pretzels in her hair, slipping ice down her back, or placing her hands in a glass of water (to make her urinate).

Since normal growth involves not only progression and integration but also regression, writes Oxrieder, the girls may act like children half their age. Some might call neighbors and strangers to ask if their refrigerator is running ("It is? Then you'd better catch it!").[25] They may play practical jokes on each other, such as tying up a girl in her sleeping bag, hiding her clothes, or freezing her bra. They dare one another to do something embarrassing. "It should be obvious that the dares serve just the same function as the pranks; the girls are testing each other and winning respect from one another through the accepted responses," Oxrieder contends.

The slumber party is "not simply frivolous, silly, and a waste of time as many parents might describe it," admonishes Oxrieder. Rather, it is a traditional way in which American girls meet a variety of needs in the course of normal development. Sleeping over provides a setting "where girls feel free to talk about things they couldn't talk about in front of their parents. ... Since they do not have strong and stable self-images, they cannot be satisfied with what they are, and they need someone to tell them they are all right." Yearning for peer approval in many areas of their lives, they behave in certain expected ways. By becoming an adequate member in the society of adolescents, a girl is prepared for the next step, that of entering successfully into the society of adults. "Having mastered most of the problems of childhood within the slumber party framework," concludes Oxrieder, "the girl gains confidence in her ability to direct her own life, and in so doing she discovers who she is and what she is becoming."

In contrast to Oxrieder's study of a custom among adolescent and preadolescent females, Barbara Skov draws on some tenets of developmental psychology to analyze the telling of Polack jokes by her teenage children and their friends—representing both sexes in their adolescence.[26] Examples of the jokes include:

How many Polacks does it take to put in a light bulb?
Five. One to hold the bulb and four to turn him around.

* * *

How can you tell the bride at a Polish wedding?
She's the one with the tennis shoes and the braided armpits.

* * *

What does a Polack do before he picks his nose?
He says grace.

Barbara Skov heard the youth—males and females alike, ages 14, 15, and 16—telling these jokes to one another in the kitchen, the family room, and the car. She documented twenty examples, which the teenagers usually referred to as "stories." All found them funny. Despite frequent queries couched in varied terms, Skov was unable to discover ethnic prejudice in the teenagers. Several said they know people of Polish descent, none of whom exhibits any of the characteristics—stupidity, dirtiness, disgusting habits—portrayed in the jokes. When they tell the jokes, the teens insisted, they do not intend to disparage Poles.

Not only do the jokes seem devoid of ethnic significance to tellers and listeners, but they also lack shock value because the topics are not taboo. The teens openly discuss sex, bodily changes they have experienced during puberty, and so on. Therefore, the jokes appear not to function as a sanctioned means of mentioning subjects otherwise inappropriate for public discourse.

Why did these teenagers tell and enjoy the jokes? Participating in this joking behavior serves as "an unconscious means of coping with ambivalent feelings associated with puberty," hypothesizes Skov, who draws on the writings of Erik Erikson.

"Briefly, psychoanalytic theory states that all human individuals pass through certain stages in their early development when the biological needs of the organism are centered in specific regions of the body," writes Skov. Because biological needs become intimately tied to emotional ones, "the libido (sexual energy) is directed toward these regions: first the oral, then the anal, and finally the pre-genital, the last of the childhood stages." Puberty—the true genital stage, i.e., adulthood—"releases masses of libidinal energy with which the maturing individual must cope according to the values and mores of his [or her] society." Regression is one means of coping. This involves "a harking back to earlier stages of emotional development, a reawakening of oral and anal sexuality, and a vacillating between these infantile stages and the developing reproductive sexuality," she writes.

Within this interpretative framework, "it would be expected that any folkloric form which provides a means of expressing verbally some of the inner conflict attendant upon the onset of puberty would contain references to matters oral and anal, as well as genital, or sexual," contends Skov. Evidence of oral, anal, and genital content abounds in the Polack jokes.

Orality (coupled with dirtiness or disgusting habits) informs the following:

How do you break a Polack's fingers?
Punch him in the nose.

*   *   *

What happens when a Polack picks his nose?
His head caves in.

Anal content—focusing on elimination of bodily waste and/or defilement through contact with it—can be seen in such examples as

How do you drive a Polack insane?
Put him in a round room and tell him to crap in the corner.

*   *   *

What about the one about the Polish village?
The toilet paper is hanging out to dry.

*   *   *

How do you know when you're at a Polish party?
When they flush the punch bowl.

*   *   *

How does a Polack take a bubble bath?
["Oh, Matt, this is disgusting," said Sandra; "I don't even want to hear it."]
He sits in the gutter and cuts farts.

Several "Polack stories" refer to genitality or sexuality, such as the following:

How can you tell a Polish airliner?
Hair under the wings.

*   *   *

How do you know when a Polack has been in your back yard?
Your trash can is empty and your dog is pregnant.

Yet other jokes dwell on stupidity or ineptitude, lack of cleanliness, or diminishment in value and esteem:

How many Polacks does it take to paint a house?
Five hundred. One to hold the paint brush and 499 to turn the house.

*   *   *

How did the Polish fight the Germans in World War I?
With dynamite.
How did the Germans fight the Polish?
They lit it and threw it back.

*   *   *

How do you sink a Polish battleship?
Put it in water.

*   *   *

Who discovered Poland?
Rotorooter.

* * *

How do you get 18 Polacks in a VW?
Throw in a penny.
How do you get them out?
Throw in a bar of soap.

* * *

A Polack and a pig were walking down the
    street, and a man came up to 'em and
    said, "Where'd you get that?" and the pig
    said, "At a raffle."

* * *

Who won the Polish beauty contest?
No one.

* * *

What was the total cost of the damage after
    the atom bomb was dropped on Poland?
    $67.50.

"It strikes me that the numerous references to dirtiness, stupidity, and unattractiveness are related to uncertainty about the desirability of the changes which adolescents undergo," writes Skov. "Pubic hair is beginning to appear; sweat glands commence to secrete; their skin breaks out. Their peers, their parents, and/or television commercials point out the horror of failing to guard against some of these secretions and eruptions, which are referred to as if they were dirty." The excitement of growing up, however, counters "feelings of unworthiness."

Skov contends that the Polish stories express this ambivalence in teenagers "by drawing verbal pictures of a repulsiveness that is unmistakably connected with the changes taking place in their bodies and then in cherishing and enjoying those pictures (of oneself) to the fullest." In sum, these jokes "can provide teenage tellers with one means of handling some of the strong feelings and the ambivalent attitudes that are aroused at the onset of puberty."

Physical maturation may also result in changes in social relations that challenge self-image and self-esteem, affecting personality development. In a study of verbal dueling among inner-city African American males—based on two years of fieldwork in South Philadelphia—Roger D. Abrahams considers how "playing the dozens" provides these adolescent youth with a means of coping in a social environment that alters as they develop physically into young men.[27] According to Abrahams, "the dozens stands as a mechanism which helps the Negro youth adapt to his changing world and trains him for similar and more complex verbal endeavors in the years of his manhood."

In Abrahams's observations, only crowds of boys take part in the ritualized verbal duel. "One insults a member of another's family; others in the group make disapproving sounds to spur on the coming exchange. The one who has been insulted feels at this point that he must reply with a slur on the protagonist's family which is clever enough to defend his honor (and therefore that of his family)." The first youth returns the insult. "This can proceed until everyone is bored with the whole affair, until one hits the other (fairly rare), or until some other subject comes up that interrupts the proceedings (the usual state of affairs)."

The following are some of the less scurrilous examples:

I hear your mother plays third base for the
    Phillies.
At least my mother don't work in a
    coalyard.
Your mother is a bricklayer, and stronger
    than your father.
At least my mother ain't no cake—everybody get a piece.
Least my mother ain't no railroad track, lay
    all around the country.

The vilification of the mother increasingly involves sexual matters as the youths' sexual awareness grows, Abrahams contends. Many of the "dozens" or "sounds" also involve rhymes or puns, and later subtlety and innuendo, as verbal dexterity blooms. "Among the older males the references to the family of the other are fleeting," but for younger adolescents "the insults are much more rigidly constructed and are directed toward or against certain things. Most prominently, they are concerned with sexual matters. Usually both the rhymes and the taunts are directed against the other's mother, alleging sexual wantonness," Abrahams writes. Changes in pitch, stress, and sometimes syntax signal the beginning of a contest.

Abrahams notes that the function of the "institution of playing the dozens" is that "the game acts as a release mechanism for the anxieties" of African American youths. As such, the "dozens are an expression of boys in transition to manhood," he contends. "In fact, 'sounding' is one of the major ways in which boys are enabled to become men."

Abrahams elaborates, describing the male adolescent's social environment as one in which he is a black man in a white man's world as well as a male in a matriarchy with family life dominated by the mother. "Women, then, are not only the dispensers of love and care, but also of discipline and authority." The most important attitude in this system "is the absolute and divisive distrust which members of one sex have for the other." Mothers teach their daughters "early and often about how men are not to be trusted. Men learn to say the same thing about the women."

When male youths reach puberty, insists Abrahams, "they must eminently be rejected as men by the women in the matriarchy; and thus a period of intense anxiety and rootlessness is created at the beginning of adolescence." For a boy, life becomes "a mass of oppositions. He is both a part of his mother-oriented family and yet not a part of it. His emotional attachments are wholly to his mother; but as a male he must seek his masculine identity, and consequently must

be rejected from his family to some extent because of this." The result, writes Abrahams, is "a violent reaction against the world of women which has rejected him, and to a life filled with expressions of virility and manliness."

At the outset of this stage of a reversal of values, the boy cannot openly attack his own mother because "his oedipal attractions fasten his affections on" her. Yet, to survive, he must reverse his affections. "He therefore creates a playground," writes Abrahams, "which enables him to attack some other person's mother, in full knowledge that that person must come back and insult his own." Between them, they castigate all that is feminine, begin "to build their own image of sexual superiority," and "also affirm their own masculine abilities," he writes. "Through the dozens the youth has his first real chance of declaring the differences between male and female and of taking sides in the struggle." Abrahams concludes: "As an institutionalized mechanism, the dozens is most important to the lower class Negro youth in search of his masculine identity. It represents a transition point in his life, that place at which he casts off a woman's world for a man's."

Since Abrahams's research in the early 1960s, other folklorists have documented playing the dozens or sounding—also known as *burning, raking, dusting, icing, putting down, cutting down,* and *tearing down*—among African American females as well as males, and also among white Euro-American adolescents of both sexes.[28] They have recorded nonobscene as well as non-mother insults, and also personal insults referring to alleged shortcomings in the other individual, not to his or her family. (The 1992 Hollywood film *White Men Can't Jump* contains numerous examples of this variety of insults.[29]) Moreover, they have discovered that verbal dueling is a widespread tradition, seemingly without racial or national bounds. Not everyone in a group knows about the ritualized insults, however; among those who do, only some participate. On one level, according to this research, the game is a duel of wits and verbal ability. The participant most skillful in using standard sounds and artful in innovating new ones may draw admiration and praise from his listeners, thereby gaining prestige and status. When playing the dozens among males involves insults about one another's mother, a youth may be trying to establish or maintain his male identity and independence within his primary reference group. Rather than an assault weapon against an enemy, it may be a symbol of peer bond. Whatever the interpretation, much of the research on the American tradition of playing the dozens is set within a framework emphasizing psychosocial development.

Law-Prescribed and Rule-Governed Behavior

Another way that scholars have sought to explain stability in traditional expressive behaviors is by uncovering behavioral laws or rules that individuals seem to follow when generating and communicating folklore. Researchers assume that people learn these rules, usually intuitively, and follow

Figure 8–5: Reasons for playing the dozens, an exercise in verbal skill and wit, vary widely from a mode of attack to a means of bonding (photo by Edwin L. Coleman, II).

them (most often unconsciously) when they tell stories or pose riddles, compose and sing songs, deliver sermons, design and construct buildings, and so on. Whether referred to as laws of composition, rules of competency in performance, or an artifactual grammar, these principles are thought to regulate traditional expressive behavior and account for folklore's nature, predictability, and durability.[30]

Interest in the laws or rules that govern expressive behavior has a long history in folkloristics. In an 1899 essay, for instance, Edwin Sidney Hartland defined folklore as "the science of Tradition" and stated that it "obeys laws as yet imperfectly understood."[31] Writes Hartland,

> The human mind, alike in Europe and in America, in Africa and in the South Seas, works in the same way, according to the same laws. And the aim of the science of Tradition is to discover these laws by the examination of their products, the customs and beliefs, the stories and superstitions handed down from generation to generation, to ascertain how these products arose and what was the order of their development, and so to co-operate with physical anthropology and archaeology in writing, as it has never yet been written, the history of civilization.

Ten years later (in 1909) Danish folklorist Axel Olrik published an essay on the epic laws of folk narrative (*epische Gesetze der Volksdichtung*).[32] Noting that those who are exposed to "the folklore of a faraway people" often feel "a sense of recognition" in "certain characteristic details," Olrik postulates a set of laws of composition for myths, fairy tales, legends, epic songs, narrative folksongs, and heroic sagas (which he identifies collectively by the German term *Sage*). These principles "apply to all European folklore and to some extent even beyond that. Against the background of the overwhelming uniformity of these laws, national characteristics seem to be only dialect peculiarities," he writes. "We call these principles 'laws' because *they limit the freedom of composition of oral literature* in a much different and more rigid way than in our written literature" (emphasis added).

Orally told and sung stories neither begin with sudden action nor conclude abruptly, observes Olrik. Hence, the best known of these laws of folk narrative are the *Law of Opening* (*das Gesetz des Einganges*) and the *Law of Closing* (*das Gesetz des Abschlusses*). "The *Sage* begins by moving from calm to excitement, and after the concluding event" it "ends by moving from excitement to calm," Olrik writes. "Before ending, it needs to relax the clenched fist of the sword-hand. . . . Hundreds of folksongs end, not with the death of the lovers, but with the interweaving of the branches of the two roses which grow up out of their graves. In thousands of legends, one finds the revenge of the dead or the punishment of the villain appended to the principal action." A multitude of Danish fairy tales concludes with the release from enchantment, but not by simply stating that "she was set free." Rather, "the storyteller always adds a long jesting closing formula in order to quiet the mood. He hangs a fig leaf on the *Märchen* as it were, in order to cover its nakedness."

Subsequent researchers have noted that folktales often begin with opening formulas such as "Once upon a time" and conclude with "And they lived happily ever after," or similar formulaic endings.[33] They have remarked that American joketellers typically ask, "Have you heard the one about . . . ?" before actually telling a joke, and end their joketellings with punchlines.[34] They have observed that many Anglo singers in northeastern Canada and the United States conclude their ballads by speaking rather than singing the last few words, their voices trailing off as they do so. In addition to such linguistic cues, performers of traditional expressive forms also signal their intention to adopt a particular communicative role or to conclude their performance by changing intonation or syntax or by employing nonlinguistic behavior, such as assuming a certain attitude or posture, gesturing, or altering facial expressions.

Another principle, indicates Olrik in his 1909 essay, is the *Law of Repetition* (*das Gesetz der Widerholung*). "In [written] literature, there are many means of producing emphasis, means other than repetition." For instance, the writer can depict the dimensions and significance of something by the degree and detail of description. Not so in oral composition and communication in firsthand interaction. Here, "for the most part," folk narrative's "spare descriptions are all too brief to serve as an effective means of emphasis." There is but one alternative, that of repetition. A youth kills three giants, one on each of three successive days. A hero tries to ride up the glass mountain once, then again, then a third time. The hero or heroine must perform three tasks, described in turn. "When a folklorist comes upon a three, he [or she] thinks, as does the Swiss who catches sight of his [or her] Alps again, 'Now I am home!'" (In other cultures, the significant number may be four or five rather than three.) This repetition, writes Olrik, "is necessary not only to build tension, but to fill out the body of the narrative. There is intensifying repetition and simple repetition, but the important point is that without repetition, the *Sage* cannot attain its fullest form." Bruce Rosenberg makes the same points about American folk preachers, whose sermons—orally composed during delivery—depend on the use of formulas and repetition.[35]

Turning to numbers other than three or four, Olrik writes, "Two is the maximum number of characters who appear at one time. Three people appearing at the same time, each with his own individual identity and role to play, would be a violation of tradition." It would also be far more difficult for narrator and listener alike to try to differentiate and keep track of more than two principal characters in the dynamics of oral communication. By contrast, readers of written literature can reread passages or interrupt the flow, stepping back from the text to reflect and reconsider. "The interaction of three or more characters, which is so popular in literary drama, is not allowed in folk narrative," writes Olrik.

The *Law of Two to a Scene* (*das Gesetz der scenischen Zweiheit*) correlates with the *Law of Contrast* (*das Gesetz des Gegensatzes*). The folk narrative "is always polarized," writes Olrik. "This very basic opposition is a major rule of epic composition: young and old, large and small, man and monster, good and evil." For example, the Danish King Rolf is celebrated because of his generosity; hence, he requires a stingy opponent, whether that be the Skoldung Rörik or the Swede Adisl. A great king has an insignificant and short-reigning successor. The hero dies because of the murderous act of a villain.

Leaving the subject of numbers, Olrik mentions another law, the *Importance of Initial and Final Position*. "Whenever a series of persons or things occurs, then the principal one will come first." Coming last, though, will be the person for whom the particular narrative arouses sympathy. Using nautical terms, Olrik designates these relationships "the Weight of the Bow" (*das Toppgewicht*) and "the Weight of the Stern" (*das Achtergewicht*). His identification of these theorems evokes comparison with research on the psychology of perception with its discovery that the first and last elements in a series are perceived best and recalled most often. Although the first element in an enumerative list seems most important, in narrative "the center of gravity . . . always lies in the" final position, writes Olrik, who reminds us "how

much the last attempt of the younger brother in *Märchen* signifies" (as in Motif H1242, "Youngest brother alone succeeds on quest," and L10, "Victorious youngest son"). "*Actergewicht* combined with the Law of Three is the principal characteristic of folk narrative—it is an epic law," Olrik writes. He adds that in a religious context, the *Toppgewicht* rules—e.g., the Teutonic god Odin or Wotan (All-Father, the chief of the gods of the Aesir pantheon) is greater than his two attendants.[36] But when these figures appear in folktales they are governed by *Achtergewicht*; the principal member is not Odin, but "the last of the three gods—Loki."

Olrik identifies and discusses several other aspects of the "essential structure" of folk narratives. One is that each attribute of a person or thing must be expressed in actions, and that the threads of the plot are single stranded (*einsträngig*) rather than entangled as in written literature. "With its single thread, folk narrative does not know the perspective of painting; it knows only the progressive series of bas-reliefs. Its composition is like that of sculpture and architecture; hence the strict subordination to number and other requirements of symmetry," writes Olrik.

"This rigid stylizing of life has its own peculiar aesthetic value," he continues. "Everything superfluous is suppressed and only the essential stands out salient and striking." For example, the *Sage* rises to peaks in *tableaux scenes* (*Haupsituationen plastischer Art*). The actors draw near to one another, "the hero's sword is scorched by the dragon's breath," the maiden stands on the back of a bull or snake to survey the scene. The tableaux scenes convey "a certain quality of persistence through time," writes Olrik, who mentions the image of Samson among the columns in the hall of the Philistines, Perseus holding out the head of Medusa, and other examples. "These lingering actions . . . possess the singular power of being able to etch themselves in one's memory," he observes.

"In summary," writes Olrik, "we find that folk narrative is formally regulated to a far greater degree than one would think. Its formal rules we may call the epic laws." Among these are not only those discussed above but also the *Law of Patterning (die Schematisierung)*, *Unity of Plot (die Einheit der Handlung)*, and *Concentration on a Leading Character (Konzentration um eine Hauptperson)*. "Life itself must be sufficient to create these types," Olrik contends.

In other words, when people generate and communicate folklore in face-to-face interaction, their behavior conforms to norms or standards by means of which others realize they have assumed a particular communicative role (e.g., that of riddle poser or narrator). Moreover, without learning and following these rules or conventions of behavior, communication would be impaired. Making use of known formulas or nonlinguistic conventions to begin and end a narrative, focusing on actions, emphasizing contrasts, addressing one theme at a time rather than entangling it with others, evoking vivid images, relying on repetition—these are essential features of oral narrative communication. They attract and hold an audience as well as enable narrators to describe events without confusing themselves or listeners. Through awareness of such stable features in folklore and of laws prescribing the behaviors necessary to generate and communicate it, Olrik suggests, "we can determine the characteristics of particular peoples, their special types of composition and cultural themes."

Other researchers share with Olrik the assumption that when people generate and communicate folklore, the ways they behave are dictated by laws or lawlike principles whose nature can be inferred and described through systematic inquiry. Finn-ish folklorist Kaarle Krohn, for instance, accounts for variation in folklore by attributing it to "laws of transformation."[37] Krohn notes that folk narratives can be transformed (and hence vary) for numerous reasons, including the fact that individuals may inadvertently forget or add something to a tale; misperceive what a narrator has said and perpetuate the misperception when they communicate the story themselves; deliberately change names to make them locally relevant or linguistically appropriate; or alter details to make them compatible with the way of life in a particular cultural environment. "For the most part," states Krohn, "it is the *mechanical laws of thought and imagination* that prevail in the rich variation of oral tradition" (emphasis added).

By contrast, Walter Anderson focuses on stability in folktales by attributing it to what he calls the "law of self-correction."[38] According to Anderson, a person hears a traditional tale many times before he or she tells it, constructing a normalform consisting of elements common to all or most of the versions heard. Because people are exposed to the same stories over and over again, Anderson notes, they are apt to correct performers who make readily perceptible changes, prompting narrators to try to emulate past performances rather than to be innovative.

Investigators such as Olrik, Krohn, and Anderson are concerned with inferring laws that appear to be valid for selected expressive forms universally or cross-culturally. Other researchers focus on rules that govern the behaviors of performers of specific kinds of traditions in particular societies but that they and/or others feel have implications or applications in other cultures or for human beings generally. In describing "the boundaries within which" Zuni storytellers operate, for instance, Ruth Benedict presents what amounts to a set of behavioral rules indicating the constraints on and freedoms enjoyed by narrators in Zuni.[39]

Constraints include the obligation to tell stories that are appropriate to one's gender (discussed in chapter 7). All narrators are expected to localize events and be certain that appropriate characters inhabit traditional settings and behave in predictable ways. Audiences expect narrators to tell them long stories and to construct their narratives from a common stock of familiar themes, incidents, and "folkloristic devices," combined and presented in innovative ways. In addition, storytellers are expected to conclude their narrating with explanatory endings ("and that's why's").

Zuni narrators are free to utilize whatever conventional themes, incidents, and descriptions they choose from the available cultural stockpile, and to determine how best to configure them into satisfying wholes. They may also incorporate their own experiences and personal knowledge into their narrating. If a storyteller "has taken part in a Corn Dance," notes Benedict, "his incidents of the Corn Dance practice reproduce his own experience, which is then of course retold by others." Narrators also have the freedom to create or use whatever explanatory endings they judge appropriate, with the result being that the same story may have different and varied endings, and sometimes even multiple concluding explanations, each time it is told. (See Box 8–6 for examples of alternative explanations with which Zuni narrators documented by Benedict and other fieldworkers ended their tellings of the same tale.)

In noting that tales people tell do not exist in any one fixed form or version, that variation is the norm rather than the exception in storytelling, that narrators telling traditional tales have the freedom to be creative as well as the obligation to follow precedents, and that storytellers' and audiences' behaviors during narratings are interdependent and complementary, Benedict

---

BOX 8–6

Alternate Closings to the Zuni Tale "The Deserted Children"

Hence to this day the dragonfly comes in early summer humming from one plant to another, yet never content with its resting place.

For this reason the dragonfly is painted on the priests' ceremonial bowls.

Hence we have today Guardians of the Corn, i.e., priesthoods.

Hence to this day the priests or hosts of Zuni cast a morsel of food into the fire with a prayer to the ancestors.

That is why the yellow wolves who live on animals they kill are in hills in every direction.

That is why we worship the dragonfly and why we are not allowed to kill it.

That is why we always choose honest people for the priesthoods.[40]

---

raises and addresses issues that emerged as principal foci in twentieth-century folkloristics. Implicit in her comments that a narrator's skill is evident in his or her selection and use of "stock incidents" in developing "stock themes" and building up a plot, Benedict implies that storytellers create the tales they communicate as they are telling them.

This point is the central thesis of Albert B. Lord's study (published 25 years after Benedict's) of South-Slavic epic singers in Yugoslavia, for whom, Lord notes, "the moment of composition is the performance," since "[s]inging, performing, composing are facets of the same act" and occur simultaneously.[41] Benedict's assertion that there is a communal stockpile of traditional components and conventions from which all Zuni narrators draw and of which all Zuni stories are composed antedates by more than a quarter of a century Claude Lévi-Strauss's characterization of myths as having as their source a heterogeneous but limited corpus of components (1) that are "remains and debris of events" or "fossilized evidence of the history of an individual or a society," and (2) that are continuously ordered and reordered by a particular mode of thought (called "mythical thinking" by Lévi-Strauss).[42]

Benedict's view that the behavior of individuals telling traditional tales is governed by unwritten rules that are restrictive, on the one hand, and permissive, on the other, is one shared by some of her predecessors and many of her followers. Russian folklorist Vladimir Propp, for instance, addresses the issue briefly in his 1928 book on fairy tale structure (discussed in chapter 4). Propp asserts that the storyteller cannot violate the logic of the *Märchen*'s plot structure by presenting components out of sequence or ignoring correlations between or among interrelated ones. But narrators are free to decide which optional structural components to include and exclude; the specifics of the incidents that the structure orders; and the "nomenclature and attributes of the dramatis personae."[43] Linda Dégh similarly stresses this dichotomous but complementary constraint and freedom in her 1962 study of traditional taletelling in a Hungarian peasant community: "From the narrator's viewpoint, authority and credibility play an important part, as well as faithfulness and respect for tradition," writes Dégh. But a storyteller's "language, style, and . . . dramatic recital" all shape a story being told, making it "inconceivable" that he or she "should repeatedly tell a long tale, letter-perfect," since "constant transformation of a tale" with repeated telling "is logical and follows its own law."[44]

That different behavioral rules obtain for men and women who assume the same performing roles, as Benedict notes is the case with storytellers in Zuni, also became a much-explored and discussed issue in late twentieth century folkloristics. Like Benedict, Rosan A. Jordan describes themes (in-cluding that of the vaginal serpent, discussed in chapter 6) which recur in Mexican-American women's narrating, implying that choice of subject matter for the stories people tell is dictated by gender-specific experiences.[45] Carol Mitchell's discussion of differences in men's and women's preferences for and reactions to selected jokes (characterized in chapter 7) similarly reveals how sex-based behavioral rules manifest themselves in a popular traditional mode of expression.[46] In her studies of Pentecostal women preachers as "handmaidens of the Lord," Elaine J. Lawless illustrates what behavioral rules women follow to gain more direct access to power within the church.[47]

According to Lawless, the way for a woman to be selected for the chief post of pastor and to authenticate religious power in a system of conservative fundamentalism is by emphasizing traditional reproductive images and maternal strategies, thereby reinforcing the view that they are subservient to men. "By firmly basing their role as preacher and pastor within the very frameworks that support a traditional, fundamental religiosity, these women pastors are able to employ the system to their advantage," writes Lawless. "The maternal and reproductive images they [use] as religious strategies serve to strip their presence behind the pulpit of its most threatening aspects."

For example, women pastors act out the role of the symbolic mother to their congregations. Group members in turn respond, "She takes good care of us," or "She's just like a mother; she cares for everybody." Women pastors also realize that they must be biological mothers, filling their sermons with references to their own children, to rearing their offspring, and to the family as a unifying image. Comments by one woman pastor (Sister Ruth Hatley of Mexico, Missouri) express the significance of this portrait of women pastors as first and foremost wives, mothers, and caretakers: "When my own kids were little, I'd hold two kids and preach, you know. They'd be crying without me, you know, so I'd hold them and preach," said Sister Hatley. "I've always said I've got more sermons over the ironing board and the dishpan than I ever did on my knees."

Fundamentalist women pastors and preachers must be both loving and tough, writes Lawless, but they also must deny seeking an equal footing with men. The Mother of the church is not the equivalent of the Father. Male deacons comprise the governing body of the church. Males determine much of the organization of the service. Women dare not appear to usurp the God-given authority of men. "I always present myself as a handmaiden of the Lord," said Sister Wanda Nelson of Bloomington, Indiana. "Let the men take the part of the ministry and the government of the church because they are the head. The Bible clearly says we are the weaker vessel," she continued. "Relax, I don't call myself a preacher. Let the men do that; it's all right. But you have got to give me the right to be a handmaiden of the Lord," she insisted, "and he has poured out his spirit unto me and he has called me into his work and I'm here."

Handmaiden, caretaker, teacher, mother—these are the terms for Pentecostal women preachers and pastors. Although liberated from being the cloistered wife and mother, writes Lawless, these women pastors are not free from "the prejudices and restrictions that hamper other women in this conservative, fundamentalist milieu." The woman pastor must be a "supermom," writes Lawless. "She must declare her 'motherly' nature, exclaim her delight in being a wife and mother, her joy in her children, her home. And she must deny her sexuality as a possible temptress while at the same time she must acknowledge her inferior status as woman and submit herself

to all men. The role is complex," concludes Lawless, "full of pitfalls and possible infractions." And the rules for aspiring to and succeeding in the pastor's role are clearly determined by, unique to, and different for each gender.[48]

As noted and exemplified throughout the preceding discussion, the unwritten rules which govern the behavior of individuals when they generate and communicate folklore are usually intuitively learned and unconsciously followed. But people are also often consciously aware of these rules; and they frequently exploit other human beings by violating rules, thereby not fulfilling others' expectations. This is the case when individuals manipulate folklore, as when someone's seeming presentation of the normal form of a familiar folklore example turns out instead to be a deliberate transformation of it. As discussed and exemplified in chapter 1, advertisers do this repeatedly by transforming and contextualizing proverbs, fairy tales, and nursery rhymes to sell their products; and as noted earlier in this chapter, many examples of children's folk speech are parodies of popular prayers ("Now I Lay Me Down to Sleep"), songs ("The Battle Hymn of the Republic"), table graces, etc., which have themselves become traditional and hence are folklore examples. But one's conscious awareness and exploitation of rules to manipulate people are sometimes covert instead of overt, as Kenneth S. Goldstein's study of the practice of children's counting out clearly illustrates.[49]

Goldstein conducted fieldwork in a racially integrated middle-class neighborhood of northwest Philadelphia between January 1966 and June 1967. He observed the play of 67 children, ages 4 to 14, who comprised eight separate play groups. These children used counting-out rhymes and techniques to choose individuals for games where an "it" had to be selected, and for games for which sides were chosen. According to Goldstein, toddlers as young as two learned the rhymes but did not participate in the activity until they were four or five years of age. Those aged 11 to 14 tended to count out less frequently, relying instead on other techniques such as coin tossing, bat holding, drawing lots, or spinning bottles. Girls employed counting out more frequently for choosing sides than for determining who would be "it," whereas boys did the opposite. When they numbered more than 10, a group used some technique other than counting out.

When counting out is suggested, and a counter selected (the person proposing the game, a recognized leader, or someone else agreed upon), other members of the group gather in a circle or line up by the counter. The counter begins, sometimes with himself or herself and at other times with the nearest person on the left, and counts clockwise. Counting continues until the counter designates someone as "it" or until sides have been chosen.

The reasons children count out include the following:

1. Equal chance 90% ("it's more democratic")
2. Avoids friction 18% ("we don't fight about it")
3. Supernatural decision 8% ("fate decides")

These justifications clearly imply that counting out is a game of *chance*. But in fact counting out may be a *game of strategy* in which rhymes and movements of players are manipulated to limit or remove chance as a factor in selection. Goldstein discovered that a few individuals engaged in this ruse, particularly one youth gifted in math.

One technique involves extending the rhyme. "If the counter finds that the rhyme ends on a child whom he does *not* want to be 'it,'" writes Goldstein, "he may add one or more phrases or lines to the rhyme until it ends on the one whom he wishes to be 'it.'" In the example in Box 8–7, the rhyme ends on "mo" with person #4.

But the counter can extend the rhyme by adding, "My mother says that you are it" to pick player #5, or by appending to that line, "But I say that you are out," in order to select player #6. "Controlling selection of 'it' by extending the rhyme is the most common 'counting-out' strategy, with better than fifty per cent of both boys and girls in the two oldest age groups employing it," writes Goldstein.

Another method of control derives from the counter's having a repertoire of rhymes with varying numbers of stresses. The counter notes the number of players, mentally recalls the appropriate rhyme with the

---

BOX 8-7

Manipulating Counting Out By Extension of Rhyme

The rhyme ends on "mo" with person #4; but by extending the rhyme with one or two lines, the counter is enabled to pick player #5 or #6, respectively.

Position of Players					
1	2	3	4	5	6
Eenie	meenie	meinie	mo,	Catch	a feller
by the	toe;	if he	hollers	let him	go,
Eenie	meenie	meinie	***mo*#**	(My	mother
says	that	you	are	***it*.)#**	(But
I	say	that	you	are	***out*.)#**

—John J., age 10[50]

necessary number of stresses, and then begins counting—commencing with herself or himself instead of the person to the immediate left. The last rhyme stress will fall on the counter, who thereby is himself or herself designated "it." If the counter does not want to be "it," she or he will select a rhyme according to the number of players in which the last stress falls on someone else. (See the examples in Box 8–8 containing four rhymes that have 7, 8, 9, and 16 stresses respectively.)

The counter also can insure against being "it" by skipping over himself or herself on the second and successive times around. According to Goldstein, one-third of his informants had used this technique at one time or another, making it the second most common form of strategically manipulating others while counting out. However, while the children considered other strategies "clever," they frowned on this one as

---

BOX 8–8
Manipulating Counting Out through Rhyme Repertory

The counter can assure or avoid being "it" by using a special set of rhymes, the choice depending on the number of players involved. The counting begins with the counter, not with the first person to the left. Each rhyme contains a different number of stresses, the last of which will end on the counter.

Seven stresses:
> Andy / Mandy / Sugar / Candy //
> Out / Goes / **He**.#

Counter is "it" when there are 3 or 6 players; *not* "it" when there are 4, 5, 7, or 8 players.

Eight stresses:
> Inka / Blink / A Bottle / Of Ink //
> I / Say / You / **Stink**.#

Counter is "it" when there are 7 players; *not* "it" when there are 3, 4, 5, 6, or 8 players.

Nine stresses:
> Apples / Oranges //
> Cherries / Pears / And A Plum //
> I / Think / You're / **Dumb**.#

Counter is "it" when there are 4 or 8 players; *not* "it" when there are 3, 5, 6, or 9 players.

Sixteen stresses:
> Eena / Meena / Mina / Mo //
> Catch / A Tiger / By The / Toe //
> If He / Hollers / Let Him / Go //
> Eena / Meena / Mina / **Mo**.#

Counter is "it" when there are 3 or 5 players; *not* "it" when there are 4, 6, 7, or 8 players.

—Sarah M., age 11[51]

being "dishonest" and "against the rules."

Stopping or continuing constitutes a fourth method. Consider this familiar rhyme:

One potato, two potato, three potato, four,
Five potato, six potato, seven potato, more

The "potatoes" are the fists that players extend for counting (on "more," that fist is withdrawn). "The counter repeats the rhyme until both fists of one player have been withdrawn and that person may be designated 'it,'" writes Goldstein; "or if the counter wishes someone else to be 'it,' he may continue repeating the rhyme until there is one player left who has not been 'counted-out' and that player is 'it.'" Most counters don't know on which players the first or last 'out' will fall; they simply shift the chance factor from first to last, but not to any specific player.

Changing positions is yet another strategy. One boy had memorized the 'first out' position in "one potato, two potato" for any number of players from two through ten. After counting each player, he would start the rhyme again from his own position after first moving to a new position or else forcing the next player he wanted to count out to take up a new position. In doing so, the youth followed a memorized list of "first out" positions for the number of players remaining (see Box 8–9). "The 'changing position' strategy was used by one extremely precocious nine year old boy who was considered somewhat of a mathematical genius at school," writes Goldstein.

A child wishing to remove himself or herself from the possibility of becoming "it" or to thwart any of the strategies above

---

BOX 8-9
Manipulating Counting Out by Changing Positions

The Counter is in position number 1.
The rhyme used is "One Potato, Two Potato":

> One Potato / Two Potato / Three Potato / Four //
> Five Potato / Six Potato / Seven Potato / **More**.

After counting out all players, the counter began again after first relocating himself or the next player he wanted to count out, according to the memoried list of "first out" positions for the number of players remaining.

	Position of Player	
Number of Players	First Out	Last Remaining
10	2	1
9	8	3
8	8	4
7	7	4
6	6	3
5	3	1
4	3	2
3	1	3
2	1	2

—Samuel G., age 9[52]

could call out "safe," "free," or "in-or-out," with the specific expression depending on the group. Only one child was permitted to do so during a round of counting, and only after counting had begun.

Goldstein's data clearly indicate that sometimes, for some children, counting out is a game of strategy rather than of chance, although it is often said to be only the latter. Knowing and understanding the implications of this are crucial. "If games serve as mechanisms through which children are prepared for adult roles in life," writes Goldstein, "then identifying a game as one of chance when it, in fact, is one of strategy may complicate any attempt at relating the end result of a socialization process with prior childhood activities." Moreover, "if one sees in the play activities a mirror of the real adult world and its values, concepts, tendencies, and ways of thought, then incorrect classification of a society's games may result in a wholly reversed or otherwise inappropriate or false picture of that world." We would add that ignoring how a child alters the rules of play or employs strategies to turn chance into something to be controlled and exploited overlooks an important fact of human behavior. Individuals do not just passively inherit a culture. They actively use a cultural heritage as a resource. They personalize folklore, utilize it for psychological or spiritual ends, and even exploit it as a means of self-aggrandizement. This personalization process and its implications are the subjects of the chapter that follows.

Notes

1. Hugh Miller, *Scenes and Legends of the North of Scotland* (Edinburgh: Adam and Charles Black, 1835), reprinted in Richard M. Dorson, ed., *Peasant Customs and Savage Myths: Selections from the British Folklorists* (Chicago: University of Chicago Press, 1968),

vol. 1, pp. 30–36. The quote is from the reprinted version, p. 31.

2. Dan Ben-Amos, "Toward a Definition of Folklore in Context," *Journal of American Folklore* 84 (1971):3–15. Quotes are from pp. 12 and 13. This essay also appears in Américo Paredes and Richard Bauman, eds., *Toward New Perspectives in Folklore,* Publications of the American Folklore Society, Bibliographical and Special Series 23 (Austin: University of Texas Press, 1971), pp. 3–15; and it has been reprinted in Dan Ben-Amos, *Folklore in Context: Essays* (New Delhi: South Asian Publishers, 1982), pp. 1–19.

3. Albert B. Lord, *The Singer of Tales,* Harvard Studies in Comparative Literature 24 (Cambridge: Harvard University Press, 1960), reprinted by Atheneum (New York, 1965). Quotes are from p. 21 of the reprinted edition.

4. For a discussion of informal learning as a concept in folkloristics, see Simon J. Bronner, "'Learning of the People': Folkloristics in the Study of Behavior and Thought," *New York Folklore* 9 (1983):75–88. In his book *The Silent Language* (Greenwich, Conn.: Fawcett Publications, 1966), anthropologist Edward T. Hall identifies three learning modes: the formal, informal, and technical (pp. 63–91). He states that in informal learning, the "principal agent is a *model* used for imitation" (p. 70), an assertion that makes explicit what many folklorists imply.

5. B. F. Skinner, *Science and Human Behavior* (New York: Macmillan, 1953). Quotes are from p. 65.

6. B. F. Skinner, *Verbal Behavior* (New York: Appleton-Century-Crofts, 1957), p. 206. For further discussion of selected views of Skinner's and their relevance for folkloristics, see Robert A. Georges, "Skinnerian Behaviorism and Folklore Studies," *Western Folklore* 49 (1990):400–405.

7. Clyde Kluckhohn, "Myths and Rituals: A General Theory," *Harvard Theological Review* 35 (1942):45–79, reprinted in Robert A. Georges, ed., *Studies on Mythology* (Homewood, Ill.: Dorsey Press, 1968), pp. 137–167. Quotes are from the reprinted version, p. 159. For a filmed example of a curing ceremony (held by the Kashia group of the Southwestern Pomo), see *Sucking Doctor* (1964, William R. Heick and Gordon Mueller, Filmmaker's Library, black and white, 16mm. and VHS, 50 min.).

8. *The Navaho* (Cambridge: Harvard University Press, 1946), pp. 231–232.

9. Kenneth L. Ketner, "Superstitious Pigeons, Hydrophobia, and Conventional Wisdom," *Western Folklore* 30 (1971):1–17. Quotes are from pp. 10, 11, and 12. For a characterization of the history and use of madstones in a particular state, see Joseph D. Clark, "Madstones in North Carolina," special monograph issue, *North Carolina Folklore Journal* 24:1 (1976):1–40.

10. Alan Dundes, "Earth-Diver: Creation of the Mythopoeic Male," *American Anthropologist* 64 (1962):1032–1051. Quotes are from pp. 1036, 1037, 1038, 1039, 1042, 1043, and 1046. The essay is reprinted in Alan Dundes, ed. *Sacred Narrative: Readings in the Theory of Myth* (Berkeley and Los Angeles: University of California Press, 1984), pp. 270–294. For a sampling of other essays illustrating the various examples and kinds of folklore he has analyzed psychoanalytically in Freudian terms, see Alan Dundes, *Parsing through Customs: Essays by a Freudian Folklorist* (Madison: University of Wisconsin Press, 1987).

11. Cited in Kenneth L. Ketner, "A Study of the Use of Madstones in Oklahoma," *The Chronicles of Oklahoma* 46 (Winter 1968–1969):433–449. The first example is an excerpt from the transcript of an interview with Mr. and Mrs. John Salisberry of Oilton, Oklahoma, in November 1961; the second is from the Tarborough, North Carolina, *Free Press*, October 21, 1848; the third is a reminiscence reported in W. H. Crockett, "The Madstone," *Frontier Times* 38 (1964):1, 64.

12. Willie Smyth, "Challenger Jokes and the Humor of Disaster," *Western Folklore* 45 (1986):243–260. Quotes are from pp. 243, 244, 245, 251, 252, 253, and 254. Three other essays concerned with *Challenger* jokes are Elizabeth Radin Simons, "The NASA Joke Cycle: The Astronauts and the Teacher," *Western Folklore* 45 (1986):261–277; Patrick D. Morrow, "Those Sick Challenger Jokes," *Journal of Popular Culture* 20 (1987):175–184; and Reinhold Aman, "Challenger Shuttle Jokes," *Maledicta: The International Journal of Verbal Aggression* 10 (1988–1989):167–181.

13. From Smyth, pp. 246, 249, and 250.

14. C. G. Jung, "On the Psychology of the Trickster Figure," in Paul Radin, *The Trickster: A Study in American Indian Mythology*, Schocken Paperback Edition (New York: Schocken Books, 1972), pp. 195–211. Quotes are from pp. xxv, 20, 52, 53, 168, 169, 200, 201, 202, 207, 208, and 209.

15. From Radin, pp. 17–18.

16. Carlos C. Drake, "Jungian Psychology and Its Uses in Folklore," *Journal of American Folklore* 82 (1969):122–131. Quotes are from pp. 124, 126, 129, and 130. See also Carlos C. Drake, "Jung and His Critics," *Journal of American Folklore* 80 (1967):321–333.

17. The message on Jack's belt varies with tellers. According to C. Paige Gutierrez, "The Jack Tale: A Definition of a Folk Tale Sub-Genre," *North Carolina Folklore Journal* (26 (1978):85–111, Jane Gentry says, "Old stiff dick, killed seven at a lick," which Richard Chase altered in his published collection of tales from her and others in Beech Mountain, North Carolina, to "Strong Man Jack, killed seven at a whack" (p. 105). A relative of Gentry's, Marshall Ward, says, "Stiff Dick kills fifty-six at one lick," while yet another relative, Ray Hicks, uses the phrase "Big man Jack, killed seven at a whack." Hicks can be heard telling a version of "The Brave Tailor" on the phonograph recording *Ray Hicks Telling Four Traditional "Jack Tales,"* recorded and edited by Sandy Paton, texts transcribed by Lee B. Haggerty (Huntington, Vt.: Folk-Legacy Records, 1964). For a filmic example of Ray Hicks telling another Jack tale ("Whikity-Whack, into My Sack"), see *Fixin' to Tell about Jack* (1974, Elizabeth Barret, Appalshop Films, color, 16mm., 28 min.).

18. Drake also proposes in his article on "Jungian Psychology and Its Uses in Folklore" that concepts such as archetype, psychological type, unconscious complexes, and unconscious projections be considered by folklorists in their fieldwork to understand their own psychology, their projections onto others, and the unconscious factors affecting their informants' behavior. Michael Owen Jones devotes a section of his doctoral dissertation to "Personality Types in Relation to Creativity and Verbalized Aesthetic Responses," in which he undertakes a Jungian analysis of several craftsmen and their customs; see his "Chairmaking in Appalachia: A Study in Style and Creative Imagination in American Folk Art (Ph.D. diss., Indiana University, 1970), pt. 1, pp. 433–480. Ellen Stekert's dissertation, "Two Voices of Tradition: The Influence of Personality and Collecting Environment upon the Songs of

Two Traditional Singers" (Ph.D. diss., University of Pennsylvania, 1965), is one of the first studies to examine at length the relationship of personality and fieldwork situation to repertoire, albeit through the use of psychological tests rather than psychoanalysis.

19. Dorothy Mills Howard, "The Rhythms of Ball-Bouncing and Ball-Bouncing Rhymes," *Journal of American Folklore* 62 (1949):166–172. Quotes are from pp. 166 and 170.

20. Mary Sanches and Barbara Kirshenblatt-Gimblett, "Children's Traditional Speech Play and Child Language," in Barbara Kirshenblatt-Gimblett, ed., *Speech Play: Research and Resources for Studying Linguistic Creativity* (Philadelphia: University of Pennsylvania Press, 1976), pp. 65–110. Quotes are from pp. 94, 102, 103, and 105. See also Courtney B. Cazden, "Play with Language and Meta-Linguistic Awareness: One Dimension of Language Experience," in Jerome S. Bruner, Alison Jolly, and Kathy Sylva, eds., *Play—Its Role in Development and Evolution* (New York: Basic Books, 1976), pp. 603–608, and Richard Bauman, "Ethnography of Children's Folklore," in Perry Gilmore and Allan A. Glatthorn, eds., *Children In and Out of School: Ethnography and Education* (Washington, D.C.: Center for Applied Linguistics, 1982), pp. 172–186. For filmic treatments, see *Children's Chants and Games* (1972, Bernard Wilets, BFA Educational Media, color, 16mm., 18 min.), and *Children's Games from Afro-American Tradition* (1980, Smithsonian Institution, Office of Folklife Programs, black and white VHS, 42 min. [pt. 1], 49 min. [pt. 2], and 60 min. [pt. 3]).

21. Brian Sutton-Smith, "A Developmental Structural Account of Riddles," in Kirshenblatt-Gimblett, pp. 111–119. Quotes are from pp. 118–119. See also Brian Sutton-Smith, *The Folkstories of Children* (Philadelphia: University of Pennsylvania Press, 1981), in which the author discusses children's development of verse stories (ages two through four) and plot stories (ages five through ten) as they acquire storytelling competence.

22. From Sanchez and Kirshenblatt-Gimblett, pp. 106–110.

23. For additional examples of conundrums, see Iona and Peter Opie, *The Lore and Language of Schoolchildren* (Oxford: Clarendon Press, 1959), pp. 79–81; C. Grant Loomis, "Traditional American Wordplay: The Co-nundrum," *Western Folklore* 8 (1949):235–247; and Alan Dundes and Robert A. Georges, "Some Minor Genres of Obscene Folklore," *Journal of American Folklore* 75 (1962):222.

24. Julia Woodbridge Oxrieder, "The Slumber Party: Transition into Adolescence," *Tennessee Folklore Society Bulletin* 43 (1977):128–134. Quotes are from pp. 128, 129, 132, and 133. See also Simon J. Bronner, "'Left to Their Own Devices': Interpreting American Children's Folklore as an Adaptation to Aging," *Southern Folklore* 47 (1990):101–115.

25. See also Norine Dresser, "Telephone Pranks," *New York Folklore Quarterly* 29 (1973):121–130.

26. Barbara Skov, "Field Research Project" [Polack jokes told by her teenage children and their friends], Archive of California and Western Folklore, UCLA Folklore and Mythology Center (circa 1973). Quotes are from pp. 1, 7, 8, 9, and 10.

27. Roger D. Abrahams, "'Playing the Dozens,'" *Journal of American Folklore* 75 (1962):209–220. Quotes are from pp. 209, 210, 211, 213, 214, and 215.

28. For a summary of some of this research and an overview of alternative explanations of playing the dozens, see Simon J. Bronner, "'Who Says?': A Further Investigation of Ritual Insults among White American Adolescents," *Midwestern Journal of Language and Folklore* 4 (1978):53–69.

29. *White Men Can't Jump* was directed by Ron Shelton and stars Wesley Snipes, Woody Harrelson, and Rosie Perez. It dramatizes playing the dozens, particularly during the film's opening minutes.

30. The authors of many so-called "performance-oriented" studies of folklore have as their objective to infer and characterize behavioral rules that are distinctive to telling stories, singing songs, celebrating, etc., in one particular society or group. While behavior is a focus in such works, their principal preoccupation is to provide insights into the nature of the culture of the group in question. This is the case, for instance, with Dell Hymes, "Breakthrough into Performance," in Dan Ben-Amos and Kenneth S. Goldstein, eds., *Folklore: Performance and Communication* (The Hague: Mouton, 1975), pp. 11–74; Richard Bauman, *Story, Performance, and Event: Contextual Studies of Oral Narrative* (New York: Cambridge University Press, 1986); and

Charles L. Briggs, *Competence in Performance: The Creativity of Tradition in Mexicano Verbal Art* (Philadelphia: University of Pennsylvania Press, 1988). Authors of other performance-oriented studies of folklore are concerned with behavioral rules that are multicultural or universal rather than culturally relative and either state or imply this in their works. This is the case with many studies characterized elsewhere in this book, including William A. Wilson, "On Being Human: The Folklore of Mormon Missionaries," 64th Faculty Honor Lecture, Utah State University (Logan: Utah State University Press, 1981) (discussed in chapter 6); Dorothy Eggan, "The Personal Use of Myth in Dreams," in Thomas A. Sebeok, ed., *Myth: A Symposium* (Bloomington: Indiana University Press, 1958), pp. 107–121 (discussed in chapter 9); and Barre Toelken, "The 'Pretty Language' of Yellowman: Genre, Mode, and Texture in Navaho Coyote Narratives," *Genre* 2 (1969):211–235 (discussed in chapter 9). Two examples of works whose authors discuss rules for traditional behaviors by drawing an analogy with grammars and the way they work cognitively are Mary Douglas, "Deciphering a Meal," *Daedalus* 101 (1972):61–81, and Henry Glassie, *Folk Housing in Middle Virginia: A Structural Analysis of Historical Artifacts* (Knoxville: University of Tennessee Press, 1975).

31. Edwin Sidney Hartland, "Folklore: What Is It and What Is the Good of It?" *Popular Studies in Mythology, Romance and Folklore*, No. 2 (London: David Nutt, 1899), reprinted in Dorson, vol. 1, pp. 230–251. Quotes are from the reprinted version, pp. 231, 233, and 234.

32. Axel Olrik, "Epische Gesetze der Volksdichtung," *Zeitschrift für Deutsches Altertum* 51 (1909):1–12, translated into English by Jeanne P. Steager and published in Dundes, *The Study of Folklore*, pp. 129–141. Quotes are from the English language translation in the Dundes book, pp. 131, 132, 133, 134, 135, 136, 137, 138, 139, 140, and 141.

33. On opening and closing formulas in fairy tales, see Max Lüthi, *The Fairytale as Art Form and Portrait of Man*, trans. Jon Erickson (Bloomington: Indiana University Press, 1984), pp. 49–53. For a description and analysis of opening and closing formulas in storytelling in a single society (the Bahamas), see

Daniel J. Crowley, *I Could Talk Old-Story Good: Creativity in Bahamian Folklore*, University of California Folklore Studies 17 (Berkeley and Los Angeles: University of California Press, 1966), pp. 32–39.

34. For a discussion of punchlines in jokes, see Elliott Oring, *Jokes and Their Relations* (Lexington: University Press of Kentucky, 1992), pp. 81–93. For an analysis of anecdotes in which punchlines consist of quoted speech that is the focus of narratives, see Richard Bauman, *Story, Performance, and Event: Contextual Studies of Oral Narrative* (New York: Cambridge University Press, 1986), pp. 54–77.

35. Bruce Rosenberg, *The Art of the American Folk Preacher* (New York: Oxford University Press, 1970).

36. For more information about Odin and other gods, see Marjorie Leach, *Guide to the Gods*, ed. Michael Owen Jones and Frances Cattermole-Tally (Denver: ABC-Clio, 1992).

37. Kaarle Krohn, *Die folkloristische Arbeitsmethode* (Oslo, 1926), trans. into English by Roger L. Welsch and published as *Folklore Methodology*, Publications of the American Folklore Society, Bibliographical and Special Series 21 (Austin: University of Texas Press, 1971). "Laws of Transformation" is the title of chapter 11 (pp. 78–98 in the English translation). The quote is from the English translation, p. 98.

38. Walter Anderson, *Kaiser und Abt*, Folklore Fellows Communications 42 (Helsinki, 1923), pp. 379ff. For a characterization in English of Anderson's principal points, see Stith Thompson, *The Folktale* (New York: Dryden Press, 1946), pp. 436–438.

39. Ruth Benedict, "Introduction to Zuni Mythology," in *Zuni Mythology*, Columbia University Contributions to Anthropology 21 (New York: Columbia University Press, 1935), vol. 1, pp. xi–xliii, reprinted in Georges, *Studies on Mythology*, pp. 102–136. Quotes are from the reprinted version, pp. 121, 123, 124, 125, 126, 129, 130, and 133.

40. Benedict, in Georges, p. 130.

41. Lord, p. 13. For an overview and discussion of subsequent research into the oral composing process, see John Miles Foley, *The Theory of Oral Composition: History and Methodology* (Bloomington: Indiana University Press, 1988).

42. Claude Lévi-Strauss, *The Savage Mind*, trans. George Weidenfeld and Nicolson Ltd.

(Chicago: University of Chicago Press, 1966), p. 22. For further discussion of the pervasiveness of this conceptualization of storytelling, see Robert A. Georges, "The Kaleidoscopic Model of Narrating: A Characterization and a Critique," *Journal of American Folklore* 92 (1979):164–171.

43. V. Propp, *Morphology of the Folktale,* rev. ed., trans. Laurence Scott, ed. Louis A. Wagner, Publications of the American Folklore Society, Bibliographical and Special Series 9 (Austin: University of Texas Press, 1968), pp. 112–113. The quote is from p. 113.

44. Linda Dégh, *Folktales and Society: Story-Telling in a Hungarian Peasant Community,* trans. Emily M. Schossberger (Bloomington: Indiana University Press, 1969), pp. 168 and 183.

45. Rosan A. Jordan, "The Vaginal Serpent and Other Themes from Mexican-American Women's Lore," in Rosan A. Jordan and Susan J. Kalčik, eds., *Women's Folklore, Women's Culture* (Philadelphia: University of Pennsylvania Press, 1985), pp. 26–44.

46. Carol Mitchell, "Some Differences in Male and Female Joke-Telling," in Jordan and Kalčik, pp. 163–186, and Carol Mitchell, "The Sexual Perspective in the Appreciation and Interpretation of Jokes," *Western Folklore* 26 (1977):303–329.

47. Elaine J. Lawless, "Piety and Motherhood: Reproductive Images and Maternal Strategies of the Woman Preacher," *Journal of American Folklore* 100 (1987):469–478. Quotes are from pp. 469, 470, 473, and 477.

48. For additional essays on gender-determined behavioral rules as they manifest themselves in folklore, see the book edited by Jordan and Kalčik and the "Folklore and Feminism" issue of the *Journal of American Folklore* 100:398 (October-December 1987).

49. Kenneth S. Goldstein, "Strategy in Counting Out: An Ethnographic Folklore Field Study," in Elliott M. Avedon and Brian Sutton-Smith, eds., *The Study of Games* (New York: John Wiley & Sons, 1971, reprint edition, Huntington, N.Y.: Robert E. Kreiger Publishing, 1979), pp. 172–178. Quotes are from the 1979 reprint edition, pp. 173–178 passim. Reprinted by permission of John Wiley & Sons, Inc.

50. From Goldstein, p. 173.

51. From Goldstein, pp. 174.

52. From Goldstein, p. 178.

9. Folklore as Personal Resource

The behavioral perspective in folkloristics reveals that folklore is learned, reinforced, and rule-governed. It also indicates that folklore can be viewed as an expressive manifestation of physical, cognitive, and psychological states and processes. But those employing the behavioral perspective also recognize the fact that every human being is unique. Therefore, while a given example of folklore may be expressive of such things as an unconscious repression, a stage in psychosocial development, or an intuitively learned behavioral law, it is the way a folklore example fits into a person's distinctive continuum of experience that makes it relevant and meaningful for the individual.

Although folklore can be defensibly characterized as a collective or communal phenomenon because every example of it is known to and shared by two or more human beings, every individual can also be said to have his or her own folklore *repertoire*. Two people exposed to the same traditional stories, songs, games, tunes, etc., never remember (or forget) precisely the same ones; and they do not perceive and recall in exactly the same way the ones they both do learn. Furthermore, people do not necessarily share with others the folklore examples they have in common; but when they do, the way they generate and transmit the common examples is affected by and reflective of the differences as well as the similarities in their experiences and behaviors. Finally, not only is every teller of a traditional tale, singer of a traditional song, player of a traditional tune, maker of a traditional basket, etc., unique, but so is each telling, singing, playing, and making of the same story, song, tune, and basket by

the same individual. For behavior is situationally idiosyncratic, with the purpose, the setting, and the number and nature of people involved all determining what form a folklore example takes. Further developing and illustrating these points are the purposes of this chapter.

Folklore in Biographical Context

Studies of folklore and the individual frequently focus on selected kinds and/or examples of folklore a person knows and the ways these relate to other aspects of her or his life history. Determining what these relationships are entails obtaining and analyzing information about a person's folklore repertoire and about selected events and experiences in the individual's life with which the folklore under consideration correlates. Studies of folklore in *biographical context*, as they can be called, reveal means by which researchers obtain information pertinent to such investigations; questions they pose and answer; and insights their inquiries provide into the ways folklore serves as personal resource.

Folklorists sometimes set out to determine what part selected kinds and/or examples of folklore played in the lives of individuals who are deceased. In such cases, one obviously cannot obtain information at first hand from the research subject himself or herself, but must instead rely on other individuals' oral, written, tape-recorded, and/or filmed records that document potentially pertinent events and experiences in the subject's life history. Finding such secondary sources and constructing from the

information they provide a biographical
context in terms of which the personal use
and meaningfulness of folklore can be determined are frequently tedious and frus-
trating, as well as rewarding, tasks, as
Gladys-Marie Fry's lengthy but successful
search for information about long-deceased
African American quilter Harriet Powers
clearly illustrates.[1]

Fry's research reveals that Harriet Powers was born a slave in Georgia on October
29, 1837 (and died in 1911). According to
census data Mrs. Powers could not read or
write. "Her entire communication with the
world was visual and oral," writes Fry,
"which she expressed in narrative quilts
using themes from her own experience and
techniques from the age-old crafts of African Americans."

Two of these quilts have survived, one
owned by the Museum of Fine Arts in
Boston (Figure 9–2) and the other by the
Smithsonian Institution (Figure 9–3). The
two are narrative quilts, an American art
form; but they use an appliqué technique
traceable to historic Eastern and Middle
Eastern civilizations, yet also having roots
in African culture, writes Fry. The quilts of
Harriet Powers form "a direct link to the
tapestries traditionally made by the Fon
people of Abomey, the ancient capital of
Dahomey, West Africa." Slaves brought
knowledge of this technique "in which
design elements are cut from cloth and
sewn onto background fabric after first
being narrowly turned under to form a
hemmed edge," contends Fry. "The two
quilts Mrs. Powers is known to have made
follow the narrative tradition of depicting
stories circulating orally, in different versions, and believed to be true." These include biblical stories on one quilt, and local
legends and astronomical phenomena on
another

Fry notes that two local legends that
Mrs. Powers transformed visually concern
"an independent hog named Betts, who ran

*Figure 9–1: Harriet Powers (1837–1911) with sun
motif appliquéd to her apron, possibly a religious
symbol derived from the concept of circularity
and the omniscience of God among the Bakongo
of Africa (Neg. #B20615; courtesy Museum of Fine
Arts, Boston).*

from Georgia to Virginia (this is a traditional motif that became fastened to Georgia), and a man frozen at his jug of liquor."
Most of the images on one quilt present
biblical heroes (Figure 9–2), "usually those
who had struggled successfully against
overwhelming odds—Noah, Moses, Jonah,
and Job." She portrays the serpent in the
Garden of Eden with feet, before he suffered
God's curse. She calls attention to Adam's
rib, from which Eve was begat. "The
miracle of creation itself provides the subject matter for several blocks."

Figure 9–2: Appliqué Bible quilt by Harriet Powers that was discovered by Jennie Smith at a Cotton States Exposition in 1886 and later purchased by Ms. Smith for $5.00 (69039, courtesy Smithsonian Institution).

Harriet Powers's fascination with biblical personages and animals may have stemmed from hearing vivid sermons in church. According to Jennie Smith, Mrs. Powers had a fondness for animals (she wanted to attend the Barnum and Bailey Circus when it came to Athens, Georgia, about 1890); and she also committed sermons to memory.

Jennie Smith had bought one of Mrs. Powers's quilts. Born Oneita Virginia Smith in Athens, Georgia, in 1862 (and died in 1946), she was an artist renowned locally. She saw a quilt by Mrs. Powers at a Cotton Fair in 1886 (Figure 9–3). Wishing to buy it, she tracked down the maker, whom she later described as "a negro woman, who lived in the country on a little farm whereon she and her husband made a respectable life. She is about sixty-five years old [actually, she was 46; work-weary, she seemed older], of a clear ginger cake color, and is a very clean and interesting woman who loves to talk of her 'old miss' and her life 'befo de wah.'" Mrs. Powers did not wish to sell the quilt. But about 1890, she experienced financial difficulties. She offered the quilt to Jennie Smith. In a handwritten account (about 1891), Ms. Smith describes the events that led to her purchase of the quilt, including the following remarks:

> Last year I sent her [Mrs. Powers] word that I would buy it if she still wanted to dispose of it. She arrived one afternoon in front of my door in an ox-cart with the precious burden in her lap encased in a clean flour sack, which was still enveloped in a crocus sack.
>
> She offered it for ten dollars, but I told her I only had five to give. After going out and consulting with her husband she returned and said "Owin to de hardness of de times, my ole man lows I'd better tech hit." Now being a new woman she obeyed.
>
> After giving me a full description of each scene with great earnestness, she departed but has been back several times to visit the darling offspring of her brain.
>
> She was only in a measure consoled for its loss when I promised to save her all my scraps.

Gladys-Marie Fry observes that although Mrs. Powers "could neither read nor write [she] nevertheless felt an obligation to record the meanings of the pictorial representations on her quilts," which she dictated to Jennie Smith.

"In addition to biblical folk materials, Harriet Powers seemed especially interested in astronomical phenomena," writes Fry. "Legendary accounts of actual events—eclipses, meteors, and comets—were infused with traditional motifs. As these legends circulated in oral tradition, they became formularized."

Fry states that pictorial tapestries like these have been called "living history books." They vary in subject matter from one designer to another. "Tradition determines style and composition, but the individual designer decides which stories to relate, choosing from a common repertory," writes Fry. "Stories from oral tradition and oral history are associated with each of the symbols."

In the quilt in Figure 9–3, Harriet Powers depicts astronomical and meteorological events occurring before her birth which she had heard about as well as more recent phenomena. For example,

> The dark day of May 19, 1780. The seven stars were seen 12.N. in the day. The cattle all went to bed, chickens to roost and the trumpet was blown. The sun went off to a small spot and then to darkness.

Figure 9–4: Quilt panel depicting the "dark day" of May 19, 1780, which was caused by dense smoke from extensive forest fires (detail of 9–3).

For centuries people had recorded "dark days." These phenomena often occurred because forest fires filled the air with smoke, turning day into night. Eighteen dark days were documented from 1706 to 1910. "Black Friday," May 19, 1780, was the most famous, a day that grew increasingly yellow and odoriferous with burnt

Figure 9–3: Pieced, appliqué, and printed cotton quilt embroidered with plain and metallic yarns by Harriet Powers (about 1895–1898) containing panels illustrating biblical and astronomical events (Acc. #64.619, Neg. #E10161; bequest of Maxim Karolik; courtesy Museum of Fine Arts, Boston).

leaves, soot, and cinders. Although scientists contend it occurred only in New England, because of fires in New York and Canada, people throughout the country told stories about the day. "Harriet Powers heard about it in Georgia," writes Fry. "She was so deeply impressed by this spectacular occurrence, which had convinced observers that the end of the world was at hand, that she recorded it on her quilt."

> The falling of the stars on November 13, 1833. The people were frightened and thought that the end of time had come. God's hand staid the stars. The varmints rushed out of their beds.

Harriet Powers captured the famous Leonid meteor storm of 1833. For eight hours some 10,000 meteors rained on the earth, in absolute silence. Eyewitnesses exclaimed that "it was snowing fire," "the sky is on fire," and "Judgement Day is here." A white planter in South Carolina wrote that he suddenly awoke to "the most distressing

Figure 9–5: Quilt panel illustrating the Leonid meteor storm of November 13, 1833, during which 10,000 meteors rained down on the earth (detail of 9–3).

cries that ever fell on my ears." He heard shrieks of horror and cries of mercy from 600 or more slaves on three plantations. Listening closely for a possible cause, the planter heard a faint voice near the door calling his name. "I arose, and taking my sword, stood at the door. At this moment I heard the same voice still beseeching me to arise, and saying, 'O my God, the world is on fire!'" The planter yanked the door open. In flooded the "the distressed cries of the negroes," driven by the most awful scene of hundreds of fireballs hurtling toward earth, the biggest ones as large as the moon. A hundred slaves lay prostrate on the ground. Some were speechless. Others cried out. All raised their hands before them, "imploring God to save the world and them. The scene was truly awful; for never did rain fall much thicker than the meteors fell toward the earth; east, west, north, and south, it was the same."

Fry states that the event marks the beginning of scientific interest in meteors. In addition, "Eyewitness accounts were handed down, becoming the topic of comment and speculation for many generations." Also, she writes, this extraordinary phenomenon "became a time-fixing device by means of which important events, such as births and deaths, were determined by the general population, including former slaves."

> Cold Thursday, 10, of February, 1895. A woman frozen while at prayer. A woman frozen at a gateway. A man with a sack of meal frozen. Isicles [*sic*] formed from the breath of a mule. All blue birds killed. A man frozen at his jug of liquor.

The entire month of February 1895 was unseasonably cold, with heavy snowfalls. February 10 (a Sunday, not a Thursday) witnessed sleet in various parts of the state. Mrs. Powers recorded the unusual weather condition, and its toll on human lives as described in oral accounts that she heard.

Figure 9–6: Quilt panel representing "cold Thursday" in February, 1895, when people and animals froze to death (detail of 9–3).

According to Fry, Harriet Powers depicted stories about meteorological phenomena that she had only heard, not read, and these proved to be accurate, paralleling scientific records. "But times were changing in Harriet's day," writes Fry, "and she knew intuitively that the quilts she had so carefully and lovingly created should be explained, in written form, for those who would examine them in later years. This she did, with the help of someone who could write. Thus, she recorded those stories that had impressed her, just as in the quilt itself Harriet Powers expressed both her life experiences and her African heritage."

In commenting on the process of attempting to reconstruct pertinent experiences and events in a dead person's life in order to understand the part folklore played in it, Fry reveals some of the sources of frustration: "It is only from official records

that we can glimpse bits and pieces of Harriet Powers's family history," she writes. "Unfortunately, there are large gaps in the total picture because information about births, marriages, deaths, and wills was not recorded as completely for the African American community as it was for whites in the nineteenth-century." Nevertheless, "Valuable but limited information concerning the Powers family is contained in the census data, tax rolls, and records of deeds for Clarke County." With what she obtained from these official records, the quilt design explanations Harriet Powers dictated to Jennie Smith, and Smith's own written accounts of her interactions with Powers, Fry was able to contextualize Harriet Powers's quiltmaking biographically and illustrate the personal use and meaningfulness of that traditional craft to a single individual.[2]

Folklorists more commonly study living, rather than dead, persons when trying to determine the part folklore plays in individuals' lives. Late nineteenth and early twentieth century Russian folklorists first called attention to the importance of such a pursuit, emphasizing the need to determine how the personalities of tellers of traditional tales and singers of traditional songs affect repertoire and style. Pioneers included folktale collector N. Onchukov and *byliny* (narrative song) collector A. F. Gil'ferding. Following their lead, Mark Azadovskii documented and analyzed, in a 1926 publication, the storytelling repertoire of Natal'ia Osipovna Vinokurova of Siberia's Verkholensk district.[3]

"Vinokurova is completely illiterate," writes Azadovskii. "She has spent her entire life in the village where she was born, having lived in the city as a servant girl only for a short time in her early youth." The folktales that constituted her repertoire were stories she had "picked up . . . wherever she had the opportunity to hear something. Several tales she heard in the city, but most she had learned from 'knowledgeable people' among the inhabitants of her region and from travelers."

The stories Vinokurova told Azadovskii were all *Märchen*, well known in versions reported from throughout Russia and the rest of Europe. Yet while their plots were readily recognizable, they had also been localized. "Siberian life flows like a broad stream through Vinokurova's creations," writes Azadovskii. "Here it is seen in some detail of the customs, there it appears in some characteristic of the dialog, and the next time it turns up in one of the broad descriptions of typical Siberian manners and morals." Furthermore, "almost all the occupations of the Verkholensk region" are mentioned, including "ferryboating, commercial transport, and hunting." However, the "importance of the tales of Vinokurova does not lie just in this local coloration," Azadovskii notes, but rather in the creative and artful way she makes them her own by transforming the stories to make them compatible with her own experiences, biases, and preferences.

That Vinokurova's tellings of well known and widely diffused stories are *her* creations and versions unique to *her* repertoire is attested in a variety of ways. She is little interested in elaborate plots, for example, or in fantastic details. She does not like lengthy stories, and so keeps her narratings brief by avoiding unnecessary repetitions. She prefers dwelling on "local customs" and the "psychological side of the folktale" and likes realistic rather than formulaic beginnings. She "introduces gesture" into her tales by describing characters' gestures and presenting dialogue with "descriptions and movements and by pantomime." Often, through an "allusion to a single movement, to a single gesture[,] some occasionally complicated inner experience of the hero is characterized."

Vinokurova's personal dislikes and likes are also reflected in her taletelling. She avoids characterizing obscene happenings whenever she can; but when she cannot, she does so "with an unusual tactfulness" and "a certain respectability." She presents servants sympathetically and sometimes gives them greater importance than do other tellers of the same tales (an obvious influence from her work as a servant girl in the city during her youth). Furthermore, "the poverty motif assumes an important place" in Vinokurova's tales, indicative of her own economic situation. "Her love for music and for sorrow came out most clearly in the tales of Vinokurova," too, as did her "fine understanding" of "nature's beauties." Prophetic dreams are also a favorite theme, again behaviorally reflective, since she "believes in dreams, loves them and understands how to tell them." But her favorite is "the slandered, persecuted woman, the wonderful conception and birth of a son." Vinokurova always portrays the "mother picture . . . with a special sympathy and delicacy" and "surrounded by a deep reverence," writes Azadovskii. There is no place in her stories for the mother-punishment motif so common in fairy tales. Other female figures and themes are similarly carefully, positively, and sympathetically presented. (See Box 9–1 for Azadovskii's comparison of Vinokurova's and other narrators' characterizations of a scene from "The Unfaithful Sister.")

These many correlations between facts of Vinokurova's life, tales she knew and told, and the way she told them led Azadovskii to conclude that she is most accurately identified as an artist. "Vinokurova is always trying to break through the limitations of traditional poetics," he states. "Her poetic feeling and her artistic talent draw her instinctively to nature descriptions." Furthermore, "one can follow her attempts to expand the traditional framework, to destroy the obligatory norms and to find words and colors in order to portray her feelings for nature directly."

BOX 9–1

Comparison of Vinokurova's and Other Narrators' Versions of an Episode in "The Unfaithful Sister"

This same artistic technique [of Vinokurova's], capturing and presenting the internal reality of a happening, in order to throw light on its psychological detail, we can observe in the tale of The Unfaithful Sister. The usual scene is the following: the sister, urged on by her lover (be it a robber, a dragon, a magician, or in the case of Vinokurova, a forest demon) sends her brother out to carry out difficult tasks, at the completion of which he would necessarily have to die. With the help of various magical animals delivered to him, the brother successfully overcomes all hindrances, kills the lover and devises a punishment for his sister. This kind of punishment is generally repeated quite uniformly in all variants.

If one pursues these episodes in Russian tradition, they appear in this sort of form: in the Krasnoiarsk collection the brother chains his sister to a post and places a five bucket vat next to her: "If you fill the vat with tears, then I will believe you." It is the same with Rasdol'ski . . . and with Zelenin. . . . This last tale, however, contains unusually gruesome details: the sister is hanged with her head down on a supporting girder. With Afanas'ev the details are a little different . . .: Ivan the czar's son locks up his sister in a stone tower, places a bundle of hay over her and places two vats next to it, the one with water, the other empty. "If you drink this water up, eat this hay and fill this vat with tears, then God has forgiven you and I forgive you too."

This same type of punishment we also find in a more complicated form: two vats are put out which the unfaithful sister is supposed to fill with tears, the one for her brother, the other for her lover. Occasionally the punishment is formulated in a more complicated way through the choice motif: in Iavorskii's collection (where an unfaithful wife appears instead of an unfaithful sister) the husband puts out two vats as a test. The one is empty, the other is filled with coal. If she rues her deed then she will fill the first one with tears; if she is still worrying about the devil (her lover), then she will eat up all the coal. On the next day it turns out that she has wept no tears, but has eaten up all the coal, down to the last piece. Thus the husband commands his dogs to tear her to pieces and to throw her into the grave to the devil. . . .

In the case of Vinokurova this tale follows, in its format, the variants just mentioned. It contrasts sharply with them, however, surpassing them in strength and splendor of presentation.

The brother led his sister to the place where he had slain her lover, the forest demon: "There is your lover!" "*She wept and wept, she rummaged and rooted in the ashes and found a boar's tusk, pressed it to her heart, wept over this tusk, this tusk of the forest demon.*" Then the brother puts up two posts, between them he hangs a chest and puts his sister inside. Next to her he places two barrels. "There," he says, "weep a barrel full for me and one for the forest demon, then I'll let you go free. Whom will you first mourn, me or this tusk?"—"*No, little brother! First I will weep for the tusk and next for you.*"

In this manner the usual scheme of the subject is indeed presented in the tales of Vinokurova, but this scheme assumes a warm, living and human coloration with her— it takes on life and movement. Instead of the torpid figure of the unfaithful sister, the vivacious, powerful person of a woman filled with passion and grief appears before us. In this picture of confusion, presented in such detail, in which she presses the tusk of her lover to her heart, sprinkling it with tears, [and] in her proud and forthright confession one senses the living picture of a loving and suffering woman, not the marionette figure of epic [folk] poetry.[4]

Speaking more generally about the telling of traditional tales, Azadovskii writes:

> The goal of [folktale] research is to determine those formative forces which govern the generation of a folktale. The narrator is faced, consciously or unconsciously, with the same assignment as the creative writer: the arrangement of his [or her] material, choosing and sifting the latter, and the formulation of his [or her] artistic intention.
>
> Thus we must . . . look at each tale as a completely artistic organism.
>
> The folktale, like every other product of art, has as its basis a definite artistic purpose. This [artistic purpose] serves as a structuring basis for a series of pictures, the examination of which reveals all the individual elements and small stylistic details.
>
> The discovery of this artistic purpose, the analysis of this artistic plan appears thus to be one of the [folklorist's] most important tasks. This task is inseparably bound up with the study of the creative individuality of the narrator.

Azadovskii finds and assesses correlations between biographical facts and the content and style of a corpus of stories that constitutes one narrator's repertoire. Pamela Jones, by contrast, focuses on the ways different individuals tell and interpret a common story and how their tellings and interpretations tally with their personal plights.[5]

Jones documented Mexican immigrants' accounts of the haunting figure La Llorona (earlier characterized and exemplified in this book, in chapter 6) while working as a nutrition counselor for a federal program in Oregon. The 19 women and one man who told her about La Llorona lived in difficult circumstances, including poverty.

"I knew little about the legend previous to my collection of these texts," writes Jones. "I believed it to be the story of a woman who murdered her children, born out of wedlock, because they were evidence of her shame. In the version I had heard, she returned after death and wept because of her lost children—eternally wandering as punishment for her sins." But "after listening to only a few variants of the story told by my informants I realized that the *llorona* is *an endlessly changing legend, modified by storytellers to address themes central to their own psycho-social development and lifestyles*," writes Jones (emphasis added). "The way the story was told, the tone of voice, the attitude, the recently discussed patient and family health history, and the actual content of the legend as it was told, all contributed to the final analysis."

Those who told her about La Llorona seemed to consider the legend "a valued memory, often related to childhood experience," writes Jones. "In each of the twenty texts I collected, all the events took place in Mexico, and at times the transmission of the legends had a nostalgic quality." Jones discovered that one woman considered the Weeping Woman to be guiltless and deserving sympathy; another told the story to children to frighten them so they would be good. That individuals with a common cultural heritage hold very different ideas about what happened to La Llorona, and why, became obvious when Jones interviewed Rosalba and Antonia.

These women, who are sisters-in-law, were present at the same interview. Rosalba, who was not actually married to the father of her children, had (along with her brother) been abandoned by her parents as a child. In her account, Rosalba reports that the Weeping Woman did not kill her children; rather, someone else came and took them away in her absence, and then threw them over a cliff.

"No, no, no," interrupted Antonia, "didn't *she* kill her children?"

"No, someone else came, and took them away," Rosalba replied.

Antonia responded: "Oh no, I am sure that *she* threw her children into the arroyo and then she went crazy and spent all of her time wandering up and down the arroyos weeping and weeping and sometimes you can still hear her weeping in the arroyos."

"By the time I had heard Rosa's story it was becoming clear that storytellers did not always consider the *llorona* to be a promiscuous murderess who deserved eternal punishment for her sins," writes Jones. "In fact, up to this point the informants had demonstrated considerable empathy for her." But it was Francisca's tale that first suggested to Jones that accounts of the Weeping Woman expressed some narrators' own feelings, concerns, and circumstances rather than being just a part of a collective cultural heritage.

At the time she told the story, Francisca had five children, her husband earned $125 a month, and she was awaiting the outcome of a pregnancy test. "She told the story of the *llorona* with great sympathy and gentleness, lingering over the description of the lady's beauty," writes Jones. Said Francisca:

> There was once a beautiful woman, oh she was so beautiful, with beautiful hair and fair skin. She had many suitors and she had a handsome husband; he was a gallant gentleman [pause of 3 seconds]. Well she had three children [pause]. She didn't like her children [pause]. She didn't like the crying that they did [pause]. One day all three children were crying and she became so upset that she killed them all with a knife. She killed them, all three, and she lived near by the river. She put them in the water, deep in the water with the fishes. Now the woman is in the river and you can hear her crying, *ayyy mis hijos,* and weeping in the river. [Pause of several seconds; the story is over.]

"Do you mean she was walking by the side of the river crying in the water?" asked Jones.

"No, I mean she was *in* the river, like a fish," Francisca replied. "You know there is *la sirena* of the sea? Well *la llorona* is the fish woman of the river—weeping in the river, half fish, half woman."

"There was no doubt that the telling of this story was cathartic for Francisca, her facial expression and body language indicating her involvement with this woman who had everything—beauty, admirers, a handsome husband," writes Jones. "Her only problem was three screaming kids. Francisca knew exactly how the *llorona* felt. . . . As she spoke about the *llorona's* children, all crying at once until the woman could no longer stand it, Francisca plainly spoke from her own experience."

In regard to another narration Jones writes: "Ofelia's version of the *llorona* legend addressed parental anxiety about children who wander near large bodies of water, as well as the guilt feelings of mothers who, occupied by work or household duties, are not always able to watch their children closely." Yet other narrators seemed to relate the legend to their own circumstances by citing poverty as a motivation for the murder. Apparently, then, these individuals who were involved with raising a family "in many cases modified the *llorona* themes to express their unconscious anxieties about taking care of their children."

Jones contrasts these women with two other sets of narrators. One consists of female students of Mexican descent at the University of Oregon. "In the students' stories, the lover was repeatedly cited as the cause of the *llorona's* predicament. In the [married] women's tales, the motive for the disappearance of the children was more often unstated, and in most of these cases the implication was that the *llorona* was the unfortunate victim of circumstance. When a motivation was stated, the informants tended to relate it to child-care issues." By contrast, "The stories told by the younger students highlighted the *llorona/lover* figure, who best exemplified their own situation and addressed anxieties related to the natural desire of these young adults to form intimate relationships."

The other set of narrators consists of juvenile delinquents at the Las Palmas

School for Girls, a residential facility of the Department of Corrections of the County of Los Angeles. Bess Lomax Hawes had published an essay on these teenagers' stories 20 years before Jones's research. Their accounts included a variety of ghostly apparitions and encounters, most of which were menacing female revenants, including La Llorona.[6]

According to Hawes, "the girls of Las Palmas School appear to have selected out of the traditional materials available to them certain themes which they state again and again in as many guises as their imaginations allow.... Taking the corpus of tales as a whole," Hawes continues, "the themes that occur most frequently are infanticide and other aggressive crimes committed *by* women, punishment or aggressive crimes committed *against* women, unconsolable grief or loss, and mutilation (another kind of loss)."

Consider the story told by Jackie G. (see Box 9–2, the second story). In Jackie's account, the Weeping Woman murders her children, who are all girls between the ages of 13 and 17—like Jackie herself. Then she seeks them in institutions and foster homes (not rivers), which is where Jackie, a juvenile delinquent, lives. On seeing a girl who

---

BOX 9–2
The La Llorona Legend Told at Juvenile Hall

La llorona has long hair and walks around crying. I heard from the counsellors at Juvie [Juvenile Hall] that she had two kids that she drowned because they were bad. She drowned them in Tijuana. She attacks bad kids in Juvie. They say it is true.
   —Rose V., born in Mexico, age 15, who heard the first sentence from her mother

* * *

It is a woman who wasn't quite all there who killed her three girls, 13 to 17 years old. She didn't want them because something had happened to her husband, and they reminded her of him, so she drowned them. Their bones are buried in her back. She doesn't know they are dead. She wears a long black cape with a peaked hood and goes around institutions and foster homes looking for her kids. If she sees a girl who looks like one of her daughters, she tries to cut out that feature. She comes around three days after it rains.
   —Jackie G., Italian-American, age 15, who heard about the Weeping Woman from a girl friend when she was 10 or 11

* * *

She had a white face and dressed in black. She had three kids—all girls I'm sure—which she drowned for her husband or husband-to-be. She was young and real pretty when she died. She must walk until she finds her kids. She appears on nights of rain or three days afterwards. She stands and looks in windows at Juvie or houses.
   —Jackie A., Negro-Caucasian, age 15, who first heard of La Llorona from two girls who saw her in Juvenile Hall in December 1965

* * *

I saw her once. She stays in the park. She is very ugly and is dressed in white. Only girls can see her face. She goes after girls to kill them.
   —Carol C. heard about the phantom when she was 10 from a Mexican woman neighbor[7]

resembles one of her daughters, she slashes her face in an attempt to cut out that feature. The narrative contains the major themes mentioned by Hawes as typifying stories told by residents of Las Palmas, and it bears directly on the narrator's situation.

In comparing the three sets of narratives, Jones writes, "Each group of informants has placed emphasis on thematic details relevant to their social roles while retaining a framework of the traditional story." Clearly, the Weeping Woman legend "carries a different message depending on who does the storytelling, delinquent girls from Las Palmas School, Chicano students from the University of Oregon, or immigrant mothers from Southern Oregon."

It should be pointed out, too, that while the narrators with families are immigrants from Mexico and the young college women are Americans of Mexican descent, the juvenile delinquents at Las Palmas School are of varied ethnic backgrounds. Many are identified as Caucasian, several as Mexican or of Mexican descent, and one as Negro-Caucasian. Jackie G. is Italian-American. The La Llorona tradition is Mexican, dating back to pre-Conquest times. Judging from these data, then, individuals may appropriate the folklore of someone else's cultural heritage when it appears relevant to their own circumstances. This includes encounters with the supernatural which, rather than being mere superstition, plays a significant role in some people's lives.

For Sam, a Hopi, supernatural entities entered into his dreams to make him more acceptable to his tribe. Among the things that Hopis value in men and that Sam lacked are fathering many children (he lost all of his), being a good hunter (he was a poor one), being sexually potent (he had suffered from impotence for a time), being a good runner (Sam was slow), and being polite to witches and supernaturals (which Sam was not). According to Dorothy Eggan, who wrote about Sam, "These are serious handicaps in Hopi society."[8]

Sam was "caught in a conflict . . . between his ambivalent desire to be *bahana* (White) and to be a good Hopi, resenting his inadequacy as a hunter and runner, concerned with the quality of his courage and with problems in his sexual life," writes Eggan. Sam used "Hopi myths to fuse his personal problems with those of his culture's heroes, thus reducing his own anxiety about them."

The Hopi, writes Eggan, learn by "associated patterns" rather than by rote. In this system, "myths, dreams, and actual experiences were told and retold, for both fantasy and storytelling had a vital role in the Hopi world" of reaffirming all things Hopi. She writes that "in reaffirmation, restatement, and reliving of beliefs and experiences, much doubt and bitterness was worked out." In addition, "Hopi philosophy and behavior were absorbed in an emotionally charged atmosphere which tended to fuse reality and fantasy." As the individual learned the Hopi way, "he tended to store in his memory related items which were representative of the group's thought processes." Not surprisingly, then, "when a myth is congenial enough to the individual he may use it as personal fantasy."

Of 310 of his dreams that Sam documented, fully one-third "use specific folklore characters or themes . . . applied effectively to Sam's personal problems," writes Eggan. Sam selected his fantasy interpretations "from the 'cultural storehouse,'" modifying or elaborating them "so that they can deal more effectively with ego-damaging reality." (See Box 9–3 for Eggan's characterization of one of Sam's dream accounts.)

A highly personalized guardian spirit appears in 73 of Sam's reported dreams. In 51 of these, the spirit is Sam's personal guide, "who once took him safely to the land of the dead; and in the other twenty-two the guide appears as various creatures—

BOX 9–3
One of Sam's Dreams

The dreamer is hunting with *bahanas* [white men] and Hopis, but suddenly finds himself with just one spirit companion who eventually proves himself to be a witch. However, practicing the Hopi doctrine of being polite to witches, Sam continues with his partner. They talk all night, make *pahos* [prayer feathers] for Tuwapongwuhti [the Mother of all Wild Game] and the game. The next day Sam is afraid of being shot by other hunters, is unlucky all day, but finally shoots a large deer. He calls for his companions to help him lift it.

Later, leaving camp he says, "I don't know why I go out there. But I was standing right by the tree and saw a fire coming up. It disappear into a valley and then come up again and change. It was a human shape coming at me. His light come out very bright and when he come near me he stopped and I watch him. It was that lady who owned the deer and rabbit, Tuwapongwuhti. She said, 'Now I'm looking for you. These twin fawns that were born to me are your sons.'" Sam, astonished, asks how that can be, and is told that he made her pregnant by urinating on a certain spot of grass the night before. Quoting again, "This frighten me for I never think I do that, but anyway the two fawns are given to me and I took them, making my few steps back to camp, but she call me back. I turn back and saw that the Mother of these fawns change herself into a most beautiful young woman. She said, 'My husband, do not fear me. I'm your lovely wife.' With that she pull me close to her and she hold me tight. I woke up and found my wife putting her arm over my chest."[9]

all of which also appear in Hopi tales— usually changing into human form for the purpose of encouraging or helping the dreamer in fear-provoking situations." Sam elaborated the concept of *dumalaitaka* (guide or guardian spirit), writes Eggan, "which is generally rather vague and unstressed [among the Hopi], into an ever present and active spirit who comes to him in dreams, takes him to witches' meetings and on treasure hunts, gives him strength, wisdom, and advice, rescues him from dangerous situations, and always assures him that he is on the right road and that his enemies are wrong."

In his dreams Sam's guide helps the dreamer (who frequently says he is a poor runner) to run with great speed to catch the Water Serpent to assure plenty of rain and good crops for the Hopi. The dreamer, a poor hunter, dreams of hunting rabbits, which change to naked, crying babies as he raises his gun to shoot. "The Guide appears and gives him small pills with which to feed the babies. Later an old man at his home village tells him that he is a good man because he fed all of these babies, and that he will now have another baby of his own." In a dream that describes a *bahana* (white man's) house, "three fair girls are ordered by an old man to bathe before they receive the dreamer, a reversal of an actual humiliating experience with a white prostitute some thirty years before this dream." The old man tells the hesitating dreamer not to fear, that nothing will hinder him. "Still hesitating, the dreamer is commanded by his Guide, appearing suddenly, to obey the old man. Eventually the girls turn into ears of corn and the informant realizes that in obeying instructions he has had a magical experience which will bring good crops to his people."

Eggan writes about Sam: "By manipulating the problem solving quality both of myths and his dreams, his fantasies not only give a sense of reality to his desire to be wise, strong, courageous, a good runner, and good hunter who is honored by his people, and pleasing to and protected by supernaturals; but he is also frequently able through fantasy to operate within the cultural stock of imaginative happenings— elaborated or distorted to be sure—but still familiar enough to give him a reassuring sense of identity with his people, even when rejected by them."

By fusing personal fears with similar ones plaguing his culture's heroes, Sam's dreams helped him deal with his anxieties. "Moreover, both familiar tales and dreams elaborated into interesting stories attract an audience, one of the few socially approved ways of becoming the center of attention among the Hopi," writes Eggan. Hence, Sam's narrating about his dreams resulted in further reinforcement.

There was one other important consequence. Eggan explains that "to the extent that he relates his dreams convincingly, he introduces new emphases and directions into Hopi lore. In the dreamer's village, for instance, we have noted a gradually increasing interest in the possibility of a more active personal guide," concludes Eggan. "The name remains the same, but in this village the spirit has become somewhat more real."

Others gain personal, spiritual, and social power by adopting a culturally familiar traditional role such as healer and becoming a specialist sought after by clients in need of therapy for emotional illness or physical injury or disease. A film by Richard Cowan called *Eduardo the Healer,* based on research conducted over a four-year period by Douglas G. Sharon, records two days in the life of Eduardo in Trujillo, northern Peru. Eduardo Calderón is a fisherman, a sculptor, and a *curandero* (male shaman or folk healer; female = *curandera*). He diagnoses others for natural and magical illnesses. Through ritual, religious objects,

and hallucinogenic drugs he cures people afflicted with emotional disturbances or suffering the effects of witchcraft (such as a hex by a *brujo,* or male sorcerer; female = *bruja*).[10]

The film opens with a panoramic view of the sky, sea, and sand on the coast at Las Delicias, Peru, where Eduardo lives. The date is March 18, 1977. Seated at his outdoor work area, Eduardo whistles softly to himself as he molds a clay figurine. He is heavyset and bare chested. His belly bulges over his baggy pants, their dark color mottled with the lighter grey of dried clay. A goatee and a head of thick black hair, pulled back into a pony tail, frame a round, expressive face. Voice-over narration in English briefly identifies Eduardo, mentioning that as a folk healer he drinks and nasally imbibes a brew made from the San Pedro cactus (a source of mescaline) in diagnosis and treatment.

At breakfast of fish, cat, and other foods, Eduardo talks with his family and sometimes jokes with his children. Juan and Alberto, who assist him in his curing, are also present. Eduardo mentions that he has "a cure" the next day. He lists some of the things he will need: a new can (in which to boil slices of cactus), corn meal, sweet limes, flowers, and San Pedro cactus ("the good ones from the north"). "I'll also need lime cones, my vest, . . . and your cap!" he says jokingly to one of his children. "We also need a 'counter hex,'" he tells his assistants.

Eduardo returns to his work with clay, wearing a dark leather vest partially covering his large torso. A woman walks in unannounced to ask if he will "cleanse" her. She removes a live female guinea pig from a bag and hands it to the healer, along with a bottle of scented water. She is ill. She thinks someone has hexed her. What can Eduardo discover?

The healer moves her to an open area of the yard, where she stands straight and still.

He makes the sign of the cross over her and says a Catholic prayer. He gulps a mouthful of scented water and sprays it near her. After spitting water in four directions, he rubs the cavy over the woman, beginning with her head and then moving down her torso—front, one side, back, the other side. He moves the guinea pig around her hips and thighs. Eduardo then holds the rodent over a trough of water, slices it down the middle, and quickly peels back the skin. The animal squeals. Blood spurts out. After spraying perfumed water over the lifeless carcass to purify the sacrifice, the healer peers carefully at the internal organs and spine.

A broken spine betokens witchcraft. Discovering that it is still intact, however, Eduardo turns his attention to the quivering viscera to perform entrail divination. Guinea pigs are thought to be sensitive enough to take on the body "humors" and ailments of the patient. In cases of organic disorders the diseased organ becomes spotted or turns black. "The liver—bad, bad, bad," mumbles Eduardo. It is black, he says. "The kidneys also . . . ," he adds, noting that they show some signs of disease beginning to affect them. "But as for witchcraft—nothing!" He sprays scented water. He recommends that the woman seek immediate medical attention. (He once completed a course in nursing from a correspondence school.) She protests. She really thought she had been bewitched, she says. Eduardo shows her the intact spinal column. No, she does not require a curing session.

This divination serves to separate patients whom he can help (either with a series of curing ceremonies or with first aid and perhaps herbs) from those whose illnesses are not serious or, like this woman's, need other medical treatment. Eduardo, we are informed, is a follower of an ancient but changing cultural tradition dating back 3,000 years. In the kingdom of Chimu the healers, known as *Oquetlupuc,* were greatly respected and well rewarded; but today Eduardo's craft is illegal in Peru. Persecuted by both Church and State, *curanderos* have gone underground, gaining much of their knowledge through oral tradition as apprentices. Nowadays they mix the trappings of Christianity with ancient shamanistic content.

Despite persecution, folk healers abound. One small town in the north of Peru had 100 at the time of Douglas Sharon's research in the late 1960s and early 1970s. Contributing to the tradition's vitality, Sharon contends, is a rigidly stratified socioeconomic system with few opportunities for individuals to break through. The unemployment rate has soared because of rapid population growth and heavy urban migration. Many people compete for a few jobs, fail to move upward economically, and suffer chronic insecurity. Such conditions produce great frustration and interpersonal conflict, writes Sharon in an article about Eduardo in *Natural History* (November, 1972). High levels of aggression result, expressed through a projective mechanism of an "envy syndrome" that supports continued belief in witchcraft. When one person feels jealous toward another, he or she can seek out a *brujo* or sorcerer to hex that individual. Someone suffering illness or personal tragedy (or guilt or fear from violating social norms) often blames it on the envy of an enemy and seeks alleviation from a *curandero.* (Sometimes a man or woman functions both as a sorcerer and a healer, although Eduardo has dedicated himself only to curing.)

"Thus," writes Sharon, "witchcraft serves as an escape valve, permitting aggression to express itself without attacking fundamental institutions." Although patients may blame their ailments on supernatural forces, the folk healer's therapy usually consists of "discovering disturbed social relationships, a procedure that rids the patient of his [or her] pathological symptoms," writes Sharon. "In this way *curan-derismo* provides individuals with channels for anxiety reduction and treatment." The folk healer can "relieve the symptoms and reintegrate the patient into society." Therefore, a cultural heritage—belief in witchcraft as well as in curing—serves as personal resource for patient and healer alike.

In the film and in various writings by Douglas Sharon we learn about Eduardo's background, including his own cure by Doña Laura, from whom we see him buying cactus and other items for the upcoming cure he will perform. Eduardo "Chino" Calderón was born in 1930 in Trujillo. His father was "an artist, a shoemaker—a good shoemaker," says Eduardo. The oldest son of the family, Eduardo had to help out financially, helping make shoes, carrying produce in the local market, raising rabbits for slaughter, and so on.

In 1947 his uncles and cousins put him in a Catholic seminary to train for the priesthood. Feeling stifled and discouraged he left at the age of 20 and headed for Lima. He had always liked art. But he wanted to be a doctor; however, it cost too much, he says in the film. He decided to become a sculptor against his family's wishes ("How can you make a living from dolls?!"). He read, practiced sculpting, and attended Lima's school of fine art. Disappointed with the school's educational philosophy and methods, he left before the end of his first year. Then he worked alone, haunting the national museum of anthropology on Sundays from the time it opened in the morning until it closed at night, making clay figures modeled after ancient ones. He accepted a poorly paid job as a bricklayer's assistant. Returning home to Las Delicias at age 21, he took up fishing, a new skill he had to learn.

For a while he did well. He met Maria, and fathered his first son of their many children (they had nine by 1972). In 1965 the fishing industry suffered a bad year, forcing small fishermen like Eduardo out of business. Having to begin anew at age 35, but having also attracted attention as an artist of considerable merit, Eduardo accepted a job as artist in charge of frieze reconstruction at Chan Chan, an archaeological site of the ancient capital of the Kingdom of Chimu (A.D. 1000–1440) and the largest adobe ruin in the world. Later he devoted more time to sculpting, making molded reproductions of ancient figurines for sale to tourists and collectors.

Throughout these years Eduardo also evolved as a *curandero*. In the film he describes some of his experiences as he interacts with Doña Laura at the market and later, at home, talking to his assistants as he slices San Pedro cactus. When he was 17 he fell victim to a strange ailment. "I was rotting alive, covered with sores." He had been up to some mischief, in love with a girl, and . . . ? Both Eduardo and Doña Laura are vague but imply that he may have been a young hellion. She treated him with herbs and made him drink a glass of San Pedro juice. "My face was all twisted," says Eduardo. His family screamed, "He's dying!" He vomited. "Everything came out black," he says, but soon he recovered his health. "Little by little I got interested in curing." He attended sessions. "I liked the rattles," he says. But he was not content with that.

He accompanied an uncle to visit a great *brujo* who "did a 'night' for us." Eduardo became his assistant, eventually gaining enough experience to serve as a *rastreador*, one who helps the *curandero* focus his supernatural "vision" on a patient's problems. "I began to 'see,'" Eduardo tells his assistants, pausing to cut another slice of San Pedro cactus. He adds jokingly: "a world champion!" The old man played the guitar and sang "a hell of a chant," he says. But Eduardo refused to work with him further. Although "I didn't believe in that witchcraft nonsense," says Eduardo, nevertheless after imbibing San Pedro juice and being thrown into a pit "I began to fly." Not ready yet to set up his own *mesa*, he worked with other *curanderos* in Chiclayo, Motupe, and Ferrañafe in the north.

Returning home Eduardo still did not begin to practice on his own until a cousin suddenly became seriously ill. Suspecting witchcraft, her father implored Eduardo to cure her. He tried, despite doubts and misgivings. In two sessions he discovered the cause as well as cured her, launching his career as a folk healer at age 28.

Essential to curing is the healer's *mesa*, an area on the ground in front of the *curandero* divided into major zones with artifacts symbolizing the duality of the worlds of human beings and nature, and the struggle between good and evil. Eduardo's *mesa* consists of two major zones (*campos*) with a neutral area between them. Called the *campo ganadero* (the field of the sly dealer), the left side contains artifacts associated with the forces of black magic and evil. Satan governs this zone, whose negative powers are focused in three staffs positioned behind the artifacts, mainly ceramic fragments and stones from archaeological ruins. The healer consults this zone in cases of bad luck, witchcraft, or adverse love magic.

The right side of the *mesa*, called the *campo justiciero* (field of divine justice), contains objects related to white magic and the forces of good—mainly saints and instruments used in healing. Christ governs this zone. His powers are focused in the crucifix and in eight staffs placed upright behind the artifacts.

Between these extremes lies the *campo medio* (middle field). It contains artifacts of neutral nature to balance the forces of good and evil. Saint Cyprian (a powerful magician who converted to Christianity) governs this zone. A serpent staff, placed behind several artifacts that can be used for either good or evil, channels his powers.

Figure 9–7: The mesa *of Eduardo, a* curandero, *with staffs and other "power objects" used in divination (photo by Douglas G. Sharon).*

Eduardo focuses his vision here, for it can reflect a case without distortion.

Eduardo has accumulated the random collection of artifacts over the years as his skills improved. He acquired each item under special circumstances, as gifts from patients or other healers or after careful search through ruins, riverbeds, and mountainous areas. Each has its own *cuenta* ("account"), activated during a night session. Each becomes a focal point of a particular force. Collectively they constitute a projection of Eduardo's spiritual power brought into action when he manipulates the *mesa* in conjunction with chanting, singing, and drinking a psychedelic brew.

When setting up the *mesa* for a cure, Eduardo positions everything so that the sea lies in back of him, a protective force preventing him from being overtaken from behind. A night healing session (which approximates the blooming cycle of the San Pedro cactus) consists of a ceremony and a curing. The former usually lasts from about 10 P.M. until midnight. The *curandero* performs prayers, rituals, and songs to the rhythmic beat of a rattle, interspersing these activities with a periodic nasal imbibition—called "raising"—of boiled San Pedro cactus and wild black tobacco juice by himself, his two assistants, the patients waiting to be cured, and relatives and friends of the patients. The first ceremony ends at midnight with the drinking of a cup of pure San Pedro brew to invoke the forces of nature and guardian spirits, to focus the *curandero*'s vision on the problem at hand, and to make the patient susceptible to therapy.

The cure lasts from midnight until about 4 A.M. Everyone present must take a turn standing in front of the *mesa* while the healer chants a song in his name. All concentrate on the swords and staffs at the head of the *mesa*. One, which is the focal point of the forces affecting the patient, is supposed to vibrate. It is then given to the

patient to hold in the left hand while the *curandero* chants the song of the staff to activate its "accounts," causing it to manifest its powers.

As Eduardo explains to his assistants in his house a few hours before the March 19 curing, he must "go back in the patient's history looking for causes." This he does through a long divinatory discourse in which he tells those assembled at the curing what he sees (to release from the patient's subconscious whatever blockages may be causing the person's problem).

The principal patient tonight, says Eduardo, is Luciano Azmat, a case that "is important—important because of its specifics." He has had much bad luck: a hex, a "spiritual shock." He lost his car through an accident, he is about to abandon his family, and he has suffered other problems as well. Tonight Eduardo, Juan, and Alberto will give him his third and final "diagnosis," and then a "'flowering' so he can move on." Eduardo explains that the healer's *mesa* is a "control panel." He can search the negative field for "factors causing the bad effects. The sickness. The illness." The staffs transmit the force "given by the master by means of bioelectromagnetic forces." The healer's assistants "are like umbilicals" extending out from the master, the generator of power, channeling the forces into curing.

In the film Eduardo, flanked by Juan and Alberto, has his back to the sea, his *mesa* before him. Artifacts fill the three fields. Staffs and swords, jabbed into the sand, stand upright to the rear of the *mesa*. Eduardo wears a black knitted cap, black vest, and black trousers. We glimpse Luciano Azmat off to the side, in the shadows. Eduardo takes a swig of scented water, then sprays it into the air to purify the *mesa*. He chants rhythmically in time with the rattle that he shakes.

Luciano Azmat stands before the healer and his assistants. Eduardo addresses him, chanting a song in his name. Juan and Alberto give Azmat a staff. Eduardo chants after saying, "I 'raise' you."

The camera switches from the patient's point of view (looking at Eduardo) to Eduardo's viewpoint, and back to the patient's. At one moment the camera is behind Azmat, the point of view of family and friends. We see him standing in a circle in the sand outlined in white. The camera moves forward gradually, over Azmat's left shoulder, coming slowly toward the healer and his assistants, ending on a close-up of Eduardo praying to Saint Cyprian.

The healer and assistants confer, speaking in low voices. No, the patient's not cured yet. Azmat trembles. Eduardo speaks. "I see a car head for an open ruin. . . . A chasm opens. It goes in." He continues, enumerating and describing some of Azmat's problems, including his daughter's having "bad thoughts" and sleepless nights.

"All this has got to change," says Eduardo, decisively but gently. "But you're coming out of it . . . in great form. . . ." Juan and Alberto rise and walk toward Azmat. They touch his face and head with small clay vessels which they then lift to their noses, imbibing the liquid. They give a container to Azmat, who imbibes slowly, tipping his head back. He coughs. He wipes his nose.

An assistant rubs a staff down Azmat's body, first the front, then the sides, then the back. Azmat sniffs.

Eduardo, Juan, and Alberto again confer. "He's better, right?" says Eduardo in a quiet voice. "Tranquil," says one assistant. "He's complete," Eduardo remarks.

Eduardo approaches Azmat with a sword and a bottle. He sprays a mouthful of scented water, then stabs the sword in front, to the left, behind, and to the right of Azmat. Eduardo returns to his place behind the *mesa* and sits. He rattles. He looks pensive.

"All's going well now?" Eduardo asks.

Azmat nods his head.

"Your car?"

"It doesn't exist any more. . . ."

"And the bad luck has passed now," says Eduardo.

Azmat no longer stands. He is at rest in the sand, his legs under him, his hands on his knees. He seems to smile slightly. "I'm more tranquil," he says. We learn that after three sessions Azmat has returned to his job as a baker, he and his family are reunited, his daughter now is able to sleep, and the bad odors in the house have gone. The scene shifts to day. We see Eduardo at his work area. Whistling, he sculpts a figurine.

As is apparent in the film, the healer Eduardo Calderón combines his own philosophy, developed from varied experiences, with a cultural heritage from which he selects elements that are meaningful and useful to him and his clients. Douglas Sharon writes that "Eduardo's *curandero* lore is the expression of a profound system of abstract thought that rivals orthodox philosophy. For, in addition to embodying traditional beliefs and practices, it is grounded in personal experience. There is a lusty, earthy quality to Eduardo's system, which reflects a direct contact with nature and a realistic perception of the joys and sorrows of the human situation." The film presents the healer's role as that of a buffer between the modern and traditional, an adaptive mechanism for the *curandero*'s people in a rapidly changing world. Eclectic and idiosyncratic, Eduardo both draws upon and contributes to tradition.

As these works by Gladys-Marie Fry, Mark Azadovskii, Pamela Jones, Dorothy Eggan, and Douglas Sharon reveal, studies which illustrate ways that folklore affects and is affected by the life experiences of particular individuals describe and analyze correlations between biographical facts and the nature of a person's folklore repertoire. As is apparent in the works of these five investigators, information about and insights into the part folklore plays in a person's life derive from researchers' observations, documentation, and/or analyses of specific events in the lives of individuals during which folklore is in focus.

By searching the historical record on slave-made quilts and documents containing information about Harriet Powers, Gladys-Marie Fry learned about the part quilting played in one person's life. In this way, Fry came to understand how Powers drew on an African heritage, American experiences, and subject matter of special interest to her from vivid Sunday sermons and dramatic oral accounts of striking natural phenomena and of individuals' reactions to them.

Mark Azadovskii recorded 26 *Märchen* from Vinokurova, meaning that on at least 26 occasions she assumed the storyteller's role and he the audience member's role, with narrating being the communicative mode through which the two interacted each of those times. Azadovskii's statistical statements about the repetitiveness with which certain themes occurred in Vinokurova's taletelling—and his descriptions of the ways she regularly began her narrating, developed the action, and portrayed characters—have their bases in his participation in, and observation and documentation of, at least 26 distinctive events.

Pamela Jones developed her sense of the ways the La Llorona legend is personalized by observing and contrasting different individuals' tellings of the story. These included the ways the narrators she interacted with behaved verbally and nonverbally and how what they told her and did so correlated with what she already knew about their life histories because of her occupation and experiences with them.

Sam was both participant in and documenter of the 310 dreams he recorded over a 16-year period. Dorothy Eggan derived her insights into the way Sam internalized and personalized Hopi mythology by studying the written records he made rather than by listening to him recount his dreams at first hand. Yet she obviously knew Sam (and Hopi culture) well; and, one can infer, she and Sam discussed his written dream accounts, giving her insight into his perceptions of and responses to those altered-state-of-consciousness experiences.

Douglas Sharon not only interviewed Eduardo and observed the healer at work on many occasions during a four-year period. He also participated as Eduardo's helper and apprentice in three 1970 curing sessions, carrying out a variety of prescribed tasks, including infusing the hallucinogenic substance made from the San Pedro cactus.[11] He knew his research subject well and was able to observe, query, and work with him and document his behavior on multiple occasions and in various ways.

Studying folklore in biographical context, then, requires a researcher to amass and analyze a considerable amount of information about some other person(s). When possible, a researcher obtains the needed information by observing and interacting directly with the individual(s) being studied. But records of all kinds supplement and often must serve as substitutes for firsthand information. Such research entails and facilitates the investigator's conceptualizing and comprehending folklore examples in terms of the experiences and events of which they are both integral and focal aspects.

Folklore as Event

Folklore can be said to "exist" because human beings continuously create stories, songs, proverbs, riddles, games, rituals, etc., and because they generate anew on multiple occasions selected examples of such phenomena through their actions and interactions. Furthermore, the nature of each of the multiple tellings of the same story, singings of the same song, utterings of the same proverb, posings and answerings of the same riddle, playings of the same game, enactings of the same ritual, etc., is determined by such variables as the identities and behaviors of the participants and the settings in which, circumstances under which, and reasons why each occurs. Hence, generating a folklore example anew is always eventful because it is a unique experience. Therefore, studies of folklore examples in terms of specific events of which they are integral and focal aspects provide additional insights into the ways folklore serves as a personal resource.

A lengthy essay by Barbara Kirshenblatt-Gimblett on a parable in context focuses on an individual's use of a traditional narrative to try to dissipate tensions in a family when a dispute arose between husband and wife. In Kirshenblatt-Gimblett's words, it examines "how one performer actually uses a particular tale on a specific occasion." The decision to narrate, the choice of narrative, and the timing of narrating depended on the narrator's inferences about what was needed, appropriate, and timely in the particular circumstances; and she acted accordingly.[12]

Dvora Katz, the individual who told the tale in question, was born in Brest-Litovsk, Poland, in 1915. She emigrated to Canada with her mother and siblings in 1929. Dvora's mother, who died in 1949, was her chief source of proverbs and parables. "In her role as mediator," writes Kirshenblatt-Gimblett, Dvora "frequently eases anxious social encounters by using about ten different parables and over one hundred proverbs which she remembers her mother applying to the foibles of human behavior in the course of conversations which took place more than twenty-five years ago." For example, Dvora learned from her mother and now tells a story identifiable as Tale Type 1682, *The Groom Teaches His Horse to Live without Food*. (The horse dies.) "In Dvora's version a stingy man is dismayed when, after weeks of reducing the horse's food, the animal is finally trained to eat nothing. 'Just when I taught him to live without food, he goes ahead and dies.' Dvora uses the parable," writes Kirshenblatt-Gimblett, "to comment on the self-defeating nature of stinginess." She also tells a story that has as its essence what folklorists identify as Motif J121, "Ungrateful son reproved by naive action of his own son: preparing for old age." A man gives his old father half a carpet to keep him warm. A child takes the other half and tells his father that he is keeping it for him when he grows old. "Dvora uses this story to comment on parent-child relationships," observes Kirshenblatt-Gimblett. "One of her favorite proverbs is 'one mother can take care of ten children but ten children cannot take care of one old mother.' In this parable, the treatment of the old man by his son exemplifies this maxim. Dvora also emphasizes how this parable shows the importance of setting a good example for your children."

Dvora described to the researcher the circumstances of family strife on one occasion on which she had told a parable. Her self-report of the performance is presented below (Box 9–4). Folklorists have recorded versions of this tale often from both Jewish and non-Jewish sources "and, in several collections, it appears as a framed narrative: the tale itself is embedded in a description of the social situation it reflects and in which it was reputedly told." Kirshenblatt-Gimblett cites the parable as containing the motif "Penitent in confession worries about little sins and belittles big ones." Dvora told the story to Ruth and Max, her sister-in-law and brother, during a tense moment culminating in an argument over Max's frequent breaking of promises to devote less time to work and more to the family. On this night he had come home too late to take the children to the movies, although he feigned not understanding why his wife wouldn't allow them to go.[13]

Through questioning Dvora on various occasions over several months, Kirshenblatt-Gimblett constructed a detailed case history of the event Dvora described, including her conception of alternative courses of action and how she chose among them. Hence, the researcher had as data "the informant's *performance*, her spontaneous and uninterrupted *report* about her performance, and her *answers* in interviews to questions about her performance."

Dvora explained in interviews how she had sized up the situation. Standing in the doorway, Dvora could see both Max and Ruth in the kitchen. Max stood near the head of the table, arguing with Ruth and asking Dvora, "Why doesn't she let the kids go [to the movies with me tonight]?" Ruth, with her back to Max, stood at the sink, washing dishes in angry silence. To Dvora, Max pleaded ignorance and innocence, repeating over and over that Ruth had strangely rejected his offer to take the family out that evening. Understanding precisely what was going on—that this was not the first time Max had refused to acknowledge prior transgressions—Dvora told the parable.

Dvora might have opted for another course of action. She could have taken Max's side and tried to convince the family to go to the movies. She might have told Max bluntly that he was in the wrong. Or she could tell a story.

Dvora might have told any funny tale as an attempt to introduce some levity, thereby (hopefully) easing tensions. She could have told the following humorous story, which in some respects is structurally similar to the parable that she did tell (Tale Type 2040, *The Climax of Horrors*):

> A wealthy nobleman goes on vacation and while he is away he phones back to the mansion to ask the servant how everything is going.

> The servant says, "Everything is great, only your favorite dog died."
> The master said, "How did that happen?"
> He said, "Well, he was trampled to death by the horses."
> The master said, "How did that happen?"
> The servant said, "Well, the horses stampeded when the barn caught fire."
> He said, "How did the fire start?"
> He said, "Well, they were burying your mother by candlelight when the barn caught fire."

"No, it doesn't apply," said Dvora when Kirshenblatt-Gimblett asked her about this tale as an alternate to the one she told. It does not apply, of course, because the situation described in the story and for which the tale is a parable differs. In the parable that Dvora told Max and Ruth, the parishioner attempts to redefine his offenses so as to minimize his guilt—which is, in Dvora's view, what Max was trying to do. Just like the story, the real-life situation involved the accumulation of offenses that built to the final act in this family drama. This is what Dvora sought to communicate to Max: that the impasse on this night had its causes in past events of which he should not pretend ignorance. Put into social interactional terms, each time Max broke a promise he precipitated an incident; the family expressed anger (challenge) and then Max made a new promise (offering) that the family accepted (acceptance), all of which constituted a ritual of corrective interchange in family negotiations.

Dvora did not confront Max directly, telling him that he was wrong, because "I don't think he was receptive to a lecture and for me to tell him. . . . He could give me many many reasons and it would, I think, it would just cause a lot of unpleasantness." In addition, "I didn't want to hurt him by emphasizing all these things. Neither would he be receptive, nor would he like it. It would only cause more guilt, as a result more anger and confused and emotional disturbance in him and then he wouldn't

BOX 9–4
"Penitent in Confession Worries about Little Sins and Belittles Big Ones"

DVORA: I have to tell you something and this was a true fact. Once I was at my brother's and the atmosphere was tense. My brother had promised the kids to take them to a show over and over again and he was busy in the office and he had no time. Are you listening?

AL: Yea.

DVORA: Next time. And he was busy and each time he made an appointment something else came up and the kids were disappointed. It was an afternoon show, a morning show. Nothing worked.

I come in and my sister-in-law, Ruth, was upset and the kids were crying and my brother says, "O.K." This was nine o'clock. "We can go to a show now." Nine o'clock nobody wants to go to a show. It was late and there was just no point. So I saw there was going to be a revolution because he couldn't understand why they can't go to a show. The kids realized that he should have gone when he made the promise to go so many times. Ruth felt that he was unfair and I thought at this point they need something to break the ice because the atmosphere was just too thick. So I says, "You know, this reminds me of a story."

No. My brother comes up and he says, "Dvora, tell me. Tell me what is wrong with a father wanting to take his children to a show? What have I done? Have I committed a crime? I want my children to go with me to a show. They all say I'm doing something wrong. What's wrong?"

So I says, "I'll tell you. It reminds me of a story my mother used to tell me."

A man once came to a rabbi to ask a *shayle* 'question regarding ritual purity,' forgiveness.

He says, "What is it? What did you do?"

He says, "I didn't wash . . . I didn't say the prayer before the meal."

He says, "How come?"

He says, "Because I didn't wash my hands."

He says, "Well, why didn't you wash your hands?"

He says, "Because I wasn't eating Jewish food."

He says, "How come you weren't eating Jewish food?"

"Because I was eating in a Gentile restaurant."

He says, "How come?"

"Because it was *Yonkiper* 'Yom Kippur,' the day of Atonement, most solemn Jewish holiday and fast day, when every man's fate for the coming year is said to be decided, and the Jewish restaurants were closed."

So this, I said, reminds me of my brother, "Why can't I take them to the show?" Here he had made so many promises and so many disappointments. He couldn't understand how come the kids didn't want to go to the show.[14]

function at all." Simply telling a funny story would have failed, too. No one was in the mood. To be effective, a story had to be humorous in order to ease tensions (and provide catharsis); but it also had to replicate what was actually happening and thereby clarify the situation.

Dvora told the parable as a definition of the situation, to pave the way for Max to make an offering to Ruth. The story presented an appropriate analogy. "In both the parable and the real life situation, the offenders make a similar mistake," writes Kirshenblatt-Gimblett. "They both distort the relationship between the final apparently trivial offenses and the entire backlog of offenses so as to make the final offense appear as a single instance, thereby making

Chart 1

[The family negotiates many corrective interchanges. Each time Max created an incident by breaking a promise, the family expressed anger (challenge) and Max made a new promise (offering) which the family accepted (acceptance). Max was relieved and grateful (thanks).]

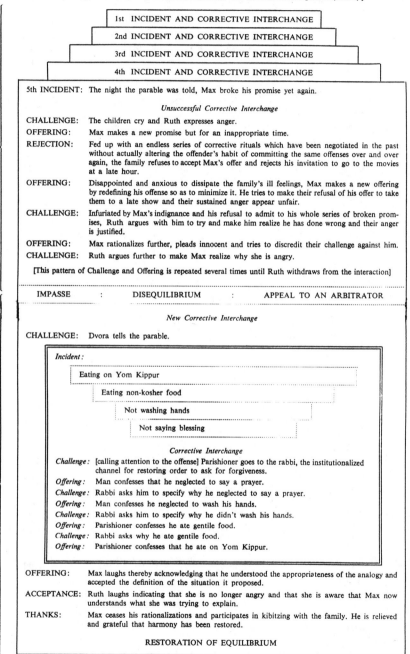

INCIDENT
AS
DEFINED
BY THE
PARABLE

| 1st INCIDENT AND CORRECTIVE INTERCHANGE |
| 2nd INCIDENT AND CORRECTIVE INTERCHANGE |
| 3rd INCIDENT AND CORRECTIVE INTERCHANGE |
| 4th INCIDENT AND CORRECTIVE INTERCHANGE |

5th INCIDENT: The night the parable was told, Max broke his promise yet again.

Unsuccessful Corrective Interchange

CHALLENGE: The children cry and Ruth expresses anger.

OFFERING: Max makes a new promise but for an inappropriate time.

REJECTION: Fed up with an endless series of corrective rituals which have been negotiated in the past without actually altering the offender's habit of committing the same offenses over and over again, the family refuses to accept Max's offer and rejects his invitation to go to the movies at a late hour.

OFFERING: Disappointed and anxious to dissipate the family's ill feelings, Max makes a new offering by redefining his offense so as to minimize it. He tries to make their refusal of his offer to take them to a late show and their sustained anger appear unfair.

CHALLENGE: Infuriated by Max's indignance and his refusal to admit to his whole series of broken promises, Ruth argues with him to try and make him realize he has done wrong and their anger is justified.

OFFERING: Max rationalizes further, pleads innocent and tries to discredit their challenge against him.

CHALLENGE: Ruth argues further to make Max realize why she is angry.

[This pattern of Challenge and Offering is repeated several times until Ruth withdraws from the interaction]

IMPASSE   :   DISEQUILIBRIUM   :   APPEAL TO AN ARBITRATOR

New Corrective Interchange

CHALLENGE: Dvora tells the parable.

CORRECTIVE
RITUAL

Incident:

Eating on Yom Kippur

Eating non-kosher food

Not washing hands

Not saying blessing

Corrective Interchange

Challenge: [calling attention to the offense] Parishioner goes to the rabbi, the institutionalized channel for restoring order to ask for forgiveness.

Offering: Man confesses that he neglected to say a prayer.

Challenge: Rabbi asks him to specify why he neglected to say a prayer.

Offering: Man confesses he neglected to wash his hands.

Challenge: Rabbi asks him to specify why he didn't wash his hands.

Offering: Parishioner confesses he ate gentile food.

Challenge: Rabbi asks why he ate gentile food.

Offering: Parishioner confesses that he ate on Yom Kippur.

OFFERING: Max laughs thereby acknowledging that he understood the appropriateness of the analogy and accepted the definition of the situation it proposed.

ACCEPTANCE: Ruth laughs indicating that she is no longer angry and that she is aware that Max now understands what she was trying to explain.

THANKS: Max ceases his rationalizations and participates in kibitzing with the family. He is relieved and grateful that harmony has been restored.

RESTORATION OF EQUILIBRIUM

Figure 9–8: A chart portraying the use of a parable to resolve family conflict (by permission of Mouton de Gruyter, a Division of Walter de Gruyter & Co.).

the trivial look significant and the significant look trivial."

Dvora chose to tell this parable in this situation at this particular moment in order to communicate her understanding of the source of tension, and to delineate the true nature and cause of conflict. Her points, writes Kirshenblatt-Gimblett, "were first, the mistake of thinking that the final offense, which was also the least serious, could be evaluated in its own right without any reference to preceding offenses; second, the opening social frame in which a guilty man confesses his sins in reverse order of their seriousness and occurrence; and third, the focus of the social interaction in the parable upon the repetition of 'challenge' and 'offering.'" Because of the aptness of its theme and appropriateness of its timing, Dvora's telling of a traditional parable helped resolve family conflict.

In his essay "The 'Pretty Language' of Yellowman," J. Barre Toelken also focuses on single storytellings, describing and analyzing one in considerable detail. He writes that during a severe winter he and others spent evenings sitting around a fire in the large hogan of Tsinaabaas Yazhi (Little Wagon) listening to the old Navaho tell stories.[15]

Toelken had lived among the Navaho on the Northern Reservation in southern Utah off and on for thirteen years, three of them "under the most intimate conditions" and for one year in Montezuma Canyon as an adopted member of the family of Little Wagon, who spoke no English. "A small [Navaho] family passing by on horseback had stopped for the night, according to the usual custom," writes Toelken. "Outside it had begun to snow lightly, and one of the travellers' children asked where snow came from." In answer, Little Wagon told a lengthy and detailed story about an ancestor who had found a piece of beautiful burning material, guarding it carefully for months until some spirits (ye'i) claimed it.

Asked if they would permit him to keep a piece of it, the spirits refused but offered to try to do something for him. Meanwhile, he had to perform several complicated tests of endurance. At last the spirits told him that because of his fine behavior they would throw the ashes from their fireplace down into Montezuma Canyon every year when they cleaned house. Sometimes they threw too much and other times they threw too little. Generally they kept their word, turning their attention to those in Montezuma Canyon. After a respectful silence following the completion of the narrating, the youth asked Little Wagon, "It snows in Blanding, too. Why is that?" The old man replied, "I don't know. You'll have to make up your own story for that."

Toelken at first assumed that the story had been composed for the occasion, but later encountered others who had heard a similar tale. He recalled that Little Wagon had commented that it was unfortunate that the boy did not understand stories; and through questioning of the old man, Toelken realized that Tsinaabaas Yazhi did not consider this an etiological story about how snow originated. Rather, writes Toelken, "if the story was 'about' anything it was about moral values, about the deportment of a young protagonist whose actions showed a properly reciprocal relationship between himself and nature." By approaching the story in terms of a traditional genre (origin stories), admits Toelken, he like the little boy had missed the point, "a fact which Little Wagon at once attributed to the deadly influences of white schooling."

Most research on the Navaho contains distortions, particularly because of the tendency for researchers to classify data from their point of view rather than the natives'. A second major area of distortion "lies in the Navaho view of information and how it may be transmitted," writes Toelken. "Sometimes an attitude may be communicated in a statement which is technically false but which uses humor as a vehicle." Aloofness may be conveyed by statements that imply the listener has missed the point of one's remarks. Other information must be requested four times for it to be revealed.

Toelken describes in detail an occasion on which one Navaho told a traditional tale about Coyote (Ma'i). Yellowman—Little Wagon's son-in-law, who lived in Blanding, Utah—almost nightly narrated to his family of thirteen children. The story has no formal title. Its plot is that with the aid of Skunk, Coyote plays dead so that he can kill and eat some prairie dogs. Toelken tape-recorded the story as Yellowman narrated to several children on the evening of December 19, 1966. Rather than giving just the text—the words of the story as transcribed from the audiotaped record— Toelken describes the narrator's actions and style in parentheses. He also indicates the audience's reactions in brackets. (See Box 9–5 for Toelken's transcription.)

Toelken's remarks about the performance and its implications cluster around the ways the narrator and audience members behaved as they interacted and some of the meaning(s) of the story inferred from the circumstances of performance and the nature of the interaction. In regard to audience, for example, Toelken notes in his transcription from the audiotape of the performance that the audience reacts at different points with "smiles and silent laughter," "quiet amusement, exchange of glances," "heavy breathing (to avoid open laughter)," "silent laughter, knowing looks," "open laughter, lasting three or four seconds," and "extended laughter, including Yellowman." According to Toelken, "the audience plays a central role" in Yellowman's "narrative style; without an audience, his tales are almost entirely lacking in the special intonations, changes in speed, pacing, and dramatic pauses which are so prominent in the specimen text given above." The drama of the narrating, and the

story itself, "emerges in response to the bona fide storytelling context."

Toelken also considers specifics of the narrator's performance style. Since many words and phrases used in telling the Coyote stories were unfamiliar to him from conversational Navaho, Toelken asked Yellowman if he used a special vocabulary when telling the tales. The narrator explained that "these were 'older' words and phrases, and that he used them because they were the vocabulary he had always heard used in the tales. But then he added with a smile a comment which I have taken to mean: 'They are beautifully old-fashioned.'" From asking them, Toelken learned that to Yellowman's children this vocabulary added a "valued sense of antiquity to the stories" and also "lent to the narratives a kind of pleasant humor," providing "a ready context for the humorous scenes within the story."

When Toelken inquired of Yellowman whether or not "he told the tale exactly the same way each time, he at first answered yes," perhaps thinking about the prototype tale that he had learned and that served as a model for his narrating. Comparison of audiotaped records of performances of the story on different occasions, however, reveal differences in wording each time because Yellowman "recomposes with each performance, simply working from his knowledge of what ought to happen in the story and from his facility with traditional words and phrases connected, in his view, with the business of narrating Ma'i stories."

As is apparent in the transcript, Yellowman starts his narrating about Coyote and Skunk by speaking in a factual, conversational tone with regular intonation and pronunciation and long pauses between sentences, "as if tired." He begins to nasalize vowels as he assumes the persona of Coyote. At one point, he pauses for four seconds between descriptions of events. He

BOX 9–5

Yellowman's Story about Coyote and Skunk

(style: slow, as with factual conversational prose; regular intonation and pronunciation; long pauses between sentences, as if tired) Ma'i was walking along once in a once-forested area named after a stick floating on the water. He began walking in the desert in this area, where there were many prairie dogs, and as he passed by them they called him mean names, but he ignored them. He was angry, even so, and it was noon by then, so he made a wish:

(slower, all vowels more nasalized) "I wish some clouds would form." He was thinking about killing these prairie dogs, so he wished for clouds, and there were clouds. [audience: smiles and silent laughter]

Then he said: "I wish I could have some rain."

He said: "I wish the ground to be damp enough to cool off my hot feet." So the rain came as he wished, and cooled off his feet.

"Now I want a little more, so the water will come up between my toes." [audience: quiet amusement, exchange of glances] Every time Ma'i wishes something it comes about.

(pause, four seconds) "Now I want the water to come up to my knees." When it reached his knees, he wanted it to be even deeper so that only a small part of his back would show. Then he said: "I wish the water would rise some more so that only the tips of my ears will show." [audience: amusement, heavy breathing (to avoid open laughter)] Now he began to float. Then he said: "I wish I could float until I come to a stop along with some flood debris near the middle of the prairie dogs' area." [audience: quiet laughter] So that happened.

The pile of debris was made up of sticks, pine cones, and other fragments of vegetation, and mud. When he came floating to that place it had stopped raining. Ma'i lay there for a long while, pretending he was dead.

Skunk was on his way by that place to get some water [audience: silent laughter, knowing looks] Ma'i was pretending he was drowned [audience: quiet amusement] and Skunk didn't know he was there. [audience: open laughter; two girls now giggling almost constantly throughout the rest of this scene] Skunk had a dipper, and put it into the water.

"Shilna'ash [the equivalent in English of "old buddy"]." (Yellowman speaking very nasally, through side of mouth, lips unmoving and eyes closed, in imitation of Ma'i) [audience: open laughter, lasting three or four seconds].

Skunk turned around in fright, but he didn't see anyone. So he put his dipper in the water again, and Ma'i said:

"Shilna'ash." (nasal, eyes closed, mouth unmoving, as before) [audience: quiet laughter] He said it four times, and on the fourth time Skunk came to that place where Ma'i was lying. (using normal intonation)

(still nasal, lips unmoving, eyes closed, for Ma'i's speech) "Go back to the village and tell the prairie dogs that you were on your way to get water and you came across the body of a dead coyote that got drowned, shilna-ash. Tell them 'It looks to me like he's been there for some time because it looks rotten and wormy.' Before you go there, get some t'loh ts'osi [a desert grass whose heads resemble small, twisted green worms] and stick some under my arms, in my nose, in the corners of my mouth [audience: mild amusement], in my ears [audience: quiet laughter], in the joints of my legs; tell them how rotten I look. Tell them, 'He must have come down the wash and got drowned.' [audience: quiet laughter] And one last thing before you go there: go make some clubs, four of them, and put them under me. Tell them: 'Since the coyote is dead, why don't we go over there where he is and celebrate?' When they get here, have them dance around in a circle. Keep one of the clubs, and when the prairie dogs beat me with their clubs, you do it, too. When they start dancing and beating, don't forget to tell them to take it easy on me; beat me slowly and not too hard,' he said. [audience: laughter]

(normal tone) So Skunk went back to the prairie dogs' village and told the whole story as he was directed by Ma'i. He said: "I was just now on my way to get water and I came across the body of a dead coyote that got drowned. It looks to me like he's been there a long time because it looks rotten and full of worms. He must have come down the wash and got drowned. Why don't we go over there and have a ceremonial to celebrate his death?"

(normal conversational tone, perhaps a bit more slowly pronounced than usual) At the village there were also jackrabbits, cottontails, ground squirrels, and other small animals that Ma'i usually likes to eat. They couldn't believe it. They said: (nasal, high pitch) "Is it really true?" "Is it true?" "Is it true?" "I don't know; why doesn't someone besides Skunk go over there and see?" (back to regular discourse, somewhat nasalized) So the jackrabbit went over to where Ma'i was and came back and told them it was all true. Then the cottontail went over there and came back and said it was all true. Then one of the prairie dogs went over there and came back and said: "It's true." On the fourth time they all went over there and gathered around Ma'i to celebrate. They began to dance around him; we don't know exactly what they were singing, but the noise sounded like they were all saying "Ma'i is dead" as they danced around and beat him slowly and gently. As they danced, more of them came along, and Skunk began to get ready to say what Ma'i had told him to say when he had said: "Don't forget to do all these things at this time, shilna'ash."

(nasal whine) Skunk said then: "Look! Way, way up there is a t'ajilgai [a special kind of bird] far above us." He said it four times, so the prairie dogs all looked up, and Skunk let out his scent [literally, "urine"] into the air and it came down right into their eyes. [audience: laughter] So the prairie dogs were fooled and they were busy rubbing their eyes.

Then Ma'i jumped up and said: "How dare you say I'm dead?" [audience: laughter] He grabbed the clubs under him and began to club the prairie dogs. [audience: laughter and giggling] He clubbed all the prairie dogs to death. [audience: extended laughter, including Yellowman (for the first time)]

(pause, after laughter, about four seconds)

"Let's start roasting the prairie dogs, shilna'ash. You dig out a place in the sand." So Skunk began to dig a place, and build a fire, and he put the prairie dogs in to cook.

"Let's have a race, shilna'ash. Whoever gets back first can have all the fat prairie dogs." [audience: laughter]

(nasal whine) "No, I don't want to. My legs aren't long enough."

But Ma'i insisted. Skunk complained that he couldn't run as fast as Ma'i, so Ma'i gave him a head start. So Skunk ran off. Skunk ran beyond a hill and hid under a rock [Yellowman uses vowel sound *aa* extensively]. Soon after that, Ma'i passed by, running as fast as he could. He had tied a burning stick to his tail so as to make lots of smoke. [audience: laughter, including Yellowman]

Skunk watched until Ma'i had gone completely out of sight, and then went back to where the prairie dogs were buried. (from this point on until midway in the next scene, the narration gets faster, with pacing related entirely to audience reaction, much in the manner of a 'stand-up' comedian in a night club) He dug up all but the four skinniest prairie dogs and took them up onto a nearby ledge. [laughter] And while he was eating he watched for Ma'i, who soon came running as fast as he could. [laughter, including Yellowman] He wanted to make a good finish to show how fast he was, so he came running very rapidly and jumped right over the fire. [laughter, including Yellowman]

"Whew!!" he said. [peak laughter, much extended, including Yellowman] "Shilna'ash, the poor old man with the stinking urine is still coming along." [extended laughter] Even though he was anxious to begin eating, he didn't want to look greedy, so he paced back and forth in the shade making lots of footprints which would show he had waited for a long time. [laughter, including Yellowman]

Then Ma'i went to the fire and began digging with a stick to find the prairie dogs. He found a tail from one of the small prairie dogs and pulled on it. "Oh oh, the tail must have come loose from being overdone." [laughter] He took out the skinny carcass and threw it over his shoulder toward the east, and said: "There will be fatter ones than this." [laughter]

Now, digging around with the stick, he came onto the second skinny prairie dog and threw it toward the south, and said: "There will be fatter ones here."

(far more slowly, almost drowsily) He came to the third one and threw it toward the west, and the fourth one he threw toward the north. Then he dug around and around with the stick and couldn't find anything. He walked around and around and finally decided to go find those skinny ones he threw away. So he ate them after all. [quiet laughter]

Then he started looking for footprints [quiet laughter] After a long time he found some tracks leading away from the roasting area to the rock ledge. He walked back and forth along this line several times without seeing Skunk, until Skunk dropped a small bone down from the ledge. [quiet laughter]

Ma'i looked up. (nasal whine) "Shilna'ash, could I have some of that meat given back to me? [quiet laughter] He was begging, with his eyes looking upward. [laughter, including Yellowman]

(pause, seven seconds)

(admonishing tone, very slowly delivered) "Certainly not," said Skunk to the begging coyote. He finally dropped some bones down and Ma'i gnawed on them. [moderate laughter]

(pause, about five seconds)

That's what they say.[16]

speaks very nasally, through the side of his mouth, "lips unmoving and eyes closed, in imitation of Ma'i." He talks in a normal tone to describe Skunk's actions. He employs a nasal whine to convey Skunk's not wanting to race with Coyote. When Coyote begs Skunk for meat, Yellowman uses an "admonishing tone, very slowly delivered" as he has Skunk reply, "Certainly not."

Most noticeable in Yellowman's delivery, writes Toelken, "are the various recitational devices" like those mentioned in the transcript.

These include a dramatic intonation put on by the narrator as he takes the parts of central characters; a kind of special nasalized delivery of all vowel sounds throughout the story (this may be a part of the "archaism" effect); a variation in phrasing, in which the opening and closing of the story are delivered quite slowly while the climax is in a passage of rapid delivery; the use of appropriate gestures, facial expressions, and body positions in taking the parts of various central characters; and, very importantly, a kind of contractual interaction which is developed by the narrator with his audience which tends to direct these other aspects of recitation and which seems based in their mutual recognition of the story type, its central characters and their importance in the Navaho world view, and their expectation that this particular performance will cause important ideas to come alive in exciting ways.

Three scenes in the story, for example, contain "an unusual overabundance of the nasal *aa* in the words chosen by the narrator," writes Toelken. Occurring naturally in several Navaho words and expressions, it is the equivalent in English of someone saying, "That's correct," or "I agree," or "Yes, I understand." The concentration of words containing this sound appears in passages in Yellowman's story where Coyote illustrates (by observing or not observing them) "some Navaho tabu, in passages where truth is being discussed, and in passages which seem to contain some key action in the development of the story line," observes Toelken. At one level, "we have a morpheme used as part of a word which communicates a particular meaning." In addition, "we have on the 'moral' (textural) level a morpheme used to suggest certainty, reliability, 'truth' within the local context." Finally, through "a subliminal chant that implies, 'Yes, there it is, now we know, this is what they say,' we are perceiving simultaneously the irony of the situation—which in nearly every case is based on our recognition that things are not as the story characters see them"; that "Coyote is not dead, a race is not really in progress (and betrayal is at hand), and the gluttonous Coyote gets finally four skinny and sandy prairie dogs." In sum, writes Toelken, "The morpheme, nasal *aa*, would seem to constitute a usable, understandable textural formula which establishes a bridge between story and meaning by helping to create irony."

Toelken also seeks to infer meanings in the telling of this story. "Does Yellowman consider these to be chiefly children's stories?" No, despite his spending more time telling them to his own children than to anyone else. Stories about Coyote's role in creation and in the fortunes of human beings and animals are told in serious adult circumstances.

"Why, then, if Coyote is such an important mythic character (whose name must not even be mentioned in the summer months), does Yellowman tell such funny stories about him?" asks Toelken.

"They are not funny stories," replies Yellowman.

"Why does everyone laugh then?"

"They are laughing at the way Ma'i does things, and at the way the story is told," responds Yellowman. "Many things about the story are funny, but the story is not funny."

"Why tell the stories?"

"If my children hear the stories, they will grow up to be good people; if they don't hear them, they will turn out to be bad."

"Why tell them to adults?"

"Through the stories everything is made possible," Yellowman remarks.

"Why does Coyote do all those things, foolish on one occasion, good on another, terrible on another?"

"If he did not do all those things, then those things would not be possible in the world," muses Yellowman.

To Yellowman, then, Toelken infers, Coyote appears less a trickster and more "an enabler whose actions, good or bad, bring certain ideas and actions into the field of possibility, a model who symbolizes abstractions in terms of real entities." On another storytelling occasion, for instance, Yellowman told about Coyote getting his eyes caught on a tree branch during a game and replacing them with amber pitch balls, ending the account by explaining "That's how Ma'i got his yellow eyes." Toelken pursued the question of how coyotes could see if their eyes were made of amber balls. "Yellowman explained patiently that the tale allows us to envision the possibility of such things as eye disease, injury, or blindness; it has nothing to do with coyotes in general; and Ma'i himself may or may not have amber eyes, but since he can do anything he wants to, the question is irrelevant—he has eyes and he sees, period."

On the basis of these and similar comments by Yellowman, Toelken infers "that Coyote tales are not simply entertainment; that they are phrased consciously in such a way as to construct an interesting surface plot which can act as entryway to a more subtle and far more important area of consideration; that the telling of, and listening to, Coyote stories is a serious business with serious consequences." Apparently, "Yellowman sees the Coyote stories not as narratives"—simply stories or texts—"but as dramatic presentations performed within certain cultural contexts for moral and philosophical reasons." Story elements such as the sequence of fours are loaded with traditional associations for a Navaho audience. The frequency of broken customs and transgressed traditions in the stories bear great interpretative weight. Admitting to fatigue or hunger is a sign of weakness, begging help from someone of lesser talents is ridiculous, begging food is contemptible; and all produce laughter in the audience.

Yellowman's tales contain humor as well as references to norms and traditions against which Coyote's morality may be judged. The humor prevents lagging interest, of course, "but far beyond that it functions as a way of directing the responses of the audience vis à vis significant moral factors," writes Toelken. "Causing children to laugh at an action because it is thought to be weak, stupid, or excessive is to order their moral assessment of it without recourse to open explanation or didacticism." One can take vicarious pleasure in the breaking of norms of behavior and simultaneously enjoy direct pleasure in moral superiority. "Why, though, would one want to feel superior to one of their own deities?"

Toelken refers to the work of Paul Radin and others who have shown that there is something psychologically compelling about Trickster. Health and order loom large in Navaho religious ideas. A common way of envisioning evil is to describe it as the absence of order. In stories told by Yellowman and other Navaho, Coyote may appear as undependable, amusing, cowardly, sneaky, skulking, tricky, exasperating, shrewd, obstinate, lascivious, dishonest, disloyal, or sacrilegious, among other qualities. Toelken hypothesizes that "Yellowman sees Coyote as an important entity in his religious views precisely because he is not ordered. He, unlike all others, experiences everything; he is, in brief, the exponent of all possibilities." Based on Yellowman's comments and his way of narrating, it seems that Coyote is "a symbol of that chaotic Everything within which man's rituals have created an order for survival." Human beings, in ordering their lives, utilize "certain devices to help conceive of order—in this case stories which dramatize the absence of it," contends Toelken.

Through their detailed documentation of a single storytelling, precise questioning of a narrator, and multifaceted analysis of an event, Kirshenblatt-Gimblett and Toelken are able to better comprehend, and enable their readers to understand, what makes storytelling in general and one kind of story in particular personally and situationally meaningful. Furthermore, these two studies reveal how documentation and analysis of single folklore-focused events can provide data and insights that have broad relevance and applicability. In Kirshenblatt-Gimblett's study, for example, Dvora's decision that telling a story would be the best way to defuse a tense family situation, and her choice of the tale she told over others in her repertoire, involve judgments about the timeliness of and appropriateness in storytelling, matters that are relevant whenever anyone assumes the narrator's role.[17] Similarly, Toelken's conclusions that the meaning of Yellowman's Coyote and Skunk story is conveyed through such aspects of the narrator's behavior as the kinds of words he speaks and the way he utters them—that is, through what Toelken calls *mode* and *texture* and not merely through plot—illustrates that there is more to storytelling than the event(s) a narrator portrays, and that focusing solely on those events may lead one to misleading or erroneous conclusions.

Other studies of single folklore-focused events include those that document and explain similarities and differences in the behaviors of particular individuals when they sing the same song or tell the same story on two or more occasions. For example, James Porter analyzed nine documented singings by Scotswoman Jeannie Robertson between the years 1953 and 1960 of the traditional ballad "My Son David" (more commonly known to folklorists as "Edward").[18] Porter concludes that the nine performances reveal three diachronic or evolutionary stages in Robertson's singing of the song.

Between the years 1953 and 1955, when Robertson was in her mid–40s and was just becoming well known (stage 1), the "individual situations [in which she sang the ballad] . . . do not appear to have affected the structure of her performance to any appreciable degree," even though the setting varied "from her own modest house" to a hall at which there was "a larger audience." During this stage, Robertson's "concept of the song was still largely the one she had formed in learning it from her mother at

Figure 9–9: Scottish singer Jeannie Robertson, April 1959 (photo by Ian Whitaker, courtesy School of Scottish Studies).

around the age of nine." She made "no attempt to 'perform' the song" but instead delivered it impersonally. Porter states that "her ego does not intrude in the sense of aiming at a personal expressiveness." Furthermore, "The tempo is fairly brisk (average duration: 3'32"), the melodic formulas moderately decorated, but the text is fluid," varying from eight to eleven stanzas. "Tonality and mode are both stable," Porter indicates, and "the pitch level . . . is E-flat, D, and F."

A single performance in 1958 constitutes stage 2—when Robertson sang the song "at the inaugural meeting of the Edinburgh University Folksong Society." During this performance, the singer's "tempo is markedly slower (duration: 5'03"), she begins to breathe not only at the end of whole lines but also in the middle of the second and fourth lines to accommodate the expanding phrases." Moreover, "the decoration of the melodic formulas becomes more prolonged, and it is in this performance that we have the first concept of 'stable' text, namely [a song of] nine stanzas."

Stage 3 represents Robertson's "performance manner, from 1959 through 1960, and later." During this stage, according to Porter, Robertson became "more aware of an audience" wider than that of her home community. The singer's "sense of spatial projection was more acute," Porter reports; and she seemed "to be externalizing aspects of her personality which had remained hidden or under restraint before she was discovered." Robertson "began to see herself as a 'folk singer,' a 'performer,' and was partially conforming to her idea of what a 'folk singer' should be like." During stage 3 her tempo "slowed considerably (average duration 5'57"), she breaks the phrase by breathing in the middle of the second and fourth lines, while the melodic formulas have become very prolonged."

Based on his analysis of Jeannie Robertson's singing of "My Son David" on nine occasions, Porter constructed a "conceptual performance model" that represents "the concept of the identity of a single song sung under a variety of conditions and over a period of time by the same singer." He emphasizes the fact that the way Jeannie Robertson conceptualized the song changed with time "through [her] contact with new audiences," and that "the performance structures of the song are derived from a complex, deep structural level in the singer's mind." Porter indicates why such a model is useful and what broader implications studies of multiple singings of the same song by the same person have:

> While it is clear that ballad singers memorize rather than improvise their material, nevertheless the performance situation, the audience, or lack of one, and the disposition and response of the singer can modify recall of

words and music so that the singing of a ballad cannot be viewed simply as an act in which a text (understood to mean a "story") is set in motion by a singer with a tune, but as a complex, existential process in which units of both cognitive and affective experience are embedded.

In noting that the behavior of ballad singers such as Jeannie Robertson is affected by "the performance situation, the audience, or lack of one, and the disposition and response of the singer," James Porter states facts that are true not just for ballad singers, but for anyone who interacts at first hand with another or others by assuming a communicative role such as singer, narrator, musician, or dancer.[19] Mutual stimulation and response are essential to and inevitable in such communicative-role-based interacting.

Precisely how coparticipants in such events stimulate and respond to each other is determined partly in advance (by enculturation and convention), but largely as the event is being generated, and hence while it is in progress. A person cast in the narrator's role may make "a long story short," for example, if he or she judges audience responses to be negative. By contrast, judging oneself to "have the audience in the palm of one's hand" may lead one to narrate at length and in detail. Audience responses, then, not only serve as feedback to a performer, but they also stimulate him or her to make decisions about how to behave as he or she continues to narrate, sing, make music, dance, etc.

Works that document and analyze the ways coparticipants in folklore-focused events stimulate and respond to each other reveal that audience behaviors are not extraneous to, but rather integral aspects of, these events. In the study discussed above, Toelken contrasts Yellowman's behavior when he told the Coyote and Skunk story to his children and when he told the same tale "when no children were present." Toelken

Figure 9–10: Storytelling after the day's work is done at the L. S. Ranch, near Tascosa, Texas, 1908 (LC S59–110, photo by Erwin E. Smith, courtesy the Erwin E. Smith Collection of the Library of Congress on deposit at the Amon Carter Museum, Fort Worth, Texas).

states that there were notable differences, for without an audience, Yellowman's stories were "almost entirely lacking in the special intonations, changes in speed, pacing, and dramatic pauses" prominent when an audience was present. Moreover, "speaking in solitude to a tape-recorder, Yellowman gives only a rather full synopsis of characters and incidents," reports Toelken, for "the narrative drama, far from being memorized, emerges in response to the bona fide storytelling context."

Audience members' perceptible behaviors are often simply overt manifestations of their reactions to stimulation. This is the case, for instance, when individuals laugh because of what a storyteller portrays and/or the way he or she does so (as was the case with Yellowman's children, for example). But audience responses may also be more obviously participatory in nature and intent. Daniel J. Crowley reports that during tellings of tales called "old-stories" in the Bahamas, audience members frequently join in on or complete the singing of a song that a storyteller sings as an integral part of her or his narrating; and audience members shout the expletive "Ehhh!" or "Ayyy!" in

response to a storyteller's calling out "Bunday!" during a pause in his or her narrating to indicate that they are paying attention and want the performer to continue.[20]

Among the Mende people of Sierra Leone, according to Donald Cosentino, tellers of stories called *dɔmɛisia* often instruct their audiences in the course of narrating to say or sing certain words on cue (e.g., "Light the fire, light it"; "Jo jajani jo / Nafoe Nafoe"). Audience members also comment spontaneously and often judgmentally on what a narrator is portraying; and they sometimes ask questions about the story characters and their actions.[21] (See Box 9–6 for Cosentino's transcription of one storytelling that indicates the part the audience plays in the narrating.) In studying the telling of stories called *yishima* while living among the Chokwe people of Zaire, Rachel Fretz discovered that audience members sometimes speak aloud to story characters as narrators portray their actions, often giving a character advice or warning him or her of impending danger.[22] During a chief's telling of a story about an antelope that appears mysteriously to rock and quiet the crying baby of a woman who is working nearby in the fields, for instance, "women in the audience advised the wife not to tell her hunter husband about the antelope." But the wife does so; and the husband sneaks up on and shoots at the antelope, which then disappears, taking the child with it. Women in the audience "begged the antelope to return the kidnapped child to her," Fretz reports; and when the narrator states that a healer is called in to help, the women in the audience "warned the villagers [in the story] not to touch the dangerous medicine prepared by the healer to bring back the child." Such research findings illustrate the varied ways that audience members coparticipate in folklore-focused events and why an awareness and understanding of audience behavior are crucial to an understanding and appreciation of the part folklore plays in individuals' lives.

Feedback comes not just from others, but also from self. One responds to one's own, as well as to others', behavior while singing, dancing, making music, narrating, etc.; and one is aware of and assesses self- as well as externally or other-generated feedback and makes decisions about how to behave based on those assessments as well. The narrator who begins laughing before delivering the punchline of the joke he or she is telling, or who breaks down and cries for no externally caused reason while telling a tale, does so because he or she reacts to what he or she perceptualizes as he or she narrates. MacEdward Leach reports one such experience when he was conducting fieldwork in Newfoundland. While a middle-aged woman was singing him a song and telling him the story of the "Rose of Branch," about a fishing boat that was rammed and sunk by a larger vessel, "tears came to her eyes and she announced that she could not go on." Leach persuaded her to finish, however; and when he asked her later if she had cried because a member of her family had lost his life in the accident,

the woman replied, "Oh, no. . . . It happened a hundred years ago, but I always think of the mothers and wives of those poor men aboard the fishing boat, all of whom perished."[23]

A storyteller's assessment of audience- or self-feedback may also motivate him or her to digress in order, for example, to eliminate a lack of understanding suggested by an audience member's furrowed brow, shaking head, or perplexedly uttered "Huh?" During a storytelling that Robert A. Georges documented, narrator George Emmanual told the tale of a king who ordered all elderly people 65 and over to be killed. One young man could not let this happen to his father. Deciding to hide the old man instead, the son "put him in a kind of pottery," stated the narrator. Aware from feedback that his audience did not understand, Emmanual immediately digressed to explain: "We have in Greece these great big potteries that we put our cheese and our oil and so forth in. So he put him in there." After several months had passed, Emmanual continued, the king gave "another order—to make a rope out of sand—in other words, to use sand as the material to make a rope." Such digressing was common during Emmanual's telling of his story, for he frequently felt the need, because of audience- and/or self-feedback, to clarify what he was portraying by explaining, restating, or exemplifying what he had said. In another storytelling Georges analyzed, 222 out of the 468 words narrator John Gonatos spoke were digressive (47%, as compared with 28% in Emmanual's case). Gonatos sometimes digressed to clarify—but more often to contextualize, supplement, and comment on—the events he was characterizing, thereby instructing the sole audience member (Georges) about Greek culture and displaying his expertise about sponge fishing, the industry in which he worked.[24] (See Box 9–7 for a transcription of Gonatos's storytelling.) As these examples suggest,

BOX 9-6
The Rope Dancer's Trick: A Dɔmɛi from the Mende of Sierra Leone

Date: February 25, 1974
Time: About 9:30 P.M.
Place: Verandah of the Blasse compound. Njɛi Woman quarter, Mattru, Tikonko
    Chiefdom, Southern Province, Sierra Leone
Performer: Aminata Blasse, a woman about 40 years old, a farmer
Audience: Two adult men and one adult woman
AMINATA: Here is one fellow, a boy. He was a rope dancer. He continued going around
    until he reached this town. He reached this town which was like the one we're in
    now. This town I'm telling you about had a name. But no one could say the town's
    name. You would have to stop half way through saying it. The town's name was
    Juwoya. If you went to that town and said Juwoya, if you, a stranger, merely said that
    they would beat you. That very night you would be looking for a way to get out.
Ah well, the young men told him. They said, "Since you've come to dance here. . ."
He said, "*Eeee*. . ."
"People must not display the town's name. If you show it, we'll beat you!"
He and these young men made a wager. He said to them now, "I'm going to show this
    town's name soon and you won't beat me."
They said "*Kooo*. . ." Then his friends added, "If you don't show the name. . ."
He said, "*Eeee*. . ."
"If you don't show the name, we won't beat you, but if you show the name, we will beat
    you."
So together they bet five pounds apiece. He said, "I'll show the town's name and you
    won't beat me." They repeated, "If you show the town's name, we'll beat you!"
When evening lowered, he staged the rope dance. The town's name was Juwoya, okay?
    The town's full name was Juwoya-vewo. A stranger could not show that name now,
    they would beat him. You could say Juwoya, but you could not say Juwoya-vewo.
    They would beat you! As soon as the evening lowered, and he proposed dancing,
    well, they built a big fire in the yard like this. Young men, girls, well they came now.
    They staged the dance. This is your part now, you say: *Ve-velo velo*.
AUDIENCE: *Ve-velo velo*.
AMINATA: *Juwoya*.
AUDIENCE: *Ve-velo velo*.
AMINATA: Now he was going to show the town's name. Now he wanted to arrive at
    this Juwoya-vewo. You see, now I'll be singing any town's name; whenever I reveal
    it, you sing the accompaniment, okay? You accompany me and I'll come to Juwoya-
    vewo. When I get to the name you won't know, okay?
AUDIENCE: *Ve-velo velo*.
AMINATA: *Mongerey*   AUDIENCE: *Velo-o*
              Senei hu   *Velo-o*
              Kenema.   *Velo-o*.
[Shouting and clapping of audience increases as Aminata sings out the name of towns
    in Sierra Leone. During the confusion engendered by the enthusiastic singing,
    Aminata sings out Juwoya-vewo and no one in the audience seems to catch it. The
    actual audience has now become the fictive audience.]

AUDIENCE: O this man can really sing sweetly!
AMINATA: *Sumbuya*   AUDIENCE: *Velo-o*
             Saloŋ   *Velo-o*
             Bo.   *Velo-o.*

That man continued doing that dance, and he continued showing that town's name. For
that reason, don't let a person come to town and say he'll do something and you
make a wager he won't. One shouldn't make a wager with such a person. You don't
know his own mind.

AUDIENCE: Even for these people who came here, they said they would do this, and
they couldn't prevent them.

AMINATA: No, they couldn't overcome them. They said they would do this and you
didn't know the steps they had planned to take.

If he's determined in his own heart now, even if he's telling lies, leave him alone. Let
him carry on.

AUDIENCE: All of them . . . Kenema and the others, *"velo-o."*

AMINATA: Yes, Kenema and all these towns in this country, he was showing their
names. He spent the whole night showing that name and they never caught him at
all. It came long ago, and it ended thus. So even if a person is lying, you should say
it's the truth, for tomorrow's sake.

AUDIENCE: That's the truth![25]

feedback and digressions are integral aspects of communicative-role-based interacting such as storytelling; and they provide insights into the ways individuals
make folklore personally meaningful for
other individuals.

Sometimes feedback from others and
self is so reinforcing that communicative
roles such as storyteller, singer, musician,
dancer, or craftsperson become avocational
or occupational identities as well for individuals. Although all human beings narrate, sing, dance, play, make objects, and so
on, some are notably adept, often so much
so that they come to identify themselves
and/or to be identified by others in terms of
these roles. In an analysis of traditional
taletelling, folklorist C. W. von Sydow calls
such individuals *active tradition bearers*,
noting that these persons—who are relatively few in number and "equipped with a
good memory, vivid imagination, and narrative powers"—are the principal tellers of

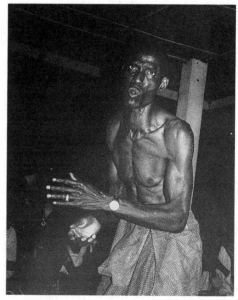

*Figure 9–11: Lele Gbomba, a premier Mende
storyteller in Sierra Leone, in performance, 1973
(photo by Rebecca Busselle, courtesy Donald
Cosentino).*

BOX 9-7
John Gonatos's Story

This is a little Greek joke that I heard on the sponge boats. Of course, like I say, you know, in the sponge boats, there are all seamen. It's like the United States Navy. You know, you hear little spicy things you wouldn't hear in a church or a house gathering.

So being that we were all men, one of the Greeks told a little spicy story regarding the olive, see—olives which grow in Greece. The olives that we eat in our salads. Well, if you notice a bottle of olives that you buy, you very seldom see the little stems, see, because when they pick the olives off of the tree, so I understand, never a stem comes off. One in a million you'll see with a stem. So it's very rare sight to see an olive with a small stem on it.

So this sponge fisherman went, kissed his wife good-bye, and went out in a sponge boat. Now, in the old country, when they go out—the fishermen go out in the Mediterranean Sea—they go across the Mediterranean to the coast of Africa. There's sponge all along those waters. So they go out and stay three or four months before they return home. Well, this time, this fisherman had engine trouble, see, or sail trouble, or some sort of trouble. And he returned back to shore. So while he was going home, his wife was not one of the true women—true wives. She had a boyfriend in the house. And you know, if that happens in a *Greek* home, you don't go to court and settle out and find judges and a jury. You just take the matter into your own hands.

So this woman, she had to immediately think up some excuse, see, to not let her husband come into the house. So he knocked at the door.

She says, "Oh, George! You've come back." In the meantime, she had *John* in there. He says, "Yes, Honey. I'm just returning because we had some trouble. Open the door." She says, "Before I open the door," she says, "I want you to prove to me that you love me."

He says, "Honey, I'll do anything you want me to."

She says, "I want you to go out and bring me one dozen olives with stems. If you can do that, then you will prove to me that you love me."

So he haul-tails out and goes in search to find an olive with a stem. It took him all night. That gave her time to make love to her—to her lover.

And John got out in time and all. And here came her husband back, and he brought her a dozen of those olives with stems on it.[26]

traditional tales and hence the ones responsible for their dissemination and perpetuation. "Most of those who have heard a tale told and are able to remember it remain passive carriers of tradition," von Sydow asserts; and their "importance for the continued life of the tale consists mainly in their interest in hearing it told again." Passive tradition bearers "point out the active carrier of tradition, the *traditor*, as a good narrator, and call upon him to narrate."[27] Von Sydow's distinction between active and passive tradition bearers applies not just to storytellers, but to the full range of communicative roles folklorists study, including singer, musician, dancer, riddler, punster, weaver, builder, and player.

That behaving with notable competency in a communicative role can be reinforced positively by self and/or others and result in a communicative role's becoming one of the multiple identities that collectively constitute an individual's social persona has been demonstrated throughout this book. As we noted in chapter 3, Helen Cordero's initial attempts to make pottery were unsuccessful. After following a relative's suggestion that she abandon that pursuit and try making clay figures instead, Cordero's doing so "was like a flower blooming," for "small frogs, birds, animals, and, eventually, 'little people' came to life in abundance."[28] Feedback from self was positive, for Cordero not only continued to make clay figurines, but also decided to display her creations publicly. Feedback from others was also immediate and positive. As we noted earlier, when Cordero showed her figures at a Santo Domingo feast day, folk art collector Alexander Girard not only bought what she had already produced, but encouraged her to make more and larger figures, which stimulated Cordero to create her first storyteller. As she continued to work at and perfect her craft and to receive positive reinforcement from self and others for her skill, Cordero's role as clay figure maker also became a way—and in some cases the principal way—for her to identify herself and to be identified by others. It also became a means for her to make a living and hence the principal way to identify herself and be identified occupationally.

The discussion earlier in this chapter of Eduardo Calderón's evolution as a healer similarly illustrates the way a communicative role is transformed into an occupational identity. Eduardo's most memorable early experience with traditional healing was through his interactions with Doña Laura, whose herbal remedies cured the seventeen-year-old when he was close to death because of a strange ailment. Afterwards, Eduardo notes in the film, "Little by little I got interested in curing." Eventually he became a *brujo*'s assistant and later worked with several *curanderos*. But it was only after he agreed to help, and succeeded in curing, a very ill cousin that Eduardo began to take healing seriously enough to devote increasing amounts of time and attention to it. By setting up a *mesa*, Eduardo

identified himself and came to be identified by others as a healer. It was then that he began performing divinations and conducting curing rituals for clients, one of several ways he was able to earn an income for himself and his family.

The process by which a role evolves into an identity is also vividly illustrated in Sharon Sherman's 1991 video *Spirits in Wood: The Chainsaw Art of Skip Armstrong*.[29] "I do what I do because I live in Oregon," one hears artist Armstrong say as the video begins and the viewer is oriented to the landscape and engaged by footage that captures the natural beauty of central Oregon. "I mean, Oregon is very much a vital part of this sculpt thing," Armstrong continues. "Wood is inherently Oregon. We have a wood culture here; chainsaws are a part of our everyday events."

Wood and chainsaws are indeed very much a part of Armstrong's life, one quickly learns. As we see him selecting an ordinary-looking log from the forest floor, taking it home in the bed of his pickup truck, and then deftly transforming it with chainsaw in hand into a recognizable object, Armstrong's voice-over details his evolution as a chainsaw wood sculptor.

His childhood home was filled with wood carvings from the Far East, Middle East, and other parts of the world, Armstrong reports. "There's a folk art wood carving that's alive and well out there, and I grew up with it," we hear Armstrong say. "My mother was an avid collector," he explains. "And I really credit her with my feeling for wood and wood carving to this day."

He studied and marveled at these family artifacts throughout his childhood, Armstrong asserts; and as he got older, he "kept comin' back" to them because "there was a real love there." He also had "a real appreciation for wildlife," which he associates with his growing up in California.

Armstrong was introduced to the

Figure 9–12: Oregon artist J. Chester "Skip" Armstrong using a router to create accents on an otter piece carved with a chain saw (photo by Susan Estep).

chainsaw while living in Vermont. He worked for farmers, clearing fields and cutting down trees. He reports that "one of the farmers down the road had an old chainsaw that he wasn't using. And I'd take that chainsaw, and I built barns with it, I cleared fields. It became my everyday companion. It was my ticket."

Armstrong returned to the West and got a job as a YMCA camp director. He "wanted to introduce the kids to wood-carving"; and while teaching the campers, he'd also teach himself. Armstrong used a chainsaw to cut down trees, from which the boys made totem poles. When the campers left at the end of the summer, he "just kept goin' at it—and that was the beginning." Armstrong left camp when it started to snow, taking with him the "boatload full of sculptures" that he'd made "in the couple of months I'd been there." When he "docked and unloaded these things into the parking lot," Armstrong recalls, "people gathered around, ooing and aahing, and then somebody popped the big question of how much. How much is that? How much is that? So," Armstrong continues, "I sold a number of them right there on the spot, and I ended up with $300 in my pocket. And I thought this was the new world—this, this would

work."

As the video proceeds, the viewer sees Armstrong transforming logs into animals, alone in the yard of his Sisters, Oregon, home, and before a group of onlookers at a craft fair in the town park. In his voice-overs he describes his craft. He notes that "the block is my initial core beginning. It has a certain height and width; it has a mass to it." He studies the rings, "the way the circular rings go in the log." He looks at the log from different angles. "I might daydream a bit about it, walk away. Then I start looking at the log a little differently. I start—in my mind, I try to see a little clearer that shape that I see might work in that piece." He seeks "just a beginning," a "way of getting into that log." Then he starts making cuts. "I have that one little seed idea, and as I start to cut and I start to really deal with the physical mass of that log, the idea starts taking shape." As he proceeds, "Each cut begets another cut. I see from that cut to this cut to this cut, oh, yeah, I need to go over here. I need to do this. This is now the piece." Armstrong states that "there's a discovery process going on. My idea in the head is random. It scatters out. It has no defining boundaries."

While listening to these words, the

viewer sees Armstrong doing precisely what he is describing—viewing a log, moving around it, pondering how to begin, making the initial cut, then accelerating his movements with the chainsaw and reshaping the log to turn it into the evolving form. As he finishes sculpting the piece before park onlookers, they applaud. "That's it," Armstrong announces. "Anybody know what it is?" "A bear!" the crowd responds with appreciation and enthusiasm.

Voice-over and visuals correlate throughout the video, revealing simultaneously through words and visuals more about how Armstrong conceptualizes and carries out his wood sculpting. "To me, the chainsaw applied to wood, which is a resistant media, just speeds up the creative and the doing process. There's no stale time there. It becomes a dance," and he would "like to be able to dance inside the log." Armstrong sees himself as part of a tradition, as one of a group of chainsaw wood-carvers who work throughout Oregon, Washington, and northern California. "I'm part of that," he says. "I'm branching off and going in a little different direction with it, but I'm certainly part of that bigger group."

While acknowledging the traditionality of his craft and seeing himself as one with other chainsaw wood-carvers, Armstrong also emphasizes his own distinctiveness and creativity. "Every piece is a unique piece," he asserts. "It isn't just the same repetitive process. . . . Even though it's still a horse, there's something about the randomness. You don't know exactly what that horse is gonna be in the end, which movement it's gonna have, what expressions it's gonna have." He continues, "I'm always willing to try the piece again and again and again just to see what will come of it. And I've noticed in the course of doing that over and over, the process grows—there's a growing process." He elaborates: "There's more animation, there's more life-likeness. There's a livingness comes out of it. That's

the beauty of doing wildlife," he continues. "There's so much variation and diversion. And I really see altogether the harmonic balance that it represents—not that there isn't violence and death everywhere. 'Eat or be eaten' seems to be the major thrust of this life plane. But taken as a whole, there's something beautifully harmonic about it."

Armstrong states that he feels like he's "part of the elemental forces that this world has in it," and that he's "tapped into those forces," including the wind and the waves. "There's an elemental earth force energy that's working through me," Armstrong asserts. "Taken together, there's a point where all of those things coalesce and you suddenly become an explosive force of energy that can basically do anything."

Armstrong's love of and way with wood are illustrated in other scenes and voice-over remarks throughout Sherman's video. We see his sprawling house (itself a "sculptural entity") with a fifty-foot-high section Armstrong added to enable him to have an unobstructed mountain view. The viewer sees and overhears him talking to owners of his sculptures—to a man who had to build a room to accommodate a massive mobile suspended from its cathedral ceiling, and to a couple whose house entrance is guarded and graced by twin dragons Armstrong carved intricately and imaginatively into the two massive wooden front doors. That his clients value his work and appreciate his skill is clear from their comments and expressions. That Armstrong is positively reinforced by their remarks and assessments is obvious from his looks and responses as well.

Like Helen Cordero and Eduardo Calderón, Skip Armstrong did not set out consciously to transform a communicative role into an occupational identity. He, like Cordero and Calderón, began by following an established tradition, incorporating folklore into his own life by patterning his behavior after that of other wood-carvers.

Yet he also contributes to the ongoing development and continuing variation of his traditional craft because of the way he has made it personally relevant and uniquely his own.

Conclusion

Studying folklore in terms of the life histories of specific individuals and single folklore-focused events in which particular individuals coparticipate amounts to more than merely making a choice among methodological options. It also constitutes recognition of the "context" in which folklore naturally occurs. For there is no story without the telling, no song without the singing, no tune without the music-making, no game without the playing, no proverb without the speaking, no dance without the dancing, and so on. By nature and definition, folklore "exists" only because it grows out of and manifests itself repeatedly in and through the behaviors of individual human beings. Once recorded in memory, in writing, on audiotape, and/or on film, a folklore example can be conceptualized and analyzed as a discrete phenomenon that is contextualizable in the alternative ways described and discussed throughout this book. But regardless of which one or combination of these contexts one studies folklore in terms of, it is its generation by some particular individual(s) at a given place and time and for some specific reason(s) that makes it meaningful for human beings and explains its reason for being.[30]

Notes

1. Gladys-Marie Fry, "Epilogue: Harriet Powers: Portrait of an African-American Quilter," *Stitched from the Soul: Slave Quilts from the Ante-Bellum South* (New York: Dutton Books, 1990), pp. 84–91 (reprinted from "Harriet Powers: Portrait of a Black Quilter," *Missing Pieces: Georgia Folk Art*

1770–1976 [Atlanta: Atlanta Historical Society, 1976]); quotes are from pp. 84, 85, 86, 89, 90, and 91. See also Pat Ferrero, Elaine Hedges, and Julie Silber, *Hearts and Hands: The Influence of Women and Quilts on American Society* (San Francisco: Quilt Digest Press, 1987), pp. 45–47; and Patsy Orlofsky and Myron Orlofsky, *Quilts in America* (New York: McGraw-Hill, 1974), p. 306. Pat Ferrero includes the astrological quilt in her one-hour film "Hearts and Hands" (available for purchase or rental from Ferrero Films, 371 Twenty-Ninth Street, San Francisco, CA 94131).

2. Other studies that reconstruct pertinent aspects of deceased individuals' lives in order to contextualize kinds or examples of folklore biographically include Richard M. Dorson's study of Abraham Lincoln as storyteller ("Oral Styles of American Folk Narrators," in Horace P. Beck, ed., *Folklore in Action: Essays for Discussion in Honor of MacEdward Leach*, Publications of the American Folklore Society, Bibliographical and Special Series 14, Philadelphia, 1962, pp. 92–98), and Edward D. Ives's book-length studies of folksongmakers and traditional singers Larry Gorman, Lawrence Doyle, and Joe Scott (*Larry Gorman: The Man Who Made the Songs* [Bloomington: Indiana University Press, 1964]; *Lawrence Doyle, The Farmer Poet of Prince Edward Island: A Study in Local Songmaking* [Orono, Maine: University of Maine Studies 92, 1971]; and *Joe Scott: The Woodsman Songmaker* [Urbana: University of Illinois Press, 1978]).

3. Mark Azadovskii, *Eine sibirische Märchenerzählerin*, Folklore Fellows Communications 68 (Helsinki, 1926); translated and published as *A Siberian Tale Teller*, trans. and ed. James R. Dow, Center for Intercultural Studies in Folklore and Ethnomusicology, Monograph Series 2 (Austin: University of Texas Press, 1974). Quotes are from the English translation, pp. 12, 13, 14, 21, 22, 23, 24, 25, 26, 29, 39, 41, 42, 43, 44, 45, and 46. Gil'ferding carried out his *byliny* fieldwork in the summer of 1871; N. Onchukov's *Northern Folktales* (in Russian) was published in 1908.

4. Azadovskii, pp. 36–37.

5. Pamela Jones, "'There Was a Woman': *La Llorona* in Oregon," *Western Folklore* 47 (1988):195–211. Quotes are from pp. 195, 197, 198, 203, 208, 210, and 211.

6. Bess Lomax Hawes, "La Llorona in Juvenile Hall," *Western Folklore* (1968):153–170. Quotes are from p. 164.

7. From Hawes, pp. 162–164.

8. Dorothy Eggan, "The Personal Use of Myth in Dreams," in Thomas A. Sebeok, ed., *Myth: A Symposium* (Bloomington: Indiana University Press, 1958), pp. 107–121. Quotes are from pp. 107, 109, 110, 111, 115, 116, 117, and 118.

9. Eggan, pp. 73–74.

10. *Eduardo the Healer* (1978, color, 16mm., 55 min., in Spanish with English subtitles) by Richard Cowan with research by Douglas G. Sharon. Distributed by Serious Business, 1145 Mandana Blvd., Oakland, California 94610. See also Douglas G. Sharon, "Eduardo the Healer," *Natural History* 81 (November 1972):32–47; "The Symbol System of a North Peruvian Shaman" (Ph.D. diss., University of California, Los Angeles, 1974); and *Wizard of the Four Winds: A Shaman's Story* (New York: Free Press, 1978). Quotes are from Sharon's 1972 essay, pp. 42 and 44. For selected studies of individuals who have adopted the role of folk artist, see Simon J. Bronner, *Chain Carvers: Old Men Crafting Meaning* (Lexington: University Press of Kentucky, 1985); Doris Francis, "Artistic Creations from the Work Years: The New York World of Work," in John Calagione, Doris Francis, and Daniel Nugent, eds., *Workers' Expressions: Beyond Accommodation and Resistance* (Albany: State University of New York Press, 1992), pp. 48–67; Amy Kitchener, *The Holiday Yards of Florencio Morales, "El hombre de las banderas"* (Jackson: University Press of Mississippi, 1994); Ysamur Flores-Pena and Roberta J. Evanchuk, *Santeria Garments and Altars: "Speaking without a Voice"* (Jackson: University Press of Mississippi, 1994); and John Michael Vlach, *Charlestown Blacksmith: The Work of Philip Simmons* (Athens: University of Georgia Press, 1981).

11. Douglas Sharon, "The San Pedro Cactus in Peruvian Folk Healing," in Peter T. Furst, ed., *Flesh of the Gods: The Ritual Use of Hallucinogens* (New York: Praeger Publishers, 1972), pp. 114–135.

12. Barbara Kirshenblatt-Gimblett, "A Parable in Context: A Social Interactional Analysis of Storytelling Performance," in Dan Ben-Amos and Kenneth S. Goldstein, eds., *Folklore: Performance and Communication* (The Hague: Mouton, 1975), pp. 105–130. Quotes are from pp. 106, 108, 111, 114, 117, 126, and 129.

13. See D. P. Rotunda, *Motif-Index of the Italian Novella in Prose* (Bloomington: Indiana University Publications, Folklore series: no. 2, 1942), which indexes the principal motif in this story and identifies it as U11.1.1.2, "Penitent in confession worries about little sins and belittles big ones."

14. From Kirshenblatt-Gimblett, pp. 109–110.

15. J. Barre Toelken, "The 'Pretty Language' of Yellowman: Genre, Mode, and Texture in Navaho Coyote Narratives," *Genre* 2 (1969):211–235, reprinted as "The 'Pretty Languages' [*sic*] of Yellowman: Genre, Mode, and Texture in Navaho Coyote Narratives," in Dan Ben-Amos, ed., *Folklore Genres* (Austin: University of Texas Press, 1976), pp. 146–170. Quotes are from the version in *Genre*, pp. 212–213, 214, 216, 218, 219, 220, 221, 222, 224–225, 226, 228–229, and 230–231. Toelken later retranslated Yellowman's storytelling in poetic form, with the assistance of Navaho Orville Tacheeni Scott, and modified some of the interpretive assertions made in the version of the essay we characterize in this work. See Barre Toelken and Tacheeni Scott, "Poetic Retranslation and the 'Pretty Languages' of Yellowman," in Karl Kroeber, comp. and ed., *Traditional Literatures of the American Indian: Texts and Interpretations* (Lincoln: University of Nebraska Press, 1981), pp. 65–116.

16. From Toelken, pp. 215–219.

17. For further discussion of this point, see Robert A. Georges, "Timeliness and Appropriateness in Personal Experience Narrating," *Western Folklore* 46 (1987):115–120.

18. James Porter, "Jeannie Robertson's *My Son David:* A Conceptual Performance Model," *Journal of American Folklore* 89 (1976):7–26. Quotes are from pp. 12, 13, 14, 15, 17, and 26. Other studies of varying ways that a single individual sings the same song or tells the same story on different occasions, to different audiences, and/or with differing senses of self or communicative responsibility include the following: Ilhan Başgöz, "The Tale-Singer and His Audience," in Ben-Amos and Goldstein, pp. 143–203; George Carey, "The Storyteller's Art and the Collector's Intrusion," in Linda Dégh, Henry Glassie, and Felix J. Oinas, eds., *Folklore Today: A Festschrift for*

Richard M. Dorson (Bloomington: Indiana University Research Center for Language and Semiotic Studies, 1976), pp. 81–91; James Porter, "Parody and Satire as Mediations of Change in the Traditional Songs of Belle Stewart," in Carol L. Edwards and Kathleen E. B. Manley, eds., *Narrative Folksong: New Directions: Essays in Appreciation of W. Edson Richmond* (Boulder: Westview Press, 1985), pp. 303–338; and Richard Bauman, "'I Go into More Detail Now, to Be Sure': Narrative Variation and the Shifting Contexts of Traditional Storytelling," in Richard Bauman, *Story, Performance, and Event: Contextual Studies of Oral Narrative* (New York: Cambridge University Press, 1986), pp. 78–111.

19. For a discussion of the concept of *communicative role* and the way in which and reasons why communication serves as the basis for interaction when individuals assume such roles, see Robert A. Georges, "Communicative Role and Social Identity in Storytelling," *Fabula: Journal of Folktale Studies* 31 (1990):49–57.

20. Daniel J. Crowley, *I Could Talk Old-Story Good: Creativity in Bahamian Folklore,* University of California Folklore Studies 17 (Berkeley and Los Angeles: University of California Press, 1966), pp. 21–24.

21. Donald Cosentino, *Defiant Maids and Stubborn Farmers: Tradition and Invention in Mende Story Performance* (Cambridge: Cambridge University Press, 1982), pp. 73, 88–116 passim, 220.

22. Rachel Fretz, "Storytelling among the Chokwe of Zaire: Narrating Skill and Listener Responses" (Ph.D. diss., University of California, Los Angeles, 1987). Quotes are from pp. 307–308.

23. MacEdward Leach, "Celtic Tales from Cape Breton," in W. Edson Richmond, ed., *Studies in Folklore in Honor of Distinguished Service Professor Stith Thompson,* Indiana University Publications, Folklore Series 9 (Bloomington: Indiana University Press, 1957), p. 40. For further discussion of feedback from others and self, see Robert A. Georges,

"Feedback and Response in Storytelling," *Western Folklore* 38 (1979):104–110, and "'I Go into More Detail Now, to Be Sure,'" in Bauman.

24. Robert A. Georges, "Do Narrators Really Digress? A Reconsideration of 'Audience Asides' in Narrating," *Western Folklore* 40 (1981):245–252. The tale Emmanual told was a version of Type 1174, *Making a Rope of Sand.* Gonatos's story is a version of Type 1417J*, *Husband Sent for Water.* For another discussion of digression in traditional storytelling, see Ilhan Başgöz, "Digression in Oral Narrative: A Case Study of Individual Remarks by Turkish Romance Tellers," *Journal of American Folklore* 78 (1986):5–23.

25. From Cosentino, pp. 133–134.

26. Georges, "Do Narrators Really Digress?," pp. 247–248.

27. C. W. von Sydow, "Folktale Studies and Philology: Some Points of View," reprinted in Alan Dundes, ed., *The Study of Folklore* (Englewood Cliffs, N.J.: Prentice-Hall, 1965), p. 231.

28. Barbara A. Babcock and Guy and Doris Montha, *The Pueblo Storyteller: Development of a Figurative Ceramic Tradition* (Tucson: University of Arizona Press, 1986), p. 21.

29. *The Chainsaw Art of Skip Armstrong,* a video by Sharon Sherman, 1991. See also her book *Chainsaw Sculptor: The Art of J. Chester "Skip" Armstrong* (Jackson: University Press of Mississippi, 1995).

30. For further discussion of the concept of *event* and its relevance to the study of folklore, see Robert A. Georges, "Toward an Understanding of Storytelling Events," *Journal of American Folklore* 82 (1969):313–328, and Bauman, pp. 1–10. A study that examines many particular events in which objects were made (and discusses the craftsman's personality, previous experiences, relationships with others including customers, and process of conceptualizing form) is Michael Owen Jones, *Craftsman of the Cumberlands: Tradition and Creativity* (Lexington: University Press of Kentucky, 1989).

In Retrospect

The thesis of this book is that folklore has been, and can be, conceptualized and studied as artifact, describable and transmissible entity, culture, and behavior. As we have noted throughout the work, these four perspectives are interdependent, not mutually exclusive. Moreover, they have been inherent in folkloristics since its inception in the early nineteenth century.

The Four Perspectives

Researchers such as Sir Walter Scott, the Grimm brothers, and Elias Lönnrot hypothesized that many songs, tales, customs, beliefs, proverbs, and examples of other expressive forms endure over long periods of time, perpetuated solely or principally through a process of oral tradition. These early investigators were also aware that many such traditions eventually pass into oblivion as a result of social change, technological development, and personal preference. Therefore, pioneering scholars conceived such phenomena to be artifacts and regarded the study of them as an historical science. They established the precedents of eliciting examples of folklore directly from living human beings (doing *fieldwork*) and of locating parallels and analogues in manuscripts and early published works. They called others' attention to these "popular antiquities" by describing them and making examples available in print. Through their publications and urgings, they also stimulated others to collect such phenomena and to preserve them for the edification of future generations.

Before Englishman William John Thoms coined the word *folklore* in 1846, field-workers and library scholars had already amassed a sizable and diverse data base for the emerging discipline of folkloristics. Furthermore, despite their inclination to view examples of folklore as survivals from the past, pioneering researchers were also aware that folklore can be disseminated through space as well as time; that it exists in relation to, rather than independently of, other cultural phenomena and behaviors; and that it persists as long as it is communally and personally meaningful and useful.

Folklorists today, as in the past, assume the artifactual nature of folklore *a priori*. When they identify a phenomenon as an example of folklore, they posit or hypothesize that it has existed through time and hence that it has a history. Since a principal characteristic of folklore is its traditionality, documenting its temporal existence is a primary research responsibility (illustrated by Barbara Babcock's reconstructed evolution of storyteller figurines, discussed in chapter 3, and Wolfgang Mieder's "Three Wise Monkeys" study, characterized in chapter 5, for instance). That folklore examples can be configured into sets identifiable as *types* provides further evidence of folklore's historicity. The multiple versions of a folklore example that constitute members of a type set reveal both the stable and the variable nature of folklore and attest to its durability and adaptability (exemplified by the "Our Goodman" ballad type, discussed in chapter 5, and by the mixed-up-report tale type that William A. Wilson describes, characterized in chapter 6).

That folklore is both durable and adaptable is also demonstrated by its existence through space. Folklore examples themselves do not move from place to place.

Rather, they become diffused spatially as a result of movements by and contacts among individuals and social groups (exemplified by Anna Birgitta Rooth's study of American Indian creation myths and Alan Dundes's essay on African tales found among Indians in the American Southeast, both discussed in chapter 5), as well as through print, audio, and visual media. To be relevant and meaningful to new groups and individuals, folklore examples must often be modified (undergo *variation*). Frequently the modifications are slight, as when personal or place names in stories and songs are changed for recognition or appropriateness (*localization*). At other times the variation is more substantial, as is the case, for instance, when sobering didactic story endings replace happy ones or narrative structures are altered to make a story plot culturally compatible or aesthetically satisfying (*transformation*).

Folklore's cultural nature is apparent because it is created and shared by human beings rather than being biologically determined or inherited. Because of its expressive nature, folklore is both an aspect of culture and a mirror of and reaction to other cultural phenomena. Through folklore, people can educate or enculturate each other; perpetuate, challenge, or modify a group's social norms and values; inform others about the bases for or nature of their culture; reveal or display their identity, traditionality, knowledge, or competence; and entertain or be entertained.

All human beings can and do assume the communicative roles through which folklore is generated and transmitted. These roles (e.g., storyteller, singer, musician, dancer, potter, quilter, healer) become avocational or occupational identities for those judged to be particularly proficient in communicating in terms of them (as is the case, for instance, with Eduardo the healer and Skip Armstrong the chainsaw sculptor, both described in chapter 9). Communicative roles may also become social identities for individuals entitled to them because other social identities of theirs require them to be performers, as when only a tribal chief or elder is allowed to tell a society's sacred stories.

To assume the communicative roles necessary to generate and transmit folklore is to behave in learned and expected ways (illustrated by Ruth Benedict's and Barre Toelken's studies of storytelling, discussed in chapters 6 and 9 respectively). For example, narrators everywhere assume the responsibility of stimulating their audiences in ways that enable individual audi-

Figure 10–1: Emile and Louis Ancelet at annual family cochon de lait *(pig roast), Ossun, Louisiana, 1989 (photo by Philip Gould).*

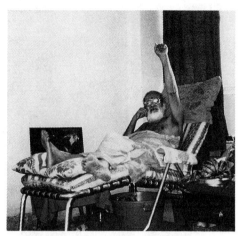

Figure 10–2: Guru Swamiji in India telling "That's Good, Very Good," and demonstrating how the tribal priest lifted his sword over the king (photo by Kirin Narayan).

ence members to perceptualize and experience vicariously the events the storytellers portray. Judgments audience members make of narrators are dependent on their assessments of the extent to which, and effectiveness with which, storytellers succeed in stimulating them. Singers need positive feedback from other people and self to be motivated to continue to interact

with others in that communicative role on a particular occasion, and to be motivated to do so again subsequently (as James Porter's study of Jeannie Robertson, described in chapter 9, suggests). That both the same and different individuals repeatedly tell the same stories, sing the same songs, play the same games, utter the same proverbs, pose the same riddles, make the same objects, play the same tunes, dance the same dances, etc., reveals that behaving in such ways is sufficiently reinforced by self and others to make the repetitiveness understandable and each repetition meaningful.

As we demonstrate repeatedly throughout this book, the four perspectives described and discussed are not just complementary. They are inherent in and essential to all folkloristic inquiry, even when only one or some combination of less than four is the explicit focus of a work.

For instance, in his study of traditional counting-out and other rhymes (discussed in chapter 3), Charles Francis Potter focuses on what he calls "word fossils" and "relics of old systems of counting." He traces selected English rhymes back to the Middle Ages, demonstrating thereby their antiquity and justifying his characterizing them

Figure 10–3: Mustafa Baydemir, master potter, Kinik, Turkey (from Turkish Traditional Art Today, photo by Henry Glassie).

Figure 10–4: Mary Vanderhorts sewing sweetgrass basket in her small shed behind her roadside stand on Highway 17, Mt. Pleasant, South Carolina, 1987 (photo by David A. Taylor).

Figure 10–5: Saddlemaker Bill Gardner with Sheridan style roping saddle, Sheridan, Wyoming, 1994 (photo by Richard Collier, courtesy Tim Evans).

as survivals. By noting the existence of parallels in Sanskrit, Latin, Old Welsh, and ancient Irish, moreover, he also indicates the widespread geographical and cultural distribution of such rhymes and the kinds of linguistic designations in them. Furthermore, in reporting that counting-out rhymes were recited by Scottish shepherds "counting their sheep, Cornish fishermen their mackerel, and old ladies their knitting-stitches," Potter describes in passing a variety of behaviors and cultural practices while carrying out his principal objective of supporting his thesis that the rhymes on which he focuses are survivals from the past.

Similarly, in reconstructing the history of what he calls "the Shanghai gesture"

Figure 10–6: Saddlemaker Bob Douglas in the saddle shop at his ranch, Wyarno, Wyoming, 1992 (photo by Richard Collier, courtesy Wyoming State Museum).

(discussed in chapter 5), Archer Taylor not only traces back in time this practice of thumbing the nose. He also cites examples of the Shanghai and analogous gestures reported from "a dozen or more countries" and over a period of "four centuries." Taylor thereby attests to the popularity of such gestures in multiple eras and cultures; to the ways those making the gestures behave; and to similarities and differences in uses and meanings of the gestures in differing periods and sociocultural contexts.

The foci of Ruth Benedict's study of Zuni mythology (discussed in chapters 6 and 8) are the ways the stories she analyzes tally and don't tally with other aspects of contemporary Zuni culture and what explanations one can propose to account for the correlations and noncorrelations. Yet despite her cultural and synchronic orientation, Benedict relies not only on tales she recorded from Zuni narrators herself, but also on those documented by other researchers working among the Zuni over the preceding 50-year period. Her use of such a data base attests to Benedict's concern with demonstrating the continuity over time of selected tale types, and hence the traditionality and historicity of the stories with which she is concerned. Furthermore, Benedict notes that some nontallying elements in Zuni tales are really survivals, for they describe ways of life and behaviors that were normative in the past but that have long been passé (e.g., the use of stone knives, the practice of entering houses through ladders up to and down through a hole in the roof).

Similarly, while he chooses to examine "Johnny Says His ABCs" in "the context out of which the joke grows" (discussed in chapter 6), C. W. Sullivan, III, also reports that the tale "has been collected in many regions of the country [i.e., the United States] over a period of at least thirty years" and that it has also been reported from elsewhere. Thus, despite his concern with

"why it is so consistently popular among children," Sullivan acknowledges the fact that "Johnny Says His ABCs" is a distinguishable tale type that exists in multiple versions; that generically the joke belongs "within the larger framework of 'dirty' jokes and, therefore, joking narratives in general"; and that it shares motifs with many other jokes "about school and about teachers."

Recurrent Questions in Folkloristics

Conceptualizing folklore in terms of the four perspectives discussed in this book reveals that folklore is not an historical artifact *or* a describable and transmissible entity *or* an aspect and manifestation of culture *or* an aspect and manifestation of behavior, but rather all of these. Thus, one must combine the concepts inherent in each of the four perspectives to answer the question *"What is folklore?"* Furthermore, one must draw on insights obtained from studying folklore in terms of all four perspectives to answer three other questions that are central to folkloristics: *(1) how and why does folklore come into being; (2) why is folklore perpetuated; and (3) how and why does folklore remain stable and change?*

Insights gained by conceptualizing and studying folklore from the four complementary perspectives enable one to answer the question *"How and why does folklore come into being?"* Folklore comes into being when a particular song, story, game, saying, tune, rhyme, riddle, chair, basket, or example of some other form of expression created by some particular human being becomes known to others, who find it meaningful enough to make it known to still others, who, if they also find it meaningful, similarly share it with others, and so on. An example of an expressive form or

BOX 10-1
Tornado Stories

Narratives akin to the tall-tale tradition and an occasional ballad are to be found in the oral traditions of twister country, but much more typical are brief accounts of the eccentric incident, the freakish detail, the arresting artifact left in the tornado's destructive path.

... [For example, a] narrator described his cousin's curious discovery after another Kansas tornado had destroyed her school building, this time emphasizing the eccentric artifact: "when she came back [to the school] her desk was still sitting there, although the building had been obliterated, and her glasses were still sitting where she'd left them on top of the desk."

... A Kansan ... described another curiosity: "when I lived in Newton a tornado hit the outskirts of town and I fled for cover at that time.... [T]he thing I remember about that was the filling station where . . . three walls were missing, one wall was remaining, and that was the wall that has the oil cans and everything. The shelves with the cans on it were still standing. There was a floor, and one wall, with things on the shelf."

In time these stories become traditionalized in one's personal repertoire through their performance in different storytelling situations. As they are told and retold, sometimes to the same audiences, their artistry is refined and their treatment of selective details sharpened. Often they enter the storm-story repertoire of captivated listeners, who may be family members or friends.

Their life is a vigorous one in midwestern talk.

—Larry Danielson[1]

behavior thus becomes identifiable as folklore when, through repetition, it is known or hypothesized to have a history of use temporally and/or spatially, and hence to constitute evidence of continuity and/or consistency in human behavior through time and/or space.

The fact that multiple individuals find an example of an expressive form or behavior meaningful enough to remember it and make it known to others, thereby contributing to its eventual transformation into or its continuing perpetuation as an example of folklore, in no way assumes or implies that any given folklore example is meaningful in the same way(s) and/or for the same reason(s) for all who come to know and share it, as studying folklore as an aspect and manifestation of culture might predispose one to assume or conclude. Quite the contrary is the case, as those viewing folklore as behavior make clear. For people are individuals as well as members of societies and other groups. Examples of expressive forms must be meaningful to people as individuals as well as to people as group members. Hence, human expressive creations must have the potential to be meaningful in different as well as similar ways and for both similar and different reasons to become folklore in the first place. Folklore can be said to exist, then, because individual human beings can and do express themselves creatively, and because individual human beings find selected human expressive creations to be meaningful and shared by or sharable with others.

"Because it is meaningful to and shared by individual human beings" is also the answer to the question *"Why is folklore perpetuated?"* However, folklore examples can lose their meaningfulness. When they do, they can be said, metaphorically, "to die out," as those regarding folklore as artifact often conclude. But as fieldworkers seeking out and documenting examples of folklore repeatedly discover, folklore is ever-becoming as well as ongoing and ever-dying. Just as examples of folklore are continuously falling into disuse and being forgotten (exemplified, for instance, by some of the grave decorating practices described by Lynwood Montell, discussed in chapter 3), so are others constantly evolving and being shared intimately face to face and disseminated widely via mass media (as the Gulf War and *Challenger* jokes presented in chapters 5 and 8 respectively illustrate). Therefore, the data base for folkloristics is always evolving and changing. But phenomena that become, are, and were data for folklorists' inquiries—and hence that are a part of the folkloristic data base—are all individually created examples of expressive forms or behaviors that have histories of use among multiple individuals through time and/or space, and hence that can be regarded as phenomena that are collective or communal rather than individual or idiosyncratic.

The third question central to folkloristics—"*How and why does folklore remain stable and change?*"—can also be answered only by combining results of studies conducted in terms of the four perspectives discussed in this work. Examples of folklore can be said to remain stable because the essence of what they communicate and the basic way they do so remain constant and hence recognizable over time (as multiple versions of the Sphinx riddle and of the death-car legend presented in chapters 2 and 5 respectively reveal). For instance, many people identify stories they tell or are told as versions of "Cinderella" because the basic action sequence the narrators depict—the plot—is kept intact as the tale is repeatedly retold, regardless of the language in which the story is narrated or the cultural or situational context in which it is shared. Individuals recognize and identify certain clay figurines as "storytellers" (described in chapter 3) because those objects all consist of one large human

Figure 10–7: A traditional meal, 1986, Allen's Neck in southwestern Massachusetts, where every third Thursday in August since 1888 Quakers have gathered for a community clambake (photo by Kathy Neustadt).

figure with multiple smaller ones clinging to and/or sitting on or by the larger one, even though there is considerable variation in the number of small figures, the ways they are attached or positioned in relation to the larger figure, the colors the figures are painted, the nature of the figures' facial features and clothing, etc.

Hence, while there are both similarities and differences in multiple versions of a phenomenon, the similarities must always be judged to be more significant than the differences, either quantitatively or qualitatively or both, for the phenomenon to be identifiable as an example of folklore. When the reverse is true and one judges the differences to be more significant than the similarities, the phenomena are not identified as the same phenomenon or as members of a single set or versions of a specific type. Instead, they are regarded either as different folklore examples, as members of different sets or versions of different types, or as phenomena that are not really folklore examples at all or any longer.

Change occurs in folklore because no one can ever really reproduce exactly a story, song, tune, basket, pot, ritual, game, etc., even if one makes a concerted effort to do so, as those viewing folklore as aspects and manifestations of behavior emphasize. As those conceptualizing and studying folklore as historical artifact correctly note, individuals often misperceive, forget, and confuse or combine parts of different traditional stories, songs, or games and procedures for making chairs, baskets, or rugs, resulting in inadvertent changes when they attempt to reproduce them. As those conceptualizing and studying folklore as behavior also note correctly, individuals often depart consciously and deliberately from traditional patterns and procedures by behaving in alternative and creative ways to give an old story a new twist, a well-known song a peppier tune, a popular riddle a new answer, or to make a familiar game more challenging, a conventional handmade chair more attractive, or a time-honored ritual more personal. As studies viewing folklore as an aspect and manifestation of culture reveal, stability may be valued over change or change over stability because of the part a given kind or example of folklore plays or the way it functions in the daily life of a society or group; and folklore borrowed by one group from another often has to be changed to make it relevant and meaningful in a new cultural environment. Thus, by drawing on multiple perspectives, one realizes that stability and change in folklore are not oppositional but complementary, for without both, folklore could not exist.

Frequent Issues in Folkloristics

In addition to enabling one to answer the questions just discussed, conceptualizing folklore in terms of all four of the perspectives characterized in this book helps one to better understand many recurrent issues in folkloristics and to reconcile seemingly conflicting positions. As we indicated in chapter 2, the issue of whether folklore examples found cross-culturally have single or multiple origins (*monogenesis* or *polygenesis*) was resolved commonsensically by the end of the nineteenth century. Scholars generally agreed that monogenesis is the more defensible hypothesis for folklore examples that are relatively lengthy or complex and found among peoples known or hypothesized to have had a common ancestry or a history of contact with each other. Polygenesis seems more plausible for short, relatively simple folklore examples, particularly if they are found widely diffused geographically and among peoples who neither share a cultural heritage nor are known or believed to have interacted with each other historically. Studies that view folklore as behavior, however, suggest that because of similarities in all peoples biologically, psychologically, and experientially, polygenesis may be more likely and common than the nineteenth-century compromise indicates. Furthermore, because of what is now known about the mobility of individuals and groups historically and about the impact people have on each other indirectly, whether electronically or via print and other mass media, folklore created at one place and time can easily be disseminated widely and among peoples of diverse cultural backgrounds, either with or without human movement. Hence, when considering the four perspectives together, monogenesis versus polygenesis emerges not as an issue that has been resolved once and for all, but rather as one that must be the subject of ongoing discussion, since what seems plausible in commonsensical terms may not be defensible in terms of what we now know about the human species and human behavior.

Also easier to understand by conceptualizing folklore in terms of the four perspectives discussed in this book are issues raised by apparent dichotomies between traditionality and creativity and between communality and individuality. Viewing folklore as artifact emphasizes its traditional nature and implies a commitment, if not a necessity, to imitate (often expressed metaphorically as "to hand down" or "to pass on"). This seems to be opposed to or to rule out creativity. Regarding folklore as an aspect and manifestation of culture focuses on its communal nature and suggests a responsibility, if not an obligation, to conform. This seems to disallow individual innovation. But the other perspectives resolve the implied contradictions and make complementary what seems oppositional when viewed in terms of a single perspective. The nature and number of differences, as well as similarities, discernible in versions of folklore examples as they are diffused through time and space indicate that in the process of reproducing those examples, human beings are not just imitative tradition bearers, but also innovative re-creators, for the folkloristic data base reveals indisputably that variation is more often normative than it is anomalous. Furthermore, as viewing it as behavior reveals, folklore must be personalizable as well as shared and sharable with others. To make it so entails both having and taking the freedom to make the familiar and communal personally relevant and meaningful; and doing so is a creative and individual act.

Taken together, the four perspectives also resolve other issues that have arisen because a single perspective or set of fewer than four has been privileged. For example,

to argue that folklore examples should be studied only in terms of their relationships to other examples of folklore, or that the only defensible way to study folklore is to do so "in cultural context," is to attempt to limit inquiry by championing a bias or onesidedness that ignores or downplays the equal importance of the other perspectives. To insist that all folklore is preserved and perpetuated through processes of memorization and reiteration is to ignore the generative nature of behavior and the personal and cultural variables that determine it. To contend that folklore is always being created at the time it is being "performed" and/or transmitted is to overlook the fact that verbatim or near-verbatim repetitions are common in folklore (in proverbial speech and counting-out rhymes, for instance) and that there are similarities too striking to be coincidental in the specific nature of and interrelationships among the structure, content, and style of multiple versions of any given tale or ballad type. Hence, many matters that seem to be "issues" in folkloristics *are* issues only when or because those who present or address them as such judge the perspectives employed in folkloristics to be competitive rather than complementary.

The Four Perspectives in Applied Folkloristics

The complementary nature of the four perspectives is also apparent in the ways trained folklorists use their discipline's methodologies and research results. Those teaching folklore organize courses in varying ways, often making either selected expressive forms/genres or societies/social groups their focus, for example. But one cannot characterize and analyze folklore as examples of expressive forms/genres without considering the human and cultural identities of the individuals who are the sources of the folklore examples selected to illustrate those forms/genres. Similarly, one cannot characterize and analyze a society's/social group's folklore without discussing what forms its people's expressiveness takes and how it manifests itself in the behaviors of individual group members. Furthermore, because all examples of folklore, by definition, have a history of use temporally and/or spatially, then a course focusing on either selected expressive forms/genres or societies/social groups must also consider such pertinent questions as the ways folklore is transmitted intergenerationally and spatially, requiring one to conceptualize and analyze folklore as artifact and transmissible entity as well. Hence, while those teaching folklore often highlight one of the four perspectives in their courses, the nature of folklore makes it impossible for them to ignore the other perspectives, even though they may treat them as subordinate to or of lesser importance than the one on which they focus.

Folklorists who make films and videos also use all four perspectives in their creations. Deciding what to focus on in a folklore film entails conceiving of folklore as artifact and choosing a phenomenon whose traditionality is attested by its documentable history. The film on Klamath traditions described in chapter 7 and those on Eduardo Calderón and Skip Armstrong discussed in chapter 9 are all concerned with behaviors that are identified by their makers explicitly as traditional, in both human and cultural terms. Furthermore, the traditions in all three films are presented as resources that manifest themselves uniquely as well as traditionally in the behaviors of specific individuals.

Folklorists employed by public agencies such as state arts councils or city cultural affairs divisions similarly find all four perspectives essential to their work. Often those in such positions are expected to locate and document the behaviors of individuals who are the active tradition bearers in their communities. Deciding who qualifies entails determining who tells *traditional* tales, sings *traditional* songs, performs *traditional* music, makes chairs in *traditional* ways, etc. Making such a determination involves distinguishing the traditional from the nontraditional and hence utilizing in the investigation the concept of folklore as artifact. The communities to which these tradition bearers belong may be defined by such criteria as their members' collective ethnic, occupational, or generational identity, requiring the researcher to consider folklore as both an aspect and a manifestation of the culture of the group in question. The ways folklore manifests itself behaviorally in, and is used by, individual tradition bearers makes viewing folklore as aspects and manifestations of behavior relevant to the public sector folklorist's work as well.[2]

Folklorists working for museums employ procedures and apply research results from each of the four perspectives, too. Soliciting or purchasing folk art objects involves first establishing the traditionality of such items, and frequently their cultural representativeness as well. Research on folk art in museum collections also involves authenticating the traditionality of objects historically, and often culturally, and noting the authentication in acquisitions or inventory record books and/or on identifying labels for exhibits. Records and exhibit labels often comment on an object's use or function, relating it to other cultural phenomena in the process. Such statements are sometimes corroborated audibly and/or visually in exhibits by accompanying excerpts from audiotaped or videotaped interviews with individuals who made the specific objects, or who create the kinds of objects, on display, which acknowledges folklore as behavior.[3]

Folklorists who work in the medical, legal, business, and other professions sup-

Figure 10–8: Folklorist Miriam Camitta (L), coordinator of a workshop series in conjunction with the 1987 exhibition "New Jersey Pinelands: Tradition and Environment," and Leslie Christofferson of Whiting, New Jersey, conduct a workshop for schoolchildren; Mr. Christofferson built the 112-room purple martin house behind him (photo by Rita Moonsammy, courtesy New Jersey State Council on the Arts).

Figure 10–9: The Oakland Museum's "hippie" exhibit (part of its "California Dream" exhibition) includes a beaded mosaic dresser made by hand in 1976, Country Joe's decorated guitar, and hand-embroidered clothing (photo by Joe Samberg, courtesy The Oakland Museum History Department).

plement and complement the knowledge and skills of their coworkers because their training prepares them to document, analyze, and explain relevant traditions in historical, cultural, and behavioral ways.[4] For instance, they inform doctors and other medical personnel about health beliefs and healing practices that are traditional cross-culturally or for members of a given society or group, suggesting ways to integrate them with "scientific" medicine and to "translate" concepts from one system of body and mind care to another. They explain similarities and mediate differences in alternative ways of conceptualizing human beings' rights and responsibilities in their relationships with each other and with those who serve in and represent national, state, and

---

BOX 10-2
The Cedarburg Cultural Center

As a folklorist, I feel privileged to have worked so closely with the Cedarburg [Wisconsin] community in realizing its dream of a cultural center. It has been gratifying to see exhibitions addressed to traditional culture attended and appreciated; to see the relationships between past and present, folk culture and fine arts understood and accepted; to see long-time residents and newcomers united in their efforts to learn about and learn from Cedarburg's past. If I have helped this community's lifelong members to value their heritage more highly, if I have helped Cedarburg's many recent arrivals to understand what daily life was like for early settlers, if I have helped the many tourists drawn to the community by its historic structures and antique shops to grasp the forces of ethnicity, occupation and religion that shaped its character, I feel I have made good use of my training as a folklorist. I have returned to the community all that it has given to me.
          —Robert T. Teske[5]

---

local institutions. They document examples of tales, rituals, and other expressive forms that are traditional in business establishments; and they determine the ways folklore unifies and factionalizes employees and how it can perpetuate and change corporate structures. Carrying out any of these tasks entails drawing on and utilizing all four perspectives employed in folkloristics, not merely one or some combination of less than four of them.

The Distinctiveness of Folkloristics

As the nature and organization of this book reveal, to know what folklore is and to comprehend and appreciate the part it plays in the daily lives of every human being are achievable goals only when one understands the origin of the concept of folklore and the ways those who have made folklore the focus of their inquiries conceptualize and study it. The discipline of folkloristics had its inception in the conviction shared by individuals of varied national backgrounds that much of what human beings think and say and do has a long and continuous history that is sustained over time

solely or principally through firsthand interaction and direct or face-to-face communication. Convinced that such phenomena have the potential to enable us to better understand our species, our culture, and ourselves, pioneering researchers laid the intellectual foundations for folkloristics by documenting, describing, and studying examples of such traditions and encouraging other individuals to do the same. Others who shared their conviction followed in their footsteps.

As their discipline has evolved, folklorists have conceptualized and studied folklore from the four perspectives described in this book. At different times in the history of folkloristics each one of these perspectives has been dominant, as indicated by the kinds of questions researchers have addressed and the nature of the scholarly works they have produced. But since the inception of folkloristics, the nature, complementarity, and importance of all four perspectives have been recognized and acknowledged.

Folkloristics is multidisciplinary because it shares concepts, concerns, and information with those in other disciplines that focus on human history, culture, or behavior. But folkloristics is a distinctive discipline because of the complementary way folklorists use the four perspectives in their investigations and because of what and how their multiperspective orientation enables them to learn about human nature and share what they discover with others.

Further distinguishing their field is that folklorists typically have focused on populations ignored by others. From the inception of folkloristics two centuries ago, folklorists have recorded at firsthand the songs, stories, proverbs, and other traditions of ordinary people and of women, children, ethnic minorities, and those lacking a public forum. This has led some folklorists to become advocates for particular groups. But whether or not they assume the role of activists, through their publications, museum exhibits, films, folklife festivals, consulting, and other vehicles of education folklorists have always provided a forum for underrepresented groups or individuals and their traditions.[6]

Another characteristic of the field is that folklorists appreciate the artistry, aesthetic qualities, wisdom, and meaningfulness of what people make, say, and do in everyday life. Collectors have filled archives and publications with examples of individuals' expressive forms and behaviors, their words recorded exactly as spoken, their movements described in detail, and their objects faithfully documented. When describing

---

BOX 10–3
The Goals of Folkloristics

No other discipline is more concerned with linking us to the cultural heritage from the past than is folklore; no other discipline is more concerned with revealing the interrelationships of different cultural expressions than is folklore; and no other discipline is more concerned, or no other discipline should be concerned, with discovering what it means to be human. It is this attempt to discover the basis of our common humanity, the imperatives of our human existence, that puts folklore study at the very center of humanistic study.
—William A. Wilson[7]

---

their traditions, folklorists present people's own points of view, often extrapolating and generalizing from them in presenting their own hypotheses, interpretations, and conclusions.

Folklorists also document and present variable tellings of a story or performances of a song, ritual, celebration, or proverb. They realize the uniqueness of each storytelling event, the different ways a song might be sung by different singers or for different audiences, and the multiple meanings that individual participants find in a ceremony or festive event.

Figure 10–10: Alice Cunningham Fletcher (seated in center holding letter), first woman president of the American Folklore Society (1905), with women at the Omaha Indian Mission (ca. 1883–1884); in addition to studying Winnebago and Omaha traditions, she lobbied for passage of federal legislation giving Indians greater control over their lands (Neg. #4473, courtesy National Anthropological Archives, Smithsonian Institution).

BOX 10-4
Folklore and Medicine

Despite the very broad authority that our society has granted to the medical profession it is clear that official medicine does not and cannot provide *everything* needed to deal with sickness, suffering, and death. No matter how many professional resources are developed and added, from social work to counseling and so forth, such official efforts never serve all needs. . . . Official medicine has always been surrounded by additional community health resources, which is good because by itself it cannot fulfill such functions as explaining the meaning of suffering or providing all of the support that a chronically disabled person requires.

. . .[The primary methods of folk medical research] involve rich and complex descriptions of actual behavior using a great variety of techniques, from interviewing to participant observation to photographic documentation. . . . [T]he descriptions are readily applied to an understanding of clinical situations, whereas the more heavily quantitative descriptions characteristic of medical sociology are often more easily used for public health purposes. Folklore studies also has a tradition of combining humanities and social science perspectives. This allows the folkloristic study of folk medicine to be broadly interdisciplinary and to include insights ranging from history and philosophy to epidemiology and psychobiology.

But in the last analysis, perhaps folklore's greatest advantage in this kind of work is its strong populist orientation. That is, cast into a clinical situation all of a folklorist's training immediately suggests questions aimed at understanding the patient's point of view and describing it in the most sympathetic manner possible. This is a central part of the discipline's intellectual history and development: the assumption that ordinary people tend to be underestimated and that their knowledge tends to be discredited by authorities. The folklorist seeks to understand that overlooked knowledge, especially by learning the traditional idioms and modes of thought from which it arises. This does not make the folklorist a critic or adversary of medicine, but it does make her or him an informed advocate of the patient, one who has the intellectual tools necessary to render physicians and patients mutually intelligible.
—David Hufford[8]

BOX 10-5
Folklorists' Training

Folklorists . . . are trained to take texts, pots, pictures and designs apart, to develop taxonomies and make lists, without getting lost in cultural descriptions of the whole. They are trained to follow up information gained in one interview with information gained elsewhere. And they are trained to look at and where scientists never look—at those artistic, expressive materials that are the antithesis of [Western] science and the essence of culturally based science.
—Rayna Green[9]

In sum, folklorists have a particular set of values and outlook. They value human creativity, expressiveness, commensuality, history, and tradition. They champion and appreciate what other researchers usually overlook: the patterns of behavior, movements, figures of speech, festive events, modes of communicating, traditional knowledge, and other expressive forms and behaviors that define and typify routine daily interactions. The questions that folklorists repeatedly ask—what is folklore, how and why does it come into being, why is it perpetuated, and how and why does it both remain stable and change—are questions that arise from a curiosity about and fascination with the fundamental nature and continuity of the human species and the desire to better understand and appreciate what all members of our unique species have in common despite their seeming diversity. Because the behaviors, forms, and processes that folklorists document and study are universal and fundamental to our existence as social beings, folkloristics is the discipline with the greatest potential to enable us to comprehend what it is that makes our species unique.

Conclusion

In this book, we have characterized folklore and the study of it principally by describing selected works and, through extensive quoting, letting their authors and creators speak much of the time for themselves. The four perspectives we focus on are ones we infer have dominated folkloristics historically, based on our perusal and analysis of both past and current scholarship. We are aware that not all folklorists will share our view that these are, indeed, *the* (or the *only*) perspectives in folkloristics or that all will agree with our characterizations of them. Nevertheless, we contend, and feel we demonstrate, that

the four perspectives have been inherent in the scholarly literature through time and central to the discipline of folkloristics since its inception. We also believe that a perspectives approach is the most meaningful way to contextualize folklore study, since it is in terms of concepts that are central to the four perspectives that folklorists conduct their inquiries.

In addition, we consciously chose to be reporters rather than critics in order to make readers aware of the varied and interesting phenomena that folklorists document and study; the numerous and significant questions they address; and the insights their investigations provide. In doing so, we do not mean to imply that there

Figure 10–11: Wedding rituals and other "rites of passage" (a term coined by French folklorist Arnold van Gennep in a book whose title bears this term, 1909), are pervasive in human society (photo by Tom Myers).

is unanimity in orientation and methodology or lack of debate and controversy in folkloristics. Throughout the history of their discipline, in fact, folklorists have always engaged in spirited exchanges and confrontations—about what folklore is, what research questions they should address and privilege, and how and why they should document and study folklore, for example.[10] Yet despite their differences, all folklorists share the conviction that the kinds of phenomena they focus upon, and their attempts to comprehend them and make them understandable to and appreciated by others, are important and worthwhile pursuits. In this book, we make this shared conviction apparent by highlighting folklorists' common concerns and demonstrating the complementary nature of their scholarly pursuits and accomplishments.

Notes

1. "Tornado Stories in the Breadbasket: Weather and Regional Identity," in Barbara Allen and Thomas J. Schlereth, eds., *Sense of Place: American Regional Cultures* (Lexington: University Press of Kentucky, 1990), pp. 30 and 33.

2. See, for example, discussions in Charles Camp, "Developing a State Folklife Program," in Richard M. Dorson, ed., *Handbook of American Folklore* (Bloomington: Indiana University Press, 1983), pp. 518–524, and Susan Auerbach, "The Brokering of Ethnic Folklore: Issues of Selection and Presentation at a Multicultural Festival," in Stephen Stern and John Allan Cicala, eds., *Creative Ethnicity: Symbols and Strategies of Contemporary Ethnic Life* (Logan: Utah State University, 1991), pp. 223–238.

3. See, for example, essays in Patricia Hall and Charlie Seemann, eds., *Folklife and Museums: Selected Readings* (Nashville: American Association for State and Local History, 1987), and Michael Heisley, "Collections and Community in the Generation of a Permanent Exhibition: The Hispanic Heritage Wing of the Museum of International Folk Art," in Kenneth L. Ames, Barbara Franco, and L.

Thomas Frye, eds., *Ideas and Images: Developing Interpretive History Exhibits* (Nashville: American Association for State and Local History, 1992), pp. 65–102.

4. See the essays in Michael Owen Jones, ed., *Putting Folklore to Use* (Lexington: University Press of Kentucky, 1994).

5. "The Folklorist as Public Servant," in Charles Camp, ed., *Time & Temperature: A Centennial Publication of the American Folklore Society* (Washington, D.C.: American Folklore Society, 1989), p. 37.

6. See Richard Kurin, "Why We Do the Festival," *1989 Festival of American Folklife* (Washington, D.C.: Smithsonian Institution, 1989), pp. 8–21; Thomas Vennum, Jr., "American Indian Problems of Access and Cultural Continuity," *1989 Festival of American Folklife* (Washington, D.C.: Smithsonian Institution, 1989), pp. 22–35; and essays in Burt Feintuch, ed., *The Conservation of Culture: Folklorists and the Public Sector* (Lexington: University Press of Kentucky, 1988).

7. "The Deeper Necessity: Folklore and the Humanities," *Journal of American Folklore* 101 (1988):157–158.

8. "Folklore and Medicine," in Jones, pp. 128–129.

9. "Culturally-Based Science: The Potential for Traditional People, Science, and Folklore," in Venetia J. Newall, ed., *Folklore Studies in the Twentieth Century: Proceedings of the Centenary Conference of the Folklore Society* (Totowa, N.J.: Rowman and Littlefield, 1980), p. 212.

10. According to some researchers, one controversy in American folkloristics has been that between literary- and anthropologically oriented researchers. This is the thesis presented and developed in Rosemary Lévy Zumwalt, *American Folklore Scholarship: A Dialogue of Dissent* (Bloomington: Indiana University Press, 1988). A related debate concerns whether textual records or records of folklore as it is documented in cultural contexts should be the focus of folklore study. See, for instance, Dan Ben-Amos, "Toward a Definition of Folklore in Context," *Journal of American Folklore* 84 (1971):3–15 (reprinted in Américo Paredes and Richard Bauman, eds., *Toward New Perspectives in Folklore*, Publications of the American Folklore Society, Bibliographical and Special Series 23 (Austin: University of Texas Press, 1971), pp. 3–15, and

in Dan Ben-Amos, *Folklore in Context: Essays* (New Delhi: South Asian Publishers, 1982, pp. 1–19); D. K. Wilgus, "'The Text Is the Thing,'" *Journal of American Folklore* 86 (1973):241–252; Steven Jones, "Slouching Towards Ethnography: The Text/Context Controversy Reconsidered," *Western Folklore* 39 (1979):42–47; Dan Ben-Amos, "The Ceremony of Innocence," *Western Folklore* 38 (1979):47–52; Steven Jones, "Dogmatism in the Contextual Revolution," *Western Folklore* 38 (1979):52–55; and Robert A. Georges, "Toward a Resolution of the Text/Context Controversy," *Western Folklore* 39 (1980):34– 40. Criticisms of existing scholarship and proposals for, or characterizations of, "new perspectives" in the study of folklore are presented in the essays in Parades and Bauman (see above) and in Charles Briggs and Amy Shuman, eds., *Theorizing Folklore: Toward New Perspectives on the Politics of Culture*, special issue of *Western Folklore* 52:2–4 (April, July, October 1993):109–400. See also the essays in Robert A. Georges, ed., *Taking Stock: Current Problems and Future Prospects in American Folklore Studies*, special issue of *Western Folklore* 50:1 (January 1991):1–126.

Index

Robert A. Georges is Professor Emeritus of English and folklore at the University of California, Los Angeles. He is editor of *Studies on Mythology*; author of *Greek American Folk Beliefs and Narratives*; co-compiler (with Stephen Stern) of *American and Canadian Immigrant and Ethnic Folklore: An Annotated Bibliography*; and co-author with Michael Owen Jones of *People Studying People: The Human Element in Fieldwork*.

Michael Owen Jones is Professor in the Folklore and Mythology Program at the University of California, Los Angeles. He is the author of *Exploring Folk Art: Twenty Years of Thought on Craft, Work, and Aesthetics* and *Craftsman of the Cumberlands: Tradition and Creativity*, and editor of *Putting Folklore to Use*.